A View of the Eng
1944-1965

Kenneth Tynan's reputation as a giant among post-war theatre critics is already secure, crowned by his influential spell as Literary Manager of the National Theatre. The 112 pieces in this book represent the whole span of his twenty-one years of regular reviewing, making up, as Tynan says, 'a record of the most memorable things I saw on English stages between the last year of the war and the early 1960s'.

These were the years of the great performances of Olivier, Wolfit, Gielgud and Richardson, the flowering of Eliot and Fry, the maturity of Rattigan and Coward, and the coming of the new drama, first from Europe with Sartre, Brecht, Ionesco and Beckett, then home-grown from Osborne, Wesker, Pinter et al.

What is remarkable is not only Tynan's fabled brilliance with the turn of a phrase but how often, reviewing new work under the pressure of deadlines, he can be seen to have got it absolutely *right*.

A View of the
ENGLISH STAGE
1944-1965

KENNETH TYNAN

Methuen
LONDON

This collection first published in 1975
by Davis-Poynter

First published as a Methuen Paperback in 1984
by Methuen London Ltd,
11 New Fetter Lane, London EC4P 4EE

Copyright © 1950, 1961, 1967, 1975
by Kenneth Tynan

ISBN 0 413 50430 1

Reproduced, printed and bound in Great Britain by
Hazell Watson & Viney Limited,
Member of the BPCC Group,
Aylesbury, Bucks

Contents

CONTENTS

CONTENTS

CONTENTS

Introduction

I started serious metropolitan theatre-going in 1943, when I was sixteen years old. Until then, except for odd matinées and pantomimes seen with my mother on brief shopping trips to London, I knew very little of theatre outside Birmingham, my home town, and Stratford-on-Avon, which was near enough to, yet far enough from, home to be the ideal place for Birmingham teenagers to take girls: the Memorial Theatre was incidental to Stratford's over-riding virtue, which was that there were no trains home after the show. ('I'm terribly sorry, darling, I really should have checked. No, no buses either. Suppose we might as well try this boarding-house . . . No good, they've only got one room left . . . Unless, of course, you wouldn't mind, um . . .') From 1943 onward, I kept elaborate notes on the plays and performances I saw, although nobody paid me for the right to print them until after I came down from Oxford in 1949. By then I had seen John Gielgud's repertory seasons at the Haymarket in 1943–4, Donald Wolfit on tour and in town in most of the major Shakespearian roles, and everything in the Old Vic repertoire at the New Theatre since 1944. These were the experiences that hooked me. What I found irresistible about theatre in the 40s and early 50s was the chance it offered of seeing outsize personalities operating at full blast – people who were never less than fascinating even when wildly miscast (e.g. Edith Evans as Cleopatra).

There were, of course, one or two directors about. Pre-eminent among them was the giant gadfly, the inspired puppet-master, Tyrone Guthrie, but there were others, notably the much underrated Michael Benthall, whose postwar productions at Stratford (especially *Midsummer Night's Dream* and the Paul Scofield *Hamlet*) had a vivid poetic intelligence that still thrills me in recollection. Meanwhile, encouraged by Sir Barry Jackson, first at Birmingham Rep. and later at Stratford, there had emerged the slight, dapper and perfectly invincible figure of Peter Brook, who established himself with his 1951 production of *Measure for Measure* as the best director in England. But on the whole the theatres into which I first ventured belonged to the actors. What turned me into a critic was the urge to commemorate these astonishing men and women, whose work would otherwise die with the memories of those who saw it.

Hence the first part of this book deals mainly with great performances – with the English career of the exiled Czech actor Frederick Valk (undoubtedly the most *elemental* player I ever saw, compelled by his imperfect English to convey emotion almost by pure sound); with the versatility and virtuosity of Donald Wolfit, who provided several generations of provincial playgoers with their best and often their only gateway to Shakespeare; with great stage comics from Sid Field at the Prince of Wales to Danny Kaye at the Palladium (and there were many more: the Crazy Gang, Monsewer Eddie Gray, Murray and Mooney, Jack Benny, Jimmy James: try to name their equivalents today); and, overwhelmingly, with the tremendous Old Vic seasons just before and after the end of the war. It was a very shaping experience to see, for example, Olivier's *Richard III* and *Oedipus Rex*, Richardson's *Peer Gynt* (directed by Guthrie) and the Olivier-Richardson *Henry IV*, Parts I and II, if one was fully aware that new standards of classical acting were being set before one's eyes for a generation to come and that, in Olivier at least, one was witnessing that most exciting of theatrical spectacles, a great actor in his first maturity. And a year or so afterwards, in the same company. Alec Guinness was coming up to challenge on the rails. Then, later in the 40s, the new young lions made their bids: Paul Scofield and Richard Burton, whom one saw as a pair whose careers might well interact as fruitfully and contrastingly as those of Gielgud and Olivier. (But Burton went his own way, which was the theatre's loss, and, really, not much of anyone's gain.)

In the 50s, as these pages faithfully record, the directors began to take over. So – particularly from 1956 onward – did the authors. Formerly, a playwright in postwar England had been either a man who wrote box-set small-cast plays about the minor emotional crises of the middle and upper classes; or a man who wrote broad farces about the lower orders, often in uniform, sometimes in civvies; or a man who (like Christopher Fry and T. S. Eliot) wrote sclerotic verse plays and was dubbed, doubtless to his own embarrassment, a 'new Elizabethan'; or a man who wrote flops. (I exclude from these categories Noël Coward, who at this time was devoting himself to writing bad Noël Coward plays.) After the launching of the English Stage Company at the Royal Court in 1956, and the revelation of John Osborne, a semblance of serious thought and a flood of non-refined feeling invaded the theatre after a long absence. One of the many things about theatre that I realized during this period was that, like William Hazlitt a century and a half earlier, I had seen very few great performances in non-classic plays, and not all that many in plays that were not by Shakespeare. Now the modern English repertoire seemed at last to be making room for the great actor; and we had, among other pleasures, Olivier in *The Entertainer*. Moreover, one found, in the wake of the Royal Court innovations (and the simultaneous exploits of Joan Littlewood's company at Stratford, East), that one's social and political beliefs were being engaged and challenged in a way that English drama since Shaw's heyday had rarely attempted. It was around this time, the usual two decades late, that the English discovered Bertolt Brecht — a discovery that had enormous and still reverberating repercussions on almost every aspect of theatrical style : on playwrights, obviously, but also on directors (of classics not less than contemporary plays), on designers (e.g. Jocelyn Herbert and John Bury), on composers, and on such other departments of stagecraft as lighting, wardrobe and make-up. Shaftesbury Avenue today (apart from a few genuine novelties like *Oh! Calcutta!* and a great deal more freedom of speech, thanks to the abolition of stage censorship) remains much as it was a quarter of a century ago; but the rest of our theatre has been permeated, for good or ill, by Brecht, and no influence of comparable magnitude is yet in sight.

Nor, I might add, does the present horizon hold a

young director with anything like the transforming power of Peter Brook. It is a worrying thought that Brook, who must be fifty, is the last authentic *enfant terrible* of stagecraft that the English theatre has produced. We have a tiny quorum of distinguished and sometimes very exciting directors, perhaps enough to crew a college boat; but when these gentlemen have turned your play down you are apt to find it falling into the hands of halfwits. The reason, I suppose, is that young directorial talent nowadays goes straight into TV and cinema, by-passing the theatre altogether.

The pieces in this book make up a record of the most memorable things I saw on English stages between the last year of the war and the early 1960s, when I gave up regular reviewing to work with Laurence Olivier at the National Theatre. They have all appeared before in hard-cover form, though not between the same hard covers. Many come from my first book, *He That Plays the King*, which was published when I was freshly down from Oxford and has long been out of print; the rest are chosen from two other collections of my work called *Curtains* and *Tynan Right and Left*. The era they record ended, or radically changed its nature, with the rise of the great institutional theatres – the Royal Shakespeare and the National – in the 1960s. I was mixed up in the latter from its inception, and my account of it is matter for another book. Meanwhile here is my guide to the previous epoch : it contains full descriptions of landmarks, ancient monuments, *curiosités historiques* (* * * *vaut le détour*), follies, mountain peaks, and even disaster areas.

Please understand that I claim no intrinsic superiority for the actors of the immediate postwar period over those of today. What is undeniable, however, is that the equivalent actor of today spends far less of his time on the stage than his predecessors did. We may see their like again, but we shall not see the like of their theatrical careers. It may therefore be possible to see this book as a kind of elegy. Although some of it was written in fury, the best of it was, I think, written in gratitude.

Richard III

by WILLIAM SHAKESPEARE
at the New

From a sombre and uninventive production this brooding,
withdrawn player leapt into life, using the circumambient
gloom as his springboard. Olivier's Richard eats into the
memory like acid into metal, but the total impression is
one of lightness and deftness. The whole thing is taken
at a speed baffling when one recalls how perfectly, even
finically, it is articulated : it is Olivier's trick to treat
each speech as a kind of plastic vocal mass, and not as
a series of sentences whose import must be precisely
communicated to the audience : the method is impression-
ist. He will seize on one or two phrases in each paragraph
which, properly inserted, will unlock its whole meaning :
the rest he discards, with exquisite idleness. To do this
successfully he needs other people on the stage with him :
to be ignored, stared past, or pushed aside during the
lower reaches, and gripped and buttonholed when the
wave rises to its crested climax. For this reason Olivier
tends to fail in soliloquy – except when, as in the opening
speech of *Richard*, it is directed straight at the audience,
who then become his temporary foils. I thought, for example, that the night-piece before the battle sagged badly,
in much the same way as the soliloquies in the *Hamlet*
film sagged. Olivier the actor needs reactors : just as
electricity, *in vacuo*, is unseen, unfelt, and powerless.

I see that I have used the word 'trick' to describe this
characteristic; I want to make it clear thus early that
it is used in this book with connotations of applause and
admiration. A 'trick', when we set about defining it and
stop using it in the vaguely pejorative sense in which an
unsuccessful actor will always describe a successful one
as 'a bundle of tricks', is nothing more despicable than
a unique piece of technique, a special catch of the voice,

tilt of the head, or manual gesture. It becomes offensive only when it is used in a part irrelevant to the aspect or aspects of the actor's personality which it represents: for instance, if Olivier were to use his famous 'traffic-policeman' pose while playing Morell in *Candida*, it would almost certainly jar, and would thus become a 'mannerism'. But tricks can quite legitimately be used to eke out dull parts or heighten good ones. It is surprising how many of the most exciting and exhilarating performances one has ever seen are written off by the profession as 'naughty – terribly naughty'. By this is meant that the actor has outstripped the classic norm of part-interpretation, and imported ingenuities and subtleties of his own: he is naughty as a schoolboy is who asks unanswerable questions. (For the standard exemplar of naughtiness, look at Charles Laughton.) Tricks are to acting what phrase-making is to poetry; within a good formal contour they are luminous gems. The opposite of a 'tricky' or 'naughty' actor is a 'lovely' or 'charming' one, by which the profession means that in him it recognizes a player severely enough type-cast and self-effacing enough not to be counted as a possible rival.

Craggy and beetlebrowed, Olivier's face is not especially mobile: he acts chiefly with his voice. In Richard it is slick, taunting, and curiously casual; nearly impersonal, 'smooth as sleekstone', patting and pushing each line into shape. Occasionally he tips his animal head back and lets out a gurgling avuncular cackle, a good-humoured snarl: and then we see the over-riding mephitic good humour of the man, the vulgar joy he takes in being a clever upstart. Ingrowing relish at his complotting kindles him, making him smoulder with laughter. We laugh, too; and some attempt has been made to prove that we laugh too sympathetically. T. C. Worsley in the *New Statesman* very ably took up this cudgel, and said that Richard's humour should arouse the chuckle that is born of nervous fear, not the belly-laugh. Now in ideal terms this argument is not refutable: it would be impossible to *demonstrate* that though no single detail or trick in the whole performance is in itself macabre in the correct manner, the total gesture is one of unpleasant and vulgar nastiness: in the same way an obscene statue can be made of pure gold. The kind of laugh Worsley is objecting to and I am supporting is that which Olivier gets when the head of Hastings is brought on in a bag: he peeps in with wistful intentness, looking almost elegiac – then, after a pause, hurriedly turns the bag as he realizes he has been looking at the head upside down. That gets its laugh, and it is, I agree, not unsympathetic to Richard. Only afterwards are we struck with the after-thought that we have just laughed at a very foul piece of casual dissembling: and we are rather ashamed. What, in fact, would Mr Worsley have us substitute? a crazy peal of laughter? or that oldest of film-Gestapo tricks, a slow, meditative, malevolent smile? The point about evil is surely that one does not notice until afterwards that it is evil at all: it is a door through which, unwitting, we pass, and which we observe only as it slams behind us. To me cats, sunflowers, white tiles in suburban kitchens, urinating horses, silk-scarved youths on Sunday, marionettes and glades of fir trees, all innocent in them-selves, are unaccountably among the harbingers of evil. I say all this to indicate that an evil thing need not be horrid or repellent in itself: it must deceive us into thinking it good. To tempt at all, Satan must charm us. I do not think it would be true to say that Olivier's Richard ever makes us warm to him; we never feel de-light or admiration; we simply laugh, and that implies neither encouragement nor hostility, but mere acceptance of an act performed. I think of Sidney: '. . . though laughter may come *with* delight, yet cometh it not *of* delight.' The two things are different: and Olivier rightly taps only the former.

In this Richard was enshrined Blake's conception of active, energetic evil, in all its wicked richness. A lithe performance, black at heart and most astutely mellow in appearance, it is full of baffling, irrational subtleties which will please while they puzzle me as long as I go to theatres. I remember the deep concern, as of a bustling spinster, with which Olivier grips his brother George and says, with sardonic, effeminate intentness: 'We are not safe, Clarence; we are *not safe*'; while, even as he speaks, the plot is laid which will kill the man. The persistent *bonhomie* of middle age shines in his face as he jests with his chosen victims: how often he skirts the footlights, his eyes tipped skyward, on some especially ironic aside: with what icy disregard he slights his too ambitious minion Buckingham! 'I am not in the giving vein to-day': the words fall like drops of frozen dew. The rejection of Buckingham is beautifully prepared, too, in the moment at the end of Shakespeare's Act III after Gloster has been coaxed into accepting the crown. From the window in Baynard's castle where he stands, Richard leaps down, tossing his prayer book over his shoulder, to embrace Buckingham and exult over their triumph. In mid-career he stops, mindful of his new majesty; and instead of a joyful hug, Buckingham sees the iron-clad hand of his friend extended to him to be kissed, and behind it, erect in horrid disdain, the top-heavy figure of the King of England.

Vulgar pride is an important point of departure for many of this Richard's major effects. The monstrous, inquisitive nose (aquiline in elephantiasis), boorishly intruded where least welcomed, emphasizes it, and the dog-like sniff and cock of eye when he points a comic line. In movement he is gawkily impulsive, with a lurching limp reminiscent of the stage gait of Mr Jimmy James: only the arms, wonderfully free and relaxed, are beautiful. He flings them out and they come to rest in grace. The secret of the passion Olivier generates is that intuition and impulse, not premeditation, control Richard's actions. The vulgar heart beats through it all: with a marvellous tact he suggests its presence in the contemptuous emphasis he gives to: '. . . you, *Lord* Rivers and *Lord* Grey'. Secure in triumph, conscious of his failings, he revels in exposing them, since none may gainsay him. And when the end approaches, his hoarse, strangled roar for a horse sums up all the impotent fury of a Machiavellian who must yield up his life and the fruits of his precise conspiring because of an accident of battle. To be vanquished by the ill luck of being unseated is a final ignominy to this enormous swindler. His broken sword clutched by the blade in both hands, he whirls, dreadfully constricted, and thrashes about with animal ferocity, writhing for absolute hate; he dies, arms and legs thrusting and kicking in savage, incommunicable agony, stabbing at air.

When Olivier revived this production in 1949 with a vastly inferior supporting company, the part of Lady Anne was given to Vivien Leigh, who quavered through the lines in a sort of rapt oriental chant. It was a bad performance, coldly kittenish, but it made the wooing credible, since this silly woman would probably have believed anything. And Olivier managed even to draw pathos from the grisly courtship, and put me in mind of Sidney's elegiacs:

> Unto a caitiff wretch, whom long affliction holdeth,
> And now fully believes hope to be quite vanished,
> Grant, grant yet a look to the last moment of his anguish.

For a moment the hunchback *histrio* joined the stricken ranks of repulsed Renaissance lovers, and one could have wept for him.

Has anyone, I wonder, discovered this neat summary of the general significance of the history plays? It comes in Gorki's *Lower Depths*:

LUKA: Everybody is trying to be boss, and is threatening everybody else with all kinds of punishment – and still there is no order in life . . . and no cleanliness –

BUBNOV: All the world likes order, but some people's brains aren't fit for it. All the same – the room should be swept. . . .

(1944)

Hamlet

by WILLIAM SHAKESPEARE
at the Haymarket

Body and soul seem always to be at odds in John Gielgud's work: during the 'O what a rogue' speech, I found myself thinking of Blair's lines in *The Grave*:

> ... *how the frantic soul*
> *Raves round the walls of her clay tenement.*

His voice is all soul, injured and struggling: but the body is curiously ineffectual, with the result, for me, that his acting lacks stomach and heart. He prances fluently enough, but with the grace of ballet rather than of animals and men. One thinks of Olivier in terms of other species, of panthers and lions: one thinks of Gielgud in terms of other arts, of ballet and portrait painting. His face is best in repose: in the eyes there is noble rebuke, in the pursed lips and sunk cheeks you discern a defiant melancholy, overcast by wisdom and the traditional poet's sadness. The voice is thrilling and bears witness to great suffering; an east wind has blown through it. In quieter times it has the same authority I used to feel in schoolboy stories, when the school captain confronts the bully of the upper fifth tormenting a fag. ' "Stop that, Stoker," said Jimmy Silver quietly.' Whoever compared Gielgud to Steerforth was not hopelessly at fault. Yet with all these powers, he is not an intemperately exciting actor: too wire-drawn, too thin-spun and fugitive, essentially unanchored to earth. The voice, too, tends to fly too high, and resorts too often to a resonant alto head-note which, though it certainly expresses demoniacal possession, will not do for all the variety of demoniacal rage, terror, love and scorn.

George Rylands's production was brown. I know that that is not nearly enough, but neither was the production : dim, flatly lit, and snail-paced, it dragged its slow length along, committing nearly all the obvious errors of Shakespearian production as it went, including the fault, born of uninventiveness and an unwieldy permanent set, of playing half the scenes before a travers curtain. Nothing so clearly and swiftly anaesthetizes Shakespeare as the travers curtain.

When I saw this *Hamlet*, Leslie Banks had been replaced as Claudius by Abraham Sofaer, who, with the Jewish actor's gift for appearing to be a dignified but slightly pathetic intruder, managed to capture an altogether remarkable slice of the audience's sympathy, and so restored the balance of a play too often obscured by the eclipsing charm of its hero.

In the same season, Gielgud played in Somerset Maugham's *The Circle* and Olivier in *Arms and the Man*, as Sergius. Both performances, able and diverting as they were, left me unhappy : there is no real place in modern comedy for the rhetoric, the expansiveness of gesture, on which these actors thrive; both men were constantly bursting the seams of their parts. It is of the first importance nowadays in intelligent comedy to get across the footlights the precise meaning of the lines; every speech, instead of being a gesture of character, as it is in Jonson, tends to be a contribution to an argument. It is not for Olivier and Gielgud to argue on our stages : that lesser men can do better. Only the Americans still write comedies of humours in Jonson's and Dryden's sense : plays like Kaufman and Hart's *You Can't Take it With You* and *The Man Who Came to Dinner* retain much of the zeal for eccentricity, the delight in odd, obsessed, ludicrous creatures, which inform *Volpone* and *The Alchemist*. Modern American farce is artificial and rhetorical in a manner of which English dramatists since Pinero have completely lost sight.

(1944)

Love for Love

by WILLIAM CONGREVE
at the Haymarket

Here is a comedy in which Mr. Gielgud can properly
abandon himself: there is plenty of elbow-room, arm-
room, and leg-room for pyrotechnics. I like this play
better than the intricate, better-mannered *Way of the
World*: it is more extravagant, with its hoyden, its wild
astrologer, and its busteous seaman, and it has a wittier
hero. The stage pictures conjured up by Rex Whistler
in this production were among the loveliest I have ever
seen, and Gielgud, as Valentine, postured beautifully before them. Tongue-in-cheek and hand-on-heart, he played
the mock-madness scenes as a sort of burlesque of his
own Hamlet: he extended the intense raptness, the silent
inner lightnings which he shares with Irving, until they
reached delicious absurdity. Gielgud is an actor who refuses to compromise with his audience: he does not offer
a welcoming hand, but binds a spell instead. They must
accept him on his own intellectual level, or not at all.
This aloofness and rigid dignity of his represent his only
unique quality: some day he must read the tragedies
of Chapman, when he will discover that he is the only
actor in Europe today who could play Bussy, Clermont
or Byron with anything like the icy poise the parts
demand.

The contrast between Gielgud and Olivier is instructive.
It can be roughly equated with the contrast Dr Johnson
pointed out between Milton's ability to carve a colossus
out of granite, and his inability to carve heads on cherry-
stones. For the large, shattering effects of passion, we look
to Olivier; for the smaller, more exquisite effects of
temper, to Gielgud. To use an old and respectable critical
terminology, it is the contrast between Nature and Art.
For the best-ordered idealizations of that with which we

are familiar, Gielgud carries off the palm; for the exploration of new, strange territories and planets, Olivier is our guide. In another medium, the comparison between Pope's Homer, gracious, supple and light of foot, and Chapman's, rugged and obstreperous, indicates the same distinction. In Book XXIII, for instance, it needs no extraordinary skill to divine that Gielgud would prefer to utter Pope's 'Ah! whither wanders thy distempered mind?' while Chapman's rendering, 'The gods have made thee mad,' is undoubtedly for Olivier. The whole matter has already been discussed, with magnificent eloquence, by Burke in the *Enquiry into the Nature of our Ideas upon the Sublime and the Beautiful*: in which the best and deepest statement is made of this radical aesthetic fission. In poetry and painting, I am for the Beautiful: in drama and sculpture, for the Sublime; hence, for me, Olivier is the better actor of the two. By just so much, Tom Tower in Oxford is greater than All Saints Church.

(1944)

Donald Wolfit

in SHAKESPEARE

In the course of 1944 I saw Wolfit in nearly all the considerable parts in the Shakespearian repertory, and out of that surfeit I think I can form an opinion. There has never been an actor of greater gusto than Wolfit: he has dynamism, energy, bulk and stature, and he joins these together with a sheer relish for resonant words which splits small theatres as Caruso shattered wine glasses. His Iachimo is a vast, gloating reptile; his Iago is sly on a very large scale, almost to the point of crudity; his Richard III is a visionary Sweeney Todd. It is grossly unfair, as well as inaccurate, to accuse him of being a 'ham'; if 'ham' means what I take it to mean, one who rants and roars and strikes poses of unnecessary and grotesque

23

altitude. Wolfit does none of these things: on the contrary, he moves very slowly and predatorily, with immense finesse, and rises to his climaxes in clear and cogent steps. There is a great deal of almost paternal authority and decision in everything he does (his great fault is to pat the audience's head instead of hitting it between the eyes): he never roars unless the text compels roaring. When it does, his voice, instead of caressing the syllables, whips them up to a frenzy, and hits a frightening, dilapidated whining note; and though my words sound comic, the effect is not. Wolfit is called 'ham', I fancy, largely because he is a middle-aged actor-manager who goes on provincial tours with an unimpressive supporting cast: that is certainly a clue to his weakness, but it is not the weakness we label 'ham'. He is an instinctive actor, and, I suspect, as blind to his own good points as to other people's bad ones. Wolfit's error lies in cherishing what I can only describe as a provincial inferiority complex to the extent of being unable or unwilling to work for anyone but himself. If he can overcome that, the West End will acquire an actor of greater technical power than it currently possesses; but there is not much time left.

Four performances stand out in my memory of Wolfit. His Macbeth, a piece of acting which displays so overwhelmingly and consistently the effect of a tenebrous obsession eating away the heart of a warrior that it deserves the name of castle-storming rather than barn-storming; his Volpone, a solid caricature overflowing with *bourgeois* wickedness; his imperious Shylock; and, of course, his Lear, majestic and devastated. His exit at the end of Act I, after the curse upon Goneril, with a dogwhip in his left hand and his right resting for comfort on the Fool's shoulder, is an irresistible tug to the tears he has so carefully delayed in us throughout the scene; we are prepared for the hurricane in his lungs which later, on the heath, threatens to scorch the stage. Wolfit's Hamlet is a fascinating but fruitless adventure into realms where he may not tread: it exposes his principal failing, which is not insensitiveness, but a physical equipment inadequate for dealing with poetry. He appears coarse-grained, and seems to lack taste: these are blank spots which we do not notice in Lear or Macbeth, where they lie at the periphery of the characters, but which damage the core of Hamlet. Wolfit has no flair for delicacy, no ear for Chesterfield's reiterated cry of 'The Graces! the Graces!' That critic was right who called his Hamlet a private detective keeping tabs on the Danish Royal Family. In comedy, too, the gap is wide: his Malvolio, Touchstone, and Benedick are all *obvious* performances, and his Bottom is sheer music-hall. Only in a catch-as-catch-can middle-class farce like *The Merry Wives* can he prosper: his Falstaff in that expertly contrived and very funny play is easily the best low performance I have seen him give.

As a character, Wolfit belongs to Tudor England; not to the days of Elizabeth, but to the upstart tyrannical *bourgeois* who reaped the fruits of the English Reformation. He dominates a stage not with the effortless authority of kingship, but by a mighty exercise of talent, thrust and will. He came into prominence by a hard path, and arrived grimy, dusty and travel-torn: and in every part he plays, the psychological marks left by the battle show sorely through his make-up.

(1944)

The Skin of Our Teeth

by THORNTON WILDER
at the Piccadilly

At last a pale featherweight beauty has found her own pretty level: Sabina is the flirtatious self-sufficient housemaid who accompanies the Antrobus family on its desperate emergence from the cave to the centrally heated apartment, and Miss Leigh's particular brand of frail,

unfelt *coquetterie* fits the part like an elbow-length glove.
When I first saw *Our Town*, I suspected Thornton Wilder
of being a fraud: he was, I said, creating a spurious
excitement by performing without scenery a piece of
writing which would be as banal as Richmal Crompton
if staged with normal décor; just so, a man might raise
a furore by playing *The Bells* in bathing trunks. But when
I met Mr Wilder, and saw the almost horrified passion
in his face as he spoke of the modern theatre, and heard
him say: 'We don't need new dramatists. We don't need
new actors. What the theatre needs is a new architect' –
then, cowering under the tough little man's glare, I conceded him profoundly genuine. And *The Skin of Our
Teeth* confirmed this, and added an impression of wit,
and of zany Heath-Robinson structural genius.

Miss Leigh passes the evening in a thigh-length caricature of a frilly housemaid's dress, flicking idly at non-
existent mantelpieces with a feather broom. She executes
all the accepted repertoire of femininity – vapid eyelash-
fluttering, mock-unconcern, plain silliness – with convulsive effect and yet always with her brows slightly
arched in affected boredom. She treats her lines as if
she were going through a very fluent first reading, with
little variation of pitch or tone; and puts important
phrases in prodigiously inverted commas. The picture
of chithood is unerring and the comparison with an
adolescent Katherine Hepburn slightly bemused by drugs
is irresistible. I can sum up all with a quotation:

> With so sweet voice, and by sweet nature so
> In sweetest strength, so sweetly skill'd withal,
> In all sweet stratagems sweet art can show.

Miss Leigh is likewise sweet; but when you have said
that half a dozen times, you have said everything.

(1945)

Oedipus Rex

by SOPHOCLES
at the New

It is bitter to have to confess that the one unmistakable phrase for this performance has already been coined: out of I know not what journalistic intuition it came, and it stands undeniable: 'a panther among doves.' Before John Piper's décor, garishly sunset and focused on to a formidable idol, stood Chorus, a cluster of decent eld, forming and reforming themselves as Montague tells us William Poel arranged his chorus in *Samson Agonistes*. Into their midst strode Olivier, black fingercurls surmounting an arrogant, sensitive built-up nose. Both literally and in Meredith's sense, you saw that he had a leg: it needed no effort of the mind to deduce that, if pricked, he would bleed purple gore, not blood. The thick, intolerant voice syncopated perfectly with the lithe, jungle movements of the man: intellectually and physically he was equipped for the heaviest suffering: his shoulders could bear disaster. I know that from the first I was waiting breathlessly for the time when the rack would move into the final notch, and the lyric cry would be released: but I never hoped for so vast an anguish. Olivier's famous 'Oh! Oh!' when the full catalogue of his sin is unfolded must still be resounding in some high recess of the New Theatre's dome: some stick of wood must still, I feel, be throbbing from it. The two cries were torn from beyond tears or shame or guilt: they came from the stomach, with all the ecstatic grief and fright of a newborn baby's wail. The point is not whether these crazy sobs were 'tricks' or whether or not they were necessary to the part: the point is that they were overwhelming experiences, and that no other actor in England could have carried them off. A man seeing the horrors of infinity in a trance might make such

27

a sound : a man awaking from a nightmare to find it truth might make such a sound; but no other man, and no other actor. I thought of Robert Greene's words in his last sickness, when a priest revealed the nature of hell to him; and summoning up all his hypochondriacal guilts, he wrote that 'for very anguish of mind my teeth beat in my head, my looks waxed pale and wan, and fetching a deep sigh I cried unto God and said, if all this be true, Oh, what shall become of me?'

Sybil Thorndike played Jocasta in an entirely different convention, which I found jarring. The *prima donna* tragedienne (an oracular Sybil), with plump arms and a bellowing contralto, given to sudden hawk-like sweeps up and down the stage, she played with that traditional blazing intensity which, so far from illuminating the personality, strangles it into a sort of red-hot anonymity. She treated every line as if it were the crucial line of the play : it was all so ponderously weighted that when the big hurdles approached, the horse couldn't jump.

Oedipus was played as a curtain-raiser to Sheridan's *The Critic*, in which Olivier was Puff. This meant that the wittiest play in English must be galloped through lest the patrons miss their last tubes : and the result was fast and infuriating. *The Critic* is one of the very smallest group of great plays in that it attains the most uproarious effects of fun by sheer verbal ingenuity. It has no 'situations', no plot, no shape, no development : it has only words, and words chimed subtly together into a pattern of wit that Sheridan could never afterwards repeat. It is a play to be taken at a leisurely pace, easy and delicate, as its single theme, that of undressing the eighteenth-century tragic muse, is slowly unwound. Sheridan always worked best from a Restoration model, and here he had Villiers's telling parody of Dryden's tragic method, *The Rehearsal*, to follow : his imagination ran wild in the manner of an eighteenth-century *Hellzapoppin*, and we owe it to him and ourselves not to lose a word of what it produced. Olivier, I thought, made the cardinal error of not trusting his author : feeling that the part was not funny enough, he donned yet another nose, this time foolishly *retroussé*, to make it quite clear that this was a comic character. Ralph Richardson, playing Burleigh (who, you remember, appears once, sits, thinks, shakes his head and makes a stately exit, never to be seen again), fell victim to the same plague of over-elaboration: determined to make what is known as 'a delicious little cameo' out of a part already hysterically amusing, he made Burleigh into an elderly jitterbug, twitching and hopping about like a maimed insect. This was all very flat, and made me sweat with embarrassment. But nothing was unforgivable except Olivier's handling of the precious words, which he scattered abroad as if they were no more than an expendable accompaniment to his own physical antics: some were lost in the wings, others in the footlights, and very few can have reached the gallery. The whole performance was a bad slap in the face for Sheridan, and its failure arose out of Olivier's blindness to the fact that it is to no purpose that one embroiders that which is in itself embroidery. To try to substitute a physical equivalent for the unearthly wit of Sheridan is as difficult as to retouch a photograph with a tar-brush: you cannot help seeming clumsy and intrusive. I thought the production of this play at the Arts two years earlier a much more satisfying piece of work; Hugh Burden, by more tenderly respecting Puff's lines, made a much funnier shot at the part.

(1945)

Henry IV

by WILLIAM SHAKESPEARE
at the New

From a production so unobtrusive that at times it looked positively mousy, three very great pieces of acting emerged. The Old Vic was now at its height: the watershed had been reached, and one of those rare moments in the theatre had arrived when drama paused, took stock of all that it had learnt since Irving, and then produced a monument in celebration. It is surprising, when one considers it, that English acting should have reached up and seized a laurel crown in the middle of a war, and that the plays in which the prize was won should have been plays of battle, tumult, conspiracy and death, as the histories are. There was a bad atmosphere then amongst the acting clubs of London – an atmosphere such as one finds in the senior common-rooms of the women's colleges at Oxford: an air of pugnacious assurance and self-sufficiency mixed with acrid misogyny. There were roughly two groups of actors: the elder, who seemed to be suffering from thyroid deficiency, a condition which induces a blunt and passive sedentariness in the sufferer: and the very young ones, afflicted by the opposite sickness, thyroid excess, whose symptoms are emaciation and nervous constriction. The good, mature players were silent: the state of society had tied their hands, and they tied their own tongues. It was left to Richardson and Olivier to sum up English acting in themselves; and this was what, in *Henry IV*, they achieved.

Richardson's Falstaff was not a *comic* performance: it was too rich and many-sided to be crammed into a single word. The humour of it, as in Max Beerbohm's prose, was in the texture: there were no deliberate farcical effects. This was the down-at-heel dignity of W. C. Fields translated into a nobler language: here was a Falstaff whose principal attribute was not his fatness but his knighthood. He was Sir John first, and Falstaff second, and let every cock-a-hoop young dog beware. The spirit behind all the rotund nobility was spry and elastic: that, almost, of what Skelton in a fine phrase called 'friskajolly younkerkins'; there was also, working with great slyness but great energy, a sharp business sense: and, when the situation called for it, great wisdom and melancholy ('Peace, good Doll! do not speak like a death's head: do not bid me remember my end' was done with most moving authority). Each word emerged with immensely careful articulation, the lips forming it lovingly and then spitting it forth: in moments of passion, the wild white halo of hair stood angrily up and the eyes rolled majestically: and in rage one noticed a slow meditative relish taking command: 'Marry, there is another indictment upon thee, for suffering flesh to be eaten in thy house, contrary to the law; for the which I think – thou – wilt – howl': the last four words with separate thrice-chewed pungency. Richardson never rollicked or slobbered or staggered: it was not a sweaty fat man, but a dry and dignified one. As the great belly moved, step following step with great finesse lest it overtopple, the arms flapped fussily at the sides as if to paddle the body's bulk along. It was deliciously and subtly funny, not riotously so: from his height of pomp Falstaff was chuckling at himself: it was not we alone, laughing at him. He had good manners and also that respect for human dignity which prevented him from openly showing his boredom at the inanities of Shallow and Silence: he had only recently sunk from the company of kings to the company of heirs-apparent. None of the usual epithets for Falstaff applied to Richardson: he was not often jovial, laughed seldom, belched never. In disgrace, he affected the mask of a sulky schoolboy, in the manner of Charles Laughton: in command, he would punch his wit at the luckless heads of his comrades, and their admiration would forbid response. The rejection scene at the end of Part II came off heartrendingly well: with his back to the audience Richardson thumped forward to welcome the new king, his whilom jackanapes: and after the key-cold rebuke which is his answer, the old man turned, his face red and working in furious *tics* to hide his tears. The immense pathos of his reassuring words to Shallow even now wets my eyes: 'I shall be sent for soon at night.' He hurried, whispered through the line very energetically, as if the whole matter were of no consequence: the emptiness of complete collapse stood awfully behind it. It was pride, not feasting and foining, that laid this Falstaff low: the youthful, hubristic heart inside the corporeal barrel had flown too high, and must be crushed. Cyril Connolly might have been speaking of this performance when he said : 'Imprisoned in every fat man a thin one is wildly signalling to be let out' – let out, and slaughtered. Beside this Falstaff, Nicholas Breton's picture of a drunkard seems almost blasphemous : 'a tub of swill, a spirit of sleep, a picture of a beast and a monster of a man.'

Enough has already been written of Olivier's Hotspur, that ferocious darling of war. With the roughness and heedlessness of the warrior chieftain, he mixed the heavy-handed tenderness of the very virile husband : and knotted the performance into a unity by a trick, the stammer which prefaced every word beginning with the letter 'w'. This clever device fitted perfectly with the over-anxiousness, the bound-burstingness, the impotent eagerness of the character. The long speech of explanation to the king about the unransomed prisoners, beginning 'My liege, I did deny no prisoners', is essentially an apology : for this Hotspur it was an aggressive explosion of outraged innocence :

> . . . for it made me mad [almost a shriek]
> To see him shine so brisk and smell so sweet
> And talk so like a waiting-gentlewoman
> Of guns and drums and w-w-

(Here the face almost burst for frenzy : the actor stamped the ground to loosen the word from his mouth. Finally, in a convulsion of contempt, it sprang out)

> w-wounds – God save the mark!

This impediment dovetailed so well with Hotspur's death that one could not escape concluding that Olivier had begun his interpretation of the part at the end and worked backwards : the dying speech ends thus :

> . . . no, Percy, thou art dust,
> And food for –
> HENRY : For worms, brave Percy.

I need not add that Olivier died in the throes of uttering that maddening, elusive consonant.

The most treasurable scenes in these two productions were those in Shallow's orchard: if I had only half an hour more to spend in theatres, and could choose at large, no hesitation but I would have these. Richardson's performance, coupled with that of Miles Malleson as Silence, beak-nosed, pop-eyed, many-chinned and mumbling, and Olivier as Shallow, threw across the stage a golden autumnal veil, and made the idle sporadic chatter of the lines glow with the same kind of delight as Gray's *Elegy*. There was a sharp scent of plucked crab-apples, and of pork in the larder: one got the sense of life-going-on-in-the-background, of rustling twigs underfoot and the large accusing eyes of cows, staring through the twilight. Shakespeare never surpassed these scenes in the vein of pure naturalism: the subtly criss-crossed counterpoint of the opening dialogue between the two didderers, which skips between the price of livestock at market and the philosophic fact of death ('Death, saith the Psalmist, is certain; all must die'), is worked out with fugal delicacy: the talk ends with Shallow's unanswered rhetorical question: 'And is old Double dead?' No reply is necessary: the stage is well and truly set, and any syllable more would be superfluous. The flavour of sharp masculine kindness Olivier is adept in: for me the best moment in his *Hamlet* film was the pat on the head for the players' performing dog which accompanied the line: 'I am glad to see thee well.' And it was in the very earth of this Gloucestershire orchard. Olivier was the Old Satyr in this Muses' Elizium; 'Through his lean chops a chattering he doth make, which stirs his staring, beastly-drivell'd beard.' This Shallow (pricked with yet another nose, a loony apotheosis of the hook-snout he wore as Richard) is a crapulous, paltering scarecrow of a man, withered up like the slough of a snake; but he has quick, commiserating eyes and the kind of delight in dispensing food and drink that one associates with a favourite aunt. He pecks at the lines, nibbles at them like a parrot biting on a nut; for all his age, he darts here and there nimbly enough, even skittishly; forgetting nothing, not even the pleasure of Falstaff's page, that 'little tiny thief'. The keynote of the performance is old-maidishness, agitated and pathetically anxious to make things go with a swing : a crone-like pantomime dame, you might have thought, were it not for the beady delectation that steals into his eyes at the mention of sex. (Shallow was, as Falstaff later points out, 'as lecherous as a monkey'.) His fatuous repetitions are those of importunate female decrepitude : he nags rather than bores. Sometimes, of course, he loses the use of one or more of his senses : protesting, over the table, that Falstaff must not leave, he insists, emphasizing the words by walking his fingers over the board : 'I will not excuse you, sir; you shall not be excused; excuses shall not be admitted; there is no excuse shall serve; you shall not be excused' – and after his breathless panic of hospitality, he looks hopefully up : but Falstaff has long since gone. Shallow had merely forgotten to observe his departure : and the consequent confusion of the man, as he searches with his eyes for his vanished guest, is equalled only by his giggling embarrassment at finding him standing behind him.

Of all the wonderful work Olivier did in this and the previous Old Vic season, I liked nothing more than this. A part of this actor's uniqueness lies in the restricted demands he makes on his audience's rational and sensual capacities. Most actors invite the spectator either to pass a *moral* judgement on the characters they are representing : or to pass a *physical* judgement on their own appearance. A normal actor playing a moderately sympathetic part will go all out to convince the audience that he is a thoroughly good man, morally impeccable; playing a villain, he will force them to see the enormity of the man's sins. He will translate the character into the terms of a bad nineteenth-century novel. An attractive actor playing the part of a *jeune premier* will try primarily to arouse the admiration of the women and the envy of the men; a player of farce will rely chiefly on grotesque make-up to establish the character for him. But most actors do insist on a judgement of one kind or another: and they are better or worse actors according to the degree to which it is obvious that they are *insisting*. Olivier makes no such attempts to insist, and invites no moral response: simply the thing he is shall make him live. It is a rare discretion, an ascetic tact which none but he dares risk.

(1946)

Love's Labour's Lost

by WILLIAM SHAKESPEARE
at the Shakespeare Memorial Theatre, Stratford-on-Avon

A young, sage little person (in his middle twenties) established himself with this production amongst the new leaders of the English theatre, along with Peter Ustinov, Michael Benthall, and their like. The farce scenes came off badly: Costard was insensitively conceived, and the pedants, who can be made hilariously funny, were caricatured out of life: I am sure Peter Brook's biggest gap is his lack of a wide sense of humour. But the rest was exquisite in the real sense of a freely traduced word. The play was set in Watteau costumes and groupings: the Princess was accompanied wherever she went by a mute, white-faced pierrot; and the whole stage had a wonderfully decadent *ancien régime* smell about it. The sudden change into the minor key at the end, when the tonic is replaced by a sudden diminished seventh on the entrance of Mercade with the news of the death of the Princess's father, came across as a superb dying fall, and left the actors twilit, their laughter frozen on their lips. The master-performance in this most allusive and opaque production was that of Paul Scofield as Don Armado. This was the first of Mr Scofield's fine seasons at Stratford, and it followed a brilliant career at Birmingham Repertory Theatre. I do not think, at this stage, he had done

35

better than Armado, which was played, not as the conventional blustering huff-puffer, but as a fading grandee, tired and drooping, with a thin scurf of moustache curling down over his upper lip. He walked pensively, and a little rheumatically, tapping and describing slow circles with the head of a long swagger stick : Mr Scofield, not yet twenty-five, suggested a most delicate senility, modulating the shrill honk of his usual juvenile voice to an urgent, breaking murmur. Only one flaw faulted the characterization : it made the horseplay at the end, when Armado is baited by the rest of the court, seem unnecessary and unpleasant; even cruel.

(1946)

The Brothers Karamazov

adapted from DOSTOEVSKY *by* ALEC GUINNESS
at the Lyric, Hammersmith

This was a 'shock' production from the moment the lights went down : the first sound to emerge from the darkness was the double bang of a pair of revolvers being fired. Then a spot slowly came up on the idiot grinning face of Smerdyakev, leaning against the proscenium arch. 'These are my new pistols,' he said maliciously. The play had begun. Alec Guinness's adaptation of the novel was a little too complex for the stage : the pity was that the speech of the Inquisitor, which is the marrow of the book, was untranslatable into theatre. Guinness played Dmitri with nail-biting ardour; Ernest Milton was a silver-tongued Father Zossima, modulating in a moment from dry feminine hypocrisy to a rigid invincible piety; and Valk, as the lousy, boorish old patriarch, was shattering. His bull neck, thrust out defiantly as he drove home some crapulous jest; his colossus stride of feet; his laborious guttural voice; his thunder-darting eyes – Valk is preeminently an actor in whom physical attributes obtrude to the extinction of all other values. Yet he is subtle: the

timing of his interminable pauses, which defy interruption, is uncanny. He is the most insidious of battering-
rams, the most persuasive of earthquakes; he burns like a
hard, gem-like holocaust. He acts with his sweat and
stamina; rock-like and immobile, he exudes power, and
in action he is a fighting *toro*, too wily for the slimmest,
most cajoling matador to cite and kill. Valk is a wild
beast who has acquired cunning and cynicism by living
amongst men : he is a veritable legend for Aesop or
Rudyard Kipling. He is the ignoble savage, whose hunger
for lost paradises is replaced by a hunger for red meat
and battle. So, at least, I felt from this performance.
Bomb-like, it blasted you : and temporarily blinded me to
the rest of what was going on. For the other details, I can
add no more than that the lighting had all the infinite
care that one associates with Mr Brook; and that Alyosha
was as unconvincing on the stage as he is in the book.

The question of shock (Smerdyakev's pistols) is worth
pursuing. Eisenstein has studied the shock effect of sound,
and so has Welles. *Citizen Kane* is stunning even if one's
eyes are shut : my ears recall especially the screech of the
crested cockatoo. Regular visual shocks are equally important to prod an audience into expectancy (for example,
a house falling down, a thug dressed in white satin. a
thick yellow fog). This may appear false and shallow :
but the producer who can cunningly mix aural and visual
assaults remains the most exciting thing that can happen
to an audience. Shock is the denial of what is expected :
to cast a man of Francis L. Sullivan's lordly bulk as Osric
in *Hamlet* would be indifferent Shakespeare, but splendid
shock. A producer approaching an old play must assume,
to avoid triteness, that his audience has either seen or
read it before; as George Moore said, all that is not new is
negligible. And not only negligible : too easy. The producer should steel his wrists, not to interpret, but to
remould the commonplace. He should be able to say :
'All that I can ultimately comprehend is the importance
of devoting myself to one end : to investigating, by curious
squints, what combinations of aural and visual shocks,

performed on a lighted stage before a darkened auditorium, can cause the great white mottle of watching faces simultaneously to flush, blench, gasp, shriek, recoil, or stare in awe. I must admit myself to the audience's secrets, their lowest psychological factors, and play on them quite openly, but with deep guile. I do not concern myself with slow absorption, with what they may feel before the rise or after the fall of the curtain. My business is with immediacy, the sudden start of here and now.'

In Bacon's essay, *Of Great Place*, this sentence catches my eye: 'Question was asked of Demosthenes, what was the chief part of an orator? he answered, Action: what next? Action: what next again? Action.' The same is valid for the theatre: the more so when we remember that to an Elizabethan child, training in oratory and training in acting were identical.

(1946)

King Lear

by WILLIAM SHAKESPEARE
at the New

Old myths died hard, and new myths die harder. The Old Vic is fast becoming a new myth, and if I am stern, it is because I find their audiences culpable and in need of stricture. The company at the New Theatre had a lot to commend it: it could brag of a most regal yet winning player in Margaret Leighton, and a vivid, swashbuckling pythoness in Pamela Brown; it had that master of miniaturists, Alec Guinness, and two actors of prodigious range and energy in Messrs Olivier and Richardson. It had nothing else, but that should suffice us: these are good players, intelligent enough to accept with like equanimity applause for a triumph and tittering hand-claps for a flop. My plaint is that the loud battalions of ingenuous claqueurs who nightly mobbed the New Theatre fed them

38

on nothing but cheers. And this is rank unwisdom: laurels, while they may inspire a single great man, infallibly call up staleness and insipidity in a large company. And resting on one's laurels is uncomfortable and prickly. Take for, example, this *Lear*.

Olivier is a player of unparalleled animal powers, miraculously crossed with a player of extreme technical cuteness. The guttural precision of his voice would be unmistakable at a Cup Final, and its hoarse rallying note is the most invigorating sound in our theatres. He has a smoky moodiness of visage, a smoulderingness which always suggests danger and dynamism *cachés*. He is our model Richard III and his Hotspur is unique. But he has no intrinsic majesty; he always fights shy of pathos; and he cannot play old men without letting his jaw sag and his eye wander archly in magpie fashion – in short, without becoming funny. He gave a moderate Lear at the New, built up out of a few tremendous tantrums of impotence (notice the crazed emphases and tearing fullness of tone in his 'I will do such things, what they are, yet I know not; but they shall be the terrors of the earth') and an infinite run of cadenzas on his four most overworked tricks: (1) the stabbing finger; (2) the jaw and eye movement; (3) the ceaseless fits of wrestling with his cloak, like a tortoise with claustrophobia, and (4) the nervously nodding head. All these he exploited with rare diligence of bravura; it is an absorbing display, but in no way a great Lear. Patches of it, beyond doubt, are technical triumphs – the delivery of 'Blow, winds' in jet blackness, shot only by authentic lightnings; and the riskily frail whimsy and fey lyric *gaminerie* with which he treated the Dover mad scene. Yet the performance told us nothing new either of Lear or of Mr Olivier: it merely introduced us to a few wholly unexpected facets of the private life of Mr Justice Shallow. I shall continue to hold that Mr Olivier is our best *active* player, our best agent, contriver, do-er: but Lear, after Act I, Scene 1, is wholly perplexed and passive, a tragic hero quite unsympathetic to Olivier's gifts. It is a baffling task, this matter of sustaining authority, and Mr Olivier never looked like bringing it off. Instead of the pathos of great strength crumbling, he offered the misfortune of bright wits blurred. He could not give us more than a fraction of all that massive, deluded grandeur.

But, I recall, Mr Wolfit did and does; and so, I fancy might Mr Richardson. There is a streak of sheer primitive dumbness, a wanton hooding of sensibility in Lear which is right outside Olivier's range.

George Relph dragged himself plaintively through the endless triteness of Gloucester, surely the most tiresome long part in Shakespeare. Nicholas Hannen was a Kent of notable volume, but, like too many members of this company, he protests too much. Edgar, a character of two halves, each a gift to a normally capable actor but devilishly hard to combine, was played to the limit by Michael Warre with the customary schizophrenic agonies. Peter Copley was very weedy and unenthusiastic about Edmund (what a part for Mr Olivier); and Frank Duncan thankfully made Oswald personable, instead of a loutish fop. I took most pleasure from Alec Guinness's vindictive Fool : he played the pathos of the part down to extinction (by now a recognizable Old Vic habit), and gave himself to twisting in their wounds all those strange lances of insolence which are the Fool's real strength. For an actor to follow up an exciting Dmitri Karamazov and an incomparable Garcin in Sartre's *Huis Clos* with this acid, bereft little vignette was a triumphant progression.

Mr Olivier's daughters both slouch and sulk, and both move with the same serpentine tread as their father. Miss Brown's Goneril was finely curt, a ghastly set sneer; and Miss Leighton's Regan, softer and more desirable than you would look for in a villainess, was capable of piercing insight – especially in the 'vile jelly' scene, which her heavy animal breathing made frightening, and the strangled yelps and roaring with which she succumbed to her sister's poison. Miss Leighton walks as we are told Shelley walked – like a snake standing on its tail. Joyce Redman tried unwisely to make novel use of her buxom build and strident voice by playing a strong, commanding Cordelia. Her best time came after she was dead. She lies quite loose and limp while Mr Olivier practises on her the most brutal enormities of artificial respiration, coiling her about him and pounding breast, belly and rump. Her inertia in this scene was profoundly moving.

Mr Olivier's production was pictorially unlovely, and both for him and his designer Roger Furse this was a sad falling-off from the formal beauty of *Henry V*. Alan Rawsthorne's music was an adequate backwash to the action, except that it too often became a full spate of flood. I had dry eyes and a heart quiescent throughout.

(Soon after writing this, I listened to a recording of the voice of Bernard Shaw, and knew instantly where to seek for this century's only and unexceptionable Lear.)

(1946)

Huis Clos

by JEAN-PAUL SARTRE
at the Arts

At a snap judgement I should say this was the best all-round production I have ever seen, though later Mr Brook's *Dark of the Moon* came along, in all its zest and wild chiaroscuro, to contend for the title. *Huis Clos* is a hot, cloistered play about three people in hell, and hell is furnished in Second Empire splendour, lit by an electric light which cannot be switched off. They are to remain within this room for ever; and as the play progresses we learn how and why they died, and how and why this is the completest torture that malevolence could prescribe for them : psychologically they are so juxtaposed that they cannot but prey on each other, and seek to destroy each other. At the end, when they understand their full plight, there is a pause; then all three burst into a frightful peal of laughter, exquisitely timed and protracted by

Mr Brook; and when this is exhausted, there is another terrible pause. Then Garcin, the only man of the three, a pacifist and a moral coward, leans forward. 'Eh bien,' he says, 'continuons.' Or, as ineffectively rendered in this translation: 'Well, let's go on.' On this tangled, desolate question-mark the curtain falls, and we know that the play belongs to the modern group of 'tragedies without finality'. Man is born in chains, and everywhere he is free: that is the burden of Mr Sartre's play, the terrors of free will and free conscience, and the well-nigh irresistible need to replace their tyranny by another, outside oneself.

A very intricate, super-naturalistic style is Mr Brook's. The lift which brings the three down to their room in hell is perfectly reproduced, and there is a fan slowly turning in the ceiling, which stops as soon as they are shown in; in this meticulously imagined atmosphere characters interrupt each other, hesitate in mid-word, become flurried, blush, fumble, fiddle irrationally with clothes or ornaments, mutter, suddenly land heavily on a word which was not prepared for it; they behave in that human-all-too-human manner which Sartre's plays demand. Steely, flexible underplaying is the most easily comprehensible phrase for it: normality reproduced so faithfully that it looks like eccentricity: normality in the sense in which we all imagine we are normal, and in which, to a hidden spectator of our moments of solitude, we might appear dangerously insane. Mr Brook goes all out for a small effects, and when he makes a big one, the impact is very big indeed. A famous dramatic critic used to cultivate the same trick: 'such is my accustomed placidity,' he said, 'that if I raise one finger the public will flock to the theatre. Of course,' he added, 'I can also raise two . . .'

Mr Brook's supporting cast of four are too good to quibble over. Alec Guinness's middle-ageing, vulture-domed neurotic, a pitilessly intelligent shell of a man, for ever straining and twitching his neck as if trying to fly out of his clothes; Betty Ann Davies's bitter, shallow, flamboyant Estelle; and Beatrix Lehmann's Inez, a spare and vindictive lesbian with callous eyes and a touch of the care-less vulgarity which marked Freda Jackson's Mrs Voray – these three worked together like the three sections of an unanswerable logical proposition, of which Descartes would have been proud. Finally, Donald Pleasence, as the smiling bellboy who conducts them to their home, made a sinister and self-effacing Q.E.D.

(1946)

The White Devil

by JOHN WEBSTER
at the Duchess

In the preface to this prodigious play, Webster quotes in his defence the remark of Euripides to Alcestides, who had accused him of slothfulness in composing his pieces: ' Here's the difference, thine shall only be read for three days, whereas mine shall continue three ages.' That vaunt is happily made good: Webster's skill has stood proof against three centuries, and you may see him played to-day, not on a rostrum of coffins in some dingy charnel, but in a softly padded Aldwych theatre. His rapacious men and savage women, with their barbaric morals and exquisitely civilized attitude towards death, will grip any audience vice-wise – until the millennium breaks upon us, and we are all Methuselahs, and no longer preoccupied with mortification and worms.

The White Devil is a very great play in a sort which no other dramatist ever mastered, and whose only counterpart in fatalism is the modern American 'tough' novel, the novel of James Cain and Raymond Chandler. In plot it is mechanical, a clean and direct narrative of revenge; and its people are ghastly unrealities, galvanized dolls, intrinsicate silhouettes in sheet metal. It has no message and poses no problems. Yet it is unquestionably a masterpiece – to my mind the finest play written between

Timon of Athens and *Venice Preserv'd*. Why? Simply for its poetry. I do not love spoken verse, or the effusive boom of the Shakespeare voice: but this is a new poetry, tangy and bitter, full of warning and irrepressibly sombre: a realistic, ragged poetry, which none has imitated save Beddoes (diffusely, and very much *à thèse*) and Shelley (in the detail of Beatrice's hair at the end of *The Cenci*). *The White Devil* is not fully a tragedy: it has no warmth or pity, and it is not meant to encourage tears. It has to do with Death: Death as a harsh poetic fact, not as a sorrowful possibility. Webster's characters, as they die, are as poignant as the unrepentantly slaughtered must always be: they die cruelly and suddenly, stabbed, strangled, or strangely poisoned by paints and acids: their faces are slapped in death, and their bodies neatly modelled in wax to taunt and vex the living withal. Death is Webster's friend: 'the skull beneath the skin' is slung around his neck in a hangman's cameo. Death is as close and usual as breakfast: Romelio, in Webster's rarely acted *Devil's Law Case*, can think of nothing but food on the eve of fighting for his life. 'Can you feed, and apprehend death?' a Capuchin asks him. He answers:

> *Why, sir? is not death*
> *A hungry companion? Say, is not the grave*
> *Said to be a great devourer? Get me some victuals!*

Death in Shakespeare is very different; a loving, quilted nothingness, come like a sleeping-bag to enfold the hero at the end of Act V. He is a sentimental godfather, a 'big sleep'. 'All shall die,' says Shallow placidly: we never thrill to the word as we do in Webster or Donne. Only Timon really compasses the Websterian death-wish; although Hamlet comes near it in the graveyard scene, he soon falls back into dewy lyricism. For Webster death is a real and considerable presence; he is the ultimate and the immediate adversary; he must be plotted against, cajoled, parleyed with, met in cunning and in battle, and, if strength and wits hold, defeated. No matter what the turning of the plot, each character knows his real condition: black to play and mate in two. Every moment of these turbulent lives is clouded with the dark, with him, the monstrous hint in every man's shadow. Listen to Brachiano, a few moments before he dies:

> On pain of death, let no man speak of death:
> It is a word infinitely terrible.

Not content with searing Brachiano's skull with acids, Webster has him strangled as well. So with Flamineo: having cleverly dissembled death from a pistol-bullet, he is stabbed in the belly a moment later, whereat he enjoys another, more soul-hurting, less rhetorical, less evitable agony.

I found the performance at the Duchess infinitely terrifying. You cannot relate the play to normality, as I suspect Mr Gielgud tried to do with *The Duchess of Malfi* a year or two ago. These Renaissance boolies are not real to us: the only emotion we share with them is lust. Save for one moment in *The White Devil*, when Flamineo, having murdered his brother and seen his mother insane with grief, says, awfully:

> I have a strange thing in me, to the which
> I cannot give a name, without it be
> Compassion.

That is the only kindling of what we call 'decent feeling' in all Webster's tragic writing. Unless you care to count Contarino's graceful tribute to Jolenta in *The Devil's Law Case*:

> How now, sweet mistress:
> You have made sorrow look lovely of late:
> You have wept.

Webster never uses word-chopping, never hangs moral saws, like millstone pendants, round his scenes (the closing couplets are invariably cynical): he is far directer than our Shakespeare, the very flooding copiousness of whose humanity is often an embarrassment to the action. All in Webster is to the purpose, which is death's purpose: passionless murder.

Margaret Rawlings's Vittoria Corombona stands, in my small experience, as the most stirring tragic acting I have seen in a woman. She is loud, demonstratively plangent, and convincingly voluptuous: a plump, pallid nymphomaniac. And such control! In the great Trial scene, she eschewed pathos and gave us in its stead anger, mettlesome and impetuous. A stalwart piece of rhetoric, and beautifully spoken. I am less sure about Robert Helpmann's Flamineo: the actor makes him nasty and austere, but there is no heart or spleen in the curt aloofness of his voice. He is sinister, but without being wicked; and Webster's intelligencer-assassin is nothing if not wicked. However, in the death-scene (one of the most amazing in all drama, fit to take its place beside that of Bishop Nicholas in Ibsen's *The Pretenders*), Mr Helpmann is tiptoe with nerves and topfull of power, and the result is splendid. What a scene it is, in all conscience – or rather, in its very lack of conscience! No pleading with the dark god, no sentimentality, no self-pity, no 'poor player, that struts and frets', no 'loving not wisely but too well'; no palliations, no excuses; but a panicky defiance, a terror, and an exultation: a shouting, not at God or Fate, but at the grey, masked figure with whom he has lived these many years, whose errands he has run, and whom he now meets and salutes, face to face.

Hugh Griffith's Monticelso was superbly degenerate; dryly continent – just as one had pictured the man known to history as Pope Paul IV. Bestriding the other extreme of Renaissance Italy there was Andrew Cruickshank's Francisco de Medecis, scarlet and tending to bloat. Roderick Lovell has a noble physique and swaggering costumes: add a throbbing sensuality, and you have a nearly perfect Brachiano. Martita Hunt's Cornelia soon tired me; her skull-and-flowers mad scene is too redolent of Tilburina for my eyes. (This, together with much else in Webster, reminds me of a phrase in Beckford: writing of the Escorial, he describes it as 'set out with many a row of grinning skulls, looking as *pretty* as gold or diamonds could make them.') The attendant flocks of penitent whores and homicidal monks were aptly evil; the set, a perspective of indigo pillars topped by dimly seen gilt, was excellent, and the clothes were rich (for those who are zealous about such things, Mr Helpmann's navel was visible throughout the play). Mr Benthall achieved a cruel enthusiasm of production which is exactly Webster's quality. It struck indelibly home upon me.

Virtue never prevails in Webster. No one feels tenderness, or regret, or nostalgia. The smart folk he writes of have no time for such commonplace responses. They stand hypnotized by their own reflection in the eyes of death, whose martial stalk throughout this play is no less real than that of Hamlet's father. Yet we do not leave the theatre disgusted or appalled. After so much refinement upon death and tranfiguration, after such orgiastic murdering-parties, we feel that death himself must be sated, and so spare us. The thought is a happy one.

Cyrano de Bergerac

by EDMOND ROSTAND
at The New

First, if we have the historical eye, let us turn to something C. E. Montague said of Coquelin's Cyrano : 'In the great speech below Roxane's window, clause sprang out of clause and line flowed into line with a kind of passionate logic; the way every phrase was given made some place in your mind ache to be filled by the next.'

And now to celebrate a subaltern, sublunary Cyrano.

Ralph Richardson, who dons the current Old Vic nose, is in appearance a Midland squirearch. Tyrone Guthrie has called upon him to play a grotesque, boldly sentimental Gascon swordsman. A whole culture, a whole world of manners separates the twain, and for our purposes a whole culture can be crammed into a word: panache. A braggart ostrichful of brave plumes must beckon and dance about the preposterous poetry of the man. He is a rapturous upstart, a commanding scaramouche, a grim jester, with his French loaf of a nose – yet all this gay while, we must feel stern, hammerblast qualities working within him, in redoubtable undertow.

There never was an English actor who could merge the extravagant and the bizarre into the heroic. The Englishman likes to dovetail snugly into a part which calls into play his generous modesty, and fits his inbred profile. Cyrano has no modesty and the absurdest profile before Disney drew Donald Duck, and yet he is a hero. That is a statement which no English actor has ever fully understood; which is why no Englishman will ever play Rostand's Cyrano. Unless, I should add, we rediscover the old, unsneering meaning of 'rhetoric'; which seems unlikely.

But in spite of us all, Richardson is giving a tremendous performance of *something* at the New Theatre. Not since *Peer Gynt* has he conquered a part so thoroughly. Of course, the bluff genteel rogue he is sketching for us, in his deft way, is by no means Cyrano; he is much too amiable (one of this actor's failings) and he is not nearly coarse enough. The nose was ten times as large as life, the actor hardly twice as large. But his voice is most delicate; breathlight of texture; more buoyant even than that of M. Charles Trenet. It has a power to puff itself up amongst vertiginous clouds of sweet rodomontade. It is a yeasty, agile voice. Where Olivier would pounce upon a line and rip its heart out, Richardson skips and lilts and bounces along it, shaving off pathos in great flakes.

He took Act I at a great pace, fairly whipping it across with his energetic cane, which flicked contrapuntally with the accusing nose. My impression was of a garish Chaplin turned schoolmaster. The duel with Valvert (*not* arranged by Peter Copley) left me stinging with excitement, and Act II, in which the ugly fool's hopes for

Roxane's love are dissipated, was a fine display of iron technique and stopwatch timing. The 'Kiss' scene came off well; here Richardson's idea of Cyrano reached out and caught such aristocracy of emotion as to transcend even Rostand's. He dignified the play's end, too, eked out as his powers were by Tanya Moiseiwitch's décor, which veiled the nunnery in damp, autumnal sorrow, and by Mr Guthrie's leaves, ceaselessly crisping, curling, flouncing, and falling on to the stage. He died neatly in Mr Guthrie's 'Position One' : that is to say, with his head and arm thrown backwards in abandon at the footlights, over the shoulder of a friend.

Margaret Leighton's Roxane is perhaps the best thing she has yet done in London. Not quite petty enough, I think, in its caprices, nor intellectual enough, it was complete in its insular fashion, moulding Roxane from a woman worth while loving into a woman worthy to be loved. In the battle scenes she was riotously good, in that busy, parading style of hers; and even better was the 'Kiss'. In this part Miss Leighton comes emotionally of age.

This is a nineteenth-century extravaganza, and Mr Guthrie has mounted it with true Lyceum flourish. The five sets are as scrupulous in their realism as a film studio could wish. This producer's *forte* was always the handling of crowd scenes; sometimes one feels a flatness in him when he touches smaller groups; he seems a little embarrassed. But soon the ragamuffins and *picaros* come vaulting back, and ideas flow again. Rostand's rhetoric sustains the whole. This is the best, most blatant romantic stage poetry I know – better at times than Shakespeare's, for Rostand strikes home far less obliquely and deployingly than our master-equivocator. All manner of genuflexion, then, to the Old Vic, for having given us a racy, heart-bumping and obviously very expensive evening-out. And thanks, too, to the translator : in a better version, Mr Richardson's shortcomings in the part would have been intolerably obvious.

(1946)

49

Antony and Cleopatra

by WILLIAM SHAKESPEARE
at the Piccadilly

For the most part, I am a student of equanimity. I fail to recoil from the grossest errors of taste, and infelicity is innocuous to me. Yet at this I was shocked. When Edith Evans began to play her Cleopatra, I felt anarchy stirring. Lady Bracknell had been involved in a low Alexandrian scandal, and soon, I cried, all our firmest standards will flex and fall, and we shall start to envisage Mrs Browning among the Medmenham Monks, or Sophie Arnould climbing a tree in knickerbockers. Someone had committed an error so stunning in its blindness that one's critical muscles were momentarily disarmed. Dame Edith, robed in frumpery resplendence, is a comic performer of the first order. She has an enviable facial mobility with one unique attribute; the gift of suggesting vulgar-hearted disdain. It is a gift to comedy. Her mistake lay in confusing the pompous disdain of the comic dowager with the ingrained *daungier* of the tragedy queen. Bereft of fan, lace, and sedan-chair, Dame Edith is nakedly middle-aged and plain. A talent for comedy, frequently enough indulged, may dry up all sympathy in an actress. Dame Edith has mislaid this sympathetic power, and is thus outlawed for ever from tragedy. Her Cleopatra is as hostile as a glacier.

Expertly she gave us the coarse hoyden of the early acts, but she bungled the inspired strumpet. The ravenous gleam of eye and band of bland teeth with which she quizzed, coaxed and tantalized her Antony belonged rather to the armoury of the aunt than the quiver of the lover. When he was half a Roman world away, and she came to reminisce over riots long past, we believed her; with what cloyless complacency, for instance, she stroked the line: 'Ha! Ha! You're caught!'

When death seemed close, she unbound her voice, and let it roam up and about, with intemperate gusto, rather like a drunken Gingold at large on a viola. The end was Grand Gingold: one felt always the need for a more mundane context than tragedy. She remained, even in the last cold moment, a vociferous slut, a barmaid among the Barmecides. Dame Edith's Cleopatra was Heredia's 'grand oiseau d'or' with its wings clipped.

Godfrey Tearle's Antony was much less earthbound. He was a tired, solitary exile from immemorial slaughters. Through many weary decades he had borne the sword of Rome among a hundred spanielled legions, yet like the gouty Napoleon at Waterloo, he was still an eager warrior, and a terrible. Like the man in Bunyan, he would hack his way into heaven, after giving and receiving many wounds. About him legends would gather and multiply; upon him the greying time of life had bestowed consolation and plenty. I found myself respecting and almost loving, not the actor, but the man. He communicated all the sadness of middle-aged lust, without a vestige of its repulsiveness. His suicide scene, which he took ruefully, generously, wisely, was impeccable: he ran gnarled fingers across one's heartstrings, and left them resonant with noble arpeggios. Such playing asks for a monument, and Oxford has provided it, for a passable likeness of Mr Tearle crowns most of the pillars outside the Sheldonian Theatre.

Michael Goodliffe has vigour, polish, and a grim black watchfulness; these, together with a costume to outshine Olympus, made a fine Octavius. Better still, there was Anthony Quayle's Enobarbus. Mr Quayle gave Enobarbus all the qualities which a novelettist would give a fighting English gentleman: amiable self-confidence, shockheaded frankness, humorous eyes, a bewildered forehead, and pensive lips. George Carr made a considerate Clown, and finally Olaf Pooley, by a flip of yellow eyelids and a terrifying slink of humped shoulders, made a character out of Mardian the Eunuch. As Colley Cibber once said, 'there is very near as much Enchantment in the well-governed Voice of an Actor, as in the sweet Pipe of an Eunuch.' Combined in one performance they are irresistible.

All permanent sets look much like miniature motels, and Glen Byam Shaw's is no exception. None the less he uses it with no serious awkwardness, save in Act V, when Cleopatra's Monument is made to appear about as impregnable as the men's dressing-room in the open-air theatre at Regent's Park. Elsewhere the production was admirable: I liked particularly the unremitting speed of it all. Most memorable was the feast on Pompey's galley, where the great men gratefully unbend, toast each other, stamp their way noisily and unsteadily through a complex Egyptian quadrille, laugh, plot and part friends. There was something very rare about Mr Byam Shaw's evocation of all this kindly fribbling.

But of course that may have been Mr Tearle's doing. For Mr Tearle is positively the kindliest actor in the world.

(1946)

The Relapse

by SIR JOHN VANBRUGH
at the Phoenix

This production (the best of Anthony Quayle's that I have seen) fairly scampered along, and Cyril Ritchard held court within it with magnificently tipsy grandeur. This was a performance singular for its effrontery: Mr Ritchard's affected, feline voice, rising and dropping a seventh to point the funny lines, was the only completely masculine thing about it. (He dealt wonderfully with the catch-phrases – 'Stap my vitals', 'Split my wind-pipe' and so forth – uttering them very deliberately as if it were vital that the audience should grasp and estimate their precise contribution to the sense.) He played Fop-

pington as a corsetted pantomine dame, cosily effeminate, rising at times to the seraphic *hauteur* of a *déclassée*
Lady Bracknell, slightly ashamed of wearing red flannel
underwear. Like so many other fine comic performances
(Olivier's Shallow, Sid Field's Photographer, for example),
it made me wonder whether one root of comedy is not
the exposure of all that is womanish in man, the unveiling of feminine traits beneath the masculine exterior.
In the case of Bob Hope, the exposure is of physical
frailty and cowardice (the comedian boasts of courage and
leaps on a chair at the sight of a beetle); in Jack Benny,
of a womanish fear of wrinkles and old age (he is constantly being embarrassed by his *toupée*); in Arthur Askey,
of goggle-eyed schoolgirlishness ('Ooh, you are filthy!'
he will roguishly scream); in Johnny Puleo (the gnome-
like dwarf of Borrah Minnevitch's Harmonica Rascals)
of grim spinsterishness, contrasted with his aggressive
prizefighter's nose and witch-like malignant eyes ; and in
Cyril Ritchard, of a sort of district-nurse effusiveness. His
Foppington is horsy in a feminine, not a masculine way.
This hip-waggling humour is, I feel, a recent vogue : I
cannot believe that Little Tich practised it. Though, I
bethink myself, George Robey certainly did : in the tones
of a flamboyant Sairey Gamp, fruitily aggrieved, he would
insist : 'Do shut up!' when the laughter from the pit
began to stir his resentment. The very greatest modern
comedians (Chaplin, Barrault, Danny Kaye) exploit only
one feminine trait – neatness, fastidiousness, finical tidi-
ness : but to them I shall turn later, for we are wandering too far from Mr Ritchard.

He was chiefly excellent because he was vulgar : he
showed us what we had long suspected, that Restoration
comedy outside Congreve is not witty and artificial, but
broad and boisterous. Foppington is an upstart, ineffectively arrogant, desperately clinging to what he imagines
is his dignity. Perhaps the most inventive touch was
Ritchard's attempt at dignified locomotion with his ankles
tied together : he slunk along in a series of minute
shuffling movements, like a dowager in a hobble skirt.

The kind of vulgarity this illustrates is social: a man trying to behave above his class of mind and manners. It made belly and mind laugh together; like Samuel Butler's *Huffing Courtier*: 'He flutters up and down like a butterfly in a garden; and while he is pruning of his perruque, takes occasion to contemplate his locks and the symmetry of his breeches . . . the beggars call him "My lord" and he takes them at their word, and pays them for it.'

The supporting cast was not quite so good as its fame led us to expect. Madge Elliott is too settled a merry widow for this sort of thing; and Esmond Knight over-balanced the delicious mockery of the ending, with its hypocritical paean to Platonic love, by taking it too seriously, and becoming bitter and teeth-grinding about it. Jessie Evans made amends with a superbly abandoned hoyden; it sounded and tasted like a pot of aphrodisiac treacle. And Richard Wordsworth made a horrible pro-curer, a fading fairylegs whose appetites, if one adopted the trick of pronouncing the long 's' as 'f' around which Alan Melville wrote a parody of this production, would certainly be described as 'fecund to none'.

(1947)

Romeo and Juliet

by WILLIAM SHAKESPEARE
at Stratford-on-Avon

'Torrid', I think, may be the word. Or 'sultry': if, that is, we can free them of their associations with Tahiti and Southern California, and make them mean what they ought to mean: something intemperately dry, tawny and madding. Peter Brook plays out this young tragedy under a throbbing vault of misty indigo: the streets crackle underfoot with aridity: it is very warm indeed. Canopies, loosely pendent from the flies, are a necessary shield against this daze of heat. Mr Brook's colours are dusty whites, sun-bleached reds and dull greys: and the brown, somnolent crowds in his market-place are all bemused and fly-blown. The sets, designed by Rolf Gérard and poised, tenuously erect, on slim flimsy pillars, are thrown open to the bare sky: silhouettes balancing in the naked sun. Everyone sweats. When they are not sprawled in a stark Mediterranean torpor, when they are moved to seize at their swords, they do so moodily, savagely and à outrance. The beggars, clowns and men-at-arms who people Mr Brook's Verona shape themselves into groupings of splashed tints and high noon-tide frenzy: witness the Capulet revelry and the deaths of Mercutio and Tybalt. The music (by Roberto Gerhard) is tired: wan reeds, distant timbrels, and the lazy beat of tight-strung drums. The whole work is a miracle of masks, mists, and sudden grotesquerie. We come to wait intelligently for the pure drops of un-expected naturalism which Mr Brook teaches his actors to wring out of Shakespeare's lines; for that novelty of inflexion which, taken with the rest, tells us that he has acquired a recognizable style. There is an elderly group of critics which insists that Mr Brook is not nearly old enough to appreciate *Romeo*: to them I say (and I hope rudely) that they are not nearly young enough. *Romeo* is a youthful play about miserable young people who confuse catastrophe with tragedy: it is precious, repeti-tive, superpathetic, overbold – all the tiresomeness of adolescence is in it. How it languishes in the wastes between Juliet's feigned and Romeo's real death! (Mr Brook does not help matters by cutting the preceding scene between Juliet and Friar Lawrence.) These lovers are not big enough figures; they are too weak for the true woe of tragedy. 'Alack, alack,' says Juliet, 'that Heaven should practise stratagems upon so soft a subject as myself!' That is the key to the play's lameness: they are both too soft, too easily dead.

All that a bizarre imagination and perfervid scholar-ship can do for the play Mr Brook has done. Consider the strange solitary tree (can it be a medlar?) which he plants, spear-shaped, in Romeo's Mantuan exile: touches like this are foreign to our stages, and welcome. His cast is obedient to him. I commend Myles Eason (Tybalt), lithe and tigerish, with hat smugly tilted and voice thin-lipped enough to match the insolent swish of his *passado*: Paul Scofield's Mercutio, not the noisy bragger who usually capsizes the play and then leaves it to founder, but a rapt goblin, ruddy and likeable (his pensive delivery of the Mab speech, with demoniac masquers grouped around him, crowns the scene with authentic faery); Beatrix Lehmann's Nurse, wrinkled in teak (when, by the way, is this part to be played as the evil old relict she is?); John Ruddock (Friar Lawrence), who expelled nearly all the boredom that interlards the holy garrulity of that frocked Pandarus; Robert Harris's Escalus, angry under an ensign of scorpions; and the unnamed figure of Chorus, shrouded in greys and far-off blues. I shall remember him for a long time, speaking the lovers' epitaph (rightly belonging to Escalus) at his decent, grave-side pace: it pelted one's ears with magic.

I did not wholly sympathize with Lawrence Payne's stocky Romeo. There was not an ounce of spontaneous melancholia in all his downright body. Masterly staging, however, came often to his aid: the first encounter with Juliet was a lovely prelude. The stage is emptied for them – he alone in perfect white, she drawn through the upstage fogs to touch lips with him. And the balcony scene was so poignant that one almost forgave Mr Brook his anomalous orchard, which was both wall-less and tree-less.

About Daphne Slater I am surer. She is not beautiful: physically she is dissonant with the hard, thick-lipped charm of Mr Payne. But her pride is her youth; with some other, less *modern* Romeo, I can imagine no better Juliet. Rightly she is excitable and impetuous; and she communicates this convulsive ardour until it becomes our panic as well as hers.

(1947)

Othello

by WILLIAM SHAKESPEARE
at the Savoy

To be present, to assist at the spinning out of events which will surely plume up and refurbish the tapestry of Western culture – is not this a pleasant thing? Had it not been fine to have snapped up and savoured the first copy of *The Rape of the Lock* as it came, cool and acid and fair, from the press? To have seen and shaken at the face of Swift as he penned the last cruel, grimy pages of *Gulliver*? To have sat by and quivered at the embarrassed wriggles of some poor questioner, swallowed up in the terrific finality of a Johnsonian 'No, sir'? My point, when at last it comes wheeling round to us, is that I have seen a public event of constellated magnitude and radiance. I have watched a transfusion of bubbling hot blood into the invalid frame of our drama. Some, I am told, boast of having seen the Chicago fire; others of having escaped the Quetta earthquake by the merest pebble's breadth; and I have known men swell as they recalled the tremendous and bloody exploits at Hiroshima. My vaunt is this: I have lived for three hours on the red brink of a volcano, and the crust of lava crumbles still from my feet. I have witnessed a performance of *Othello* in which Donald Wolfit played Iago, and Frederick Valk Othello. How hushed I was! How young and how chastened: so much so that for days afterwards, long after I had sent my final particular roar of 'Bravo' coursing and resounding about the theatre, I could speak of little but these twin giants, and the authentic ring of their titles to greatness. In the mind's middle distance, I think I perceive that other players flickered intermittently across that bare stage – that flat scene of astounding war; I can, if I screw up my memory, hear them now, grunting and twittering and shrilling. Who they were, I have not the slightest notion. They lie *perdu* : an irrelevant flurry of colour and dim noise in the midst of which gigantic things were going forward. They it was, as I think, who buzzed and rattled when the big gladiators fell fatigued. I should prefer to ignore them, thus dismissively.

Othello is, of course, a moral play : rigidly and cruelly so; though I confess I had inclined to skirt glibly round this central part of its structure and fortification. I should not have neglected Johnson, who said : 'We learn from Othello this very useful moral, not to make an unequal match. . . . I think Othello has almost more moral than any other play.' What paroxysms of fright and foreboding must have consumed Shakespeare's Jacobean audiences! Here, proudly booming before them, was a monstrous blackamoor, a black gargoyle, concealing within him racks on which to stretch himself and those about him until the excruciated lyric cry was released; and bearing in his baggage explosive coils of taut, dangerous springs. Anything might happen while this nigger devil yet lived. Horrors and Domdaniel excesses crowded the horizon. I had never fully shared this expectancy of terror until Mr Valk pressed me, at pistol point, to accept it.

Shakespeare, perhaps for fear of too much alarming his spectators, has dealt very unfairly with Othello. Up to the crucial temptation scene (III, iii) he utters only 240 lines of verse to Iago's 574. And Mr Wolfit took full advantage of this early ascendancy. What a muscular actor he is! Yet his ponderous gait contrasts oddly with his rasping whine of a voice. I need not celebrate again the virtues of his Iago : its stout craft, its unhurried certainty and precision. I would append only a tiny animadversion, upon his treatment of poetry. To listen to Mr Wolfit speaking good verse is an experience analogous to watching a rebellious rogue elephant walking a tight-rope. It is enjoyable because it is very, very strange. Like a prize-fighter nursing a young flower, like John Steinbeck's Lenny petting a puppy, so is Mr Wolfit when a line of poetry is delivered into his hands. He has doubtless cultivated a love for the stuff, but I trace hints of an unwilling courtship that went badly against a rather uneven grain. This quibble apart, I salute a performance which laid quite bare that 'diseased intellectual activity' of which Hazlitt spoke: a performance worth seeing if only to hear Mr Wolfit giving the hapless word 'Nature' its full eight or nine syllables.

But this was Mr Valk's private adventure, no other near, and we were soon made to realize it. In appearance he was quintessential teddy-bear; 'not' (I hear Coleridge grumbling) 'thoroughbred gentleman enough to play Othello'. No aristocracy of bearing; no regularity of profile; in short, no flair. Yet temperamentally (and this is the unseekable key) there is no other such tragic player on our stages. This was (to borrow another phrase from Coleridge) Shakespeare by flashes of lightning, with a pall of heavy thunder over all, and a sullen Southern sky. I cannot believe there is blood in the man's veins: it must be some vile compound of corrosive venoms, arcane and nameless; some crazy river having its dayspring in spleen, and adulterated with black bile. Why, he was to be touched into mad, lambent flame in an instant; he broke every law of our stage-craft, this berserk Colossus. Following the imperious rules of his agony, his voice would crack and pause, minute-long, in midline: and there would be speechless signallings the while, and rushes as of a wild bull. Then the voice would rise and swoop again into unknown pastures of word-meaning, scooping up huge vasty syllables of grief as though carving an ancient bed of clay. He seemed, at times, almost to sing, so unlike our custom was his elocution; a bully's song, a bludgeoner's song, yet its strains moved to pity, as great verse should. I shall see him always in a dim dusk-light, singing impious lullabies to soothe his own congenital disquiet. You could almost hear thin skins splitting and half-shut minds banging and locking themselves around you; the theatre was perturbed, but pin-still.

Usually I go to Shakespeare for the poetry, worn though it now is: there seems to be little else, in an averagely good performance, to enrapture the mind. Under Valk, I discover, verse collapses. I have heard it plausibly objected to him that, with his Czech emphases, he loses all the music in words. Now I believe that words are neither harmonious nor discordant in themselves: the verse is either smooth and end-stopped or it is not. It is very hard to write an unmelodious heroic couplet. But this kind of minuteness is blankly impertinent when Valk is acting, piercing to the core of elemental and therefore wordless things, willing to tear a heart from sheer granite. There was no time for R.A.D.A. modulations and exquisiteness: a man was hacking a horrid path for himself, and it was not pretty, or fanciful: it was inviolable rage, and there were gulfs awash with tears opening all round him. He stood, petrifact, bellowing in their dreadful midst. Cadence, and that careful forethought by which English actors contrive to ignore the existence of consonants, went quite by the board. The highest praise I can summon up for Valk is that he gave what could by no standards be described as 'a beautiful performance': for beauty is regular and predictable, and this was neither. The fury of sound had overcome him: yet with grave *naïveté* he seemed to be listening to himself as he spoke. And when the time came, and Chaos returned, this three hours' sojourner in Olympian charnels lifted his great lion's head and sent his poor voice piping into the vaulted roof above him: 'Oh the pity of it, Yaggo – the pee-ee-eety of ee-eet!' You could hear the terrible, derisive echo.

The play, the words, all plays, all words were too small for this passion. It transcended the prescribed limits of acted drama, and strode boldly through Hell-lake and bade the white-clad recording imps take notice of foul disorders and evil conceits; of the climax of a great anguish; of the dilapidation of a sturdy tower; of the molten intoxication of a warrior and demi-god. We who saw these things passing were caught up with Valk to his own pinnacles and when the curtain fell, it was if an end had been put to the tales of mortal suffering; after this death, there could come no more refinement of woe. The sense of relief preceded the permanent sense of awe: the full tragic action was communicated like the hot breath of the ferocious antique gods.

I cannot tell whether this was a good Othello. I do not even know whether it was a good stage performance. Indeed, at this distance of time I would not care to say that it was a stage performance at all. Except, of course, that I know it chose to be made known in a public theatre, and that might have been accident: lightning may strike anywhere, and even the Savoy 'scapes not the thunderbolt. With every line he uttered and motion he compassed, Mr Valk left behind him a heap of rules triumphantly smashed and discarded; he trampled on them, and took glory from it. ('There is no such thing', I have heard him insist, 'as an ungainly position.') He battered Othello to dust, and I wish him long life to pursue his angry stampede across other plains: let us see his Lear, with Mr Wolfit's Edmund at his elbow. And here, I am sure, is at last an adequate Timon. The thick reverberations of that great voice, the killing sureness of its every tremor towards the avalanche; the athletic pathos of that giant frame in motion, stuttering, lurching, toppling; the rhetorical clawings of those hands – gifts like these must not set their bounds in one performance. They must expand, and then Mr Valk may do still more to strike us free of the old formal bonds of dramatic decency.

But I am hoarse with protest. To pray that there may be no quick cessation of his energies were, as Johnson might have built the phrase, a superfluous genuflexion. Such power is lawless, and bears kinship with the elements. As Chesterton said of Mr Belloc's voice:

Nor does it cease. Nor will it cease.

There is nothing perishable in this great Czech.

('After a long succession of noise, as the fall of waters,

or the beating of forge hammers, the hammers beat and the waters roar in the imagination long after the first sounds have ceased to affect it: and they die away at last by gradations which are scarcely perceptible.' Thus Burke. I am yet conscious of no such slipping away. But Burke is, I suppose, right: those hammer-strokes and top-less cascades will cease, in long time, to roar in my ears and bewitch me.)

(1947)

Richard II

by WILLIAM SHAKESPEARE
at the New

As Richard said on the walls of Flint Castle: 'We are amazed.' The Old Vic has let us down heavily; and, what is more disastrous, they have let Mr Guinness down. I wonder what kind of Richard we expected from him. Not, perhaps, the faithful and capable artist which Montague tells us Benson made of the part; nor yet Hotspur's 'sweet lovely rose'; more likely the sad neurotic whom Mr Guinness lets us glimpse in the deposition scene, a man seething and sorrowful at his own impotence, at his sheer inability to come to intellectual grips or mix minds with the burly, well-meaning politicians who are making off with his birthright. Most of all smacking of the Richard that was inside Mr Guinness was the line with which the weary springtime king surrenders the crown to Bolingbroke. Balancing it lightly in his fingers, an inch from the usurper's nose, he says gently and with infinite scorn: 'Here cousin – *seize* the crown.' The eyes spoke most compellingly as the actor dwelt, with pensive irony, on the long 'ee' of 'seize'. I would almost cast a Richard on eyes alone: they must be the only wholly regal attribute he possesses, attuned to cow the worst rebel with a passing glance. Mr Guinness had this icy stare, and it was one fragment of the performance we should like to have called his Richard. Another spread itself over the opening scene, when Mr Guinness showed us the true picture of a cant phrase: 'exquisitely bored'. Shouted insult and counter-shout of accusation are flying between Bolingbroke and Mowbray: to all of which Richard pays not the slightest attention, save to direct a pained, impassive gaze upon the contender who should offend his ears with over-much tumult. For the rest of the scene he passes the time in stroking and tending, with the severe raptness of the true dandy, what might be an incipient beard. I thrilled to the delicacy of this; but the prosperous sequel I promised myself was ruined by the dowdy unsuggestiveness of Ralph Richardson's production. Sir Ralph, I begin to think, has a common-place mind behind all that marketable technique; a mind mole-like in its earthiness. He tries to make Mr Guinness bellow, which is like casting a clipped and sensitive tenor for Boris Godounov; he would have him speak at the top of a voice whose peculiar quality it is to have no top. Richard is a character part; he is not one of Corneille's waxwork grandees. The key to him is the line: 'O that I were as great as is my grief!' If he were, he might be a tragic figure. But the circumstances are wrong, and he remains merely a misfit. Sir Ralph's production, fettered to the textual footnotes, gave us nothing of this. The Richard we saw — to abandon guesswork about the Richard we might have seen — was a mercurial prig; in silence, smugly prim, in speech, ardently royal. If you can imagine Bloomsbury turned full-throated monarchist, you have some notion of the intellectual climate around him. At his best (in the deposition scene), Mr Guinness recalled to me a phrase of Henry James's about a 'Bohemian wanting tremendously to be a Philistine'.

So far the production was shamefully blinkered. The rest was just quietly and miserably dull. People would march down to the footlights, point at the upper boxes, and say with complete conviction: 'Yonder stands Pomfret Castle'; everyone was constantly seen in angry profile and from no other angle; and the verse was punctuated by flips of the fingers and glances into the wings which served indiscriminately to call up a flourish of trumpets, a rattle of drums, or the sudden entry of a clutch of heralds. Michael Warre's columnar set is possibly the most impracticable that ever man devised. One cannot but stare when Northumberland, swarming with difficulty through a maze of pillars and posts, complains of 'these high wild hills and rough uneven ways'; and it is even odder when Bolingbroke, in similar plight, extracts a splinter from his arm and refers to the set as ' the grassy carpet of this plain'. It was about as carpet-like as a porcupine. But none of this was as funny as the immaculate, unhurried entrance of Ross and Willoughby, who are instantly dubbed 'bloody with spurring, fiery-red with haste'.

The cast, Mr Guinness apart, made heavy going of the ordinariness Shakespeare and Sir Ralph had lavished on them. The producer himself, a sedentary lion, roared John of Gaunt tediously to his grave; Sir Lewis Casson and the prompter played York as an appallingly well-rehearsed cross-talk act; Frank Duncan presented a tousled pot-boy which the programme had the insolence to call Hotspur; on the credit side, Harry Andrews, well cast for once, struts a stern Bolingbroke, Margaret Leighton lounges affectingly through Richard's Queen, and 'makes her bends adornings'; and Michael Warre, the only man onstage not openly embarrassed by the set, makes a bold and likeable assassin of Pierce of Exton. Of the other lords who keep ratting on one another, I cannot remember much, except that the fooling of those gay tumblers, Bushy, Bagot and Sunshine Boy Green, went over very big.

Herbert Menges's music – portentous drums and muffled hunting-horns – was all that we expect of an Old Vic Shakespeare. And all we ever get.

(1947)

The Alchemist

by BEN JONSON
at the New

It is hard to over-praise this play. It mingles together
sweet dirt, smart gulling and coxcombry into a wonderful theatrical confection. It thrives on malice and savagery
and makes them palatable. This is the heart of our
native humour, a vein of bitter, harsh venom : Jonson's
angry caricatures take a central place in our comic
literature, and project themselves by homespun craft
into the work of all our indigenous satiric artists, blazing
up furiously in Swift and Hogarth, and finally rekindling
in Dickens, whom, in their last weak days, they
strengthened.

And there is such a thing as a good episodic play : *The
Alchemist* is such a thing. Like bead after bead, the
episodes click together upon the connecting string, which
is chicanery and chiselry. Singly or in pairs, the gulls are
drawn to the chisellers to be snared and trimmed. What
is piquant, they like it : humble and gladdened, they
depart penniless, sometimes upon a servile errand for their
cheaters. They have come in search of panaceas, of the
Philosopher's Stone, and they are beguiled by three
glorious impostors : the exuberant Janus, Face, the
shadow-conjuror, Subtle, and the female spiv, Doll. So far
you laugh sporadically; soon you can hardly stop, for by
Jonson's art the hoaxes start to react on one another, wires
cross, gull is involved with gull, and there is a buzz of
entrance and exit, accompanied by a fine slamming and
reslamming of doors. The peak of the hubbub comes, I
suppose, with the belated release of Dapper, locked blindfold in a privy, and freed after a whole act in smoking
darkness.

The Old Vic production missed none of this. Morris
Kestelman's agreeable Augustan set abounded in doors

and queer coigns, and nothing seals a scene as tellingly as a slammed door. I query Mr Burrell's wisdom in shifting the setting to the eighteenth century; a move which made nonsense of Dame Pliant's line about the Armada having sailed three years before her birth.

George Relph plays Subtle: heavy lids, bright eyes, sagging bulbous face and somehow a sagging bulbous voice. I remember vividly the slow, jovial smile of anticipated triumph which greets the news of some new arrival to the cozenage; his eyes pop with avidity. Mr Relph plays gallantly down to allow Ralph Richardson, as Face, to climb on to his back and then hoist the play squarely on to his own shoulders. Sir Ralph's Face is a performance of great versatility, but (I thought) considerable professional dishonesty. He is opportunism itself, shuffling and grimacing most impertinently, pushing in his lines swiftly and selfishly, as if each were a last straw at which the play might clutch. Sir Ralph acts as if he were an eager, benevolent but tired scoutmaster, diverting himself by watching a rabble of tenderfeet practising first-aid. At first he condescends to simulate equality with them, and partakes of their ingenuousness; but this is bogus, and you know that he will soon have to show them himself how it is really done. With no real hope: for, worst of all, he makes you sense that this has been going on for months, to his increasing bewilderment and boredom. He patronizes his fellows roguishly and provokingly, and needless to say, every minute of his performance is a sheer delight to watch.

Joyce Redman's neckline appeared to get nearer to her nipples in every part she played that season, and this was distracting. She gave Doll Common the right abandon, though I got no sense of *rapport* with the other cony-catchers. Of the gulls: there are the rich who come out of greed, and the poor who come out of a need for illusions. Nicholas Hannen made a Balzacian figure of Sir Epicure Mammon, and even pulled pathos out of the sauces in his golden cauldron of a belly: I know of no better voluptuous writing than this part. Peter Copley's

Ananias, tatty and outraged, swaying like a black eel and gesticulating, is the best thing he has yet done. I was less happy about Margaret Leighton's Dame Pliant. This is an attempt to coax a certain facile kind of phrase out of a certain facile kind of critic – 'a brilliant little study, delicately etched in' – 'makes a character out of a few lines'. There *is* a character to be made out of the widow, but so far Miss Leighton has not found it. A similar but successful experiment is Alec Guinness's Abel Drugger. He, you remember, is the puny tobacconist who becomes Face's creature, and brings his paltry gifts to Subtle as to a shrine. Mr Guinness manages to get to the heart of all good, hopeful young men who can enjoy without envy the society of wits. I was overjoyed to watch his wistful, happy eyes moving, in dumb wonder, from Face to Subtle : a solid little fellow, you felt, and how eager to help! At last he puts in a tolerable contribution to the conversation. *O altitudo!* His face creases ruddily into modest delight, and he stamps his thin feet in glee. In a later scene, Mr Guinness demonstrates a very rare gift, that of suggesting the change that comes over a man when he is alone. Drugger is commissioned by Face to bring him a Spanish costume as disguise. He trots away, and returns shyly, clad in its showy cloak and hat. Waiting for Face to answer the door, he begins to execute timid dance-steps under the porch. He treads a rapt, self-absorbed measure with himself, consumed with joy. Then Face appears : the pretence is over, he recognizes his intellectual master, and, not regretfully or pathetically, but smartly and prosaically, he sheds his costume and hands it over. It is most touchingly done.

Mr Guinness, in spite of Sir Ralph's exertions, carried off every scene in which he appears, and one or two in which he ought not to appear at all. Drugger used to be Garrick's part, but, Mr Guinness having now appropriated it, I name him the best living English character-actor. But not, while Mr Valk is here, the best actor in England.

(1947)

The Master Builder

by HENRIK IBSEN
at the Arts

This performance is the most towering single thing to be
seen in the West End for many months. It is also the
strongest, and I am not excepting public buildings, works
of sculpture, or even the pavements we tread on. Like
everything Mr Valk does, it is inordinate. I take leave to
deny the proposals of some of his critics, that the dreadful
duets between Hilda and Solness should be played in taut,
twanging calm. Solness's is a considerable agony; that of
the genius and idealist, moving ungraciously into middle
age, and shockingly confronted by an embodiment (Hilda)
of the evil 'servers and helpers' who had pushed him to
the acropolis of his profession. Hilda stands for the 'robust
conscience', the Viking spirit of frigid plunder and savage
acquisitiveness. Examining himself, Solness finds that time
has woven a tough shroud around him, a shroud of
domestic custom and circumstance, whose pettiness
enrages him but whose envelope is so tight about him that
he feels guilty at the thought of breaking free. His conflict
(as Hegel would say of all tragic action) is between two
intrinsically good things : the impulse to self-advancement
(involving surrender to his vocation) and the impulse to
debonair home-contentment. The crux of the play is
Solness's conclusion that homes are no longer worth building, since the lives lived within them are wretched beyond
all salvaging. Hilda's contagious romanticism spurs him
on to erect extravagant castles in the air, and he dies in
this final, impossible conviction. The battle in *The Master
Builder* is not between youth and age, but between cruel
idealism and safe, responsible materialism.

Mr Valk's Othello was like a great dam bursting; his
playing in *The Brothers Karamazov* was a triumph of
coarse *gouaillerie*; and now his Solness has made his star

blaze red across all this continent, and other lights are tapers. You felt at once that this man had built monuments, stone upon stone, and was capable of sheer, muscle-tight toil; you could not consent to it as mere stage pretence. I noticed a strange tendency in myself to begin to compare him with Frank Lloyd Wright. I see now that I must have been temporarily insane, for as I sat watching him I could cheerfully have measured his bulk against that of the Palace of All the Soviets, and not found them disparate by one solitary inch or stress. He seemed an Alp. And when he fell from his crazy tower, the very fall of the House of Usher seemed like crackling matchwood. Mr Valk rules our stages, but not with the negligent assurance of a constitutional monarch. Mr Valk is a dictator.

His Hilda, Valerie White, plays sternly up to him with a mixture of matter-of-factness and mischief. Her deep, clear voice is right for Hilda, who must be trollish and asexual; an impulse, not a dream-vision. Jane Henderson underplays Aline very movingly, save that I found her a shade too unlikeable : she must be rival as well as contrast to Hilda. But one saw Solness's point, for Jane Henderson, unlike John Anderson, is not everybody's Jo. Donald Houston, in the pink of condition, and our lovely adenoidal Yvonne Mitchell complete Peter Ashmore's clever cast.

(1947)

Twelfth Night

by WILLIAM SHAKESPEARE
at the New

When the curtain fell on this production of Mr Guinness's the stage was littered with red herrings : one in particular sprawled across one's mind : this was Feste. Robert Eddison is made to play the clown as a tall, consumptively gaunt exile with a hollow baritone voice and great (though fey) dignity. He has a little drum, on which he thumps when things look bad: but apart from this musical accessory, you would tip your hat to him, rather than acknowledge him as a professional entertainer. Mr Eddison moves with his own random, big-boned clumsiness and succeeded in giving a fine first sketch for a performance of *He Who Gets Slapped*: but he and the spirit of the play hardly touched hands for a moment. Anyone who has read Bradley knows that Feste is a wistful zany: but to argue from this that he knew all the time that Viola-Cesario was a girl and that his soul was consumed with a raging love for Olivia is to postulate a play which Shakespeare never wrote, a play whose resolution can only come when Feste marries Olivia and usurps the dukedom from Orsino. Mr Guinness's interpretation merely added another major character to a play which has too many to begin with. And this Feste would never have stooped to haggling over the halfpenny tips bestowed on him for running errands.

Apart from Peter Copley's lank-haired motherless child of an Aguecheek, there was only one really sculptural performance in this production: Cedric Hardwicke's Toby. Sir Cedric has now done for Sir Toby exactly what Sir Ralph did for Sir John Falstaff: he has restored him to the knighthood. This Sir Toby is gruff and soldierly; not a glowing, tosy old buccaneer, but rather a retired staff officer; too intelligent even to be called Anglo-Indian. He was a Somerset Maugham beachcomber, with twinkling eyes which deserve to be called humorous rather than merry. He preserved an impassive, resigned visage, broken only by occasional eyebrow movements of mild contempt, accompanied by the faintest of shrugs. This was mock-pomp at its subtlest: he never roars with laughter, belches, spits or raises his voice, yet an impression of extreme, almost disintegrating alcoholism was perfectly conveyed. He lets rip but once, in the carousing scene, when the catch is being sung. Slowly, with tatterdemalion dignity, he rises and climbs on to the barrel on which he has been sitting, and, with pursed lips, devout nose and only slightly roguish eyes, he executes a stately stomach-dance, his hands gently resting behind his ears. The grave, unself-conscious concentration of this had the genuine world-blindness of all great comic characters. Sir Cedric made Toby the apogee of all uncles who have thrown up everything and taken to drink, and whose name is never mentioned in the drawing-room; but whose unmannerly brusqueness and sense of fun annoyingly delight the children when they meet him. With such men lavish speech is a great effort, only sparingly made: all is done with a flicker of a jaundiced, bloodshot eye and a telling grunt. For delicacy of insight and shady, cock-eyed charm I have seen no performance in Shakespearian comedy much better than this.

(1948)

The Gioconda Smile

by ALDOUS HUXLEY
at Wyndham's

This was an unusually well-written murder story, full of early Huxley (such as the time when the hero says he would be happiest of all sitting on a little hill contemplating a glorious sunset and picking his nose), and rising to later Huxley (in the condemned cell at the end, when the doctor preaches acceptance of death to the hero). The two fit together without undue jarring: the eldritch nastiness of the very latest Huxley never intrudes at all. Clive Brook, as the middle-aged connoisseur who is wrongly accused of murdering his wife, gives one of his richest, sulkiest performances: Mr Brook has the power, which none but English actors possess, of suggesting centuries of decadence behind every syllable he utters. You feel that the family is inbred to the point of deformity; you know that he has travelled, had mistresses, seen Fiesole and Fiji with the same sardonically appraising eye. Heavy sour lips, drooping lids, swift sense of humour, and ripening bulk sum up Mr Brook: but it is the suspicion of Lorenzo the Magnificent lurking in his ancestry that gives him his charm. He is a florid Renaissance growth buttoned tightly down into tweeds, and gone rather to the dogs. Miss Brown, who plays the real murderer, a jealous spinster, gives a most commanding display: her dark brown voice, alternately silky and hatchet-sharp, can lash and soothe more readily than any woman's in England. Her red hair tumbles in eruption down her back: and she laughs. Miss Brown's laugh shows off her teeth; she tips her head back and is loudly jolly. Or so you think until you notice the wide, blazing, mad eyes: and then you shiver, and change the subject. Miss Brown laughing is dangerous; Miss Brown quiescent is dangerous. You can never tell with Miss Brown: there is no real point of rest, no middle place of calm in her wild soul-wandering. She is undoubtedly the loveliest murderess on the English stage.

(1948)

Hamlet

by WILLIAM SHAKESPEARE
at Stratford-on-Avon

Hamlet, as it is printed and played to-day, is an *uncomeatable* text. Its sinews are perplexed and self-involved, like strands of weed in a furious river: as Landor said of *Paradise Regained*, here and there a prominent muscle swells out from the vast mass of the collapsed. It is too long, and its length is spun out of frayed and trailing nerve-ends, growing wispier, as time passes, and less relevant: they cloud our vision at curtain-fall, ill-digested nothings, unresolved and unregarded. Our *Hamlet*, a judicious blend of the Second Quarto and First Folio, compares, dramatically and psychologically, very ill with the brief and unpolished First Quarto. It is confused where the First Quarto is clear, legato where the First Quarto is staccato; but its very complications tempt us to act it and make physical sense of its contrariness. The customary latterday Hamlet has tended to be the kind of man Cyril Connolly was indicating when he wrote of Chamfort: 'His predicament is one with which we are all familiar . . . that of the revolutionary whose manners and ways of life are attached to the old régime, whose ideals and loyalties belong to the new, and who, by a kind of *courageous exhibitionism*, is compelled to tell the truth about both.' It is a good compromise, more grateful to the eye than the egomaniac savage which Salvador de Madariaga has recently commended to us: but it fails to make the play a unity. Only the beholder-critic can do that, as only a beholder can discern in the random hoofprints of a horse the pattern of an exquisite tesselation. *Hamlet* remains a mangled, racked body of a play. Reflect, for example, upon the placing of the two central soliloquies. In our text the incisive plotting of 'The play's the thing Wherein I'll catch the conscience of the king' (an end to indecision and a signpost to action at the end of Act II) is inexplicably followed up, sixty lines later, with 'To be or not to be'. The core lies here of the arguments adduced to prove the mercurial, delaying quality of Hamlet's distraction; a subtlety which the First Quarto sensibly circumvents by putting the suicidal soliloquy into his mouth on his first entrance in Act II, when the last words we have heard from him have been: 'The time is out of joint; O cursed spite That *ever I was born* to set it right.' 'O what a rogue' (here changed to 'O what a dunghill idiot slave') does not occur until long after 'To be or not to be': their relative positions are *reversed*, thus making what is, to my mind, a much more likely progression.

But given the jumbled psychology of the received text, and given the jumbled psychology of our times, it is right that our young actors should continue to make their guesses at the part. The kind of modern Hamlet we had all been waiting for is beautifully defined by C. S. Lewis:

> I am trying to recall attention from the things an intel-
> lectual adult notices to the things a child or a peasant
> notices – night, ghosts, a castle, a lobby where a man can
> walk four hours together, a willow-fringed brook and a
> sad lady drowned, a graveyard and a terrible cliff above
> the sea – and amidst all these, a pale man in black
> clothes . . . with his stockings coming down, a dishevelled
> man whose words make us at once think of loneliness
> and doubt and dread, of waste and dust and emptiness, and
> from whose hands, as from our own, we feel the richness
> of heaven and earth and the comfort of human affection
> slipping away.

What I am going to contend is that Paul Scofield, the
Hamlet of Michael Benthall's production at Stratford is,
for this generation, that pale man. A pale man; not even
embryonically a pale hero; for Hamlet is perhaps the only
Elizabethan protagonist with nothing heroic about him.
'He was likely, had he been put on, To have proved most
royally'—he was *likely*, but he was never put on: the
frustrations of fear and conscience intervened.

Mr Scofield underplays his Hamlet in a manner of
which verbal analysis can never explain the success. Its
very outlines are sketchy: the actor does not aim at any
specific emotion at any given time. He does not aim at
youth (he is a man, not a *young* man); he is not eager, he
is not pathetic, not scornful, nor brutal. He is nothing
definite, nothing capable of imprisonment in a few labels:
he shares with Olivier this strange technique of not
insisting. (And with Alec Guinness's Abel Drugger, his
Clown in *The Winter's Tale* shares an ability to make
goodness funny without deriding it.) I think even Lamb,
who could not bear to see the play acted, would have
applauded this Hamlet: Lamb, who said:

> . . . such is the actor's necessity of giving strong blows to
> the audience, that I have never seen a player in this
> character who did not exaggerate and strain to the utmost
> these ambiguous features, these temporary deformities in
> the character. They make him express a vulgar scorn at

Polonius which utterly degrades his gentility . . . they make him show contempt, and curl up the nose at Ophelia's father – contempt in its very grossest and most hateful form: but they get applause by it: it is natural, people say: that is, the words are scornful and the actor expresses scorn, and that they can judge of: but why so much scorn, and of that sort, they never think of asking.

(What a clear picture is here of the nineteenth-century Hamlet! In the court scenes, behaving like Gulliver in Lilliput; in awful soliloquy, like Gulliver in Brobdingnag.)

Lamb is here getting at a very important point: he represents the decay in the spectator of an instinctive response to stock, stylized gestures and vocal tones; and the beginning of that embarrassment in the face of intensified stage emotion which finally produced the naturalistic style. Mr Scofield's gift, like that of many great modern actors, is that he never aims his whole being at any one bull's-eye of emotion. That is too easy: the art is in missing by inches, and thus creating for us a human being incidentally expressing anger, instead of an embodiment of anger who is only incidentally a human being. The lines serve to illuminate a man, not a passion: only the very greatest actors can fuse the two inalienably, and the rest are better advised not to try. Of the rest, Mr Scofield is among the finest.

Lamb's ideal Hamlet is (like himself) 'shy, negligent, and retiring'. Negligent and retiring we may concede, but Scofield is never shy, for that supposes a self-consciousness of which he knows nothing. Helplessness he has: to a nearly comic degree he needs strength and comfort; and the wan, stricken fullness of his face cries out to be soothed. Unconvinced and tentative, he pads about the wide solitary stage, his turned-out feet going two ways in two minds, his tired hands flickering, his lips pursed and worried, inly hopeless of ever grasping joy. The matronly spectator may meditate adopting him as a pet, lean and shaggy in his hunger for solace. No sound he utters, no step he takes is fixed or purposed: there are no roots, he is a wandering plant, in sapless perambulation. Sometimes

he will seem to make stern his lips with terrible earnest-
ness; he will prowl around, inclined stiff-necked forwards,
surveying the ground with the beady-eyed intentness of a
schoolmistress rolling up her sleeves to investigate an evil
smell in the changing-room; but always the fraily shrugging hands contradict his designs. Again the plaintive
voice breaks, and the unsought squalor of being tightly
involved in murders and adulteries bursts afresh on his
intelligent soul. Nothing he does is confidently predictable.
Even the simplest move over the stage may be dammed
and diverted by some new roaming of his vague, merciful
eyes. He commands all the silent agonies of childhood; in
him the gravity of extreme youth and the puckishness of
old age commingle. To have these qualities, and yet
resolutely repel any hint of pathos, is one negative mark
of great acting. Two things await this Hamlet; of these
alone, as we watch him, we can prophesy. He will be
trapped, and die. What time he will not weep.

Mr Benthall has dressed him in the black frock-coat and
fly-away tie of the 1860s, thus putting one constantly
in mind of Matthew Arnold; except that Mr Scofield's
vagrant beauty is nothing like Arnold, but closer to his
Scholar Gipsy:

> . . . that Oxford scholar poor,
> Of pregnant parts and quick inventive brain,
> Who, tired of knocking at preferment's door,
>   One summer morn forsook
> His friends. . . .

The poem is full of lines which call up Mr Scofield's
raptness in repose:

> . . . thy figure spare,
> Thy dark vague eyes, and soft abstracted air. . .

– or best of all:

> seen by rare glimpses, pensive and tongue-tied

– for it is the crown of this Hamlet that, in one of the
longest parts ever written, he never seems verbose or even
anxious to speak at all. He must 'unpack his heart with

words', but he does so with a reluctance, a dour and humble delicacy, which makes the privilege of listening to him seem all too sparingly granted.

This is the best Hamlet I have seen. I have admired the supple hysterics of Mr Gielgud's and stared aghast at the giant technical prowess of Mr Wolfit's; more nearly I have cherished the courtier of Mr Clunes and the agile puppet, sodden in tears, which Jean-Louis Barrault made of the part. Mr Scofield has ousted them all from my memory, and I know that there is now in England a young actor who is bond-slave to greatness, and can stand beside the other exciting young men (Mr Benthall, Mr Ustinov, Mr Quayle) who are going to make our theatre in the coming decade a thing of great pride and fruition. I think, in fine, that we can now speak of Paul Scofield as 'Scofield', and know whom we mean.

Something now of the pace and passion of Mr Benthall's production. By setting and costuming the play in a nineteenth-century Ruritania, hung with vast crimson curtains and gilt tassels, he has sidestepped any comparison with previous *Hamlets*: everything is new; there is no point of contact: we are seeing a new play. The soldiers are Life Guards; Polonius (played very tactfully by John Kidd) is a dwarf elder statesman, prim and monocled; Claudius becomes a nasty and boorish Prince Consort. Mr Benthall's mastery of the unexpected inflexion, the striking vocal novelty, is nearly as complete as Mr Brook's. Witness the first appearance of the Ghost to Hamlet: he does not even look at it as the others recoil, but stares fixedly away, deliberately crosses himself, and, with perfect steadiness, *murmurs*: 'Angels and ministers of grace, defend us.' Look, too, at the handling of Ophelia's madness: one cannot quickly forget the rising poignancy of 'If − thou − hadst − not − come − to − MY − BED!' and her subsequent collapse, writhing and whimpering. Better still is Mr Benthall's quite original treatment of the scenes after the death of Polonius between Hamlet, Rosencrantz and Guildenstern. These are usually played up to the comic hilt, but Mr Benthall makes them prickly with menace.

The two spies, immaculate in evening dress, advance on Hamlet with swords lazily at guard; he hysterically jests with them, edging towards escape between the pillars; only to discover, by a gleam of helmet and another and yet another advancing figure, that the whole palace soldiery is joining in the man-hunt. The sense of trappedness is complete. Almost my only quibble with the production is Mr Benthall's resort to the traditional hair-triggered cannon when Fortinbras bids the soldiers shoot: this was an obvious cue for a volley of muskets, and the producer missed it.

After grateful praise to Anthony Quayle (Claudius), Claire Bloom (Ophelia), and Diana Wynyard (Gertrude), I must open the full throat of acclamation for Esmond Knight's Ghost. This overwhelming performance sent terror and alarm into one's very stomach : consternation rippled across the whole audience as it listened to Mr Knight's ghastly care in reaching after breath, an agonized inhaling as if he were scouring up the deepest fumes of hell to bear the noxious pain of his message to Hamlet's ears.

> *If ever thou didst thy dear father love*
> (intake of breath)
> *Revenge his foul and most unnatural MURDER*
> (the voice rising to a shriek)
> HAMLET : *MURDER?* (A horrified yell)
> GHOST : *MURDER – most foul as in the best it is. . . .*

Those three full-volume 'Murders' and their endless echoing down corridors and along galleries of pillars, sent the scene swimming up to a climax of banging horror. I was out of my seat for fright.

(I ought to add that Robert Helpmann alternated the leading part with Scofield, and gave a very clean-cut and passionless performance – not indeed of Hamlet, but Hamlet's moral tutor at Wittenberg University.)

(1948)

Medea

by EURIPIDES
at the Edinburgh Festival

I am humbly at a loss to account for the miracle by which every aspect of Mr Gielgud's latest adventure was contrived to appear so uniformly, harmoniously, and continuously bad. To begin with the translation.

Robinson Jeffers's 'free adaptation' of the play has left it roughly as close to the original as Settle's *Fairy Queen* is to *A Midsummer Night's Dream*, or as processed cheese is to Roquefort. For boldness of invention, for literal faith, for any of the translator's possible virtues, Mr Jeffers tamely substitutes a sort of vulgar, unearthly disrespect. In terms of writing, his play is a pedestrian crisscrossing of richly empty resonances (e.g. 'the *marble music* of the Greek temples') and arch, idiomatic modernisms (e.g. Medea's reaction to Creon's notice of expulsion: 'This is *it*.') New characters and speeches have been most diligently spawned: Miss Cathleen Nesbitt's excellent performance as the nurse owes a fabulous debt to the fact that her part has been doubled in length and quadrupled in significance by the wanton amalgamation into it of the meatiest passages of the Messenger's speech. Whether Miss Nesbitt refused to play the part unless it was lengthened to fit her, or whether the actor originally engaged to play the Messenger was below standard (this, when I think of the rest of the supporting cast, would hardly be conceivable), we shall probably never discover. It is an inexplicable and unpleasant piece of rewriting.

After so many minor excisions and replacements in the play's internal structure, it will not surprise you to learn that, in a final despairing slash, Mr Jeffers has cut off its head. The legendary chariot of Zeus which, unsummoned, bears Medea off after the catastrophe, lifting her like an eagle above the stain of blood and the guilt into the passionate peace for which Seneca so clearly prepared her in his 'Medea superest', and Corneille in his

Dans un si grand revers, que vous reste-t-il?
MÉDÉE :   *Moi!*

– this devastating triumph over mortal retribution is reduced to the status of a flagged taxicab. (How appropriately, we shall discuss later.) Medea makes some remark about having her chariot waiting at the gate, and, having stifled the supernatural thrill as it rose in our throats, she marches down the garden path and is off, without so much as a Home, James, and don't spare the Thracian horses.

The Chorus is decimated: only three young women are left, dressed in scrupulously authentic costumes that make them look like derelict mermaids. The first (Miss Elspeth March) is Wagnerian; the second is somewhere between a starved pre-Raphaelite heroine and Mr Robert Cummings made up as Charley's Aunt; and the third is just a sprat. To the pre-Raphaelite falls the flattest line in the play (and there is stiff competition): when the bells of hell have really begun to ring for Medea, she stirs uneasily, sensing that things are not quite as they used to be, and, after some deliberation, commits herself to this: 'Several frightening and *irrational* things seem to have been happening lately.' After a triple murder that is crazily outspoken; Miss E. M. Delafield's Provincial Lady, in similar circumstances, would have felt the same. I wonder how many members of the audience remembered, as I did, Alexander Woollcott's story of the schoolmaster who, coming upon a mutilated torso in the Lower Third dormitory, remarked: 'Some dangerous clown has been here.'

Mr Gielgud's production is most threatening. He has given the play three (some say four) sunsets, thus demolishing Euripides' strict unity of time. And he has collected positively the least inviting group of secondary players I have ever seen. I isolate, for pity's sake, Mr Hector MacGregor, absurdly young for Creon, and disfigured by a make-up which put me in mind at once of Fig. 3 (Anger) in any Actor's Manual. Mr Ralph Michael makes Jason thick-skinned and regimental, eliminating that benighted sensibility which is an actor's one hope of success in this tedious part: he does away, too, with any idea of varying pace or volume – except, not unnaturally, at the end, when a pair of serpents that have been coiled innocuously about Medea's door throughout the play suddenly become neon-lit, giving the place an understandably vexing resemblance to a certain dingy boîte in the West Central postal district. It puts Jason right off, as Mr Jeffers might phrase it.

(On the credit side, Mr Gielgud has invented a good piece of business for Jason's interview with his sons: the children, shortly to be stabbed to death, play with their father's sword, and make mock-passes at each other with it. Little do they know, and so forth.)

I have considered carefully what I am to say next, and my conclusion is that the only way to arrest Miss Eileen Herlie in her headlong plunge into an oblivion which she has no need to seek so prematurely, is to be thoroughly rude to her. Let me set down two passages from the criticism of Shaw which jumped unbidden to my mind as I watched this Medea. In the first, he is speaking of the Irish actor Barry Sullivan, 'who would . . . when led into it by a touch of stateliness and sonority in the lines, abandon his part, and become for the moment a sort of majestic incarnation of abstract solemnity and magnificence'. In the second, he reviles an actress for playing in '. . . a somnambulistic, hysterical, maudlin condition in which the most commonplace remark will seem fraught with emotions from the very ocean-bed of solemnity and pathos.' I had better reveal to Miss Herlie at once that either of those excerpts might have been written about her. (Before going on, I ought to add that, while I bear Miss Herlie no ill-will, I bear the skill of Euripides and the craft of heroic acting still less.)

Medea's entrance line in this version, of which there is no sign in Euripides, is directed at the sun: she says she has come to look upon its face for the last time. This line Miss Herlie delivered as I think she imagines Rachel delivered the line in *Phèdre* of which it is so faithful a translation:

> *Soleil! je te viens voir pour la dernière fois.*

I do not believe Miss Herlie can have breathed freely until the day when a provincial reporter rose to the bait and compared her to Bernhardt; and it was this, as much as anything, that squeezed the spleen into what I am writing. For Miss Herlie's idea of a performance in the grand manner is almost incredibly ingenuous. Sarah at least had three tricks, if we can trust Walkley's fingers; Miss Herlie has but one. This consists of uttering every speech, every sentence, as if it were a curtain line – that is to say, with hollow eyes and in a sepulchral, desolating moan, sinking to a plummy bleating sound which is intended to coax the critic into saying: 'I shall never forget the *awful finality* with which Miss Herlie . . .' When you have heard twenty consecutive lines recited in this way, with gusty pauses between each of them, you begin to wonder whether you were not wrong in doubting the efficacy of water dripping on the head to produce insanity. After ten minutes the whole of Miss Herlie's performance is predictable, and transparently pretentious: she simply has not the dignity, the inner thundering, nor even the technical polish for these alarming parts she plays. Willingness to act plus a preternaturally loud voice have conquered in Miss Herlie the willingness to learn how to act and how to control the voice. I admit that in repose she is gracious; but she lunges rather than moves, and she has common hands. In this part she looks about as savage and exotic as the advertisement in which the lady discovers blood on her toothbrush; her every gesture, every maenadic clutch at her vast wig, proclaimed the naked, reinless freedom of Kensington Gravel Pits.

When I saw *The Eagle has Two Heads* I felt, contrary to what was then being written, that Miss Herlie was not good enough for the play, which is, after all, a perfect exercise in a rare genre, artificial philosophic melodrama. After Medea, I shall refuse to accept her as a good, far less as a potentially great actress until she shows a range and a finesse of which we have hitherto seen no token. There is a story of a visit paid to Miss Herlie's dressing-room after a matinée of the Cocteau play by a recently lamented actress and wit. She extended her congratulations; Miss Herlie, supine and perspiring, waved a listless arm and said that her guest ought to have come to an evening performance. 'I give my all to the evening audiences,' she said. Her visitor regarded her benignly. Then, baring her teeth: 'You little spendthrift, you,' she crooned. If Miss Herlie does not take care, she will shout herself silly in a couple of years, and all her golden coins will be spent. It is not a beguiling thought.

To a few innocent people caught up in this disaster, I must apologize. But, when all is done, you need pretty formidable excuses for putting on the Medea at all: you must have fulfilled one at least of three conditions: (a) discovered an actress as good as Agnes Moorehead at her best; (b) discovered a new and ingenious translator; (c) discovered yourself to be a producer of genius. Now none of these conditions could reasonably be argued by Mr Gielgud. The thing is ruled out of court: on such in-existed.

(1948)

Peter Brook

Peter Brook, at 25, is probably the most mature and certainly the most exciting producer in England. He has all Guthrie's genius for invention, and adds to it a Continental delicacy and finical flair: he selects far more critically than the older man. He has all Benthall's electrical prowess, and throws in a few tricks of his own : and his decorative sense is such that he designed, impeccably, both costumes and scenery for his production of *Measure for Measure* at Stratford. His professional productions have included *Man and Superman* and *King John* (Birmingham Repertory Theatre); *Love's Labour's Lost, Romeo and Juliet, Measure for Measure* (Stratford); *Huis Clos* (Arts Theatre); *The Brothers Karamazov, Men Without Shadows, The Respectable Prostitute, Dark of the Moon* (Lyric, Hammersmith); *Boris Godounov, La Bohème, The Olympians, Salomé* (Covent Garden); *Ring Round the Moon* (Globe). Peter Brook is a small, sausage-shaped man : he looks edible, and one gets the notion that if one bit into him he would taste like fondant cream or preserved ginger. His snub face creases readily into a thuggishly wicked little grin : his forehead meanwhile is deeply wrinkled. He gives you the impression that the sun is dazzling him as he talks to you : the eyes are tiny and deep-set – twinkling ice-picks. His miniature hands are limp, and flutteringly expressive : the rest of him stands quiet, dapper, and smug. Occasionally he will chuckle, but generally he will be casual, almost affected in his sly, throwaway sophistication. His voice is flat and high-pitched, like a kazoo. One feels he has never travelled anywhere on foot or on buses, but is wrapped up in silk and carried. He talks on : stubby, sunny, and immovable; a great knowingness beams through every pore. He is almost a perfect producer, and, sedately, he knows it.

Brook has a fine ear for aggressive novelties of vocal inflexion, for sound effects such as frail woodwinds and muttering crowds; and a bright eye for fantastic bustle; for peace, too, and nostalgia. Mists, all that veils or is faraway and untouchable, have always fascinated him; by contrast, he loves hurly-burlies, the sweat and stench of prisons and gutters. At his best he skips nimbly between these two poles. He can impart a bitingly keen edge to nostalgia : he likes to show us distant minarets, ice-pure slim pillars against the sky, exquisite filigree work, blue hazes, palaces dissolved into mist. Alternately he loves suddenness, shock, noise and immediacy: his *Brothers Karamazov* opened with two revolver shots fired into the dome of the darkened auditorium.

Dark of the Moon was a mediocre American play about witchcraft. Brook grasped it, filled it with a cast of rowdy young unknowns, and cast a spell over it. It became a crazily orchestrated symphony of black and amber: a jigsaw of wild superstitions and hot loveliness, reaching its perspiring climax in a revivalist meeting which tore the heart out of the play and held it in its hand. *Ring Round the Moon*, in striking opposition to this dirt, noise and savagery, is complete wedding-cake: it has been traced with an icing-gun on gossamer. Brook has a way of getting the best out of his designers. Oliver Messel has done nothing for twenty years as good as the flimsy conservatory in which Anouilh's lovers flirt and part. It is a testimony to the cunning of the set and the lighting that, though there is no change of scene, there was a round of applause every time the curtain rose. Brook's fireworks display (in the literal sense) at the end of the play is a superb *bonne bouche*; a dewdrop, you might say, from the lion's mane.

Measure for Measure is his maturest work to date. The presence in the cast of John Gielgud may have been an influence to moderation: at all events the outcome is a perfect marriage of shrill imagination and sober experience. Brook permits himself only one 'trick': the grisly parade of cripples and deformities which Pompey introduces in that leprous Viennese gaol. Last of all appears ' Wild Half-Can who stabb'd pots': a very aged man, naked except for a rag coat, twitching his head from side to side, and walking poker-stiff, bolt upright on his bare heels, with his toes turned up. All the ghastly comedy of the prison scenes was summed up in this horridly funny piece of invention. Brook's triumph, however, is his fifth act: a scene of such coincidences and lengthy impossibilities, such forced recon-

ciliations and incredible cruelties that most producers flog it through at breakneck speed towards the
welcome curtain. Fully aware of the tension his flawless timing has created, Brook here has the effrontery
to sit down and let it ride: into this dreadful act he
inserts half a dozen long pauses, working up a new
miracle of tension which Shakespeare knew nothing
about. The thirty-five seconds of dead silence which elapse
before Isabella decides to make her plea for Angelo's
life were a long, prickly moment of doubt which had
every heart in the theatre thudding. Three years ago
Brook would have added much more to *Measure
for Measure*: he has learnt to prune and be sparing,
and any moment now will be at the height of his
powers.

(1949)

Four Eccentrics

So far I have had something to say about the big personalities on the narrative stage, the stage on which stories
are told. I want now to go on to the other kind; the revue
stage, the music-hall stage, in which personality develops
less inhibitedly in freer air. We discovered, after a patient
scrutiny, that there was only one British born actor
(Olivier) with the right pretensions to heroic stature,
on English stages. The unique people have been moving
more and more towards the lighter atmospheres, the
less rarefied emotional climates: we can point to two
native jesters (Miss Gingold and Mr Field). Of them I
shall now speak, and of two others, one an American, the
other French.

First, then, a picture of Hermione Gingold, whose
Sweet and Low series of revues during and after the
late war established her as our mentor and exemplar
of aristocratic waspishness.

I suggested earlier that one of the reasons why we

laugh at male comedians is that they are exposing, wittingly or not, all that is feminine in them. In Miss Gingold the reverse is true: behind all her hastily assumed but beautifully draped femininity is a gloating maleness, a massive and unbreakable virility. In her bottom drawer, so to speak, there is a large bottle of rye; under the *politesse* and the urbanity lies the questing beast of the high Renaissance, wholehearted and irresistible. As Arthur Marshall would put it, we laugh when the mask drops, and she becomes a livid, gibbering Thing. She is heavily roguish: to use a phrase which she, in a sketch, once applied to Evelyn Laye, the Admiralty couldn't be more arch. You are hard put to find the right word to describe Miss Gingold's profession: she is not a *diseuse*, she does not sing, and she is not properly a satirist. She does not parody anything or anyone especially well, except herself: and if we must define what she does, we can only call it self-mockery. She explores every nook and cranny of her voice and personality, and riotously exposes what she finds: her every appearance in revue is an adventure – an inquiry into the number of unladylike things a woman can do and say without losing her poise. She can turn a melting smile into a baring of fangs more outrageously than anyone I know except Groucho Marx: and she gets her laughs by this method, of suddenly and fleetingly letting us glimpse the caged wolf pacing up and down behind the façade of the *grande dame*. She stands poised on the stage, in an attitude which would be one of finely relaxed grace, were it not that her eyes are surveying her outpost hands and toes with a sort of bemused contempt. You feel that her heart is not in her work; that she keeps up the pose of fragile womanhood purely for the money. She moves in surges from the hips; it is a slimy prowl rather than a walk, and you can almost hear her murmuring 'Heigh-ho!' for boredom as she does it. The whole impression is of an exaggerated and very much alive masculinity hiding behind an exaggerated and exhausted femininity. Her eyes tell you that she is not convinced that she ought to be doing this sort of thing at all: disinterested and casual, they give the delicious lie to the enthusiasm of her performance. They are the self-mockers, and the agents of our laughter. She affects, garishly and wantonly, the rompishness and gush of extreme youth, but always with frigid uncern. Whenever a weak pun crops up in her lines, she spits it out with shuddering coyness, averting her eyes delicately to her bosom; inwarding gloating over the absurdity of getting a laugh with material like that. Alternatively, she skims over the bad lines by assuming the manner of an ageing principal boy, and *sings* the offending word in a throbbing, throaty contralto.

I suppose, in the final categorizing, she can only be said to play two parts: one is a voracious spinster, with no lipstick, and lecherously bespectacled, and the other a rampageous courtesan, slashed with an enormous Cupid's bow. The former was last seen in her Masseuse, who can hardly keep her hands off her clients as she puts on a warmly inviting and very ginger grimace, the lower lip extended, grotesquely alluring; you become fly to her spider, and only the tiny gap in her teeth, just left of centre, warns you that there is something more macabre in her designs than meets the eye. Her voice remains much the same whether she is being a spinster or a tart: a hideous extension of all that is wrong with South Kensington vowel sounds. In her burlesque of Eileen Herlie's Medea, I recall her starting with dismay as she saw her colleagues grouped around a vast sausage-shaped pillar well upstage, and instantly lurching towards it, dismissing them frostily with the line: 'Thiss – is may parsonnul collem.' She will then chew her lower lip coyly, meditatively, but a little predatorily as she casts an idle glance over the boxes and stalls, seeking her next victim. You feel that she is always ready to pounce, and that when she does, she is not going to want to play sardines. A number ideally suited to her brand of gloating was John Jowett's *Borgia Orgy*, in which she rose to heights of full-blooded malice which she alone can scale. Her attitude towards her audiences has always reminded me of the villainous doctor in James Thurber's drawing, who looms unpromisingly over his terrified client and growls: 'You're not my patient, you're my meat, Mrs Quist.' In *Borgia Orgy* she behaved like that: 'We're pushing some people we know off a *steeple*,' she confided, her voice rising to a note of delighted and incredulous joy on the last word; and the murderous glee with which she 'wondered who'd sit on the circular saw' woke me up screaming for days. It is easy, in writing about her, to make her sound like one of the less amiable products of the imagination of Hieronymus Bosch; so I must take leave again to insist that these lines and others like them become funny because she utters them in a fatuous, tea-party effusiveness of voice, the reverse of demoniacal and poles apart from poison and passion. The same leaning towards frolicsome destructiveness was indulged in a number called *Blanchisseuse Heureuse*, in which she was a laundress making enough money to conduct her business at the Ritz in a Schiaparelli evening gown: in moments of disenchantment, she would 'crush pyjama buttons into *fragments*, with this *rather* dainty Cartier *casse-noisette*'. In lines like this, her voice is a delectable plummy rasp, emerging from her as from a cement mixer. She caresses words in an almost maternal way, but occasionally lunges into them with the masculine strength and purpose of a growling trombone; I have heard her described as being, along with Françoise Rosay, the best female impersonator of our time. Sometimes she decides to walk in an insane caricature of the thigh-slapping strides of a principal boy in pantomime, sagging forward in tiny lurches, bending at the knees, accompanied by a circular motion of the shoulders, as if she were hiking in a race. She did this most of the time in a sketch (performed with Henry Kendall) concerning a Darling of the 1914–18 war receiving in her dressing-gown a bear-skinned Guards officer. Hearing her Pongo's knock at the door, she throws herself with disgusting abandon across a divan, siezes her river of beads, and sucks them, eyeing him rapaciously the while. 'Charmaine, Charmaine,' he explodes impetuously, 'Never change, Charmaine.' '*Thart*', chants Miss Gingold, 'would be a leetle *unsanitaree*'; singing the last word as she prances gracelessly away. It has been said that she treats words like chewing-gum, and it is true to the extent that she finds great difficulty in letting go of them. During the same sketch, she used constantly, for no very obvious reason, to refer to the stage manager as 'the starge mania*geur*', purring the ultimate syllable with a distention of the lips that momentarily made the French language a thing of shame. She distorts the most innocent words quite unrecognizably; some she merely savours, others she smacks her lips over, others she belches, and many she positively drools.

Even her well-bred spinsters run wild in word-puzzles : her *Music Talk*, for instance, is full of carefully art-ic-u-la-ted in-acc-u-ra-cies. 'I have been *arst* to talk to you this evening', she begins, 'about mew-sick.' She is wearing a shapeless sack of a tea-gown, a grey wig with a bun, and another string of beads, this time dangling to her thighs; the hands are clasped across the stomach, and she pushes out the words across her bust with all the flighty determination of the woman who, in a last desperate withdrawal, has retreated to the voice, manner and mind of the male. The pianist plays an illustrative piece of Bucalossi. 'Ah!' she says, in a strained parody of eager ear-cocking, 'Ah! Does not this remind us a *teeny* bit of Mozart?' The voice has soared to an ecstatic, asthmatic shrillness. Then a pause; and finally : 'No. It does not.'

Scratch the languid veneer of Miss Gingold's stage self, and gushing barbarism flows forth; she has what Rymer said the true artificer must always have, 'flame as well as phlegm'. She makes no effort to project herself across the footlights : indeed, she treats the audience as if they were old gloves she had recently cast off. With her huge eyes, monstrously curving lips, and husky, daintily ribald voice, she deserves our wonder, though you will never catch her demanding it. I think one could even take a few lines of Carew's elegy on Donne, and apply them to her :

> . . . *to the awe of thy imperious wit*
> *Our stubborn language bends, made only fit*
> *With her tough-thick-ribbed hoops to gird about*
> *Thy giant fancy, which had proved too stout*
> *For their soft melting phrases.*

But I believe I can hear her rebuking me; very coldly, with magistral authority, she is saying : 'Take those words out of your mouth : you don't know *where* they've been.'

A revue artist does not need to be humorous, in our accustomed sense of the word, but he or she must be humorous in Ben Jonson's. A humorous person in that sense is one whose whole being is governed by some irrational, heedless inclination, some bent so innate and unreasoned that it seems to call for no explanation and never dreams of compromising with the elaborate scheme of under-statements of which our reasonable lives are constructed. A humour is a magnificent exclamation mark in the middle of a legal text-book : all Jonson's great eccentrics are like that. They possess what would be impudence and wilful blindness to normality, were it not so innocent. Your true *original* makes no attempts to satirize people who already exist : he is himself the germ of a new sort of human being. He invents, and scorns to imitate; his art is not the art of caricature, but an art akin to abstract sculpture. A modern French sculptor is reputed to have said, unanswerably, that he finds it odd to reflect that the fruits of the earth bear no resemblance to anything else upon it, whereas the artistic fruits of man often bear an unaccountable resemblance to things that already exist; and this he thinks, is a wrong tack. And so whenever his pieces of sculpture begin to look like anything that ever was on land or sea, he smashes them, and starts again.

That is how the revue artist works: in a manner as different from the cartoonist's as the cartoonist's is from the portrait painter's. That is how Miss Gingold works: and to an even greater extent, it is how Danny Kaye works. They are both projectors of their own daemons, which move and make laws outside and beyond reality. They assume that you are going to enjoy their rareness, their unnaturalness, and make no apology or concession; to them you are in the position of astronomers, who find the stars they know dull and redundant, but whose eyes spark at the sight, very distant and pinpricking, of the star that no one has ever seen before. And this thrill is very far from the thrill of the legitimate stage, which is tethered to things already seen and experienced; Holofernes said 'imitari is nothing,' and though he was wrong about the drama, he was right about revue and music-hall. The straight actor appeals to the sophisticated mind, which compares and contrasts him with the thing he is personating; the music-hall star goes to something more primitive, the simple joy of discovery. I shall be happier about our theatre when there is a place in straight plays for the personality which nowadays is being drawn more and more towards revue; and that can happen only when we go to the play and find, with the wondering shock that a child feels at its first visit to a circus, that all the people on the stage are unrecognizable: that we have never seen them before, that they are not just extensions of tricks and traits we are familiar with, but that they are strangers, unlooked-for foreigners whom we cannot relate in any way to ourselves. It will need the fecundity of a Dickens to bring it off; but if it happens, I fancy that some of the awe attendant upon a Greek tragic performance may return to the theatre. The day of ideal character is over; it died with the eighteenth century; but it was a good vein. It prevented an audience from feeling smug; it banished the friendly current of equality and mutual greeting which nowadays flows between actor and spectator. Now we must seek this other kind of awe: the awe of uniqueness. I do not mean that we must enter the stalls as if the theatre were a shrine; nor do I look for ashen reverence in the boxes; I want merely to feel in the narrative theatre the sheer elastic joy and release which I have felt on more than one occasion in the Palladium. I want drama to become aware that it is part of the same tradition as circus, where those only count who have unique skills, like that, for instance, of the contortionist: and I want it to go to work subtly, provocatively and intelligently, to adapt the technique of circus to its own better purposes. Mr Shaw is in essence a maker of farces: he puts the poor folk who must act his plays through hoops, and, as one disgruntled professional told me, 'you can almost hear the old devil giggling at you in the wings'. That rich, Irish whimsy which could invent a burglar who knits and a grocer's wife with visions, and inflict them so tellingly upon us that we almost believe they exist, was content to reserve his higher dramatic energies for gaming with ideas instead of personalities. Had he invented people as monstrous, as contradictory, as perversely serene and complacent as his ideas, he might have begun the new method I am hoping for. But he stopped short of giving ideas flesh; and when you do that, in Donne's phrase, ' a great prince in prison lies'. He excused his extravagances as *jeux d'esprit*, he made apologies for that of which he should have been most proud.

A very fine, though not a complete eccentric is Danny Kaye. He has at his finger-tips the whole technique of unreason; but he has, in the past, been forced too often to waste and discard it on sublunary things. He is a good parodist (witness his 'Lobby Song', which took the American musical film to pieces and then threw the fragments alarmingly in our faces), but there are better; he is expert at doing things for purposes of sheer outrage (during his turn at the Palladium he would call for a cup of tea and a chair, and would sit and drink it and do nothing else for about two minutes – to test his command of us); but I like him best when he is doing the things that only he has ever thought of doing, and which only he has the technical prowess to perform. I am thinking of the 'Melody in Four F', which is a description of enlistment into the American forces sung entirely in that fluent riddle-me-ree gibberish called 'scat'. Most of it goes something like this: '*Tar*degitgat-gaddlywadadadoozay - gitgat - gaddly - wikasatsoosay - *reee*-taba boozay'; and he tells us his fables in this language because it is as natural to him as Esperanto is to us. I mean English. (Louis Armstrong, Fats Walker, Billy Banks had all tried it before him; Kaye had the advantage of being white and looking, to our insular eyes, fitter for the parlour.) He does not do it because he wants to impress us, or to be obscure or affected, but because he *can*. Delacroix wisely remarked that the man of talent does anything he wishes to do, while the man of genius does only what he *can* do. Let us recall some of the other things Mr Kaye can do. He can sing 'Dinah' in a wild Slav accent which nobody ever spoke in, and which involves his pronouncing 'Dinah' as 'Deenah', and hence 'ocean liner' as 'leener'; and he prefaces the song with a few introductory words about the lady it celebrates. About how he left home and wandered 'through small willages and pretty cities; and then I met my ferrst womans. She was gowerjuss, sensash-unally beuriful; when she walked, it was like a leedle gazelle strolling in a pasture, and when she spoke her voice, her voice was like the sound of angels.' He stops here, shrieks deafeningly : 'Soft and Mellow!' and instantly returns to the dewy lyricism of their first meeting. Consider Mr Kaye's handling of that loony ragtime number 'Minnie the Moocher' : tiring of the words (though, heaven knows, they are full enough of wild references to people like the King of Sweden to satisfy most of us), he zips into a sort of game with the audience. He sings a phrase in tempo, and we must repeat it in tempo.

I saw middle-aged stockbrokers doing it at the Palladium : 'Eh-loo-seh.' he encouragingly starts; 'Eh-loo-seh,' we reply; 'Oolay-acker-*seurre*' – 'Oolay-acker-*seurre*'; 'Ouvrez la fenêtre, Jean ou Sacque' – 'Ouvrez la fenêtre, Jean ou Sacque'; 'Hee-hee' – 'Hee-hee.' It was absurd and delicious; we were not mocking anything, not mimicking anything, we were saying things we had never said. I felt like a child learning the alphabet, and was refreshed. In another number, written, like all his best vehicles, by his wife, Sylvia Fine, he is a hat-designer explaining his trade :

> *It's how I pull and chew on it,*
> *The little things I do on it,*
> *Like tracing yards of lacing*
> *Or a bicycle built for two on it.*

It is done in an astoundingly accurate French accent, and is very funny : but it only becomes hysterical when Mr Kaye broadens out from sheer satire and starts looking for a cue to be zany. He is telling us, on a rising musical scale, how joyous the odds and ends of hat-making are : 'Give me *threeaad* and needle', he screams and then, at immense speed, goes berserk : 'I itch and twitch to stitch, I'm a glutton for cuttin', for puttin' with the button : I nip and tuck and strip and pluck and rip and trim and blip and brim and – ' (suddenly 'Ol' Man River' joins the stream) 'tota-thatta-barge, and lifta-thatta-bale – ' Here, on an impossibly high note, he stops dead : the excursion has gone far enough; another moment and we shall be over the cliff. You are left panting but relaxed, as dogs always seem to be.

Two more examples and I have done : one is the name of the famous German composer which he recites in 'The Little Fiddle'. It goes, as far as I remember, like this : 'Jakob Herzheimderbofhausvonkleinstorpdaswetter-istgemütlichderpfeifeldie-keh-keh – (these sounds a sort of shrill coughing noise) – vonausterlitzeindadaeindada ', and after a pause : 'Junior.' The return to normality is complete with that last word : to me, a perfect epitome of his method. He takes off, as it were, from ground we all know; then tortuously rises to a fantastic, slippery pinnacle of aberration which he builds as he goes along, like an opossum climbing its own tail; reaching a climax of deformity in the staccato 'keh-keh'; and then slowly and gently bringing us back with the three-point landing on 'Junior'. It is done almost deferentially; surgeon-like, he anaesthetizes you, delicately makes the incision and removes your rational faculty, turns it upside down, pops it back, sews up the wound with practised fingers, and brings you back to reality. Except that, though you are not aware of it, you are not exactly the same as when you went under. He can do the same thing without having recourse to mere verbal tongue-twisting : in that very beautiful and light-footed song called 'Ballin' the Jack', he makes use of incantatory powers, charming you and luring you into a territory of soft-shoed relaxation which seems so familiar that you would swear you were dreaming. On the surface the song is no more than an unremarkable description of a new dance-step, but Mr Kaye's sorcery turns it into a perfectly legitimate lost paradise. It is the most inexplicable of all his achievements : merely by interjecting strange and irrelevant shreds of phrase into the music, he hypnotizes you : there is no other word. The effect reminded me precisely of the method and voice-movement employed by Mr Peter Casson, the only other professional hypnotist I have seen, and another soft-voiced unpredictable. What are these shreds? Things like 'Look at that man go : he's crazy. I swear he's crazy', and 'Oh, you're delicious; and a sound I can only reproduce as 'Oh dimmmmmmmmmm!' And then he tells you to go through the dance with him : 'Do me,' as he puts it, 'after me.' It is a cross between the voice of the priest at some Stravinskian ritual and the voice of the teacher at dancing-school : and you obey.

How does Mr Kaye appear on the stage? In a slipshod fashion, he dances, but not particularly keenly or well; you would take him for a youngish, nervous, mild-mannered Puck, with a curling flock of yellow hair falling awry over an unexpectedly aristocratic forehead; he would put a girdle around the earth as soon as look at you. You would not, until he begins to enchant you, guess that he was a Jew: but his disarming deviltry and insidious frankness soon make that clear. All the great variety performers seem to have had Jewish blood: it lends them an unassuming, all-displaying magnetism which they share with the dummy hand at bridge. You are not especially struck with Mr Kaye until the twangling Jew's-harp of a voice begins to run riot: and then he is possessed. He rises effortlessly to a frenzy of articulation in which not a syllable is lost: in *Lady in the Dark* he reeled off, to music, the names of a hundred Russian composers in less than half a minute, and if you play the record slowly you can identify them all – even César Cui. The end to the technical versatility of his voice has never been reached: the ultimate comic gift of split-second finesse and fastidiousness gleams blindingly in his sheer power of pronouncing. He holds you first by ingenuousness, by walking as if the coat-hanger were still in his coat; next, by fixing you with his two cocktail-shaking hands, the index fingers pointing out at the stage boxes, tugging every eye to focus on him; and finally, by the voice. He never dashes bull-headed into his songs, as Betty Hutton does: he primps, adjusts his tie, smooths his hair, and slides into them like a water-snake. When the climaxes of ingenuity approach, he does not, as Al Jolson would, hurl himself lungs and liver into them: you can tell by his anxious brow and screwed-up lips that a strange, splenetic power has taken hold of him; and it is not an easy, laughing power (the Cheshire-cat smile has frozen), but something undeniably magical, which has temporarily made him its slave as well as you. You had suspected, earlier in his act, when he would pause, inconsequently, and mouth 'Tip-toe through the tulips', prancing and eerily grinning, that he was subject to attacks of his daemon energy: and now you are sure. Dadaism, in which sounds are more expressive than mere hidebound words, has moved in: his voice will whisper, brag, disclaim, splutter and sigh without missing a beat, and it will flatten itself out on a mean, piercing, high-pitched braying note which will surely leave him dying for want of breath.

In between these mad crescendos, he tends to relax too much; at the Palladium he would sit down, dangling his feet over the footlights, ask the audience for a cigarette and a match, and chat with them, about how nice it was to have broken down the glass wall between actor and spectator and turned the theatre into a drawing-room: when all the time we were thinking that, after all, a theatre was not a drawing-room, and we had paid our money to see a freak, a unique performer so big that no drawing-room could ever hold him. Danny Kaye owes too much of his success to qualities not directly connected with his superb vocal agility and abandon: his good looks and ingenuousness, for instance. I thought he played too much on these at the Palladium, and cared not deeply enough for the powers which set him beyond our normal ken. He will never be a good straight comedian, because he cannot work with partners: he is the most solitary of clowns, working in a dimension which no one else can inhabit. He owes it to us not to care whether we like him or not: it is embarrassing when he tries to fraternize. It is like playing Daphne to his Apollo.

Male single-mindedness and female fastidiousness mix in putting across Danny Kaye's peculiar quiddity:

> *My brain I'll prove the female to my soul,*
> *My soul the father; and these two beget*
> *A generation of still-breeding thoughts,*
> *And these same thoughts people this little world.*

– a little world to which no trespassers should be admitted. It is, as C. E. Montague pointed out in his review of Benson's Richard II, the world of the isolated artist.

Audiences always love (not merely approve or prefer) perfect articulation; a sharp, cutting voice which, though it projects a very fountain of words, leaves each one distinct, shaped and crisp; each uttered (as Olivier, as Barrault utters them) with no contortion of the face. It demonstrates command: the ability to make words perform for you, skip, leap and gyrate, or, in Max Beerbohm's phrase, 'tread in their precedence, like kings, gravely'. That is Danny Kaye's treasure: and now we must wonder whether he can develop, and ask ourselves whether we can count as a great comic artist a man who is, when we reduce him to essentials, no more than a flurry of sound. He has always seemed lost without his wife's lyrics, and power like his should acknowledge no such limits.

Chevalier is a much more accomplished all-round artist than Kaye. I saw him in the flesh only once, during his season in 1948 at the London Hippodrome, when he was almost sixty. It would be quite inaccurate for me to say that I merely caught glimpses and detected adumbrations of the old splendour: because it was still there, all as deft and cunning and potent as I remember it in *The Love Parade* many years ago. I admit I went expecting to feel a delicious thrill of nostalgia for the 'twenties; I intended to applaud Chevalier's gameness and courage, and I wanted to hear again the lilting, *faux-naïf* little songs with which he made his reputation. I was disappointed: he sang none of the old love-songs, and banished nostalgia. He stood alone on the broad stage for two and a half hours with no support except an accompanist, and he never looked tired or wistful. From the moment he strode on to the stage, in that sailorly gait, with the toes turned prettily in, and began to beam irrepressibly with his apple-cheeks and sly eyes, I knew that the remarks I had been ready to make ('And when you think he's nearly sixty!') were going to be disastrously out of place. You were never embarrassed when he danced, you wanted more of it: the cat-footed grace, the almost oriental discretion of being able to suggest a complete pirouette by a flick of the heel, the long rangy stride were still as commanding as when, long ago, he was dancing partner to Mistinguette. Nor had he lost his grinning abandon (he grins where Danny Kaye smiles. A grin means a response to a joke shared, a smile implies a private enjoyment: Chevalier is more public in his glee than Kaye). I noticed it first when he sang 'Just One of Those Things' ('Chust Worn of Thoz Krezzy Theengs') and, coming to the line in which he tells us that it had been just one of those fabulous flights ('farbulous flats'), he threw his loving arms way out in space, stood tip-toe, tilting forward at the hips like a man about to throw himself off a cliff, and flung his head back in a disarming hoot of exultation. Chevalier is perhaps the greatest master alive of the art of unlocking his audience's confidence: he is always smiling knowingly at some front-row stall, as if sharing a private, wordless joke: his look says: 'You gay dog, you know why I'm grinning, don't you? Well, don't let's tell anyone else.' He gets double laughs by this method on nearly every line.

I did not know before how great was his gift of mimicry. I like his swaggering Frenchman, hopelessly in love with everything Spanish, who struts like a pouter pigeon on slick feet, singing 'A Barcelona', interposing respectful and ineffective 'Holés' into the music. I like his 'Place Pigalle', in which he draws brief thumb-nose sketches of the people one meets there, the pickpocket, the aged lecher, and, superbly funny, the leering pansy: the number is Zolaesque in its squalid diversity. Chevalier, by turning up the collar of his dinner jacket and plunging his hands deep in his trouser pockets, can become a waterfront outcast; shambling with eyes on the ground and toes turned up, he reminds you of the sort of hunted, brutish creatures that Jean Gabin is always playing: in this impersonation he touches off great trains of pathos. Then, in an instant, he will breeze into a buoyant chorus song, shuffling along on his toes in profile to the audience, jigging his shoulders up and down and winking over the left one at you. He even mimics animals: particularly, an old pet dog, once a masher of the boulevards, and now feeling the springtime again and trying disgustingly to waggle his ears. In another longish number he is an ancient Chinese mandarin co-mitting hara-kiri because of the defection of his young wife: he is careful to explain that 'I know they never commit hara-kiri in China, but you know, I had to have a strong ending for the song.'

Chevalier's is the ebullience of the overgrown school-boy who has just discovered about sex. He sulks, pouts and enthuses as schoolboys will; his little anecdotes are chuckled confidences, secretly and daringly exchanged under the headmaster's nose. He is perpetually, you feel, playing truant. You sympathize immediately, because he has obviously just learnt what it is to fall in love: it is still a delightfully risqué subject to him, and his eyes shine naïvely under provocatively arched eyebrows when he tells you about it. The gurgling voice, persuasively flat and tending to yodel its high notes, is a weapon of great sophistication; but you divine from its persistence and his anxious lips that he is very worried lest you should fail to understand him. He 'seeryoosly wornts you to eeyer' every syllable. At the end of the song, he pushes out his lower lip, and grins, and you know that he knew all the time that you were listening. He has been treating you and playing upon you like children, to whom everything must be explained: while Chevalier is on the stage, you are a vagrant mob of Peter Pans, and he your joyous ring-leader.

Very occasionally, after long and painful intervals, there emerges from a provincial city a clean comedian. The consequent fracas is always heartening: a boisterous quarterstaff is giving battle to the jagged razors of innuendo, and putting the nasty rout to flight. Late years have granted us but one theme for such talk as this: the munificent clowning of the late Sid Field, the bumpkin droll. It is wrong to be precious in speaking of a man so burly; to fantasticate one whose renown was built upon blunt ways and broad gestures. But there was a finical subtlety to Mr Field that deserves writing about. I cannot do it : yet I'll hammer it out.

With him, comparison, the critic's upholstery, must retire defeated : nobody has done such things before on our stages. He was enchanted as Bottom was, but he knew it : he was a soul in bliss. There can be no explaining that angelic relaxedness, no dissecting that contentment. He was in permanent possession of some rare and delectable secret, the radiance in the blear eyes told you : yet what he said was serenely, even pugnaciously usual. He could be very nearly a rudesby. I cannot fathom by what alchemy this blend of celestial stance and mundane observation, of nectar and beer, was contrived. You would not guess, from the moonstruck words that eased out of him, that this man would appear in guise and circumstance as other men. Yet I dare insist that no more naturalistic clown walked the land. He employed no barb of repartee, he had no niceness in returning phrase for phrase : his ordinary situation was confusion, or at best mild bafflement. The sketches he animated have, when you think about it, no intrinsic humour of line about them; and if they have, it is generally something trite beyond words (in his golfing sketch, for instance, the instructor would tell him to make the tee with sand : and Mr Field, mistaking him, would make a slightly hurt, recoiling movement and then venture defensively : 'I'm not drinking that *sterf*' : his voice climbing to a pained shrillness, and then, after a moment's consideration : 'More like *co-coa*'.) He had no use at all for pathos, or for the poignant eyes of the quick, ferret comic; to be honest, his face was sadly flat and slab-shaped. Apart from the habit of stage ease and peace, he had none of the marks of his contemporary drolls. He was elephantine. And though he did it delicately, he lumbered. His style was amorphous : he was like a man carrying about with him a number of inexplicable parcels, which he couldn't remember buying, and certainly didn't want. Yet whenever he opened one of them, something wildly funny flew out.

He was most recently seen in the American play *Harvey*, in which he played a dipsomaniac whose *fidus Achates* is a six-foot rabbit, which we cannot see. It was his first straight part, and it was not pleasant to hear : he took all the easy spontaneity out of his voice, and turned it into a carefully modulated tenor with about as much personality as a cod : he dropped the faint Midland accent, the soft uncouthness which was his birthright, and the loss was irrecoverable. His miming was still perfect, though : jocose, flaccid, topful of indiscriminate *bonhomie*, he would nudge and nod confidingly at the rabbit by his side; he would trip and turn to stare reproachfully at the invisible foot that had toppled him, and then, with a wink, extend his own foot to return the trick. Touches like this, and the scene in which he dialled a telephone number with hand-movements appropriate to a man painting a picture, made the play bearable.

But he must not be judged on this rash adventure : he was too solitary, like all great comics, for the interactions and cross-stresses of drama. I want us to remember him with a blaze of footlights before him, in small and simple sketches. Picture, to begin with, a pair of drunks, veering, with no great determination, around a lamp-post. One of them is portly and has the constricted look of a man about to vomit. That is Mr Field. The other is very tiny, and from time to time he supports his little frame by clutching at Mr Field's middle. This, on the fourth or fifth occasion (these things happen gradually), shakes Mr Field's equanimity. He surveys his partner from above in slow wonder – wonder, perhaps, that there should be men so much smaller than himself. Then, in weary exasperation : 'Get-tout-from-mund-der-neath-me-Ver-*non*!'—the last word with unmistakably effeminate emphasis. How print, the great leveller, flattens that line! and how unfairly it robs Mr Field of the convulsive squirms of dismissal which accompanied it! The written word is untender to comedians, whose every inflexion must have its record if it is to survive. Mr Field's more wayward triumphs are almost impossible to pin down. How should you see that it was, for example, very funny when he tried to be intimidating; when, after a few threatening starts and a clouded warning glance, he decided to assault his provoker. This he did, mind you, not with fist or foot, but by removing the cloth cap from his head, folding it neatly, and making curious little dabs and pokes with it, shadow-boxing the while. I asked him once how he knew that the only fitting weapon was the cap. He thought it over. Finally: 'It relieves my feelings,' he said, 'without being brutal.'

I liked him, too, when he 'put it on'. His normal accents were, as I have said, those of the suspicious West Midlander; but he could, if he wished, persuade us that he was born within sight of the Victoria and Albert Museum. He would incline, with earnest benignity, to the members of the pit orchestra, and inquire politely: 'And how are yooo to-day? R-r-r-reasonably well, I hoop?' The incongruity of all this, proceeding from those stolid peasant lips, was irresistible. He always revelled in these elocutionary achievements. I once heard him successfully pronounce that formidable word 'Shostakovich'. At first the magnitude of what he had done escaped him; he passed on, and would have finished the sentence. But all at once glorious consciousness of it overtook him, and he stopped, enthralled in recollection. After a moment's rapture, slow irradiation broke across his face, until it became a huge, blushing, beaming rose. Impulsively he turned towards the wings, and sang out: 'Did you heah *me*, Whittaker?' I do not know who Whittaker was.

Then there was the sketch in which he played all the male parts, making rushed exits which nearly tore the scenery down; one of these character studies was an aged sire, decrepitude being suggested by an uncombed white wig. The character had a paralysed hand which rotated regularly as if preparing to roll dice; it dangled over the edge of the table at which he sat. As I remember it, Mr Field was talking about the awful state of everything. 'The chimneys haven't been swept,' he complained, 'the windows won't open, the floor's dirty, the wallpaper's coming off.' Then, his gaze wandering to his infirmity, he watched it with gloomy interest and, indicating with his good hand this final item in the catalogue of decay, added mournfully: 'And *this'll* have to be seen to.' And there was his impetuous, cavorting, velvet-clad photographer, welcoming an old friend as a sitter, and making tea for him. Having drunk it, he sets the man in position, chatting cosily, paces out the correct number of steps for the camera, then turns and, in a flash of quiet aberration, runs up as if to bowl. Seeing his blunder, he blushes gauchely and fumbles out an apology. Actually, Mr Field running up to do anything was fanciful enough: in his Slasher Green sketch, which involved his wearing a vastly be-shouldered overcoat, a pencilled moustache, and all the wily self-confidence of the local boy cutting a shady dash in the city, he was constantly threatening to run up and do something. 'Stand well back, Harry,' he would warn his partner, 'stand well back, boy. I don't know what I might do.' You felt that this was quite true; squinting with determination, he pawed the ground, and was about to set off, when the inadequacy of a stage for his giant exploit hit him: 'Not enough room really. I ought to be in a *field*.' And so we never knew just what it was that he didn't know what he might do.

He was often a prey to stage children. I am think-ing of one especially, a gay and omniscient little fright, who took a hellish delight in carping at his brushwork. (For some reason he was painting a landscape.) By and by he suggested that she might like to go away and peddle her papers: 'Why', as he put it, 'don't you go and play a nice game on the railway track – with your *back* to the *oncoming engines*?' He tried to soothe her with a drink of lemonade ('Get the bottle well down your throat'). But nothing availed him, and at last the crash came. She was telling him about the difference between ultramarine (which he was using) and Prussian blue (which she would have preferred), and it was here that he went to pieces. He rounded on her, fixed her with a moistly aggressive eye, and began a terrible verbal attack .on Prussian blue, speaking at great speed and in devastating fury. As the rage seized him, he started to sag at the knees: his legs wilted, and he collapsed to the ground in a lump. The little girl, stunned, helped him to his feet, and waited, with an odd and worried look. We waited, too. At last, between gulps, and in tones of the utmost deprecation and shame, he explained. 'I am a *fool*,' he said petulantly; 'I *must* remember to *breathe* when I speak.' If that is not good enough for Lewis Carroll, I have misunderstood him badly.

His great golfing sketch was full of these things, and we have not space for them all. How would you reply to a pro who said: 'When I say "slowly back", I don't mean "slowly back", I mean "slowly back" '? Mr Field just stopped in his tracks and thought; and then: 'Let's pick flowers,' he urged hopefully. He made no attempt to reply to the pro's heavy sarcasm in its own vulgar kind; instead, he affected sublime indifference. 'I could have been having my music lesson – with Miss Bollinger,' he explained with careful scorn; 'Miss Bollinger is nice and kind. She can play the piano.' An afterthought occurred to him: ' – and the flute.' He flipped out his tongue elaborately in making the 'the' sound. I would enjoy writing about how he looked when his mentor told him to get behind the ball, and he screamed back: '*It's behind all round it!*' But others have noticed that, and the ground is covered.

I do not pretend to account for these strokes: I can only point vaguely to the quality most of them share – a certain girlishness that seeps through the silly male bulk of the man, a certain feminine intensity on the emphatic words. But Mr Field was even more bewildered. 'I suppose,' he replied laboriously when I asked him to explain some of the things he said: 'I suppose I'm just peculiar altogether.' It might be possible, in some sort, to trace his genealogy from the names of his three favourite comedians, Bob Hope, Bud Flanagan and Jimmy James. Particularly from the last-named buffoon, with whose genius he had many affinities. He is certainly not explicable in terms of scripts, a fact which ought to be clear by now : nearly all his sketches were originally ad-libbed around an inconsiderable nucleus of ideas, and many affecting tales are told of the anguish of those who tried to tie him down to what they had written for him. He never, he said, forced a laugh in his life; it embarrassed him physically to have to utter a line he did not think funny. 'Makes me perspire all over,' he would mutter. Not many comedians have that discretion. I think a saint would have laughed at Sid Field without shame or condescension.

I am a coward : it must, as they all say, be genius. Certainly it was inflexible enough, uncompromising enough, and detached enough from topicality, though it was 'ramm'd with life'. Given the technical equipment, comic genius depends largely upon the blind faith with which the comedian follows the mazy twists of his own intricacies. It is a very different thing from artistry, which is technical : genius, the hooded energy, can wreck a good artist, who must be circumspect and learn from others. Danny Kaye, for instance, is an artist nine-tenths of the time; Field never was.

(1950)

Caesar and Cleopatra
by GEORGE BERNARD SHAW

Antony and Cleopatra
by WILLIAM SHAKESPEARE
at the St James's

Overpraise, in the end, is the most damaging kind of praise, especially if you are an actress approaching forty who has already reached the height of her powers. Who now remembers Rose Elphinstoune, of whom it was said in 1865: 'Nothing can ever have moved the passions more than her Belvidera in *Venice Preserv'd*?' And in whose head does the name of lovely Lucy Mead, who in 1889 'seemed to attain a fuller greatness with each new performance,' now strike a chord?

With these ladies in mind, it may be time for a sober consideration of Vivien Leigh, for whom similarly vivid claims have been made. This summer she celebrates probably the climax of her career, a climax towards which she has climbed, with unflurried industry, for many seasons past. Stoically, she has absorbed her share of ill-judged malice. 'Vivien is a galvanized waxwork,' gibed an old and bitter friend; and how cunning her detractors have been to point out that the flower-freshness of her face is belied by her sturdy, businesslike wrists and ankles! One cynic, biting his nails furiously, described her as being as 'calculating as a slot-machine'. In the face of all this her calm has been complete, and we must admire her for it.

Now, with Miss Leigh drawing the town, it is time to scrutinize her dispassionately. Fondly we recall her recent peak, when, in 1945, she held together the shaky structure of Thornton Wilder's *The Skin of Our Teeth*. She used her soul in this display; and was sweet. About this time Laurence Olivier became an actor-manager, and almost at once I felt foreboding that the lady might protest too much and cast her net wider than her special talents would permit. Sir Laurence cast Miss Leigh as Blanche in *A Streetcar Named Desire*. She accepted the responsibility, worked with Trojan intensity, and failed. After the initial shock at hearing Williams's play described by the critics as 'a shallow shocker', we shut our eyes tightly and forgave Miss Leigh. This year, emboldened, she has invited the highest kind of judgement by venturing on both Shaw's and Shakespeare's Cleopatras. And several authorities have reached out for the ultimate word in the dictionary of appraisal and found her 'great'.

She remains sweet. In all her gentle motions there

is no hint of that attack and upheaval, that inner up-roar which we, mutely admiring, call greatness; no breath of the tumultuous obsession which, against our will, consumes us. In *Caesar and Cleopatra* she keeps a firm grip on the narrow ledge which is indisputably hers, the level on which she can be pert, sly, and spankable, and fill out a small personality. She does, to the letter, what Shaw asks of his queen, and not a semi-colon more. And how obsequiously Sir Laurence seems to play along with her, never once bowing to the command that most great actors hear, the command to enlarge on the flat symbols of the text.

Antony and Cleopatra is another world. This is a leaping giant of a play which demands 'greatness' of its performers and sleeps under anything less. 'You were a boggler ever,' says Antony at one point to his idle doxy; and one can feel Miss Leigh's imagination boggling at the thought of playing Cleopatra. Taking a deep breath and resolutely focusing her periwinkle charm, she launches another of her careful readings; ably and passionlessly she picks her way among its great challenges, present-ing a glibly mown lawn where her author had imagined a jungle. Her confidence, amazingly, never flags. Once or twice in the evening the lines call for a sort of palatial sweetness; and she scents these moments and excels in them.

Yet one feeling rode over these in my mind; the feel-ing Mr Bennet in *Pride and Prejudice* was experiencing when he dissuaded his daughter from further piano-forte recital by murmuring that she had 'delighted us long enough'. Though at times, transported by Shake-speare, she becomes almost wild, there is in Miss Leigh's Cleopatra an arresting streak of Jane Austen. She picks at the part with the daintiness of a debutante called upon to dismember a stag, and her manners are first-rate. 'She plays it', as someone said, ' with her little finger crooked.' This Cleopatra is almost always civil. Miss Leigh's piercing, candid blankness is superbly pretty; and for several years to come it will not be easy to refrain from wishfully equating her prettiness with greatness. Hers is the magnificent effrontery of an attractive child endlessly indulged at its first party. To play Cleopatra the appealing minx must expand and gain texture : and she puts on a low, mournful little voice (her first wrinkle) to suggest seediness. But for the outrageous, inordinate Queen of Egypt one must return, every few seconds, to the published version.

Miss Leigh's limitations have wider repercussions than those of most actresses. Sir Laurence, with that curious chivalry which some time or other blights the progress of every great actor, gives me the impression that he subdues his blow-lamp ebullience to match her. Blunting his iron precision, levelling away his towering authority, he meets her halfway. Antony climbs down; and Cleopatra pats him on the head. A cat, in fact, can do more than look at a king : she can hypnotise him.

Whenever I see Miss Leigh, an inexplicably frivolous little Rodgers-Hammerstein lyric starts to trot round my head. It goes :

> *My doll is as dainty as a sparrow;*
> *Her figure is something to applaud;*
> *Where she's narrow she's as narrow as an arrow;*
> *And she's broad where a broad should be broad. . . .*

It is a delightful song, and it gives me great pleasure. But it has nothing to do with the robes of queens; or with gravity; or with greatness.

(1951)

Richard II and *Henry IV, Part I*

by WILLIAM SHAKESPEARE
at Stratford-on-Avon

The Shakespeare Memorial Company at Stratford has now launched *Richard II* and the first part of *Henry IV*. Together, these make up the first half of

Shakespeare's tetralogy of kingliness, which is to be presented under the joint direction of Anthony Quayle, Michael Redgrave, and John Kidd. The exterior of the Memorial Theatre retains its touching pink ugliness, lapped on one side by the Avon; but inside, Quayle has made great changes, relining the auditorium to look warmer and more inviting, and erecting on the stage a permanent setting (by Tanya Moiseiwitsch) on which the full quartet of history plays will be acted – an imposing arrangement of beams, incorporating rough approximations of the balcony and inner recess of the Elizabethan stage.

Richard II has been less successful than its next of kin. This is a reclining, effeminate play where the 'Henry' series are upstanding and male, and Miss Moiseiwitch's timbering is out of key with its lushness. Redgrave, still missing the real heights by an inexplicable inch, makes a fine sketch of Richard, using a shaky tenor voice, a foppish smile, and damp, uncertain eyes to summon up the poor man's instability. In the early scenes, clad in sky-blue doublet and cloak of palest orange, he looked exquisitely over-mothered, a king sculpted in puppy-fat. Alternately malicious and sentimental, Redgrave's Richard is a noble booby, sincerely envious, as well as afraid, of the power to command which is not his. It was not his fault that in the later acts and the slow hysterical slide towards death one tired of him.

There can be no hesitation about *Henry IV, Part I;* oak-beamed and clinker-built, it fits the set perfectly. Memories of Olivier's Hotspur and Richardson's Falstaff inevitably taunt us, but this is undoubtedly a much more thoughtful and balanced production than the Old Vic's. Redgrave now moves into the major key with a raw-boned, shockheaded Hotspur, affecting a rasping Lowlands brogue to account for the references to Harry Percy's thickness of speech; and at least three of the best six English juveniles crop up around him. Alan Badel, the intemperately exciting flyweight whose Fool partnered John Gielgud's Lear last year, plays the tiny part of Poins with fastidious distinction; Duncan Lamont, a sour young actor with a swarthy voice, finds a complete character, glowering and long-sighted, in the involved complottings of Worcester; and finally, a shrewd Welsh boy shines out with greatness – the first this year.

I am speaking of Richard Burton, whom New York saw last autumn in Fry's *The Lady's Not for Burning*. His playing of Prince Hal turned interested speculation to awe almost as soon as he started to speak; in the first intermission the local critics stood agape in the lobbies. Burton is a still, brimming pool, running disturbingly deep; at twenty-five he commands repose and can make silence garrulous. His Prince Hal is never a roaring boy; he sits, hunched or sprawled, with dark unwinking eyes; he hopes to be amused by his bully companions, but the eyes constantly muse beyond them into the time when he must steady himself for the crown. 'He brings his cathedral on with him,' said one dazed member of the company. For all his bold chivalry, this watchful Celt seems surely to have strayed from a wayside pulpit. Fluent and sparing of gesture, compact and spruce of build, Burton smiles where other Hals have guffawed; relaxes where they have strained; and Falstaff (played with affectionate obesity by Anthony Quayle) must work hard to divert him. In battle, Burton's voice cuts urgent and keen – always likeable, always inaccessible. If he can sustain and vary this performance through to the end of *Henry V*, we can safely send him along to swell the thin company of living actors who have shown us the mystery and the power of which heroes are capable.

(1951)

Macbeth

by WILLIAM SHAKESPEARE
at Stratford-on-Avon

Last Tuesday night at the Stratford Memorial Theatre
Macbeth walked the plank, leaving me, I am afraid, unmoved to the point of paralysis. It was John Gielgud,
never let us forget, who did this cryptic thing; Gielgud,
as director, who seems to have imagined that Ralph
Richardson, with his comic, Robeyesque cheese-face, was
equipped to play Macbeth; Gielgud who surrounded the
play's fuliginous cruelties with settings of total black,
which is just about as subtle as setting *Saint Joan* in total
white; Gielgud who commanded dirty tatters for Macbeth's army and brisk, clean tunics for Malcom's, just
to indicate in advance who was going to win. The production assumed, or so I took it, that the audience was
either moronic or asleep; it read us a heavily italicised
lecture on the play, and left nothing to our own small
powers of discovery. When, in the banquet scene, a
real table and some real chairs, chalices, and candelabra
were brought on, life intervened for a moment; but
once the furniture had gone, we were back in the engulfing, the platitudinous void, with its single message :
'Background of evil, get it?' The point about Macbeth is
that the murders in it should horrify us; against Mr Gielgud's sable scenery they looked as casual as crochet-work.

In the banquet scene, spurred perhaps by the clever
handling of Banquo's ghost, which vanished dazzlingly in
one swirl of a cloak, Richardson came to life for several
consecutive sentences, and I could not help recalling a
line he had uttered earlier in the evening : 'My dull
brain was wrought with things forgotten.' Up to this
point he had appeared a robot player, a man long past
feeling, who had been stumping across the broad stage
as if in need of a compass to find the exit. Now, moment-

tarily, he smouldered and made us recall his excelling past, littered with fine things encompassed and performed. And then, and ever after, Sir Ralph's numbness, his apparent mental deafness, returned to chill me: Macbeth became once more a sad facsimile of the Cowardly Lion in *The Wizard of Oz*. At the height of the battle, you remember, Macbeth contemplates suicide, rejecting the thought in the words: 'Why should I play the Roman fool, and die on mine own sword?' Sir Ralph, at this juncture, gripped his blade by the sharp end with both hands and practised putts with it; it was as if the Roman fool had been the local pro.

His feathery, yeasty voice, with its single spring-heeled inflexion, starved the part of its richness; he moved dully, as if by numbers, and such charm as he possessed was merely a sort of unfocused bluffness, like a teddy-bear snapped in a bad light by a child holding its first camera. Sir Ralph, who seems to me to have become the glass eye in the forehead of English acting, has now bumped into something quite immovable. His Macbeth is slovenly; and to go further into it would be as frustrating as trying to write with a pencil whose point has long since worn down to the wood.

Sleep-walking, which appeared to be this Macbeth's natural condition, had an unexpectedly tonic effect on his lady. Margaret Leighton seized her big solo opportunity, waking up to give us a gaunt, pasty, compulsive reading of the scene which atoned for many of her earlier inadequacies. But two things are required for an effective Lady Macbeth: first a husband off whom she can strike sparks – and it would be easier to strike sparks off a rubber dinghy than Sir Ralph. Second, she needs to be sexless; Macbeth is unique among the tragedies in that none of the leading characters ever mentions sexuality. Lady Macbeth is painted granite, and to cast a woman as attractive as Miss Leighton in the part is like casting a gazelle as Medusa. In fact, it is probably a mistake to cast a woman at all, since Lady Macbeth offers none of the openings for nostalgia, yearning, and haggard glamour which attach to every other great female part, from Cleopatra to Blanche DuBois. No, Lady Macbeth is basically a man's role, and none of Miss Leighton's sibilant sulks could convince me otherwise.

Now what to praise? Kenneth Rowell's sculptural costumes, which sat well on everyone save, unaccountably, Sir Ralph; Siobhan McKenna's patient Lady MacDuff; and the attack, if nothing else, of Laurence Harvey's Malcolm. And that will have to do. The theatre which gave us, last year, so many pretty lessons in Shakespearian acting and production seems, for the time being, to have unlearned them all.

(1952)

The Millionairess

by GEORGE BERNARD SHAW
at the Hippodrome, Coventry

There have been no new plays this week. A prickly calm, of the kind that precedes summer lightning, has left my playgoing in the doldrums. And so, if you will bear with me, I propose to reminisce. I want to write about something which carried me away like a rocket when I saw it – five weeks ago – at the Hippodrome Theatre, Coventry. It was a play called *The Millionairess*; Katharine Hepburn was playing in it, and, by a happy coincidence, it is opening at the New Theatre tonight.

The Millionairess, as everyone knows, was written by Shaw in 1936 for Edith Evans, but it has never been performed in the West End. And no great wonder, because it is almost without wit, and contains hardly any of those somersaulting paradoxes with which, for so long, Shaw concealed from us the more basic gaps in his knowledge of human behaviour. It is that terrible hybrid, a didactic farce; in it Shaw is grinding an axe, but the sparks refuse to fly. The characters talk interminably, infectiously, and almost interchangeably.

It is not even outrageous – nobody, watching it, would ever nudge his neighbour and whisper : 'Whatever will he say *next*?', which is the correct response to most Shavian wit. In *The Millionairess*, written in the twilight of a civilization and of its author's life, the old dexterity and assurance have given place to a querulous fumbling; the dialogue is twice as noisy as Shaw's best, and roughly half as effective.

Its heroine, a steel girder in the play's house of cards, is Epifania Ognisanti di Parerga, who has inherited from her father £30,000,000 and one piece of advice; she must not marry until she finds a man who can turn £150 into £50,000 within six months. Alastair Fitzfassenden, a mindless athlete, unexpectedly performs the feat, and is duly swallowed up. Tiring of him, Epifania takes to running around with a middle-aged incompetent named Adrian Blenderbland, whose leg, in one of her saucier tantrums, she breaks. At length, still fretful, she meets an eerie Egyptian doctor, who feels her pulse, falls in love with it, and challenges her to go out into the world with thirty-five shillings and earn her living for six months. Nettled, she agrees; and returns six months later to claim her prize, having amassed yet another fortune. She is, you conclude, a shrew past taming, a force beyond resisting, a rich little rich girl with a heart of bullion.

You might think, from my simplification of it, that the play is well constructed. It is nothing of the sort. Its long first act is entirely given over to the exposition of several situations that are never afterwards developed; every scene is plastered with merciless narrative speeches wherein each character tells the others what he or she has been doing while the curtain was down. And the central character is quite hateful. Epifania, described by Shaw as 'a born boss', bangs through the play like a battering-ram, living at the top of her lungs, and barking orders like a games mistress run amok. There is something of a crowbar about her charm, and something, too, of a rhinoceros.

The part is nearly unactable; yet Miss Hepburn took it, acted it, and found a triumph in it. She glittered like a bracelet thrown up at the sun; she was metallic, yet reminded us that metals shine and can also melt. Epifania clove to her, and she bestowed on the role a riotous elegance and a gift of tears not of its author's imagining. Her first entrance was as if she had just emerged from the sea and were tossing the spray from her eyes; and it was not one entrance but two, for she had swept in, out, and then in again before I could blink. She used her mink wrap as Hitler is said to have used the Chancellery carpet, hurling it to the floor and falling upon it, pounding her fists in tearful vituperation.

Her voice is a rallying-call to truancy, a downright clarion; 'she is,' as someone once declared, 'that yell – that shriek that is simultaneous with the bell ringing at school' – the bell that provokes the rush into the playground for the break. Miss Hepburn is not versatile; she is simply unique. Like most stars of real magnitude, she can do one or two of the hardest things in the world supremely well; and *The Millionairess* scores a bull's-eye on the target of her talents. It is just hard enough for her, just close enough to impossibility, and from first word to last, star and part are treading common ground. Epifania is written on one note, but it is Miss Hepburn's note, and she makes it sound like a cadenza.

As I could have predicted, she was stark, staring, and scandalously bold, alternately shooting the lines point-blank at us and brandishing them like flags; and she reached a high point in her brazen retort to somebody who inquires, in the second act, whether she throws temperaments merely to make herself interesting. '*Make* myself interesting!' she flings at him. 'Man: I *am* interesting.' Between outbursts she curls up, cocooned in Balmain's lovely gowns, nipping intently at her sentences with sharp weasel-teeth, relaxing. What is astonishing about her is her warmth. Her grins gleam at you; and as she shapes them, she droops the corners of her eyelids and twinkles like a fire. And in her last long speech, a defence of marriage and all the risks it implies, an urchin quaver invades the determination of her voice, and coaxes the heart. At that moment James Bailey's plushy setting disappeared from my mind, and with it everyone else on stage.

The supporting cast had done much valiant and loving work. Robert Helpmann, rakish under a tarboosh, had padded pop-eyed through the role of the Egyptian doctor and made it eloquent. Cyril Ritchard had lent a flustered dignity, like that of a goosed hen, to the nonentity Blenderbland. But they vanished then, and it was, as it had been meant to be, Miss Hepburn's night. She combines the sparkle of 'Kate the Curst' with the attack of Petruchio – that 'mad-brain'd rudesby, full of spleen'; she glows like a branding-iron, and marks you her willing bond-slave.

All this, of course, was at Coventry, and many weeks ago. Much may have been changed by now, and the show that arrives at the New Theatre this evening may be quite a different thing. What I have been writing about is strictly past history; but if it should happen to repeat itself, I hope only to be within sound of the cheering.

(1952)

Romeo and Juliet

by WILLIAM SHAKESPEARE
at the Old Vic

I am told that Claire Bloom's performance in the Old Vic's *Romeo and Juliet* is a failure because Miss Bloom ignores the poetry. They say she loses all the music of the verse. To which I can only reply by exposing this alleged defect for the virtue it really is. Let me start by burning my boats and declaring that this is the best Juliet I have ever seen.

'Word-music' is a great maker of reputations. Give an actress a round, resonant voice and a long Shakespearian part, and she will have to enter smoking a pipe to avoid being acclaimed. And everyone will forget (a) that the same voice could turn last year's Hansard into poetry, and (b) that what Shakespeare demands is not verse-speaking but verse-acting. A golden voice, however angelic, is not enough. Whenever a climax looms up, the actor faces a choice between the poetry and the character, the sound and the fury, because you cannot rage mellifluously or cry out your eyes in tune. The answer, now as always is: take care of the sense, and the sounds will take care of themselves. Edmund Kean, Irving, and Olivier, on whom our whole tradition of heroic acting rests, have one thing in common: they have all been repeatedly accused of lacking poetry. Miss Bloom sins in good company.

The average Juliet sings the part sweetly, chants it demurely, dismissing passion with a stamp of the foot. Nine-tenths of Juliet, as Miss Bloom demonstrates, is not in the least demure: she is impatient and mettlesome, proud and vehement, not a blindfold child of milk. And the result is an illumination. The silly lamb becomes a real, scarred woman, and we see that it is the whole character that is poetic, and not just the lines. When she is quiet, as in the balcony scene, Miss Bloom's candour is as still as a smoke-ring and as lovely. 'I have forgot why I did call thee back' is spoken with grave amazement: there are no simpers or blushes in this dedicated young creature. From her first meeting with Romeo, as they touch hands at the Capulets' ball, she is no novice, but an initiate in the stately game of love. In silence, as in speech, her communication with Romeo is complete: their minds fit like hand into glove, and his absence wounds her like an amputation. 'Word-music' goes overboard in Miss Bloom's best scene, that in which the Nurse breaks the news of Tybalt's death and Romeo's banishment — first the superb harshness of 'Blistered be thy tongue!' after the old crone has reviled Romeo, and then a desolating panic, crowned at the end by an exit suddenly gentle and bereaved, cradling Romeo's rope-ladder to her breast. I have seen no more moving piece of acting this year. Miss Bloom was not quite adequate to the mighty obstacle of the potion speech, and the death scene seemed to catch her off guard. But enough had been done by then to make the gilded statue of remembrance, promised by Romeo's father in the last scene, quite unnecessary. We had already seen pure gold.

Alan Badel, her Romeo, is that freak, a young man with an old man's voice, an old man's snicker, and an old man's leer. Couple with these disadvantages a lack of inches and looks, and you have a problem that no amount of intelligence can solve. Mr Badel is not a romantic actor. He does some daring little things early on, but the later agonies are beyond him. He lingers over them, squirming and yearning, but the total effect is miniature – rather like a restless marmoset.

(1952)

Jack Benny

at the Palladium

There is a rumour about to the effect that Jack Benny, who has returned to the Palladium for three weeks, is a great clown. This is a dreadful slur on his reputation, so let us dispose of it at once. Mr Benny is not a clown at all; he is a straight man, or stooge, and possibly the subtlest in the history of comedy. Funny men surround him, but they are there purely for the purpose of leaving him cold. It is he who, in all good faith, asks the questions; the others provide the punch-lines. He is the duck's back; they pour the water. He receives their slights with a mask of bland resignation; his eyes glaze to a blood-curdling blue, and inwardly he meditates mayhem. At length, adjusting his smile with an effort and shrugging faintly, like an injured diplomat, at the audience, he passes on to other, happier things. He gets his laughs, in fact, not by attacking, but by suffering in silence.

Benny's is a character performance, with a clear and considered attitude towards humanity. He wants to cheat and rob it. Calm, sunburnt, and ingratiating, he is forever pondering devices by which the bite may suddenly and simultaneously be put on his wife, his family, his friends, and the United States Treasury. His fabulous repose is shaken, his small fine hands start to expostulate, only when he is accused of avarice. This hurts and disgusts him, and his eyebrows, tired and deprecating, start upwards. Benny's whole act is that of a man fatigued with protesting his innocence to a court which is disposed to hang him out of hand: it is a long yawn, with an eye to the main chance.

To be as fond of Benny as I am may easily be an eccentric taste: he is technically a buffer-state, a rarity in this country, where comedians are generally aggressors. But no one with an eye for the craft of comedy should miss the chance of studying the ease and timing of his minutely rehearsed ad libs. His company includes a nest of three hopeful song-birds, who fail repeatedly to win his heart; and a guileless Irish tenor, looking appropriately starved, called Dennis Day. Mr Day, incidentally, ventures for several minutes on end into the special hell reserved for people who impersonate Sir Harry Lauder singing 'Roamin' in the Gloamin',' complete with gestures and stick. Someone should tell him that Danny Kaye is in the Lauder business too, and that it is getting tough at the top.

(1952)

Guys and Dolls

by FRANK LOESSER
at the Coliseum

Guys and Dolls, at which I am privileged to take a peek last evening, is a hundred-per-cent American musical caper, cooked up out of a story called 'The Idyll of

Miss Sarah Brown', by the late Damon Runyon, who is such a scribe as delights to give the English language a nice kick in the pants.

This particular fable takes place in and around Times Square in New York City, where many citizens do nothing but roll dice all night long, which is held by one and all, and especially the gendarmes, to be a great vice. Among the parties hopping around in this neighbourhood is a guy by the name of Nathan Detroit, who operates a floating dice game, and Miss Adelaide, his ever-loving pretty, who is sored up at this Nathan because after fourteen years' engagement, they are still nothing but engaged. Anyway, being short of ready scratch, Nathan lays a bet with a large gambler called Sky Masterson, the subject of the wager being whether The Sky can talk a certain Salvation Army doll into joining him on a trip to Havana. Naturally, Nathan figures that a nice doll such as this will die sooner, but by and by she and The Sky get to looking back and forth at each other, and before you know it she is his sweet-pea. What happens next but The Sky gets bopped by religion and shoots craps with Nathan and the boys for their immortal souls. And where do the sinners wind up, with their chalk-striped suits and busted noses, but at a prayer meeting in the doll's mission house, which hands me a very big laugh indeed. The actors who nab the jobs of playing these apes and essences of 42nd Street have me all tuckered out with clapping them.

Nathan Detroit is Sam Levene, who expostulates very good with his arms, which are as long as a monkey's. Stubby Kaye, who plays Nicely-Nicely Johnson, the well-known horse-player, is built on lines which are by no means dinky, for his poundage maybe runs into zillions, but he gives with a voice which is as couth as a choir boy's or maybe couther. He commences the evening by joining in a three-part comedy song about the nags. In fact, it is a fugue, and I will give you plenty of eleven to five that it is the first fugue many patrons of the Coliseum ever hear. Miss Vivian Blaine (Miss Adelaide) is a very choice blonde judy and she gets to sing a song which goes as follows: 'Take back your mink to from whence it came' and which hits me slap-dab in the ear as being supernaturally comical. Myself, I prefer her to Miss Lizbeth Webb, who plays the mission doll, but, naturally, I do not mention such an idea out loud.

The Coliseum is no rabbit hutch, and maybe a show as quick and smart as this *Guys and Dolls* will go better in such a sized theatre as the Cambridge Theatre. Personally, I found myself laughing ha-ha last night more often than a guy in the critical dodge has any right to. And I am ready to up and drop on my knees before Frank Loesser, who writes the music and lyrics. In fact, this Loesser is maybe the best light composer in the world. In fact, the chances are that *Guys and Dolls* is not only a young masterpiece, but the Beggar's Opera of Broadway.

(1952)

The Way of the World

by WILLIAM CONGREVE
at the Lyric, Hammersmith

William Congreve is the only sophisticated playwright England has ever produced; and, like Shaw, Sheridan, and Wilde, his nearest rivals, he was brought up in Ireland. By sophisticated I mean genial without being hearty, witty without being smug, wise without being pompous, and sensual without being lewd. These attributes, now to be seen in John Gielgud's revival of *The Way of the World*, rarely coincide in an Englishman who has not had the benefit of a Dublin education or, at the very least, of an industrious French governess.

Because they speak precisely and with affection for the language they are using, it is usually taken for granted that Congreve's characters are unreal. Nothing could be more misguided. These people do not bare their souls (that would smack of nudism), but they are real enough.

It is the plot which is unreal; and of all plots, none more closely resembles a quadratic equation than that of *The Way of the World*. At the heart of the maze is Lady Wishfort, to whom nearly everyone in the play is related, and in whose money everyone has a consuming interest. But the labyrinth is so brilliantly peopled that you forget the goal. Congreve's genius is for mixing and contrasting human beings, not for taking them anywhere in particular.

And what glorious contrasts Mr Gielgud has provided! Having assembled what I heard described, in an enviable slip of the tongue, as 'a conglamouration of stars,' he has let them have their heads. The play sails into life with pennants flying. Mr Gielgud is at the helm, a crowd of deft character actors like Eric Porter, Richard Wordsworth, and Brewster Mason are manning the rigging, and Eileen Herlie is thrown in for ballast. To pipe us aboard there is Paul Scofield as Witwould, the amateur fop – a beautifully gaudy performance, pitched somewhere between Hermione Gingold and Stan Laurel. Gielgud's galleon would not be complete without a figurehead, and there, astride the prow, she triumphantly is – Margaret Rutherford, got up as Lady Wishfort, the man-hungry pythoness. This is a banquet of acting in itself. Miss Rutherford is filled with a monstrous vitality : the soul of Cleopatra has somehow got trapped in the corporate shape of an entire lacrosse team. The unique thing about Miss Rutherford is that she can act with her chin alone : among its many moods I especially cherish the chin commanding, the chin in doubt, and the chin at bay. My dearest impression of this Hammersmith night is a vision of Miss Rutherford, clad in something loose, darting about her boudoir like a gigantic bumblebee at large in a hothouse.

After which I am sorry to have to end my report on a minor chord. The scenes between Mirabell and Millamant, which should be the play's delicious crown, do not come off at all. The two lovers remain what Johnson called them, 'intellectual gladiators', but the strength is all on one side, and the wrong side at that. Mr Gielgud, an impeccable Mirabell in plum velvet, has Pamela Brown begging for mercy almost before the battle is joined. This is, of course, a ghastly abdication on her part. Millamant must be the empress of her sex, and her words, whether tinkling like a fountain or cascading like Niagara, must always flow from a great height. From Miss Brown's mouth they do not flow at all; they leak, half apologetically, in dribs and drabs. Instead of saving up the revelation that she loves Mirabell, she lets us know it from the outset, thereby dethroning the empress and setting an ogling spinster in her place. Miss Brown, to sum up, sees through Millamant and (what is worse) lets us see through her as well. It is a grave mistake, and I will hear no excuses. All I can offer by way of consolation is this: it is the kind of mistake which only an actress of Miss Brown's intelligence could have made.

(1953)

King Lear

by WILLIAM SHAKESPEARE
at the King's, Hammersmith

It is annoying that the Old Vic did not hold Donald Wolfit in the troupe long enough to show us his *King Lear*, which is now being alternated with *Twelfth Night* at the King's, Hammersmith. His present supporting company explores new horizons of inadequacy. Only Richard Goolden, a macabre Fool with a senile stoop and a child's skipping legs, is of much assistance to the play. Extricate Mr Wolfit's Lear from the preposterous production and you have a great, flawed piece of masonry, making up in weight what it lacks in delicacy: a tribal chieftain rather than a hereditary monarch. Mr Wolfit scorns the trick (known to many lesser actors) of flicking speeches exquisitely to leg; he prefers to bash them towards mid-off and run like a stag. In the mad scenes this impatience with finesse is a weakness: the insanity looks too much like tipsiness. And to play the last unearthly act Lear must land, as it were, by parachute on the top of Parnassus. Mountaineering, however dogged, will not take him there. At these moments Mr Wolfit seems unaccountably grounded.

His mark is still higher up the great slope than anyone else's in our time. He is magnificent in the early scenes, sulking like a beaten dog when Cordelia refuses to play ball with him; and the colloquies with the Fool are horribly moving, with the old man's thoughts staring past his words into the chasm of lunacy. Best of all is the pause that follows his fit of rage at Cornwall's cruelty. 'Tell the hot duke –' he begins, and then stops in mid-eruption, veins knotted, fighting hideously to keep his foothold on the tiny ledge which stands between him and madness. Mr Wolfit's Lear is a brilliant compound of earth, fire, and flood. Only the airy element is missing.

The Glorious Days

at the Palace

The Glorious Days can best be described – to adapt a phrase of George Kaufman's – as Anna Neagle rolled into one. Here she is, anthologized at last, available once nightly in the large economy size; dipping into the fabled store of her talents, she brings up a horn of plenty, from which she pours, with cautious rapture, three dwarf acorns. First, she acts, in a fashion so devoid of personality as to be practically incognito; second, she sings, shaking her voice at the audience like a tiny fist; and, third, she dances, in that non-committal, twirling style, once known as 'skirt-dancing', which was originally invented (or so Shaw tells us) to explain the presence on the stage of genteel young women who could neither sing nor act.

The curtain is no sooner up, disclosing a war-time pub,

than news arrives that Miss Neagle has been decorated
for gallantry; and her entrance is the cue for the opening
number, a ragged chorus of 'For She's a Jolly Good Fellow',
vivaciously led by a Chelsea pensioner. On leaving the
pub, Miss Neagle is maliciously greeted by a bomb, and
the rest of the entertainment tells, in its own illimitable
way, the story of her concussion. For some reason she is
being wooed by three men – a rake, a theatrical producer,
and a good German – who see her, respectively, as an
ideal mistress, an ideal leading lady, and an ideal comrade.
Which shall she be? Eliminating obvious improbabilities,
you are left, of course, with No. 3, but Miss Neagle's
methods are more circuitous. She has hallucinations.

She first imagines herself to be Nell Gwynn, here presented as a scheming social worker using her favours to
blackmail Charles II into building Chelsea Hospital. She
keeps returning to the subject at crucial moments in their
relationship, to the King's understandable annoyance
('That hospital for old soldiers *again*?'); but in the end
the unsavoury ruse succeeds. Miss Neagle's Nell (not
the broadest of Gwynns) was dressed by Doris Zinkeisen
and devised by Robert Nesbitt; the words were put into
her mouth by either Mr Nesbitt, Harold Purcell, or Miles
Malleson; her music was composed by – among others –
Harry Parr Davies and Henry Purcell, and her dance was
arranged by Frank Staff. From their collective guilt I except Miss Zinkeisen alone: her costume designs for the
Drury Lane dancers, bold and striking, represent the only
contact made by *The Glorious Days* with the living
theatre.

Unmoved by her failure to identify herself with pretty
Nelly, Miss Neagle goes straight into her second audition:
as Queen Victoria, the ideal comrade. While she changes
her clothes, three choruses of 'The Boys of the Old
Brigade' are sung by an army of shuffling baritones, during
which time there was some speculation in the house about
whether the star had got caught on a nail in the wings.
However, we were soon swooning back to Windsor in
1846, where Miss Neagle's idea of the young Victoria was

revealed to be a somewhat rowdier version of Mrs Gwynn. She is pictured singing a drinking song to Albert, accompanying herself on the ivories, and pleading libidinously to be waltzed with. Bang on cue, Johann Strauss drops in, establishes his origin ('*Ach, so*'), and clicks his heels; whereupon the scenery dissolves into the castle ballroom, which turns out to be a nightmare premonition of the casino at Biarritz. To cover another costume change, a curious interlude ensues, of total irrelevance to the action except that it happens twenty years after the preceding scene and twenty years before the next. It is laid in a London supper saloon, and none of the characters or events in it is ever referred to again. The first half ends with an investiture at Windsor.

There was heated division of opinion in the lobbies during the interval, but a small, conservative majority took the view that it might be as well to remain in the theatre. There was always a chance that Miss Neagle might come bowling on as Boadicea, with a knife between her teeth; or that she would be discovered, dressed like Robinson Crusoe, stepping out of a boat and saying: 'The Queen of Spain will thank us for this day's work, or she'll have Chris Columbus to reckon with!'

As it was, she spent Part Two playing her mother, meanwhile delegating the job of playing herself to three other actresses. Mother, naturally, was a star of musical comedy who flourished from 1913 to 1937; and Miss Neagle characterizes her, with remarkable ferocity, as a well-meaning *diseuse* of appallingly limited technique. We follow her career through the twenties in a series of production numbers that seem to have been recovered from the wastepaper basket of a bankrupt impresario of the period. When this is over, we are back in 1943: Miss Neagle has chosen to marry the producer and decided, against all advice, to become an actress. She departs for Burma with an ENSA troupe; and one cannot help wishing that the whole of *The Glorious Days* could go with her. If not to Burma, then at least to Birmingham.

Its prevailing tone, to sum up, is a mixture of cynicism

('They'll lap it up') and joviality ('God bless them'). *The Glorious Days* demonstrates once and for all that the gap between knowing what the public wants and having the skill to provide it is infinitely wider than most English producers ever dream.

(1953)

The Merchant of Venice

by WILLIAM SHAKESPEARE
at Stratford-on-Avon

Whenever I see *The Merchant of Venice*, I while away the blanker bits of verse by trying to pull the play together in my mind. Does Shylock stand for the Old Testament (an eye for an eye, etc.) and Portia for the New (mercy, etc.)? And if so, what does that make Antonio, the shipping magnate whose bond unites the two plots? Does he represent the spirit of Protestantism? These metaphysical hares chase each other round and round; and when I have done, the play remains the curate's egg it always was. Or, rather, the rabbi's egg, because so much depends on Shylock. Which brings us to the Problem of Michael Redgrave, now, as always, at the turning-point of his career.

The difficulty about judging this actor is that I have to abandon all my standards of great acting (which include relaxation and effortless command) and start all over again. There is, you see, a gulf fixed between good and great performances; but a bridge spans it, over which you may stroll if your visa is in order. Mr Redgrave, ignoring this, always chooses the hard way. He dives into the torrent and tries to swim across, usually sinking within sight of the shore. Olivier pole-vaults over in a single animal leap; Gielgud, seizing a parasol, crosses by tight-rope; Redgrave alone must battle it out with the current. The ensuing spectacle is never dull, but it can be very painful to watch.

His conception of Shylock is highly intelligent – a major prophet with a German accent, a touch of asthma, and lightning playing round his head. But who cares for conceptions? It is the execution that counts. And here Mr Redgrave's smash-and-grab methods tell against him. His performance is a prolonged wrestling match with Shylock, each speech floored with a tremendous, vein-bursting thump; the process also involves his making a noise like a death-rattle whenever he inhales, and spitting visibly whenever he strikes a 'p' or a 'b.'

Some things he did superbly. At the end of the court scene, even after Portia had warned him that to take the pound of flesh would expose him to the death penalty, you felt that this cheated tyrant would be maniac enough to hang the consequences and start carving. There were also hints that Mr Redgrave did not deny Shylock a sense of humour: he discovered a sensational new pun in his delivery of the speech about 'water-rats' and 'pi-rates.' But he simply could not fuse the villainy of the part with its sardonic comedy. And I begin to think that no English player ever will. It needs a Continental actor to switch from fun to ferocity in a split second: Englishmen take at least half a minute to change gear. And when they are playing in their high-tragedy manner, as Mr Redgrave is, they find it practically impossible to change gear at all.

Now, Shylock is a proud and successful financier with a chip on his shoulder; he is not an abject slave bearing a yoke of lead. Mr Redgrave cringes and crumples every time Antonio opens his mouth – you would think he had never seen a Christian before. He should, of course, out-smile the lot of them. Like the other Shakespearian rogues, Richard III, Iago, and Claudius, Shylock must wear a cloak of charm. Even Antonio describes him as 'kind', and the bond must seem to be what Shylock calls it, 'merry'. Mr Redgrave gives us nothing more merry than a twisted leer. Or perhaps I should say a twisted Lear. Because I shall be much surprised if his performance as the mad king, later in the season, is vocally or physically very different from last Tuesday's Jew. I hope one day to see this actor playing a part insincerely, with his mind on other matters. Then the defences might come down, and the great Shakespearian performance that surges within him might at last be let out.

The jewel of the evening is Peggy Ashcroft's Portia, a creature of exquisite breeding and uncommon sense. She speaks the poetry with the air of a woman who would never commit the social gaffe of reciting in public, with the result that the lines flow out newly minted, as un-strained as the quality of mercy itself. Her handling of the tiresome princelings who come to woo her is an object lesson in wit and good manners; later, in the court-room, we wept at her compassion; and the last act, invariably an anti-climax, bloomed golden at her touch.

Apart from the fiery furnace that is Mr Redgrave and the cool zephyr that is Miss Ashcroft, the production is pretty tepid stuff. The scenery (flimsy pillars, as usual) looks fine in silhouette, and on one occasion, when the sky inadvertently turned green, assumed extraordinary beauty. But I tire of settings that seek to represent nowhere-in-general; how one longs to see everywhere-in-particular! The trial was well staged – but why must Shylock always be alone? Surely all the Jews in Venice would turn up for his triumph?

I cannot imagine what Donald Pleasence was trying to make of Launcelot Gobbo, who is not, I suggest, an organ-grinder's monkey. Yvonne Mitchell is wasted on Jessica. On the credit side, Tony Britton's Bassanio is an attractive scamp; and Robert Shaw, cast as Gratiano, delighted us and himself by giving a fiery and determined performance of Mercutio.

(1953)

The Wandering Jew

by E. TEMPLE THURSTON
at the King's, Hammersmith

The present revival of *The Wandering Jew* is one of the most reassuring theatrical experiences in years. Have we really progressed so far? In 1920 the play survived 390 performances; today not a line of it but rings flat and false. Only in village pageants, and in *The Glorious Days*, do traces of its style persist. It is written in four 'phases': a trip through time with Donald Wolfit as the legendary Jew who insulted Christ and was doomed to live until the Messiah should return. In the first scene Mr Wolfit wears a burnous, a shiny red wig, and his usual make-up, a thick white line down the bridge of the nose. As ever, he delivers each line as a challenge, flung in the teeth of invisible foes; his voice roars like an avalanche of gravel; and when he swirled off, girding his rude bath-robe about him, to spit at his Saviour, I fell to wondering exactly where his ponderous, vibrato methods belong.

Not in the little club theatres, I decided; nor in the larger West End houses, where they would soon grow oppressive. Nor yet at the Old Vic – I picture Mr Wolfit erupting at the very thought. Where, then, is his spiritual home? My answer is nowhere in particular: he is a nomad, part of the great (albeit dead) tradition of the strolling player, who would erect his stage in a tavern yard and unravel his rhetoric to the winds. Mr Wolfit is not an indoor actor at all. Theatres cramp him. He would be happiest, I feel, in a large field.

Phase two takes us to the Crusades. The Jew has become a marauding knight of uncontrollable sexual appetites. And woe betide the maiden of his choice (I am slipping, as the author incessantly does, into blank verse). The Christian camp, all stripy canvas and flags, seems to be pitched backstage at Bertram Mills's circus, and Mr Wolfit comes in from jousting in the garb of the human cannon-ball. Throughout the production great stress is laid on headwear: a character in phase two affects a tea-cosy, the guards in phase four go in for tin sombreros, and Mr Wolfit's jousting kit is topped off by an inverted gal-vanized-iron bucket with two holes knocked in it. With the morrow he'll be gone, so he chases a young woman around his tent, breathing balefully into her face (having first removed the bucket) and even spitting at her, in a token sort of way. Matheson Lang, a born charmer, might have just carried this scene off. As it was, the scene carried Mr Wolfit off, prostrate as on a stretcher.

He is back for phase three, tightly encased in a kimono, to play a thirteenth-century Sicilian miser persecuted for his faith. A large trunk in the corner of his villa attracts our curiosity, which is quickly satisfied. He throws it open, and: 'What would this be worth in the open market?' he gloats, producing, with a tremendous flourish, a faded horse-blanket. In the final phase the Jew is arraigned by the Spanish Inquisition, which convicts him of un-Catholic activities and sends him to the stake. As the curtain falls, Mr Wolfit goes up in flames, aged four-teen hundred and some odd years. It is like the annual roasting of an ox on Shakespeare's birthday at Stratford-on-Avon.

(1953)

Venice Preserv'd

by THOMAS OTWAY
at the Lyric, Hammersmith

Way out in the smoky suburb of Hammersmith a prodigy has been brought to birth. By which I mean a pure, plain, clear, classical production of the last great verse play in the English language – Thomas Otway's *Venice Preserv'd*, written in 1681, its author's thirtieth year. That it should be performed at all is treat enough; that it should be performed so well is a marvel.

Otway writes grandly, with a sort of sad, nervous power, about a large subject – the ethics of betrayal. Two impoverished Venetian malcontents, Jaffeir and Pierre, join a plot to overthrow the Senate. Their motives are highly personal. Jaffeir's bride is Belvidera, whose miserly father is a senator, and Pierre's mistress is Aquilina, a prostitute whose present keeper is a senator. Rationalizing their grudges, they become crusading revolutionaries – the process is not uncommon today. But Pierre is a cynic and a man of action. Jaffeir is a romantic and a man of feeling, and when one of his fellow-conspirators attempts to seduce his wife, the romantic in him subdues the rebel, and he betrays the plot to the Senate. There is another motive for his treachery – his wife's fears for her father's life – but the key to it is private pique, masquerading as public-spiritedness. In the vacillations of poor, uxorious Jaffeir there is magnificent irony. The plotters having been arrested and condemned to torture, he wants desperately to atone. All he can do is to satisfy Pierre's plea for a quick death, and then to kill himself.

The play's major flaw is that Otway allows Jaffeir far too much self-pity, a mood of which John Gielgud, as an actor, is far too fond. The temptation sometimes proves too much for him : inhaling passionately through his nose, he administers to every line a tremendous parsonical quiver. But pictorially, if not emotionally, this is a very satisfying performance. The same goes for Eileen Herlie's Belvidera. The spectacle of Miss Herlie reeling and writhing in coils is both pleasing and appropriate, but something in her voice, a touch of fulsomeness, suggests an energetic saleswoman rather than a tragic heroine.

With the rest of the company I have no quarrel at all. Paul Scofield's Pierre, smouldering under a black wig, is the strongest, surest performance this actor has given since he came to London. Meanwhile, Pamela Brown, pop-eyed and imperious, has recaptured the fluent authority which in *The Way of the World* she seemed to have mislaid. The scene in which Aquilina caters to the masochistic whims of her decrepit senator, Antonio, was written as a scurrilous lampoon of the Earl of Shaftesbury. From this dunghill Miss Brown plucks a daisy of a performance, made up of boredom, contempt, and even a flicker of compassion. Her Aquilina is a definitive drab.

Peter Brook's production and Leslie Hurry's décor go straight to the play's atmospheric point – which is that, while reading it, you get the eerie sensation of being underground, trapped in a torch-lit vault. I shall return to Hammersmith again; but I should do so more than once if Messrs Gielgud and Scofield could be persuaded to alternate the roles of Jaffeir and Pierre, as Gielgud and Olivier alternated Romeo and Mercutio eighteen years ago.

(1953)

A Tribute to Mr Coward

To be famous young and to make fame last – the secret of combining the two is glandular: it depends on energy.

Noël Coward, who was performing in public at ten, has never stopped being in action; at fifty-three he retains all the heady zest of adolescence. Forty years ago he was Slightly in *Peter Pan*, and you might say that he has been wholly in *Peter Pan* ever since. No private considerations have been allowed to deflect the drive of his career; like Gielgud and Rattigan, like the late Ivor Novello, he is a congenital bachelor. He began, like many other satirists (Evelyn Waugh, for instance), by rebelling against conformity, and ended up making his peace with it, even becoming its outspoken advocate.

Any child with a spark of fantasy in its soul is prone to react against the English middle classes, into which Coward was born. The circumstances of his early upbringing, in Teddington, were 'liable', he wrote after-wards, 'to degenerate into refined gentility unless care-fully watched.' He promptly reacted against them, and also against his first school-teacher, whom he bit in the arm – 'an action which I have never for an instant regretted.' From this orgy of rebellion he excepted his mother, a tiny octogenarian who is now comfortably installed in a flat in Eaton Square. With the production of *The Vortex*, in 1924, notoriety hit him. He had already written two other plays and most of a revue, meanwhile announcing that his own wit and Ivor Novello's profile were the first and second wonders of the modern world.

The Vortex, a jeremiad against narcotics with dialogue that sounds today not so much stilted as high-heeled, was described by Beverley Nichols as 'immortal'. Others, whom it shocked, were encouraged in their heresy by an unfortunate photograph for which Coward posed supine on a knobbly brass bedstead, wearing a dressing-gown and 'looking', as he said, 'like a heavily-doped Chinese illusionist.' From this sprang the myth that he wrote all his plays in an absinthe-drenched coma; in fact, as he has been patiently explaining for nearly thirty years, he drinks little and usually starts punishing his typewriter at seven a.m. His triumph has been to unite two things ever dissociated in the English mind : hard work and wit. Toil is commonly the chum of serious-mindedness; and though, within Coward, a social historian and philosopher are constantly campaigning to be let out, they seldom escape into his work. His wit in print is variable – he has not written a really funny play since *Present Laughter* in 1942 – but in private it is unflagging. It took Coward to describe an American adaptation of *The Cherry Orchard*, set in the deep South, as 'A Month in the Wrong Country'; and many other theatrical *mots* have been fathered on him. We may never know, for example, whether it was he who, after seeing a certain actress as Queen Victoria, left the theatre murmuring: 'I never realized before that Albert married beneath him.'

To see him whole, public and private personalities conjoined, you must see him in cabaret. Just before his first season at the Café de Paris, I noticed him watching his predecessor, whose act was not going too well. I asked him how he was enjoying the performance, and, with a stark, stunned, take-it-or-leave-it stare, he hissed: 'Sauce! Sheer sauce!' A few weeks later he padded down the celebrated stairs himself, halted before the microphone on black-suede-clad feet, and, upraising both hands in a gesture of benediction, set about demonstrating how these things should be done. Baring his teeth as if unveiling some grotesque monument, and cooing like a baritone dove, he gave us 'I'll See You Again' and the other bat's-wing melodies of his youth. Nothing he does on these occasions sounds strained or arid; his tanned, leathery face is still an enthusiast's.

All the time the hands are at their task, affectionately calming your too-kind applause. Amused by his own frolicsomeness, he sways from side to side, waggling a finger if your attention looks like wandering. If it is possible to romp fastidiously, that is what Coward does. He owes little to earlier wits, such as Wilde or Labouchère. Their best things need to be delivered slowly, even lazily. Coward's emerge with the staccato, blind impulsiveness of a machine-gun.

I have heard him accused of having enervated English comedy by making it languid and blasé. The truth, of course, is the opposite: Coward took sophistication out of the refrigerator and set it bubbling on the hob. He doses his sentences with pauses, as you dose epileptics with drugs. To be with him for any length of time is exhausting and invigorating in roughly equal proportions. He is perfectly well aware that he possesses 'star quality', which is the lodestar of his life. In his case, it might be defined as the ability to project, without effort, the outline of a unique personality, which had never existed before him in print or paint.

Even the youngest of us will know, in fifty years' time, exactly what we mean by 'a very Noël Coward sort of person.' (1953)

Prose and the Playwright

Where the modern poetic drama is concerned, I have always been for the man Bacon quotes who, when asked his opinion of poets, said he thought them the best writers, next to those that wrote prose. But lately, among my friends, I have been finding myself in a beleaguered minority; the post-war vogue of T. S. Eliot and Christopher Fry has brought back into play that ancient battering-ram of criticism, the assumption that the upper reaches of dramatic experience are the exclusive province of the poet. This kind of talk is probably giving the prose play-wrights a brutal inferiority-complex, and I have a mind to contest it. For if Eliot is right in suggesting that there are certain subtle and rarefied states of being which can achieve theatrical expression only in verse, then a great battle has been lost, almost by default.

We tend to forget how long it took to make prose socially acceptable in the theatre. Up to the last quarter of the nineteenth century it remained a slightly dingy poor relation; the Greeks sniffed at it, Shakespeare reserved it mostly for persiflage, Molière shunned it whenever (as in *Tartuffe* or *Le Misanthrope*) he had anything ambitious in hand, and in the long eighteenth-century debates about the relative fitness of blank verse and heroic couplets for tragedy, prose seldom got more than a passing and per-functory mention. The English romantics carried on the tradition of bardolatry: Shelley, Byron, Wordsworth, Keats, and Coleridge all wrote unactable verse tragedies, thus delivering what might easily have been the death-blow to serious drama in English. Nobody seemed to have noticed that ever since Shakespeare's death poetic tragedy had been languishing and prose comedy flourishing; and it occurred to no one that the latter's prosperity might be due not so much to its being comic as to its being prose. In the Elizabethan era, before drama had been clearly distinguished from other literary forms, it naturally contained a good deal of the epic, much of the lyric, and a strong flavour of what A. B. Walkley called 'that element of mixed philosophy and rhetoric which was soon afterwards to be diverted into other channels, in England by Sir Thomas Browne, in France by the great pulpit orators.' By the beginning of the last century the process of differentiation had taken place, and the drama stolidly ignored it.

The three gigantic musketeers of prose were, of course, Ibsen, Chekhov, and Shaw; they made it respectable, and Chekhov even went so far as to show that prose, by means of what it implied rather than what it stated, could reproduce the effect of poetry in purely theatrical terms. By 1900 it began to look as if prose had gained its point – and pretty tardily, too, since the novel had started to replace the verse epic two centuries earlier. It would have surprised the drama critics of the period to be told that within fifty years the old medium would once more be asserting its claim to dramatic supremacy. Yet that is what has happened. Just as prose has started to test its wings, we are asked to believe that it can never fly. The powers of the line that stops short of the margin are again being hymned and its mysteries celebrated.

This seems to me grossly unhistorical and based on an alarming number of unproven assumptions. For an irrevocable change has been overtaking language in the last three hundred years. Poetry and colloquial prose, which are now (in spite of Wordsworth) linguistically divorced, shared in the sixteenth century rich champaigns of vocabulary and image. Elizabethan pamphlets are as generous with metaphor as Elizabethan plays; and a dramatist could inject a shot of colloquialism into a tragic aria without courting bathos. Nobody titters when Hamlet, in mid-soliloquy, exclaims, 'Why, what an ass am I!'; but when Aaron, in Christopher Fry's tragedy *The First-born*, says of Moses that 'he took me by the scruff of my heart', it is comic in much the same way as Abe Burrows's parody of the 'sophisticated-type' love song: 'You put a piece of carbon-paper under your heart, and gave me just a copy of your love.' Everyone agrees that formal poetic diction is dead; yet if you spike a dramatic verse-form with the vernacular, the experiment invariably fails – unless a comic or ironic effect was what you had in mind. Auden, Isherwood, Eliot and Fry have all exploited this trick of bathos; and it may be that the wheel has come full circle, that poetry in the theatre should be confined to comedy, where its potency still lingers.

The customary plea for verse is summed up in this extract from one of Dryden's essays: 'All the arguments which are formed against it, can amount to no more than this, that it is not so near conversation as prose, and therefore not so natural. But it is clear to all who understand poetry, that serious plays ought not to imitate conversation too nearly.' And once you admit that 'naturalness' is not enough, he continues, you are halfway to accepting poetry: 'You have lost that which you call natural, and have not acquired the last perfection of Art.' But Dryden's antithesis is a false one. The perfection of art in the theatre depends neither on naturalism nor on poetry. Drama has in its time borrowed tricks from both, but what it has built is a new and separate structure, whose foundation stones – the last acts of *The Master Builder* and *The Three Sisters* – are architectural triumphs of prose over naturalism.

On naturalism I shrink from pronouncing, because I have never (has anyone?) seen a completely naturalistic play – I doubt if one exists. What bothers me is the way in which the higher criticism equates prose with poverty of dramatic expression. 'What is the prose for God?' cries one pundit, quoting from Granville-Barker and forgetting that the answer to the question is on almost every page of the Bible. Nobody wants to banish luxury of language from the theatre; what needs banishing is the notion that it is incompatible with prose, the most flexible weapon the stage has ever had, and still shining new. Those playwrights who have followed the Ibsen-Chekhov lead are in the main stream of modern drama. Giraudoux for prime example; *La Folle de Chaillot* and *La Guerre de Troie* represent prose exulting in its own versatility, embracing slang and stateliness, gutter and glitter, in one enormous grasp. Synge and O'Casey stand beside Giraudoux in the great line; and when, earlier this year, Dylan Thomas's *Under Milk Wood* was published, nobody could doubt that only death had robbed us of another to join them. *Under Milk Wood* was commissioned by the B.B.C. for sound broadcasting, but two Sunday-night stagings of it at the Old Vic proved that it could enmesh the watcher as well as the listener. Here, unfolding in the talk and thoughts of its inhabitants, was a day in the life of a Welsh coastal town, a devout and mischievous celebration of the sea, soil, wind, and wantonness of Wales. Prose went into battle rejoicing. Take, for instance, this exchange between Mrs Cherry Owen and her errant husband.

MRS CHERRY OWEN: Remember last night? In you reeled, my boy, as drunk as a deacon with a big wet bucket and a fish-frail full of stout and you looked at me and you said, 'God has come home!' you said, and then over the bucket you went, sprawling and bawling, and the floor was all flagons and eels.

CHERRY OWEN: Was I wounded?

MRS CHERRY OWEN: And then you took off your trousers and you said, 'Does anybody want to fight?' Oh, you old baboon.

Or the letter written by Mog Edwards, 'a draper mad with love', to his 'Beloved Myfanwy Price my Bride in Heaven':

I love you until Death do us part and then we shall be together for ever and ever. A new parcel of ribbons has come from Carmarthen today, all the colours in the rainbow. I wish I could tie a ribbon in your hair a white one but it cannot be. I dreamed last night you were all dripping wet and you sat on my lap as the Reverend Jenkins went down the street. I see you got a mermaid in your lap he said and he lifted his hat. He is a proper Christian. Not like Cherry Owen who said you should have thrown her back he said. Business is very poorly . . . If this goes on I shall be in the workhouse. My heart is in your bosom and yours is in mine. God be with you always Myfanwy Price and keep you lovely for me in His Heavenly Mansion. I must stop now and remain, Your Eternal, Mog Edwards.

The whole play is a tumult of living, and its burden is compressed into the remark of Polly Garter, the town tart: 'Isn't life a terrible thing, thank God!' Philip Hope-Wallace, writing in the *Manchester Guardian*, sent his thoughts to the right place when he said: 'Not since *Juno and the Paycock* have we heard in a theatre words coming up thus, not chosen but compelled: a fountain from the heart.'

Thomas side-stepped the snare which besets the prose playwright who, though he abjures verse, secretly aspires to the condition of poetry. This fatal urge is responsible for the solemn, booming cadences, the sentences lying in comatose state, which one sometimes finds in the plays of Charles Morgan. *The Burning Glass* is a forest of prose on stilts, opulently teetering. Morgan's excuse, of course, is that Thomas had a head start on him, since (like O'Casey) he was putting words in the mouths of a people essentially imaginative. Morgan's characters are drawn from the English upper class, whose vocabulary is crippled by the restraints of social usage (no tears, no ecstasies), and about whom it is today practically impossible to write a great play. The spirit is not in them; or if it is, their tight lips firmly repress it. I doubt if even Arthur Miller or Tennessee Williams, the prose masters of the contemporary English-speaking theatre, could construct a tragedy around the country homes of Berks and Bucks. It is significant that the most successful passages of *The Cocktail Party* were those in which Eliot exposed the vacuity of *haut bourgeois* chatter:

JULIA: . . . The only man I ever met who could hear the cry of bats.
PETER: Hear the cry of bats?
JULIA: He could hear the cry of bats.
CELIA: But how do you know he could hear the cry of bats?
JULIA: Because he said so. And I believed him.

Eliot is here using verse to show how resolutely, how comically unpoetical his characters are; and, wryly but appropriately, it works.

One of the handicaps of poetry is that penumbra of holiness, the legacy of the nineteenth century, which still surrounds it, coaxing us into tolerating sentimental excesses we would never forgive in prose:

> O God, O God, if I could return to yesterday, before I thought that I had made a decision. What devil left the door on the latch for these doubts to enter? And then you came back, you, the angel of destruction – just as I felt sure. In a moment, at your touch, there is nothing but ruin.

Exit, you might expect, into snowstorm; but you would be wrong. The lines come not from Victorian melodrama but from *The Cocktail Party*, printed as prose. Their lameness is particularly vexing because Eliot has shown himself capable of writing intensely muscular dramatic prose. So has Fry: one has only to read his lecture, 'An Experience of Critics', parts of which are as speakable as a Giraudoux tirade. Much of his latest play, *The Dark Is Light Enough*, is infinitely less dramatic. Its construction rules out of court the old argument that poetic plays are deficient only in plot; *The Dark is Light Enough* abounds in plot and incident, yet remains as static as a candle-lit tableau or darkling waxwork. It happens in a château on the Austro-Hungarian border. The Hungarian rebellion of 1848 has just begun, and a crisis is precipitated by the Countess Rosmarin, who decides to give shelter to Gettner, a deserter from the revolutionary army. The play's main action is the regeneration of Gettner, nihilist and traitor, by the Countess, who stands for divine charity, the justification of God's circuitous ways to man.

The first great drawback is the fact that Rosmarin, being by definition perfect, is incapable of development; in spite of Dame Edith Evans's vocal exertions, she can scarcely avoid resembling a benignly crinolined soup-kitchen. The second and greater drawback is, I am afraid, Fry's style, which – though it is noticeably less sportive than it used to be – seems now to have taken on the texture of diatomite, a substance used in the manufacture of pipestems, which contains thousands of fossils to the cubic inch. The characters studiously express different attitudes towards life, but they use interchangeable rhythms and identical tricks of speech in which to do so. They *tell* us, with ruthless fluency, what kind of people they are, instead of letting us find out for ourselves. I needn't say that there are some fine set pieces of rhetoric; but the best of them − that in which Rosmarin likens Gettner to a blue plucked goose shivering on the water's brink − embodies in itself the germ of poetry's weakness: it describes in repose rather than illustrates in action. And one regrets the readiness with which Fry has succumbed to padding and jingle, in phrases like 'for my sake, if my sake is worthy', 'a coward, if a coward is what you are', 'splendidly sleeping', 'precariously promising', and 'inconsolable inclination.'

It is good to learn that he is at present making prose adaptations of Anouilh's *L'Alouette* and Giraudoux's *La Guerre de Troie*; perhaps the experience will lure him across the frontier into the large Gothic landscapes of prose. The chance of converting Eliot is, I imagine, much slimmer; but it may not be impertinent to suggest that even in his best play, *Murder in the Cathedral*, the most impressive pages were those which contained the speeches of self-exculpation by the four knights and the sermon delivered by Becket on Christmas Day. And these were all prose:

> I have spoken to you today, dear children of God, of the martyrs of the past . . . because it is fitting, on Christ's birth day, to remember what is that Peace which He brought; and because, dear children, I do not think I shall ever preach to you again; and because it is possible that in a short time you may have yet another martyr, and that one perhaps not the last. . . .

In poetry, Fry gilds where Eliot anoints; in neither procedure are there seeds of real dramatic vitality. If they, the foremost heretics, can be persuaded off their crosses, away from their martyrdom in a lost cause, the theatre would immediately benefit. Mallarmé once said. in lapidary despair : *'Pour moi le cas d'un poète, en cette société qui ne le permet de vivre, c'est le cas d'un homme qui s'isole pour sculpter son propre tombeau.'* But he was slightly in error. It is not our society but our theatre which rejects the poet; 'nowadays', as Walkley said, 'we expect a drama to be purely dramatic.' If poetic playwrights did not exist, it might be an agreeable caprice to invent them; but it would no longer be a necessity. And in a theatre starved by the cinema and besieged by television, necessities must come first.

(1954)

Separate Tables

by TERENCE RATTIGAN
at the St James's

(The scene is the dining-room of a Kensington hotel, not unlike the Bournemouth hotel in which Separate Tables, *Terence Rattigan's new double bill, takes place. A Young Perfectionist is dining; beside him, Aunt Edna, whom Mr Rattigan has described as the 'universal and immortal' middle-class playgoer.)*

AUNT EDNA : Excuse me, young man, but have you seen Mr Rattigan's latest?

YOUNG PERFECTIONIST : I have indeed.

A.E. : And what is it about?

Y.P. : It is two plays about four people who are driven by loneliness into a state of desperation.

A.E. (*sighing*) : Is there not enough morbidity in the world. . . ?

Y.P. : One of them is a drunken Left-wing journalist who has been imprisoned for wife-beating. Another is his ex-wife, who takes drugs to palliate the loss of her looks. She revives his masochistic love for her, and by curtain-fall they are gingerly reunited.

A.E. (*quailing*) : Does Mr Rattigan analyse these creatures?

Y.P.: He does, in great detail.

A.E.: How very unwholesome! Pray go on.

Y.P.: In the second play the central character is a bogus major who has lately been convicted of assaulting women in a cinema.

A.E.: Ouf!

Y.P.: His fellow-guests hold conclave to decide whether he should be expelled from the hotel. Each contributes to a symposium on sexual deviation. . . .

A.E.: In pity's name, stop.

Y.P.: The major reveals that his foible is the result of fear, which has made him a hermit, a liar, and a pervert. This revelation kindles sympathy in the heart of the fourth misfit, a broken spinster, who befriends him in his despair.

A.E. (*aghast*): I *knew* I was wrong when I applauded *The Deep Blue Sea*. And what conclusion does Mr Rattigan draw from these squalid anecdotes?

Y.P.: From the first, that love unbridled is a destroyer. From the second, that love bridled is a destroyer. You will enjoy yourself.

A.E.: But I go to the theatre to be taken out of myself!

Y.P.: Mr Rattigan will take you into an intricately charted world of suspense. By withholding vital information, he will tantalise you; by disclosing it unexpectedly, he will astound you.

A.E.: But what information! Sex and frustration.

Y.P.: I agree that the principal characters, especially the journalist and the major, are original and disturbing creations. But there is also a tactful omniscient *hôtelière*, beautifully played by Beryl Measor. And what do you say to a comic Cockney Maid?

A.E.: Ah!

Y.P.: Or to Aubrey Mather as a whimsical dominie? Or to a pair of opinionated medical students? Or to a tyrannical matriarch – no less than Phyllis Neilson-Terry?

A.E.: *That* sounds more like it. You console me.

Y.P.: I thought you would feel at home. And Peter Glenville, the director, has craftily engaged for these parts actors subtle enough to disguise their flatness.

A.E. (*clouding over*): But what about those difficult leading roles?

Y.P.: Margaret Leighton plays two of them, rather externally.

Her beauty annihilates the pathos of the ex-wife, who should be oppressed with crow's-feet. And her mousy spinster, dim and pink-knuckled, verges on caricature. It is Eric Portman who commands the stage, volcanic as the journalist, but even better as the major, speaking in nervous spasms and walking stiff-legged with his shoulders protectively hunched. He has the mask of the true mime, the *comédien* as opposed to the *acteur*.

A.E.: Yet you sound a trifle peaky. Is something biting you?

Y.P.: Since you ask, I regretted that the major's crime was not something more cathartic than mere cinema flirtation. Yet I suppose the play is as good a handling of sexual abnormality as English playgoers will tolerate.

A.E.: For my part, I am glad it is no better.

Y.P.: I guessed you would be; and so did Mr Rattigan. Will you accompany me on a second visit tomorrow?

A.E.: With great pleasure. Clearly, there is something here for both of us.

Y.P.: Yes. But not quite enough for either of us.

(1954)

West-End Apathy

'And how,' ask my friends, having debated the opera, the ballet, politics, and the Italian cinema, 'how is the theatre getting along?' The very set of their features, so patiently quizzical, tells me I am being indulged; after the serious business of conversation, they are permitting themselves a lapse into idleness. I shrug cheerily, like a martyr to rheumatism. A wan, tingling silence ensues. Then: 'De Sica's new film is superb,' says somebody, and talk begins again, happy and devout. I stew, meanwhile, in what Zelda Fitzgerald once called 'the boiling oil of sour grapes.'

The bare fact is that, apart from revivals and imports, there is nothing in the London theatre that one dares discuss with an intelligent man for more than five minutes. Since the great Ibsen challenge of the nineties, the English intellectuals have been drifting away from drama. Synge, Pirandello, and O'Casey briefly recaptured them, and they will still perk up at the mention of Giraudoux. But – cowards – they know Eliot and Fry only in the study; and of a native prose playwright who might set the boards smouldering they see no sign at all. Last week I welcomed a young Frenchwoman engaged in writing a thesis on contemporary English drama. We talked hopefully of John Whiting; but before long embarrassment moved me to ask why she had not chosen her own theatre as a subject for study. She smiled wryly. 'Paris is in decline,' she said. 'Apart from Sartre, Anouilh, Camus, Cocteau, Aymé, Claudel, Beckett, and Salacrou, we have almost nobody.'

If you seek a tombstone, look about you; survey the peculiar nullity of our drama's prevalent *genre*, the Loamshire play. Its setting is a country house in what used to be called Loamshire but is now, as a heroic tribute to realism, sometimes called Berkshire. Except when someone must sneeze, or be murdered, the sun invariably shines. The inhabitants belong to a social class derived partly from romantic novels and partly from the playwright's vision of the leisured life he will lead after the play is a success – this being the only effort of imagination he is called on to make. Joys and sorrows are giggles and whimpers: the crash of denunciation dwindles into 'Oh, stuff, Mummy!' and 'Oh, really, Daddy!' And so grim is the continuity of these things that the foregoing paragraph might have been written at any time during the last thirty years.

Loamshire is a glibly codified fairy-tale world, of no more use to the student of life than a doll's-house would be to a student of town planning. Its vice is to have engulfed the theatre, thereby expelling better minds. Never believe that there is a shortage of playwrights; there are more than we have ever known; but they are all writing the same play. Nor is there a dearth of English actors; the land is alive with them; but they are all playing the same part. Should they wish to test themselves beyond Loamshire's simple major thirds, they must find employment in revivals, foreign plays, or films. Perhaps Loamshire's greatest triumph is the crippling of creative talent in English directors and designers. After all, how many ways are there of directing a tea-party? And how may a designer spread his wings in a mews flat or 'The living-room at "Binsgate", Vyvyan Bulstrode's country house near Dymsdyke'? Assume the miracle: assume the advent of a masterpiece. There it crouches, a pink-eyed, many-muscled, salivating monster. Who shall harness it? We have a handful of directors fit to tame something less malleable than a mouse and a few designers still capable of dressing something less submissive than a clothes-horse. But they are the end, not the beginning, of a tradition.

Some of us need no miracles to keep our faith; we feed it on memories and imaginings. But many more – people of passionate intellectual appetites – are losing heart, falling away, joining the queues outside the Curzon Cinema. To lure them home, the theatre must widen its scope, broaden its horizon so that Loamshire appears merely as the play-pen, not as the whole palace of drama. We need plays about cabmen and demi-gods, plays about warriors, politicians, and grocers – I care not, so Loam-shire be invaded and subdued. I counsel aggression because, as a critic, I had rather be a war correspondent than a necrologist. (1954)

The Lost Art of Bad Drama

Night-nurses at the bedside of good drama, we critics keep a holy vigil. Black circles rim our eyes as we pray for the survival of our pet patient, starved and racked, the theatre of passion and ideas. We pump in our printed transfusions – 'honest and forthright,' 'rooted in a closely observed reality' – but so avidly do we seize on signs of relapse that we fail to observe that, for the moment at least, the cripple is out of bed and almost convalescent. He can claim, this season, three successes: *Hedda Gabler*, Anouilh's *Time Remembered*, and Pirandello's *Rules of the Game* – and he had a vestigial hand in *Separate Tables*,

(Mr Rattigan is the Formosa of the contemporary theatre, occupied by the old guard, but geographically inclined towards the progressives.) Further tonics lie ahead, among them a Giraudoux and another Anouilh before spring is out. Implausible as it may sound, good drama may be able to walk unaided within a year or so.

But what of bad drama, the kind which repudiates art and scoffs at depth, which thrives on reviewers who state themselves 'shocked, but I rocked with laughter'? We assume that it is healthy; in fact, it looks extremely frail. Many a frankly 'commercial' play has come smiling to town in recent months and walked straight into an upper-cut from both critics and public. Take *The Night of the Ball*, for instance – a knightly piece, glib and well-nourished, star-bright and silk-swathed, yet see how scarred and blunderbussed the critics left it! And is old *Happy Holiday* dead? As any doornail. Jesu, Jesu, the bad plays that I have seen! and to think how many of my old acquaintance are dead! How a good yoke of starlets at Cambridge Circus? Truly, cousin, I was not there.

It is now, in fact, a risky proposition to back plays that twenty years ago would have swept the boards unopposed. One imagines a box-office mogul bewailing his lot in Justice Shallow's vein: 'By the masses I was call'd every-thing. . . . There was I, and little Noël Coward of Teddington, and black Ben Travers, and Frederick Lonsdale, and Vernon Sylvaine, a Manchester man – you had not four such rib-crackers in all of Shaftesbury Avenue again; and I may say to you, we knew where the bona-robas were, and had the best of them all under two weeks' notice. . . . Is old *double-entente* of your town living yet?' Dead, sir, dead.

One begins to suspect that the English have lost the art of writing a bad successful play. Perhaps some sort of competition should be organized; the rules, after all, are simple enough. At no point may the plot or characters make more than superficial contact with reality. Characters earning less than £1,000 a year should be restricted to small parts or exaggerated into types so patently farcical than no member of the audience could possibly identify himself with such absurd esurience. Rhythm in dialogue is achieved by means either of vocatives ('That, my dear Hilary, is a moot point') or qualifying clauses ('What, if you'll pardon the interruption, is going on here?'); and irony is confined to having an irate male character shout: 'I am perfectly calm!'

All plays should contain parts fit to be turned down by Gladys Cooper, Coral Browne, Hugh Williams, and Robert Flemyng. Apart from hysterical adolescents, nobody may weep; apart from triumphant protagonists, nobody may laugh: anyone, needless to say, may smile. European place-names (Positano and Ischia) are romantic; English place-names (Herne Bay and Bognor Regis) are comic. Women who help themselves unasked to cigarettes must be either frantic careerists or lustful opportunists. The latter should declare themselves by running the palm of one hand up their victim's lapel and saying, when it reaches the neck: 'Let's face it, Arthur, you're not exactly indifferent to me.' The use of 'Let's face it' in modern drama deserves in itself a special study. It means that something true is about to be uttered, and should strike the audience with the same shock as the blast of the whistle before the train plunges into a tunnel. . . .

But I falter. I cannot convince myself that these rules, archaic already, will assure success. For bad plays, dependent on what is topical and ephemeral in mankind, are much harder to write than good ones, for which the rules are permanent and unchanging. The commercial writer must blind himself to history, close his eyes, stop his ears, shutter his mind to the onslaught of reality; he must ignore all the promptings which instinct tells him to be valid, about unity of action and the necessity of reducing one or more of his characters to a logical crisis of desperation; he must live the life of a spiritual hermit. Such self-abnegation is seldom found. The great age of the thoroughly bad play seems to be over, and it behoves the critic to sing a requiem.

A thermometer, meanwhile, might be left in the mouth of good drama. Our season's tally is certainly encouraging, but it pales by comparison with last season's record in Sweden. There, according to the report in *World Theatre*, one might have seen four Strindbergs, four Shakespeares, three Chekhovs, three Pirandellos, two Molières, two Shaws, two Ibsens, two Giraudouxs, and one each from Vanbrugh, Wycherley, Lorca, Kafka, Brecht, Ugo Betti, Arthur Miller, Anouilh, Eliot, Bernanos, and Samuel Beckett – not to mention the *Oresteia* of Aeschylus. Yet 'the season', mourns the compiler of the report, 'was not a milestone.' We have a long way to go.

(1955)

Henry IV, Parts I and II

by WILLIAM SHAKESPEARE
at the Old Vic

I suspected it at Stratford four years ago, and now I am sure: for me the two parts of *Henry IV* are the twin summits of Shakespeare's achievement. Lime-hungry actors have led us always to the tragedies, where a single soul is spotlit and its agony explored; but these private torments dwindle beside the Henries, great public plays in which a whole nation is under scrutiny and on trial. More than anything else in our drama they deserve the name of epic. A way of life is facing dissolution; we are in at the deathbed of the Middle Ages. How shall the crisis be faced? The answer takes us to every social and geographical outpost: to East-cheap drunks and Gloucestershire gentry, to the Welsh and the Scots, to the minor nobility and the crown itself.

There is much talk of death; to the king it comes as a balm, Falstaff sags at the mention of it, Shallow is resigned to it, and Hotspur meets it with nostrils flared.

The odd, irregular rhythm wherein societies die and are reborn is captured as no playwright before or since has ever recaptured it. In Hal's return to honour and justice the healing of a national sickness is implied. Implied: that is the clue — for there is no overt exhortation in these plays, and no true villain, no Claudius or Iago on whom complacent audiences can fix their righteous indignation. Hotspur is on the wrong side, yet he is a hero; Prince John is on the right one, yet his cynical perfidy at the disarmament conference would have astonished Hitler. Only a handful of plays in the world preserve this divine magnanimity. To conceive the state of mind in which the Henries were written is to feel dizzied by the air of Olympus.

We knew from Douglas Seale's handling of the *Henry VI* trilogy that he was a director of rare historical imagination; and the Old Vic company, which lacks star quality, exactly fits a pair of plays which lack star parts. Note how cleverly Mr Seale lets the two evenings illuminate each other. He gives Falstaff a page in Part I as well as Part II, using the boy as mute audience to the knight's soliloquies; taking his cue from a phrase in Part II — 'wearied and out-breathed' — he makes Hotspur and Hal in Part I so stricken with battle fatigue that they can scarcely lift their swords. The tavern scenes, writhing with squalor and pulsing with visual wit, transport us straight to pre-Crookback England.

Paul Rogers's Falstaff is fussy and perhaps too easily discomfited, but vocally it is a display of rich and immaculate cunning. Rachel Roberts hits off Mrs Quickly to perfection, and few Pistols have been fired more powerfully than John Neville's. The same actor's Hotspur was hampered by a stammer needlessly borrowed from Sir Laurence Olivier, and the best double was that of Paul Daneman, whose malign Worcester was followed by a goatish Justice Shallow, giddy with snobbery and agog with innocence.

Mr Seale's hand seems to stiffen at contact with royalty: his groupings in the court scenes were static, and the episode of the purloined crown was badly staged on a remote rostrum, high and half-visible. Eric Porter gave us all of Henry's guilt but little of his grandeur; and in Robert Hardy's Hal there was too great a show of intelligence. Mr Hardy is rightly proud of his technique, but he is in danger of developing it at the expense of his acting 'innards': the performance was well-timed but soft-centred. Ann Todd and Virginia McKenna intrude briefly and softly into what has been called the smoking-room of Shakespearian drama – though Miss Todd's irruption into the middle of the curtain-call was, to say the least, presumptuous. Audrey Cruddas's permanent setting is both rugged and regal. To sum up, Mr Seale has put the Old Vic in particular and Shakespearian production in general on the right realistic track.

(1955)

Tiger at the Gates

by JEAN GIRAUDOUX
translated by CHRISTOPHER FRY
at the Apollo

In spite of a few bad performances and a setting uniquely hideous, I do not believe that anyone could emerge from *Tiger at the Gates* unaware that what had just hit him was a masterpiece. For this is Giraudoux's *La Guerre de Troie n'aura pas lieu*, brought to us at last, after twenty years of impatience, in a methodical translation by Christopher Fry. It remains the final comment on the superfluity of war, and the highest peak in the mountain-range of modern French theatre. At the lowest estimate, it is a great occasional play, in the sense that its impact might be doubled if war seemed imminent; but to call it dated because nowadays we are at peace is to ignore its truest warning, which is that nothing more surely rouses the sleeping tiger of war than the prospect of universal tranquillity.

What is to engage us is the process whereby the Trojan war nearly failed to happen. Returning disillusioned from one campaign, Hector finds another impending; to send Helen back to the Greeks he will undergo any humiliation, even the dishonour of his wife. Paris, his brother, gives in to him easily, but Helen is harder to persuade. The Fates, in choosing her for their instrument, have endowed her with an icy indifference to Hector's enormous compassion. 'I'm sure', she says, 'that people pity each other to the same extent that they pity themselves.' Yet she, too, puts herself in his hands.

Breaking all precedents, Hector refuses to make the traditional speech of homage to his fallen soldiers; instead, we have the majestic tirade in which he rejoices with those who survived, the cowards who live to make love to the wives of the dead. His last stumbling-block is Ulysses, wily and circumspect, who reminds him, as they amicably chat, that a convivial 'meeting at the summit' is always the preamble to war; but even he agrees to gamble against destiny and take Helen home in peace. In the play's closing moments, war is declared. To reveal how would be an insult to those who know the text and a terrible deprivation to those who do not. Enough to say that history passes into the keeping of (Max Beerbohm's phrase) 'those incomparable poets, Homer.'

I cannot but marvel at the virtuosity of Giraudoux's prose. It embraces grandeur and littleness in one gigantic clasp; having carved a heroic group in granite, it can turn to the working of tiny heads on cherry-stones. No playwright of our time can change gear so subtly, from majestic gloom to crystalline wit. Sometimes, in the mass debates, the verbal glitter is overpowering, but in duologues Giraudoux has no rival. Hector's scenes with Helen in the first act and with Ulysses in the second ring in the mind like doubloons flung down on marble.

Is it objected that English actors jib at long stretches of ornate prose? Or that they are unused to playing tragic scenes for laughs and comic scenes for tears? If so, they had better relearn their craft. The player who thinks Giraudoux unactable is in the wrong profession. Harold Clurman, the director, has tried hard to teach old dogs new tricks, but the right note of vocal aristocracy is only intermittently struck. Listening to Giraudoux should be like watching a series of lightning water-colours, dashed off by a master; some of the present company make do with ponderous cartoons, licking the lead and plunging it deep into the paper. This is the case with Walter Fitzgerald's Ulysses, a dour and laboured performance; and Diane Cilento, though fetchingly got up in what I can best describe as a Freudian slip, gives us paste jewellery instead of the baleful diamond Giraudoux had in mind for Helen. It is Michael Redgrave, as Hector, who bears the evening's brunt. He is clearly much happier in the emotional bits than in the flicks of wit which spark and speckle them; but, even so, this is a monumental piece of acting, immensely moving, intelligent in action, and in repose never less than a demigod. In the presence of such an actor and such a play, I will forgive much. Especially do I feel for anyone unlucky enough to have to stumble and clamber over the obstacle-course of Loudon Sainthill's set. It is enough to make a chamois nervy.

(1955)

Macbeth

by WILLIAM SHAKESPEARE
at Stratford-on-Avon

Nobody has ever succeeded as Macbeth, and the reason is not far to seek. Instead of growing as the play proceeds, the hero shrinks; complex and many-levelled to begin with, he ends up a cornered thug, lacking even a death scene with which to regain lost stature. Most Macbeths, mindful of this, let off their big guns as soon as possible, and have usually shot their bolt by the time the dagger speech is out. The marvel of Sir Laurence Olivier's reading is that it reverses this procedure, turns the play inside out, and makes it (for the first time I can remember) a thing of mounting, not waning, excitement.

Last Tuesday Sir Laurence shook hands with greatness, and within a week or so the performance will have ripened into a masterpiece: not of the superficial, booming, have-a-bash kind, but the real thing, a structure of perfect forethought and proportion, lit by flashes of intuitive lightning.

He begins in a perilously low key, the reason for which is soon revealed. This Macbeth is paralysed with guilt before the curtain rises, having already killed Duncan time and again in his mind. Far from recoiling and popping his eyes, he greets the air-drawn dagger with sad familiarity; it is a fixture in the crooked furniture of his brain. Uxoriousness leads him to the act, which unexpectedly purges him of remorse. Now the portrait swells; seeking security, he is seized with fits of desperate bewilderment as the prize is snatched out of reach. There was true agony in 'I had else been perfect'; Banquo's ghost was received with horrific torment, as if Macbeth should shriek 'I've been robbed!,' and the phrase about the dead rising to 'push us from our stools' was accompanied by a convulsive shoving gesture which few other actors would have risked.

The needle of Sir Laurence's compass leads him so directly to the heart of the role that we forget the jagged rocks of laughter over which he is travelling. At the heart we find, beautifully projected, the anguish of the *de facto* ruler who dares not admit that he lacks the essential qualities of kingship. Sir Laurence's Macbeth is like Skule in Ibsen's chronicle play *The Pretenders*, the valiant usurper who can never comprehend what

Ibsen calls 'the great kingly thought'. He will always be a monarch *manqué*.

The witches' cookery lesson is directed with amusing literalness; the Turk's nose, the Jew's liver, and the baby's finger are all held up for separate scrutiny; but the apparitions are very unpersuasive, and one felt goose-flesh hardly at all. On the battlements Sir Laurence's throttled fury switches into top gear, and we see a lion, baffled but still colossal. 'I 'gin to be a-weary of the sun' held the very ecstasy of despair, the actor swaying with grief, his voice rising like hair on the crest of a trapped animal. 'Exeunt, fighting' was a poor end for such a giant warrior. We wanted to see how he would die; and it was not he but Shakespeare who let us down.

Vivien Leigh's Lady Macbeth is more niminy-piminy than thundery-blundery, more viper than anaconda, but still quite competent in its small way. Macduff and his wife, actor-proof parts, are played with exceptional power by Keith Michell and Maxine Audley. The midnight hags, with traditional bonhomie, scream with laughter at their own jokes: I long, one day, to see whispering witches, less intent on yelling their sins across the country-side. The production has all the speed and clarity we associate with Glen Byam Shaw, and Roger Furse's settings are bleak and serviceable, except for the England scene, which needs only a cat and a milestone to go straight into *Dick Whittington*.

(1955)

Waiting for Godot

by SAMUEL BECKETT
at the Arts

A special virtue attaches to plays which remind the drama of how much it can do without and still exist. By all the known criteria, Samuel Beckett's *Waiting for*

Godot is a dramatic vacuum. Pity the critic who seeks a chink in its armour, for it is all chink. It has no plot, no climax, no *dénouement*; no beginning, no middle, and no end. Unavoidably, it has a situation, and it might be accused of having suspense, since it deals with the impatience of two tramps, waiting beneath a tree for a cryptic Mr Godot to keep his appointment with them; but the situation is never developed, and a glance at the programme shows that Mr Godot is not going to arrive. *Waiting for Godot* frankly jettisons everything by which we recognize theatre. It arrives at the custom-house, as it were, with no luggage, no passport, and nothing to declare; yet it gets through, as might a pilgrim from Mars. It does this, I believe, by appealing to a definition of drama much more fundamental than any in the books. A play, it asserts and proves, is basically a means of spending two hours in the dark without being bored.

Its author is an Irishman living in France, a fact which should prepare us for the extra, oddly serious joke he now plays on us. Passing the time in the dark, he suggests, is not only what drama is about but also what life is about. Existence depends on those metaphysical Micawbers who will go on waiting, against all rational argument, for something which may one day turn up to explain the purpose of living. Twenty years ago Mr Odets had us waiting for Lefty, the social messiah; less naïvely, Mr Beckett bids us wait for Godot, the spiritual signpost. His two tramps pass the time of day just as we, the audience, are passing the time of night. Were we not in the theatre, we should, like them, be clowning and quarrelling, aimlessly bickering and aimlessly making up – all, as one of them says, 'to give us the impression that we exist.'

Mr Beckett's tramps do not often talk like that. For the most part they converse in the double-talk of vaudeville: one of them has the ragged aplomb of Buster Keaton, while the other is Chaplin at his airiest and fairiest. Their exchanges are like those conversations at the next table which one can almost but not quite decipher – human speech half-heard and reproduced with all its *non-sequiturs* absurdly intact. From time to time other characters intrude. Fat Pozzo, Humpty Dumpty with a whip in his fist, puffs into sight with Lucky, his dumb slave. They are clearly going somewhere in a hurry : perhaps they know where Godot is? But the interview subsides into Lewis-Carrollian inanity. All that emerges is that the master needs the slave as much as the slave needs the master; it gives both a sense of spurious purpose; and one thinks of Laurel and Hardy, the ideal casting in these roles. Commanded to think, Lucky stammers out a ghostly, ghastly, interminable tirade, compounded of cliché and gibberish, whose general tenor is that, in spite of material progress and 'all kinds of tennis', man spiritually dwindles. The style hereabouts reminds us forcibly that Mr Beckett once worked for James Joyce. In the next act Pozzo and Lucky return, this time moving, just as purposefully, in the opposite direction. The tramps decide to stay where they are. A child arrives, presenting Mr Godot's compliments and regretting that he is unable to meet them today. It is the same message as yesterday; all the same, they wait. The hero of *Crime and Punishment* reflects that if a condemned man 'had to remain standing on a square yard of space all his life, a thousand years, eternity, it were better to live so than to die at once. . . . Man is a vile creature ! and vile is he who calls him vile for that !' Something of this crossed my mind as the curtain fell on Mr Beckett's tatterdemalion Stoics.

The play sees the human condition in terms of baggy pants and red noses. Hastily labelling their disquiet disgust, many of the first-night audience found it pretentious. But what, exactly, are its pretensions? To state that mankind is waiting for a sign that is late in coming is a platitude which none but an illiterate would interpret as making claims to profundity. What vexed the play's enemies was, I suspect, the opposite : it was not pretentious enough to enable them to deride it. I care little for its enormous success in Europe over the past three years, but much for the way in which it pricked and stimulated my own nervous system. It summoned the music-hall and the parable to present a view of life which banished the sentimentality of the music-hall and the parable's fulsome uplift. It forced me to re-examine the rules which have hitherto governed the drama; and having done so, to pronounce them not elastic enough. It is validly new, and hence I declare myself, as the Spanish would say, *godotista*.

Peter Hall directs the play with a marvellous ear for its elusive rhythms, and Peter Woodthorpe and Paul Daneman give the tramps a compassionate lunacy which only professional clowns could excel. Physically, Peter Bull is Pozzo to the life; vocally, he overplays his hand. Timothy Bateson's Lucky is anguish made comic, a remarkable achievement, and perfectly in keeping with the spirit of the play.

(1955)

Titus Andronicus

by WILLIAM SHAKESPEARE
at Stratford-on-Avon

I have always had a soft spot for *Titus Andronicus*, in spite of the fact that I have often heard it called the worst thing Marlowe ever wrote. Whoever wrote it, whether a member of the Shakespeare syndicate or the chairman himself, he deserves our thanks for having shown us, at the dawn of our drama, just how far drama could go. Like Goya's 'Disasters of War', this is tragedy naked, godless, and unredeemed, a carnival of carnage in which pity is the first man down. We have since learned how to sweeten tragedy, to make it ennobling, but we would do well to remember that *Titus* is the raw material, 'the thing itself', the piling of agony on to a human head until it splits.

It is our English heresy to think of poetry as a gentle

way of saying gentle things. *Titus* reminds us that it is also a harsh way of saying harsh things. Seneca's Stoicism, in which the play is drenched, is a cruel doctrine, but it can rise to moments of supernal majesty. Lear himself has nothing more splendid than :

> For now I stand as one upon a rock,
> Environ'd with a wilderness of sea. . . .

The parallel with Lear is sibling-close, and Peter Brook cleverly strengthens it by having the fly-killing scene performed by a wanton boy. But when all its manifold excellences have been listed, the play still falls oddly short. One accepts the ethical code which forces Tamora to avenge herself on Titus, and then Titus to avenge himself on Tamora; it is the casualness of the killing that grows tiresome, as at a bad bullfight. With acknowledgements to Lady Bracknell, to lose one son may be accounted a misfortune; to lose twenty-four, as Titus does, looks like carelessness. Here, indeed, is 'snip, and nip, and cut, and slish, and slash,' a series of operations which only a surgeon could describe as a memorable evening in the theatre. When there enters a messenger 'with two heads', one wonders for a lunatic instant whether he is carrying them or was born with them.

Much textual fiddling is required if we are to swallow the crudities, and in this respect Mr Brook is as swift with the styptic pencil as his author was with the knife. He lets the blood, one might say, out of the bath. All visible gore is eliminated from the play, so that Lavinia, tongueless and handless, can no longer be likened to ' a conduit with three issuing spouts '. With similar tact Mr Brook cuts the last five words of Titus' unspeakable line, 'Why, there they are both, baked in that pie,' as he serves to Tamora his cannibalistic speciality – *tête de fils en pâte (pour deux personnes)*.

Adorned by a vast, ribbed setting (the work of Mr Brook, designer) and accompanied by an eerie throbbing of *musique concrète* (the work of Mr Brook, composer), the play is now ready for the attentions of Mr Brook, director. The result is the finest Shakespearian production since the same director tackled *Measure for Measure* five years ago. The vocal attack is such that even the basest lines shine, like Aaron the Moor, 'in pearl and gold.' Anthony Quayle plays the latter role with superbly corrupt flamboyance, and Maxine Audley is a glittering Tamora. As Lavinia, Vivien Leigh receives the news that she is about to be ravished on her husband's corpse with little more than the mild annoyance of one who would have preferred foam rubber. Otherwise, the minor parts are played up to the hilt.

Sir Laurence Olivier's Titus, even with one hand gone, is a five-finger exercise transformed into an unforgettable concerto of grief. This is a performance which ushers us into the presence of one who is, pound for pound, the greatest actor alive. As usual, he raises one's hair with the risks he takes. Titus enters not as a beaming hero but as a battered veteran, stubborn and shambling, long past caring about the people's cheers. A hundred campaigns have tanned his heart to leather, and from the cracking of that heart there issues a terrible music, not untinged by madness. One hears great cries, which, like all of this actor's best effects, seem to have been dredged up from an ocean-bed of fatigue. One recognized, though one had never heard it before, the noise made in its last extremity by the cornered human soul. We knew from his Hotspur and his Richard III that Sir Laurence could explode. Now we know that he can suffer as well. All the grand unplayable parts, after this, are open to him : Skelton's Magnificence, Ibsen's Brand, Goethe's Faust – anything, so long as we can see those lion eyes search for solace, that great jaw sag.

(1955)

Henry V

by WILLIAM SHAKESPEARE
at the Old Vic

Harry of Monmouth, butcher and sophist, is a figure hard to love for himself alone. When he protests envy of the common man, who 'all night sleeps in Elysium', we cannot but jeer, for we have just seen three common men kept up till dawn by his persistent quarrelling. By stressing the 'gentle gamester' aspect of the part and delivering the rest as a trumpet voluntary, many actors have been able to blind us to the barbarity of *Henry V*. Richard Burton takes a steeper path. He gives us a cunning warrior, stocky and astute, unafraid of harshness or of curling the royal lip. The gallery gets no smiles from him, and the soldiery none but the scantest commiseration. Though it sometimes prefers rant to exuberance, this is an honest performance, true and watchful and ruthless.

The job of creating sympathy for Henry's cause thus falls to the director, and here Michael Benthall lets us down. Bowing to the 'tradition' inaugurated by Sir Laurence Olivier's film, he presents the French as fluttering mountebanks. Charles VI is a girlish fumbler, the Dauphin an affected lout; this being so, the goal is kept by fops and Henry has nothing to beat. Instead of bearding a pride of lions, the armed might of England is employed to drown a basket of kittens. That the English were a happy few we know, but to stir our hearts they must challenge a triumphant many. We expect splendour from our Frenchmen, a robust assurance, a pomp and a power, not a weedy and beribboned defiance. Great battles may be won on the playing-fields of Eton, but not when the first fifteen is playing the third.

Apart from this central *gaffe*, there is little wrong with the production that a National Theatre and a more experienced company could not cure. Derek Francis's dogged Gower, Dudley Jones's brisk Fluellen, and Job Stewart's Nym, irretrievably glum, are perfect, as is the cosy, care-worn sketch which Rachael Roberts makes of Mrs Quickly. If I devote more space to John Neville, it is because this actor implicitly demands it. He has shown in the past that he has strong and curious views on the play. Some years ago, as Henry V, he gave a compelling performance of Richard II; now, as Chorus, he is giving a princely and effusive performance of Henry V, old style. How the plumbing stands out in his neck! And how romantically he snatches each word from the air! Yet, as Sainte-Beuve said, '*l' éceuil particulier du genre romanesque, c'est le faux*', a remark amplified by the American critic Stark Young when he condemned English actors for 'a certain sweetish piety peculiarly their own and peculiarly false.' Here we recognize Mr Neville, who played so piously to the loftier seats that they begged him, at the end, to take the 'star' curtain. The *compère* who steals the show is by definition a bad *compère*. Mr Neville's failure is pretty, seductive, 'actorish', and complete.

(1955)

Moby Dick

adapted by ORSON WELLES *from*
HERMAN MELVILLE'S *novel*
at the Duke of York's

At this stage of his career it is absurd to expect Orson Welles to attempt anything less than the impossible. It is all that is left to him. Mere possible things, like Proust or *War and Peace*, would confine him. He must choose *Moby Dick*, a book whose setting is the open sea, whose hero is more mountain than man and more symbol than either, and whose villain is the supremely unstageable whale. He must take as his raw material Melville's prose, itself as stormy as the sea it speaks of, with a thousand wrecked metaphors clinging on its surface to frail spars of sense. (You do not dip into Melville, you jump in, holding your nose and praying not to be drowned. If prose styles were women, Melville's would be painted by Rubens and cartooned by Blake: it is a shot-gun wedding of sensuousness and metaphysics.) Yet out of all these impossibilities Mr Welles has fashioned a piece of pure theatrical megalomania – a sustained assault on the senses which dwarfs anything London has seen since, perhaps, the Great Fire.

It was exactly fifty years ago last Wednesday that Irving made his last appearance in London. I doubt if anyone since then has left his mark more indelibly on every second of a London production than Mr Welles has on this of *Moby Dick*. He serves Melville in three capacities: as adapter, as director, and as star. The adaptation, to begin with, is beautifully adroit. Captain Ahab's self-destructive revenge on the albino whale that tore off his leg is over in less than a hundred and fifty minutes. And two brilliant devices reconcile us to the lushness of Melville's style. Firstly, seeing how readily Melville falls into iambic pentameters, Mr Welles has versified the whole action. Secondly, to prepare us for the bravura acting which is to come, he 'frames' the play as a rehearsal held sixty years ago by a tyrannical brandy-swigging American actor-manager. My only criticism must be that role of Pip, the mad cabin-boy, has been rather too heavily expanded. Mr Welles clearly sees Ahab as Lear and Pip as a cross-breed of the Fool and Cordelia, but the duologue between them was a very ponderous affair, not helped by the agonized inadequacy of the actress to whom Pip's ramblings were given.

The real revelation was Mr Welles's direction. The great, square, rope-hung vault of the bare stage, stabbed with light from every point of the compass, becomes by turns the Nantucket wharf, the whalers' chapel, the deck of the *Pequod*, and the ocean itself. The technique with which Thornton Wilder evoked 'Our Town' is used to evoke 'Our Universe'. The whaling-boat from which Ahab flings himself at Moby Dick is a rostrum projecting into the stalls, and the first-act hurricane is a model of imaginative stagecraft: ropes and beams swing crazily across one's vision, while the crew slides and huddles beneath. Mr Welles's films have already established his mastery of atmospheric sound: here the crash and howl of the sea is alternated with a brisk little mouth-organ theme and strange, foreboding chords played on a harmonium. Dialogue is overlapped, words are timed, syllables are pounced on with a subtlety we have not heard since *The Magnificent Ambersons*. Gordon Jackson, a much-neglected actor, gives Ishmael just the right feeling of perplexity, and Patrick McGoohan as Starbuck, the mate who dares to oppose Ahab's will, is Melville's 'long earnest man' to the life, whittled out of immemorial teak. His is the best performance of the evening.

When I say that, I am not excepting Mr Welles, who now comes before us as actor. In aspect, he is a leviathan plus. He has a voice of bottled thunder, so deeply encasked that one thinks of those liquor advertisements which boast that not a drop is sold till it's seven years old. The trouble is that everything he does is on such a vast scale that it quickly becomes monotonous. He is too big for the boots of any part. He reminds one of Macaulay's conversation, as Carlyle described it: 'Very well for a while, but one wouldn't *live* under Niagara.' Emotion of any kind he expresses by thrusting out his chin and knitting his eyebrows. Between these twin promontories there juts out a false and quite unnecessary nose. Sir Laurence Olivier began his film of *Hamlet* with the statement that it was 'the tragedy of a man who could not make up his mind.' At one point Mr Welles's new appendage started to leave its moorings, and *Moby Dick* nearly became the tragedy of a man who could not make up his nose.

Let me now turn about and say that, though Mr Welles plays Ahab less than convincingly, there are few actors alive who could play it at all. Earlier in the evening, as the actor-manager, he makes what seems to be a final statement on the relationship of actor to audience: 'Did you ever', he says, 'hear of an unemployed audience?' It is a good line; but the truth is that British audiences have been unemployed far too long. If they wish to exert themselves, to have their minds set whirling and their eyes dazzling at sheer theatrical virtuosity, *Moby Dick* is their opportunity. With it, the theatre becomes once more a house of magic.

(1955)

La Plume de Ma Tante

at the Garrick

My allegiance to M. Robert Dhéry, the star and author of *La Plume de Ma Tante*, dates from a rainy evening in Paris last winter when I attended a revue of his devising called *Ah! Les Belles Bacchantes!* Within ten minutes I had entered a new dimension of comedy, the dimension of calamity.

Everything in the show went wrong: not loudly wrong but mildly, shiftily, provoking those tiny tremors that plague the nervous system when, in a large quiet room, a small object falls thunderously to the floor. While announcing the first item (a modest scena depicting the creation of the universe), the *compère* paused and stared, without comment but with immense disquiet, at something that was happening on the stage a few feet in front of him. Whatever it was (and he did not explain), it disturbed other members of the troupe as well; they would break off, in the middle of songs and sketches, to contemplate it. Glances of horror would be exchanged, and mute appeals flashed towards the wings. At length the truth transpired: what everyone on stage knew, and had determined to hide from us, was that gas was escaping from the footlights. No action was taken, because by now the cast had other things on its mind: a lion was at large in the backstage corridors, and one of the dressing-rooms was on fire.

M. Dhéry has been presenting shows like this for more than seven years, and I was a late-comer to the cult. In *La Plume de Ma Tante* he and his squadron of harassed Stoics make their London début. Over some of their work, it must be admitted, there hangs a pall of slip-shod improvisation; and they are without their greatest clown, the irreplaceable Louis de Funès. Yet enough remains to throw serious doubt on the English definition of revue as an entertainment in which acid, modish people say acid, modish things. Nothing in the present show is satirical, and nothing is topical – how could it be, since M. Dhéry's sense of humour has no malice and is quite untethered to time and place? If we seek a parallel, we may find it in the films of M. Jacques Tati and nowhere else on earth

The deviser himself takes part, with a touch of Chaplin in his method and of Commedia dell'Arte in his lineage. He treats his company, a bright-eyed troupe to whom ghastly things are constantly happening, with enormous compassion. I am not sure why he introduces M. Christian Duvaleix as 'my brother-in-law, Amsterdam', but when M. Duvaleix slinks ogling into view, the penalty is swift: his electric guitar blows up in his face. At this he betrays absolutely no surprise. Imagine the convulsions with which an English comedian would greet a similar mischance and you have the measure of M. Dhéry's directorial tact, which amounts to a minor revolution in comic technique. Or consider Mlle. Colette Brosset's appearance as an understudy involved in a *pas de deux* with an Eton-cropped ballerina whose interest in her is not exclusively professional; vaguely aghast, Mlle Brosset confides to the audience no more than a single, horrified whisper: 'She must be *mad*!' And I have not yet mentioned the superb M. Jacques Legras, whose face is a fish-mask of utter despair and who eats dog-biscuits for solace; nor would it be fair to omit my delight in the brief item entitled 'Domingo Blazes and His Courageous Latin-American Band'. (Courageous in what sense I do not know, though I suppose it takes courage of a sort to work for a band-leader three feet high.) M. Gérard Calvi's music is wanly haunting, and the dances are led with long-limbed abandon by Mlle. Nicole Parent, who shows in a bullfight ballet that she really knows something about how bulls are fought.

M. Dhéry's speciality is the comedy of disaster, the gaiety of quiet desperation, and because of this he provides the perfect response to the alarming events of our time. He teaches us, when confronted with calamity, to react with only the faintest of shrugs. We may look foolish, but we have kept our dignity. His basic theme is embarrassment, the agony of a man discovered in a moment of private aberration, of anti-social lunacy; and he implies that such lunacy is not only funny, but healthy. I shall often return to the Garrick in the weeks to come, knowing that, however much I may chafe at the passing crudities, there will always be golden moments at which, suddenly and without warning, tears of laughter will stand in my eyes. Either M. Dhéry is a genius or the word has no meaning.

(1955)

Notes on the National Theatre

Since today begins a New Year, it is fitting that the English should be reminded of a resolution that was made in their name on 21 January, 1949. That, as the fervent will remember, was the day of the Giant Step, when the drama received its greatest (and almost its only) official boost since Charles II created the patent theatres. It was the day on which the House of Commons unanimously approved the National Theatre Bill, empowering the Treasury to spend a million pounds on building a home for the nation's drama.

Seven years have passed, and what has become of that august and imaginative resolve? One stone has been regally laid; and that, by mischance, in the wrong place. Having expressed our will, we, the people, left things to them, the National Theatre Executive Committee, and shortly afterwards relapsed into what Matthew Arnold bitterly called 'our favourite doctrines of the mischief of State interference, of the blessedness of leaving every man to do as he likes, of the impertinence of presuming to check any man's natural taste for the bathos and pressing him to relish the sublime.'

Why? Has the theatre forgotten the long passion that brought its dream to the brink of fact? Surely the classic arguments, endorsed always by the few and seven years ago by the many, need no reiteration. Must it again be urged that Britain is the only European country with a living theatrical tradition which lacks a national theatre; and that the public money which gave us a visual library, the National Gallery, is needed just as vitally to provide (in Benn Levy's phrase) a 'living library' of plays? But the points were all made in the Commons debate. The general impotence of our theatre, as opposed to the individual excellence of our actors, is the laughing-stock of the Continent; and it is unthinkable that anyone nowadays would sink to the crassness of saying, as a daily paper did in 1938: 'To have no National Theatre is a tribute to our liberty.' To whom, one wonders, is the following quotation still controversial? 'I consider it a pity, and even a folly, that we do not make some national effort to aid and assist dramatic representation . . . Think with what excitement and interest this people witnesses the construction or launching of a Dreadnought! What a pity it is that some measure of that interest cannot be turned in the direction of the launching, say, of a National Theatre!' The speech from which these extracts are taken was delivered by Sir Winston Churchill in 1906.

Geoffrey Whitworth, the pioneer of the National Theatre, died in 1951; one regrets that he did not live to see and surmount the ironies with which time has festooned his vision. One recalls William Archer and Granville-Barker, in the first flush of certainty, graciously smiling on the idea of a subsidized opera-house, but never doubting for an instant that the theatre would come first, since 'England possesses a national drama but does not as yet possess a national opera'. Well, that was in 1904. We now have a subsidized opera-house; we are soon to have a second concert-hall on the South Bank; and the L.C.C. has just agreed to spend seven million pounds on the 'rehabilitation' of the Crystal Palace. And still that lonely, misplaced stone is all we have of our theatre.

But what, the diehards may ask, will the National Theatre give us that Stratford and the Old Vic do not? Firstly, a really modern theatre, comparable with those abroad and capable of staging the widest variety of plays. Secondly, not a cast of underpaid second-stringers, like the Old Vic, nor yet a starry, short-term band, like Stratford, but a large, experienced, permanent company, drawn from our finest talent and paid accordingly. Of the several objects prescribed for the National Theatre, Stratford and the Old Vic fulfil but one – that of presenting Shakespeare. The others (those of reviving the rest of our classical drama, presenting new plays and the best of foreign drama, and preventing recent plays of merit from rusting in oblivion) have no roof at all over their heads. At the X Theatre the play is good; at the Y, the acting; and the décor at the Z is magnificent. But there is nowhere we can send our guests, confidently saying: 'This is our theatre's best. On this we stand.'

Our theatre has always been dogged by poverty; it is now dangerously close to being bitched by it. In 1880 Matthew Arnold concluded his great germinal essay with the words: 'The theatre is irresistible; organize the theatre!' To which one would add: 'The Act is irresistible; implement the Act!'

(1956)

Othello

by WILLIAM SHAKESPEARE
at the Old Vic

Even in prospect, the double *Othello* of John Neville and
Richard Burton looked fairly black. The roles of Othello
and Iago were to be alternated by two born Cassios : how
could they manage overnight the switch from black outside to black inside? And in part one's qualms were
justified. The Moor came lame from the struggle, as he
must when age is absent. Messrs Burton and Neville are
the youngest Othellos the town has seen this century, and
if they reply that both Garrick and Kean played the part
before reaching thirty, my counter-charge must be that
the audience which swallowed the fourteen-year-old
Master Betty as Hamlet would swallow anything.

Temperament alone is not enough for Othello, nor is
physical beauty. The essence is that unfeignable quality
which some call weight and others majesty, and which
comes only with age. Frederick Valk had it, a great
stunned animal strapped to the rack; but neither Mr
Burton, roaring through his whiskers, nor Mr Neville, a
tormented sheikh, could give the Moor his proper magnitude. In the grace-notes Mr Neville was exemplary, the
moments of sacrificial tenderness; he conveyed, even at the
raging climax, a sense of pain at the treachery of Iago,
whom once he had loved. The part's quiet dawn and its
quiescent sunset were both there. What escaped the actor
was the intervening tempest.

Tuesday's performance, with Mr Burton blacked up and
Mr Neville a capering spiv, was a drab squabble between
the Chocolate Soldier and the Vagabond King. Only the
best things in Michael Benthall's production held one's
attention : Rosemary Harris's Desdemona, a moth of peace
who might profitably have beaten her wings more vigor-
ously, and Richard Wordsworth's Roderigo, a wholly

credible ninny. On Wednesday we were in a different world. Mr Burton was playing Iago, and the production rose to him.

Paradoxically, the only way to play Iago is to respect Othello. Let Iago mock the Moor with cheap laughs, and the play collapses: it becomes the farce of an idiot gull instead of the tragedy of a master-spirit. Mr Burton never underestimates Othello; nor, in consequence, do we. His Iago is dour and earthy enough to convince any jury in the world. He does not simulate sincerity, he embodies it; not by the least wink or snicker does his outward action demonstrate the native act and figure of his heart. The imposture is total and terrifying. Like his author, Mr Burton cares little for the question of Iago's motive: mere jealousy of Cassio's rank is not enough, else why should Iago go on hounding Othello after he has supplanted Cassio? Discarding this, Mr Burton gives us a simple, dirty, smouldering drive towards power without responsibility. With a touch more of daemonism in the soliloquies, this will be an incomparable performance.

We may now define this actor's powers. The open expression of emotion is clearly alien to him: he is a pure anti-romantic, ingrowing rather than outgoing. Should a part call for emotional contact with another player, a contemptuous curl of the lip betrays him. Here is no Troilus, no Florizel, no Romeo. Seeking, as Othello, to wear his heart upon his sleeve, he resorts to forced bellowing and perfunctory sobs. Mr Burton 'keeps yet his heart attending on himself', which is why his Iago is so fine and why, five years ago, we all admired his playing of that other classic hypocrite, Prince Hal. Within this actor there is always something reserved, a secret upon which trespassers will be prosecuted, a rooted solitude which his Welsh blood tinges with mystery. Inside these limits he is a master. Beyond them he has much to learn.

(1956)

The Chalk Garden

by ENID BAGNOLD
at the Haymarket

On Wednesday night a wonder happened: the West End theatre justified its existence. One had thought it an anachronism, wilfully preserving a formal, patrician acting style for which the modern drama had no use, a style as remote from reality as a troop of cavalry in an age of turbo-jets. One was shamefully wrong. On Wednesday night, superbly caparisoned, the cavalry went into action and gave a display of theatrical equitation which silenced all grumblers. This engagement completed, the brigade may have to be disbanded. But at least it went out with a flourish, its banners resplendent in the last rays of the sun.

The occasion of its triumph was Enid Bagnold's *The Chalk Garden*, which may well be the finest artificial comedy to have flowed from an English (as opposed to an Irish) pen since the death of Congreve. Miss Bagnold's style recalls Ronald Firbank's *The Princess Zoubaroff*; it has the same exotic insolence, the same hothouse charm. We eavesdrop on a group of thoroughbred minds expressing themselves in speech of an exquisite candour, building ornamental bridges of metaphor, tiptoeing across frail causeways of simile, and vaulting over gorges impassable to the rational soul.

The heroine of *Zoubaroff*, entreated to wear a smile, replied that it was too hot to wear another thing; and boy met girl with the exchange: 'We slept together' – 'Yes. At the opera. "Bérénice".' Like Firbank, Miss Bagnold evokes a world full of hard, gem-like flame-throwers, a little room of infinite riches. 'Of course I'm affected,' Aubrey Beardsley is rumoured to have said: 'Even my lungs are affected!'; but there is nothing affected, or snobbish, about Miss Bagnold, unless verbal precision is a mark of snobbery.

London gives her the actors she needs. Dame Edith Evans, exasperated by 'this *mule* of a garden,' suggests a crested wave of Edwardian eccentricity vainly dashing itself on the rocks of contemporary life. Peggy Ashcroft is, beautifully, the dumpy governess who leads Dame Edith's granddaughter, a pretty pyromaniac ferociously played by Judith Stott, to forsake the sterility of her grandmother's house and rejoin her errant mama – a role in which Rachel Gurney shows once again how foolish our theatre has been to neglect her.

Something is being said about the necessity of rescuing young people from the aridity of a rich, irresponsible life; but it is being said wittily, obliquely, in a manner that one would call civilized if one thought civilization was worthy of the tribute. *The Chalk Garden* probably marks the end of an era; Miss Stott's farewell to Dame Edith, as irrevocable as Nora's departure in *A Doll's House*, represents the future taking leave of the past. But the past has its joys. In this production (by Sir John Gielgud) we see English actors doing perfectly what few actors on earth can do at all : reproduce in the theatre the spirited elegance of a Mozart quintet.

(1956)

Look Back in Anger

by JOHN OSBORNE
at the Royal Court

'They are scum' was Mr Maugham's famous verdict on the class of State-aided university students to which Kingsley Amis's Lucky Jim belongs; and since Mr Maugham seldom says anything controversial or uncertain of wide acceptance, his opinion must clearly be that of many. Those who share it had better stay well away from

John Osborne's *Look Back in Anger*, which is all scum and a mile wide.

Its hero, a provincial graduate who runs a sweet-stall, has already been summed up in print as 'a young pup', and it is not hard to see why. What with his flair for introspection, his gift for ribald parody, his excoriating candour, his contempt for 'phoneyness', his weakness for soliloquy, and his desperate conviction that the time is out of joint, Jimmy Porter is the completest young pup in our literature since Hamlet, Prince of Denmark. His wife, whose Anglo-Indian parents resent him, is persuaded by an actress friend to leave him; Jimmy's prompt response is to go to bed with the actress. Mr Osborne's picture of a certain kind of modern marriage is hilariously accurate: he shows us two attractive young animals engaged in competitive martyrdom, each with its teeth sunk deep in the other's neck, and each reluctant to break the clinch for fear of bleeding to death.

The fact that he writes with charity has led many critics into the trap of supposing that Mr Osborne's sympathies are wholly with Jimmy. Nothing could be more false. Jimmy is simply and abundantly alive; that rarest of dramatic phenomena, the act of original creation, has taken place; and those who carp were better silent. Is Jimmy's anger justified? Why doesn't he *do* something? These questions might be relevant if the character had failed to come to life; in the presence of such evident and blazing vitality, I marvel at the pedantry that could ask them. Why don't Chekhov's people *do* something? Is the sun justified in scorching us? There will be time enough to debate Mr Osborne's moral position when he has written a few more plays. In the present one he certainly goes off the deep end, but I cannot regard this as a vice in a theatre that seldom ventures more than a toe into the water.

Look Back in Anger presents post-war youth as it really is, with special emphasis on the non-U intelligentsia who live in bed-sitters and divide the Sunday papers into two groups, 'posh' and 'wet'. To have done this at all would be a signal achievement; to have done it in a first play is a minor miracle. All the qualities are there, qualities one had despaired of ever seeing on the stage – the drift towards anarchy, the instinctive leftishness, the automatic rejection of 'official' attitudes, the surrealist sense of humour (Jimmy describes a pansy friend as 'a female Emily Brontë'), the casual promiscuity, the sense of lacking a crusade worth fighting for, and, underlying all these, the determination that no one who dies shall go unmourned.

One cannot imagine Jimmy Porter listening with a straight face to speeches about our inalienable right to flog Cypriot schoolboys. You could never mobilize him and his kind into a lynching mob, since the art he lives for, jazz, was invented by Negroes; and if you gave him a razor, he would do nothing with it but shave. The Porters of our time deplore the tyranny of 'good taste' and refuse to accept 'emotional' as a term of abuse; they are classless, and they are also leaderless. Mr Osborne is their first spokesman in the London theatre. He has been lucky in his sponsors (the English Stage Company), his director (Tony Richardson), and his interpreters: Mary Ure, Helena Hughes, and Alan Bates give fresh and unforced performances, and in the taxing central role Kenneth Haigh never puts a foot wrong.

That the play needs changes I do not deny : it is twenty minutes too long, and not even Mr Haigh's bravura could blind me to the painful whimsey of the final reconciliation scene. I agree that Look Back in Anger is likely to remain a minority taste. What matters, however, is the size of the minority. I estimate it at roughly 6,733,000, which is the number of people in this country between the ages of twenty and thirty. And this figure will doubtless be swelled by refugees from other age-groups who are curious to know precisely what the contemporary young pup is thinking and feeling. I doubt if I could love anyone who did not wish to see Look Back in Anger. It is the best young play of its decade.

(1956)

The Quare Fellow

by BRENDAN BEHAN
at Stratford-atte-Bowe

'Bloddy sparklin' dialogue,' said a pensive Irishman during the first interval of *The Quare Fellow* – and sparkle, by any standards, it amazingly did. The English hoard words like misers; the Irish spend them like sailors; and in Brendan Behan's tremendous new play language is out on a spree, ribald, dauntless, and spoiling for a fight. In itself, of course, this is scarcely amazing. It is Ireland's sacred duty to send over, every few years, a playwright to save the English theatre from inarticulate glumness. And Irish dialogue almost invariably sparkles. But now consider the context of Mr Behan's hilarity. His setting is an Ulster prison, and one of its inmates is shortly to drop, rope-necklaced, through the untender trap.

> *To move wild laughter in the throat of death?*
> *It cannot be: it is impossible.*

But Berowne was wrong. To a countryman of Swift many things are possible, and this among them; this, perhaps, especially.

In adversity the Irish always sparkle. 'If this is how Her Majesty treats her prisoners,' said one of them, hand-cuffed in the rain *en route* for gaol, 'she doesn't deserve to have any.' With this remark of Oscar Wilde's, Mr Behan, who has spent eight years of his life in prison for sundry acts of I.R.A. mischief, entirely agrees; and his protest is lodged in the same spirit of laconic detachment. The Irish are often sentimental about causes and crusades, but they are hardly ever sentimental about human beings. So far from trying to gain sympathy for the condemned man, an axe-murderer known as 'the quare fellow', Mr Behan keeps him off-stage throughout the action. All he shows us is the effect on the prison population of the knowledge that one of their number is about to be ritually strangled.

There are no tears in the story, no complaints, no visible agonies; nor is there even suspense, since we know from the outset that there will be no reprieve. Mr Behan's only weapon is a gay, fatalistic gallows-humour, and he wields it with the mastery of Ned Kelly, the Australian bandit, whose last words, as the noose encircled his neck, were: 'Such is life.' Mr Behan's convicts behave with hair-raising jocularity, exchanging obscene insults even while they are digging the murderer's grave. An old lag feigns a bad leg in order to steal a swig of methylated spirits; a newcomer anxious to raise bail is blithely advised to 'get a bucket and bail yourself out.' Even the hangman is presented serio-comically as a bowler-hatted publican with a marked addiction to the wares he sells. The tension is intolerable, but it is we who feel it, not the people in the play. We are moved precisely in the degree that they are not. With superb dramatic tact, the tragedy is concealed beneath layer after layer of rough comedy.

Meanwhile, almost imperceptibly, the horror approaches. Two warders, chosen to share the murderer's last eight hours of life, thoughtfully discard their wrist-watches in anticipation of his inevitable demand: What time is it? His last letters are thrown unopened into his grave: better there than in the Sunday papers. Dawn breaks, accompanied by the ghastly, anguished clatter of tin cups and plates against iron bars that is the tribute traditionally paid by the thousand convicts who will see tomorrow to the one who will not. The empty exercise yard now falls silent. The hush is broken by a unique *coup de théâtre*, Mr Behan's supreme dramatic achievement. An unseen humorist, bawling from some lofty window, embarks on an imaginary description, phrased as racily as a Grand National commentary, of the hundred-yard dash from condemned cell to scaffold. They're coming into the straight now; the chaplain's leading by a short head. . . . A young warder, new to the ceremony, faints and is carried across the stage for treatment. A sad, bawdy ballad filters through from the punishment block. The curtain falls, but not before we have heard the swing and jerk of the drop. I left the theatre feeling overwhelmed and thanking all the powers that be for Sydney Silverman.

John Bury's two sets exactly capture the aridity of confinement. And Joan Littlewood's production is the best advertisement for Theatre Workshop that I have yet seen: a model of restraint, integrity, and disciplined naturalism. Glynn Edwards, Brian Murphy, and Maxwell Shaw, as three of Her Majesty's guests, and Dudley Foster, as one of the same lady's uniformed hosts, stand out from an inspired all-male company. Miss Littlewood's cast knows perfectly well what it is doing. She must now devote a few rehearsals to making sure that we can understand precisely what it is saying. That done, *The Quare Fellow* will belong not only in such transient records as this, but in theatrical history.

(1956)

Timon of Athens

by WILLIAM SHAKESPEARE
at the Old Vic

The best that can be said of Michael Benthall's production of *Timon of Athens* is that its cuts and transpositions are clever. The rest is aimless improvisation. Leslie Hurry's settings are as coarse as his costumes, a dissonance of sequins, Pepsi-Cola purple, and desiccated mud. And to those who imagined the play to be a study of benevolence warped by ingratitude, Mr Benthall administers a succinct slap: it is, by his curious lights, the story of a scoutmaster betrayed by his troop. To the role of the scoutmaster Sir Ralph Richardson brings his familiar attributes: a vagrant eye, gestures so eccentric that their true significance could be revealed only by extensive trepanning, and a mode of speech that democratically regards all syllables as equal. I select, for instance, Sir Ralph's thanks to the Amazons for enlivening his feast. 'You have added,' he said distinctly, 'worth, and toot, and lustre.' It took a trip to the text to reveal that 'and toot' meant 'unto't.' Yet there was in his performance, for all its vagueness, a certain energy, and it was a relief to hear Timon's later tirades spoken with irony instead of fury. The stone-throwing scene with Apemantus was the best thing of the night.

Some of the junior members of the troop carry on very oddly: killingly painted and draughtily dressed, they besiege one with an epicene intensity. Mr Benthall must really curb his love of moralizing. In a play set in Greece, there is no need to plug so savagely the reasons which pious historians adduce to explain the fall of Rome. As Sydney Smith said when Mrs Grote tried to lure him to the theatre. 'All this class of pleasures inspires me with the same nausea as I feel at the sight of rich plum-cake or sweetmeats; I prefer the driest bread of common life.'

(1956)

The Good Woman of Setzuan

by BERTOLT BRECHT
at the Royal Court

'What is style?' asked Cocteau, and answered: 'For many people, a very complicated way of saying very simple things. According to us, a very simple way of saying very complicated things.'

Many local critics have roundly consigned *The Good Woman of Setzuan* to the first category. Why, they demand, does Brecht need three hours, fourteen scenes, and thirty actors to prove that poor people are often a grasping lot? And, indeed, if that were all he was

saying, we could write the play off and turn to something more important – a musical, perhaps, needing
three hours, fourteen scenes, and thirty actors to say
precisely nothing. But in fact the rapacity of the poor
is a point made only in the play's first act. Shen Te,
a genial harlot whose goodness the gods reward with
a large cash prize, is instantly fleeced by the neighbours
she has been enjoined to love, and is saved from bank-
ruptcy only by the ruse of inventing and impersonating
a ruthless male cousin named Shui Ta.

So far, so simple. Now watch the plot proliferate,
burgeoning into paradoxes that only a simpleton could
find simple. Shen Te falls in love with a shiftless airman who needs money to buy himself a job, and how
better can she supply it than in the guise of the go-
getting Shui Ta? Only this time it is not she alone who
suffers: she raises the money, but learns that 'you
cannot help one poor man without trampling down
twelve others.' Pregnant and deserted, betrayed by two
kinds of love, she devotes herself to a third – love
for her unborn child, to safeguard whose future she once
more summons Shui Ta. With fearful results: she rapidly
becomes the richest inhabitant of Setzuan, and the most
diligently hated.

The final trial scene is one of those high moments
of art when character and symbol coalesce. Shui Ta is
accused of murdering Shen Te. 'You were her greatest
enemy!' shouts an angry peasant. 'I was her only friend,'
is the sad reply. Irony as august, as bitterly conclusive,
as this is seldom heard anywhere, least of all in the
theatre. A fallacy has been exposed: that of seeking to
be perfect in an imperfect society. Hastily mumbling
a few vague exhortations, the gods who rewarded Shen
Te nip back to heaven. Their commandments clearly
don't work – but whose will? Must good ends always
be achieved by base means? An epilogue, rashly omitted
in the present production, poses the question to the
audience, inviting it to choose between changing human
nature and changing the world. Brecht implies, of course,

a Marxist solution: let us change human nature *by* changing the world; and China embarked on just such an experiment several years after he wrote the play.

First fill a man's stomach and then talk to him about morality — that is Brecht's springboard, as it was in *The Threepenny Opera*; but the new dive is far more sophisticated. Macheath, after all, was a criminal; Shui Ta causes far more pain without ever breaking the law. Rather the opposite: 'he' is regarded by the authorities as a pillar of society. Similarly, the worthless pilot earns promotion in Shui Ta's sweat-shop by an impeccably moral act; he refuses to accept from a kindly time-keeper more money than is his due, and thereby wins the boss's eternal respect. This is a scene of the most biting subtlety.

At every turn emotion floods through that celebrated dam, the 'alienation-effect'. More and more one sees Brecht as a man whose feelings were so violent that he needed a theory to curb them. Human sympathy, time and again, smashes his self-imposed dyke: when Shen Te meets her airman on a park-bench in the rain; when she learns (disguised as Shui Ta) that he means to abandon her; when, alone on the stage, she shows her unborn son the glory of the world; and, most poignantly, at the close, when she begs the gods for aid and enlightenment.

In George Devine's production the great challenge is partly muffed. Honourably bent on directing his cast along cool, detached Brechtian lines, Mr Devine forgets that the Brechtian method works only with team-actors of great technical maturity. With greener players it looks like casual dawdling. Conscious of my heresy, I wish he had chosen an easier style and presented the play as a sort of *Teahouse of the October Revolution*. Teo Otto's tubular setting would still have fitted, and Eric Bentley's clumsy translation would, I hope, have come in for drastic revision. Anything would be preferable to hearing Mr Bentley's Americanisms spoken with North Country inflexions.

Peggy Ashcroft, in the taxing central role, is only halfway fine. As Shui Ta, flattened by a tight half-mask which helps her to produce a grinding nasal voice, she is superb; nothing tougher has been heard since Montgomery last harangued the troops. Yet her Shen Te won't do. Sexily though she blinks, all hints of whorish earthiness are expunged by those tell-tale Kensingtonian vowels. What remains is a portrait of Aladdin as it might be sketched by Princess Badroulbadour.

All the same, the production must not be missed by anyone interested in hearing the fundamental problems of human (as opposed to Western European) existence discussed in the theatre. In the context of our present prosperity, these problems may appear irrelevant. They are still cruelly relevant to more than half of the inhabited world.

(1956)

Precious Lillie

Debrett's Peerage, a thick, comely, and infallible volume, correctly refers to Beatrice Gladys Lillie by her married name, Lady Peel. *Who's Who in the Theatre* is also thick and comely, but it is not quite infallible, and one of the most fallible things about it is its habit, in edition after edition, of describing Miss Lillie as an 'actress'. Technically, I suppose the blunder might be defended, since she has been known to impinge on the legitimate stage; in 1921 she appeared in *Up in Mabel's Room* and eleven years later played the Nurse in Shaw's *Too True to Be Good*. But these were transient whims. To call her an actress first and foremost is rather like calling Winston Churchill a bricklayer who has dabbled in politics. If acting means sinking your own personality into somebody else's, Beatrice Lillie has never acted in her life. There may be some mechanical means of disguising that true and tinny voice, or of suppressing that cockeyed nonchalance; but the means might very well involve the use of masks and gags, and the end would not be worth it. She would never be much good at impersonation. One of her recurrent delusions is that she is a mistress of dialects, but in fact the only one she has really mastered is her own brand of Berkeley Square Canadian; and she can hardly open a door on stage without squaring up to the operation as if she were about to burgle a safe.

To some extent, an actress can be judged by measuring her performance against the character she is meant to be playing; but there is nothing against which to measure Miss Lillie. She is *sui generis*. She resembles nothing that ever was, and to see her is to experience, every time, the simple joy of discovery that might come to an astronomer who observed, one maddened night, a new and disorderly comet shooting backwards across the firmament. But if she is not an actress, no more is she a parodist, as some of her fans insist; she parodies nothing and no one except herself. Nor does she belong in the main stream of North American female comics. Almost without exception, American comediennes get their laughs by pretending to be pop-eyed, man-hunting spinsters. Miss Lillie is as far removed from these as a butterfly is from a guided missile. The miracle is that this non-acting non-satirist has managed to become the most achingly funny woman on earth.

Twentieth-century show business has a small and incomparable élite: the streamlined international entertainers of the twenties and thirties. Noël Coward, Gertrude Lawrence, Maurice Chevalier, Alfred Lunt and Lynn Fontanne were among the founder-members of this shining and exclusive gang. Miss Lillie is the Commonwealth representative. She was born fifty-eight years ago in Toronto, the second daughter of John Lillie, a volatile Irish schoolmaster who had served in the British Army under Kitchener. The first recorded event in her life was her summary ejection, at the age of eight, from the choir of the local Presbyterian church. It seems she upset the congregation by pulling faces during the hymns.

Both her father, who died in 1933, and her mother, who lives in a Thames-side house near London, achieved an early and lasting tolerance of their child's eccentricities. Sensing that she had something to express, but not knowing exactly what it was, they sent her to a man named Harry Rich – of whom nothing else is known – for lessons in gesture. She loathed the lessons, but they stuck, and many of the odder poses in which she nowadays finds herself are directly attributable to Mr Rich.

At fifteen she left school and embarked with her mother and sister for England, with the idea of becoming a child soprano. Her official repertoire included such ballads as 'I Hear You Calling Me' and 'Until', but secretly she and her sister Muriel were rehearsing something a little wilder, entitled 'The Next Horse I Ride On I'm Going to Be Tied On.' This clandestine seed was later to bear lunatic fruit; for the moment, however, it got nowhere.

Her career as a straight singer languished until the summer of 1914, when she was engaged for a week at the Chatham Music Hall on the outskirts of London. Here she sang Irving Berlin's 'When I Lost You', and the audience reaction indicated that she had lost them for good. Without much hope, she attended an audition held by the Anglo-French impresario André Charlot. Idly, she guyed a serious romantic number, smiled wanly, and was about to leave the theatre when Charlot, in a state verging on apoplexy, seized her arm and offered her forty-two dollars a week to appear in his next revue, *Not Likely!* She accepted, and soon the panic was on. Charlot adored and fostered the madness of her method, constantly giving her bigger spots, and it was under his banner that she made her triumphant Broadway début in *Charlot's Revue of 1924.*

Around this time she had her hair cut off, for reasons that may give some hint of the devious way her mind works. With Michael Arlen, H. G. Wells, Frederick Lonsdale, and Lonsdale's two daughters, she was cruising on Lord Beaverbrook's yacht. The Lonsdale girls were close-cropped, and Miss Lillie, who favoured plaits, was powerfully impressed by the advantages of short hair for swimming. Back in London she ordered her coiffeur to give her what would be now known as a brush cut. Only when he had finished did it occur to her that there was more to life than swimming. For a while she wore false plaits attached to her ears by rubber bands. One day the elastic snapped, and she has remained, ever since, cropped for immersion. Nowadays she hides her hair beneath a bright pink fez. There is no good reason for this, either. It is just one *idée fixe* on top of another.

Meanwhile, she had fallen in love. In 1920 Robert Peel, a young and toweringly handsome great-grandson of Sir Robert Peel, resigned his commission in the Guards and married Charlot's zany soubrette. They spent a raffish honeymoon at Monte Carlo, winning $25,000 at the tables a few hours after arriving and losing $30,000 a few hours before departing. In 1925 Robert's father, the fourth baronet, died, and Miss Lillie became Lady Peel. Her husband, a man of devouring energies, was at various times a sheep farmer in Australia and a race-horse owner in England. During the slump he generously formed an orchestra of unemployed miners and toured the country with it, often losing as much as £500 a week. He died in 1934, leaving one son. Eight years later the young Sir Robert, who had just passed his twenty-first birthday, was killed when the British destroyer *Hermes* was sunk by Japanese dive bombers in the Indian Ocean. His mother received the news in a Manchester dressing-room, where she was putting on make-up to appear in a new Cochran revue. It is one of the paradoxes of the theatre that though every actor's ambition is to stop the show, his instructions are that it must go on. The revue went on that night with Miss Lillie clowning on schedule and wishing herself ten thousand miles away. Thereafter an inner withdrawal took place; since her son's death she has entered into no binding personal relationships with anyone.

In forty years on the stage she has been seen in nearly forty shows, many of them bearing prankish, exclamatory titles like *Cheep!* and *Oh! Joy!* and most of them remembered chiefly for her part in them. Apart from the war years, when she sang for the troops in the Mediterranean area, she has seldom been far away from the big money. The movies have intermittently attracted her, but, like Coward and the Lunts, she has never thought of depending on them for a living. Pre-war residents of Hollywood remember her vividly, swinging an enormous handbag within which there rattled a motley haul of jewellery known as 'The Peel Poils'. For a talent so deeply spontaneous, the stage was always the best place. In New York, just before the war, she was paid $8,000 for a week at the Palace, and today one imagines even Las Vegas baulking at her cabaret fee.

Her title sits drolly on her, like a tiara on an emu, and for a certain kind of audience there is an irresistible savour in the spectacle of a baronet's wife shuffling off to Buffalo. There have, however, been moments of embarrassment. In 1936, billed as Lady Peel, Miss Lillie appeared in an Ohio city and rashly chose as her opening number a travesty of a suburban snob. 'Ladies and gentlemen,' she began, 'I'm sure you will appreciate what a comedown this is for me – me that's always 'ad me own 'orses. . . .' Few acts can have fallen flatter. Many women in the house began to sniff audibly, and at the end of the monologue, according to Miss Lillie, some attempt was made to take a collection to sustain her in her fight against poverty.

Offstage she leads a fairly intense social life and has arguably slept through more hours of daylight than of dark. Her conversation is an unpunctuated flow of irrelevancies which only acute ears can render into sense. As a maker of epigrams her rating is low. It is rumoured that she once said of a tactless friend that 'he doesn't know the difference between tongue-in-cheek and foot-in-mouth', but remarks like that need a degree of premeditation to which she is a stranger. She excels at the casual impromptu, as when a pigeon flew in at the window of her apartment and she, looking up, briskly inquired: 'Any messages?' To surprise her friends, she will go to considerable lengths. Her last Christmas present to Noël Coward was a baby alligator, to whose neck she attached a label reading: 'So what else is new?' Last year she stood for several hours on a draughty street corner in Liverpool in order to wave maniacally at the Duke of Edinburgh as he drove by with the Queen. She received from the carriage a royal double-take, which she regarded as ample compensation. At parties, with a little pressing, she will try out her newest hallucinations, nursery rhymes villainously revamped or bizarre attempts at mimicry; I once saw her spread-eagled on top of an upright piano, pretending to be Marilyn Monroe.

Some of her leisure time is spent painting, a difficult art for which she has evolved impossible working habits. 'I do children's heads out of my nut,' she told an interviewer. 'I paint on the floor and show my work on the piano in the dark. I call myself Beatrice Van Gone.' She habitually uses as canvases the cardboard lids of laundry boxes. One of her sitters was the child actor Brandon de Wilde. He is also one of her closest confidants. Whenever Miss Lillie is in New York, she calls up Brandon and the two journey to Coney Island, where they frequently end up in the Tunnel of Love. A radio commentator once asked Brandon what Miss Lillie did in the tunnel. 'It's very dark in there,' the child explained, as to a child, 'so naturally she doesn't do anything.' De Wilde's ingenuous imagination appeals strongly to Miss Lillie, who has a great deal of urchin in her and very little *grande dame*. She also has the kind of knockdown spontaneity that one associates with Zen masters, together with something much more mysterious – that ambiguous, asexual look that so often recurs among the greatest performers.

Her last show, *An Evening with Beatrice Lillie*, took three-quarters of a million dollars at the Broadway box office three seasons ago, and then ran for eight successful months in Britain. It enshrined her art in what seems likely to be its final form. The rebuke to Maud for her rottenness, the lament about wind round my heart – they were all there, presented with a relaxed finesse that astonished even her oldest eulogists. She looked like Peter Pan as Saul Steinberg might sketch him, and the only phrase for her face was one that a French critic used many years ago to describe Réjane – 'une petite frimousse éveillée,' which means, in James Agate's rough translation, 'a wide-awake little mug.' A supreme economy distinguished all she did. By twirling four Oriental fingers, she could imply a whole handspring, and instead of underlining her gags in red pencil she could bring down the house with a marginal tick. For any line that struck her as touching on the sentimental she would provide a withering facial comment, as if to say (the expression is one of her pets): 'Get me!' She would survey the audience with wintry amazement, until it began to wonder why it had come; she would then overwhelm it with some monstrous act of madness, such as wearing an osprey feather fan as a hat, banging her head against the proscenium arch, or impersonating Pavlova and a roller-skating bear, one after the other, in a sketch bearing no relation either to ballet or zoology.

Once, in an effort at self-analysis, she said: 'I guess it's my nose that makes them laugh,' but the explanation is as perfunctory as the nose. One thing is certain: she wrecks the old theory that all great clowns have a breaking heart. Miss Lillie has no more pathos than Ohrbach's basement. Nothing on stage seems to her tragic, though many things arouse in her a sort of cool curiosity. If a ton of scenery were to fall at her feet, she would regard the débris with interest, but not with dismay; after a light shrug and a piercing little smile, she would go on with whatever she was doing. (In wartime this insouciance was a rare asset. Quentin Reynolds, who was often her companion during the blitz, testifies that in the midst of the bombing her demeanour was positively sunny.) She reminds one of a bony, tom-boyish little girl attending what, if her behaviour does not improve, will surely be her last party. Her atti-tude toward events, if she has one, might be summed up in the comment: 'Hmmmm. . . .'

I have two theories about her: one about what she does, and another about the way she does it. What she has been doing for the last forty years is conducting guerrilla warfare against words as a means of communi-cation. Having no message to convey, she has no need of language as most of us understand it, so she either abandons words altogether or presents them in com-binations aberrant enough to crack a ouija board. Faced with the drab possibility of consecutive thought, she draws herself up to her full lunacy. She will do anything to avoid making sense – lapse into a clog dance, trap her foot under an armchair, or wordlessly subside beneath the weight of a mink coat.

Mime attracts her as an alternative to words. This imperial urchin can let winsome candour, beady-eyed tartness, and appalled confusion chase each other across her face in a matter of seconds. Consider the frosty, ap-praising regard she bestows on the waistcoat of the huge baritone who suddenly interrupts her act to sing 'Come into the Garden, Maud' straight down her throat. Though she takes an early opportunity to seize a chair in self-defence, she betrays none of her apprehension in words.

The traditional comic formula is: Tell them what you're going to do; do it; then tell them you've done it. Miss Lillie's is: Tell them what you might do; do something else; then deny having done it. Even the famous purchase of the double-damask dinner napkins embodies her basic theme: the utter futility of the English language. Nobody is a more devout anthologist of the whimpers, sighs, and twitters that the human race emits in its historic struggle against intelligibility. It is not surprising that she turns to French when deliver-ing her demented salute to the home life of cats: '*Bon-*

jour, all the little kittens all over the world!' When someone in another number fails to understand a question, she tries German, brusquely demanding: '*Sprechen Sie Deutsch?*' And once, into a Cockney sketch already obscured by her inability to speak Cockney, she inserted a sudden moan of Italian. If ever a monument is erected to her, it should be modelled on the Tower of Babel. She is like Eliza Doolittle at Mrs Higgins's tea party in *Pygmalion*, using what seems to her perfectly acceptable verbal coinage but to everyone else counterfeit gibberish. In certain moods she becomes quite convinced that she is an authority on bird talk. Coward once wrote for her a comic folk song that contained the line: 'And the robin sings ho! on the bough.' Every time she reached it she would pause. 'The robin,' she would firmly declare, 'does *not* say ho.'

In 1954, on a trip to Japan, she visited the Kabuki Theatre and was fascinated by what she saw: the colour, the weirdness, and the elaborate stylization. The idea of using Kabuki technique in a sketch at once took hold of her mind, and she was not in the least perturbed when someone pointed out that British audiences (for whom the sketch was intended) might be slightly befuddled by a parody of something they had never seen. Following instinct, she devised a number called 'Kabuki Lil'. When it was still in the formative stage, by which I mean a condition of nightmarish inconsequence, she described it to me:

'These Kabuki plays, you see, they go on for six months with only one intermission. All the women are men, *of course*, and they're simply furious most of the time, waving swords round their heads and *hissing* at each other. They take off their boots when they come on, and kneel down on cushions. There's a lot of work done with cushions, so I shall have cushions too. And they play some kind of musical instrument that goes right round the back of my neck, only one string, but I expect I shall manage. I don't think I shall say a word of English – after all, *they* don't – but I wish I could get hold of one of those terrific rostrums they have in Tokyo that sail right down the aisle and out of the theatre. I think they have rollers underneath them, or perhaps it's men? Anyway, I think I've got the spirit of the thing. . . .'

Something was dimly taking shape in the chaos of her mind, but what emerged on stage was beyond all imagining. It varied notably from night to night, but the general layout remained the same. Miss Lillie shuffled on attired as a geisha, with a knitting needle through her wig and a papoose strapped to her back. After performing some cryptic act of obeisance, she sat cross-legged on a pile of cushions. Thereafter, for about ten minutes, she mewed like an asthmatic sea gull : the sketch contained not one recognizable word. Tea was served at one point, and the star produced from her sleeve a tiny bottle of Gordon's gin with which to spike it. From time to time she would grasp a hammer and savagely bang a gong, whereupon music would sound, jittery and Oriental. This seemed to placate her; until the sixth bang, which evoked from the wings a sudden, deafeningly amplified blast of 'Three Coins in the Fountain', sung by Frank Sinatra.

It was while watching this sketch, so pointless, yet so hysterical, that I hit on the clue to her method. I reveal it without hesitation, because I do not believe that anyone could copy it. The key to Beatrice Lillie's success is that she ignores her audience. This is an act of daring that amounts to a revolution. Maurice Chevalier was speaking for most of his profession when he said in his autobiography : 'An artist carries on throughout his life a mysterious, uninterrupted conversation with his public.' To get into contact with the dark blur of faces out front is the Holy Grail of every personality performer except Miss Lillie, who converses not with her public but with herself. Belly laughter, for which most comedians sweat out their life's blood, only disconcerts her; it is an intrusion from another world. She is uniquely alone. Her gift is to reproduce on stage the grievous idiocy with which people behave when they are on their own: humming and mumbling, grimacing at the looking glass, perhaps even singing into it, hopping, skipping, fiddling with their dress, starting and stopping a hundred trivial tasks – looking, in fact, definably batty. At these strange pursuits we, the customers, peep and marvel, but we are always eavesdroppers; we never 'get into the act'.

The theatre is Miss Lillie's hermitage. It is an empty room in which she has two hours to kill, and the audience, like Alice, is 'just a thing in her dream'. She is like a child dressing up in front of the mirror, amusing herself while the grownups are out. The fact that we are amused as well proves that she has conquered the rarest of all theatrical arts, the art of public solitude, which Stanislavsky said was the key to all great acting. To carry it off, as she does, requires a vast amount of sheer nerve and more than a whiff of genius, which is really another word for creative self-sufficiency. One might add that it probably helps to have had experience, at an early age, of pulling faces in church.

Her future, like her act, seldom looks the same from one day to the next. She would like to take her solo show to South America and Asia, with a split week in Tibet, where she feels she has many fans. A musical has been written for her, based on the life of Madame Tussaud. Its title, which she finds hauntingly seductive, is *The Works*. But wherever her choice falls, the queues will form. There is no substitute for this magnetic sprite. She alone can reassure us that from a theatre increasingly enslaved to logic the spirit of unreason, of anarchy and caprice, has not quite vanished.

(1956)

The Caucasian Chalk Circle and Mother Courage

by BERTOLT BRECHT

Trumpets and Drums

adapted by BERTOLT BRECHT from GEORGE FARQUHAR'S The Recruiting Officer

at the Palace

When the house-lights went up at the end of *The Caucasian Chalk Circle,* the audience looked to me like a serried congress of tailor's dummies. I probably looked the same to them. By contrast with the blinding sincerity of the Berliner Ensemble, we all seemed unreal and stagey. Many of us must have felt cheated. Brecht's actors do not behave like Western actors; they neither bludgeon us with personality nor woo us with charm; they look shockingly like people – real potato-faced people such as one might meet in a bus-queue.

Let me instance the peasant wedding in *The Caucasian Chalk Circle,* a scene more brilliantly directed than any other in London. A tiny cell of a room, ten by ten, is cumulatively jammed with about two dozen neighbours and a sottish monk. The chances for broad farce are obvious, but they are all rejected. Reality is preferred, reality of a memorable and sculptural ruggedness. I defy anyone to forget Brecht's stage pictures. No steps or rostra encumber the platform; the dominant colours are browns and greys; and against a high, encircling, off-white back-cloth we see nothing but solid, selected objects – the twin gates in *The Caucasian Chalk Circle* or Mother Courage's covered wagon. The beauty of Brechtian settings is not of the dazzling kind that begs for applause. It is the more durable beauty of *use*.

The same applies to the actors. They look capable and practical, accustomed to living in the open air. Angelica Hurwicz is a lumpy girl with a face as round as an apple. Our theatre would cast her, if at all, as a fat comic maid.

Brecht makes her his heroine, the servant who saves the governor's child when its mother flees from a palace rebellion. London would have cast a gallant little waif, pinched and pathetic: Miss Hurwicz, an energetic young woman too busy for pathos, expresses petulance where we expect her to 'register' terror, and shrugs where other actresses would more likely weep. She strengthens the situation by ignoring its implications: it is by what it omits that we recognize hers as a great performance.

As Eric Bentley said, 'Brecht does not believe in an inner reality, a higher reality or a deeper reality, but simply in reality.' It is something for which we have lost the taste: raised on a diet of gin and goulash, we call Brecht ingenuous when he gives us bread and wine. He wrote morality plays and directed them as such, and if we of the West End and Broadway find them as tiresome as religion, we are in a shrinking minority. There is a world elsewhere. 'I was bored to death,' said a bright Chelsea girl after *Mother Courage*. 'Bored to life' would have been apter.

The famous 'alienation effect' was originally intended to counter-balance the extravagant rhetoric of German classical acting: to a debauched emotionalism, Brecht opposed a rigorous chastity. *Mother Courage* cries out for rich and rowdy performances. Brecht has staged it in a style light, swift, and ironic. In the central part Helene Weigel is never allowed to become a bawdy and flamboyant old darling: her performance is casual and ascetic: we are to observe but not to embrace her. Twice, and agonizingly, she moves us: elsewhere, even in Paul Dessau's magnificent songs, we must never sympathize with Mother Courage. She has battened on the Thirty Years' War, and must suffer for her complicity by losing her daughter and both her sons. But the clearest illustration of the 'A-effect' comes in the national anthem, which the Berliner Ensemble have so arranged that it provokes, instead of patriotic ardour, laughter. The melody is backed by a trumpet *obbligato* so feeble and pompous that it suggests a boy bugler on a rapidly sinking ship. The orchestration is a criticism of the lyrics, and a double flavour results, the ironic flavour which is 'A-effect'.

Irony crops up throughout *Trumpets and Drums*, Brecht's expansion of Farquhar's *The Recruiting Officer*, advanced by a hundred years so as to coincide with the American Revolution. This involves propaganda, but it is propaganda as blithe and irrefutable as the remark made by an American wit on first seeing the playing-fields of Eton : 'Here,' he cried, 'is where the battle of Yorktown was lost!' Farquhar's text has been surveyed by cool new eyes, against the larger vista of England at war, and there is evidence that the director (Benno Besson) does not find enforced recruitment particularly hilarious.

Captain Plume is the kind of role in which, formerly, John Clements was wont to cut a charming dash. Dieter Knaup plays him realistically, as a sallow and calculating seducer. The costumes look as if people and not puppets had worn them, and the settings, shiny Hogarthian etchings suspended on wires, are amusing without being 'amusing'. And to show that Brecht can throw his bonnet over the windmill, we have Wolf Kaiser as Captain Brazen, who does just that, entering every time with a new hat which he whips off and flings irretrievably over the nearest rooftop.

Is it mere decadence that makes us want more of this, more attack, more abandon? I think not. Brecht's rejection of false emotions sometimes means that the baby is poured out with the bath-water : the tight-wire of tension slackens so much that the actors fall off, and instead of single-mindedness, we have half-heartedness. Yet as a corrective he is indispensable. It is possible to enter the Palace Theatre wearing the familiar British smile of so-unsophisticated-my-dear-and-after-all-we've-rather-*had*-Expressionism (what *do* such people think Expressionism was?) and it is possible to leave with the same faint smile intact. It is possible : but not pleasant to contemplate.

(1956)

End of a Twelvemonth

At this time of thanksgiving and convalescence, when all is hushed save for the gentle pop of bursting facial capillaries, it is somehow fitting that we should look back on the past year and on to the new. (We can uncross our eyes later.)

1956 was full of good theatrical auguries. At the Comedy Theatre the Lord Chamberlain was smilingly flouted, while from the Royal Court there issued a distinct sound of barricades being erected. The Berliner Ensemble came, was seen, and overcame; and Angus Wilson, Nigel Dennis, Dylan Thomas, Brendan Behan, and Eugène Ionesco were exposed for the first time to London audiences. Tyrone Guthrie made *Troilus and Cressida* seem like a new play, and Edith Evans made *The Chalk Garden* seem like a classical revival. Fewer people forgave John Gielgud for appearing in *Nude with Violin* than would have forgiven him five years ago. And the play of the year, over which families were split in almost the same way as they were split over Suez, was John Osborne's *Look Back in Anger*, an oasis of reality, as Arthur Miller rightly said, in 'a theatre hermetically sealed off from life'.

By putting the sex war and the class war on to one and the same stage, Mr Osborne gave the drama a tremendous nudge forward. Much of modern thought outside the theatre has been devoted to making Freud shake hands with Marx; within the theatre they are mighty incompatibles. Social plays are traditionally sexless, and plays about sex are mostly non-social. Jimmy Porter is politically a liberal and sexually a despot. Whether we like him or not, we must concede that he is a character with a full set of attitudes, towards society as well as personal relations. Others may solve Jimmy's problem : Mr Osborne is the first to state it. No germinal play of comparable strength has emerged since the war.

Assuming that the year's good things bear fruit, what else can one predict for 1957? A lot, quite safely. Someone will present a play about a homosexual athlete with a millionaire father, whereupon many citizens will write to the papers mysteriously complaining that they get enough of that sort of thing in everyday life without going to the theatre for it. A new play by J. B. Priestley will have its *première* in Danzig. A famous actor, drawing on the rich experience of having played two modern roles in ten years, will declare that the Stanislavsky method ('all this soul-searching and pretending to be a lettuce') is ruining modern drama. The London Shakespeare method will meanwhile ruin fifty-six young actors, several of whom will be signed on for a second season at the Old Vic. A farce entitled *Giblets on Parade* will begin a four-year run at the Whitehall Theatre. Noël Coward will announce the successful completion of his five-hundredth Atlantic crossing.

The establishment of drama chairs at English universities will be triumphantly opposed on the grounds that the practical study of drama neither encourages nor requires intellectual discipline: by this means will be perpetuated the philistine myth that drama is best when most brainless. The suggestion that actors, like singers, should keep in training will be dismissed as a transatlantic extravagance, like good plumbing; and the virtues of muddling through will be illustrated by reference to the Elizabethan theatre. ('So far as actors are concerned, they, as I noticed in England, are daily instructed, as it were in a school, so that even the most eminent actors have to allow themselves to be instructed by the dramatists, which arrangement gives life and ornament to a well-written play . . .' – Johannes Rhenanus, writing in 1613.) In spite of everything, about four good native plays will be performed and supported. None of them, however, is likely to deal seriously with Suez, Cyprus, Kenya, the United Nations, the law, the armed forces, Parliament, the Press, medicine, jazz, the City. English cities outside London, or London postal districts outside the S.W. and

N.W. areas. Two thousand wish-fulfilling plays will be written about life after the next war. Ten will be staged. One will be good.

(1957)

The Entertainer

by JOHN OSBORNE
at the Royal Court

Camino Real

by TENNESSEE WILLIAMS
at the Phoenix

Mr Osborne has had the big and brilliant notion of putting the whole of contemporary England on to one and the same stage. *The Entertainer* is his diagnosis of the sickness that is currently afflicting our slap-happy breed. He chooses, as his national microcosm, a family of run-down vaudevillians. Grandad, stately and retired, represents Edwardian graciousness, for which Mr Osborne has a deeply submerged nostalgia. But the key figure is Dad: Archie Rice, a fiftyish song-and-dance man reduced to appearing in twice-nightly nude revue. This is the role that has tempted Sir Laurence Olivier to return to the Royal Court after twenty-nine years.

Archie is a droll, lecherous fellow, comically corrupted. With his blue patter and jingo songs he is a licensed pedlar of emotional dope to every audience in Britain. The tragedy is that, being intelligent, he knows it. His talent for destructive self-analysis is as great as Jimmy Porter's. At times, indeed, when he rails in fuddled derision at 'our nasty sordid unlikely little problems', he comes too close to Jimmy Porter for comfort or verisimilitude. He also shares the Porter Pathological Pull towards bisexuality, which chimes with nothing else in his character, though it may be intended to imply that he has made a sexual as well as a moral compromise.

But I am carping too soon. To show the ironic disparity between Archie's mind and the use he makes of it, Mr Osborne has hit on a stunningly original device. He sets out the programme like a variety bill, and switches abruptly from Archie at home, insulated by gin, to Archie on stage, ogling and mincing, joshing the conductor, doing the chin-up bit and braying with false effusiveness such aptly named numbers as 'Why Should I Bother to Care?' 'We're All Out for Good Old Number One', and 'Thank God We're Normal.' In these passages, author, actor, and composer (John Addison) are all at peak form. A bitter hilarity fills the theatre, which becomes for a while England in little: 'Don't clap too hard, lady, it's an old building.'

Archie has abdicated from responsibility. He despises his wife, sleeps out nightly, and morally murders his father by coaxing him back into grease-paint: yet he can still button-hole us with songs and routines that enjoin us to share the very couldn't-care-less-ness that has degraded him. The death of his son, kidnapped and killed in Egypt, restores him for a while to real feeling. He has just been reminiscing, with drunken fervour, about a Negress he once heard singing in a night-club, making out of her oppression 'the most beautiful fuss in the world.' Now, shattered himself, he crumples, and out of his gaping mouth come disorganized moans that slowly reveal themselves as melody. Archie the untouchable is singing the blues.

With Sir Laurence in the saddle, miracles like this come often. At the end of the first act Archie is struggling to tell his daughter about the proudest encounter of his life, the one occasion when he was addressed with awe. 'Two nuns came towards me,' he says. 'Two nuns. . . .' All at once he halts, strangled by self-disgust. The curtain falls on an unfinished sentence. Sir Laurence brings the same virtuosity to Archie's last story, about a little man who went to heaven and, when asked what he thought of the glory, jerked up two fingers, unequivocally parted. The crown, perhaps, of this great performance is Archie's jocular, venomous farewell to the audience: 'Let me know where you're working tomorrow night – and I'll come and see *you*.'

When Archie is offstage, the action droops. His father is a bore and his children are ciphers: the most disquieting thing about the play is the author's failure to state the case of youth. There is a pacifist son who sings a Brechtian elegy for his dead brother, but does little else of moment. And there is Jean, Archie's daughter, a Suez baby who came of age at the Trafalgar Square rally but seems to have lost her political ardour with the passing of that old adrenalin glow. She is vaguely anti-Queen and goes in for loose generalities like 'We've only got ourselves'; beyond that, *nada*. Rather than commit himself, Mr Osborne has watered the girl down to a nullity, and Dorothy Tutin can do nothing with her.

This character, coupled with Archie's wife (Brenda de Banzie, bedraggled-genteel), reinforces one's feelings that Mr Osborne cannot yet write convincing parts for women. He has bitten off, in this broad new subject, rather more than he can maul. Although the members of Archie's family incessantly harangue each other, they seldom make a human connection, and you cannot persuade an audience that people are related simply by making them call each other bastards. Tony Richardson's direction is fairly lax throughout, but I cannot see how any director could disguise either the sloth of the first act or the over-compression of the third.

In short: Mr Osborne has planned a gigantic social mural and carried it out in a colour range too narrow for the job. Within that range he has written one of the great acting parts of our age. Archie is a truly desperate man, and to present desperation is a hard dramatic achievement. To explain and account for it, however, is harder still, and that is the task to which I would now direct this dazzling, self-bound writer.

Tennessee Williams's *Camino Real* is likewise microcosmic, but in a stricter sense; it takes on the whole world.

The message shrieked by Mr Williams's garish symbols is that life is diseased and curable only by innocence. It issues from a dingy, timeless coastal town where Spanish is spoken, the police are in charge, and 'hermano' is a dirty word. On one side of the plaza is a hotel for decayed romantics such as Casanova; on the other, a squalid flophouse where people like the Baron de Charlus find what is modishly known as their adjustment. The proles are kept happy by frequent festivals, among them a burlesque fertility rite wherein a tart is ceremonially declared a virgin. Idealism is mirrored in Don Quixote, emblem of the pure romantic quest, and in Kilroy, a vagrant American prize-fighter who loves people so perilously much that the police force him to dress up as a clown.

At this stage the play goes off the rails. Its middle stretch is devoted to the tedious courtship of Casanova and Marguérite Gautier; and when we get back to Kilroy, it is merely for a comic seduction scene with the pseudo-virgin – gay in itself, but essentially irrelevant. He finally decides to venture, with Quixote, into the desert that surrounds the town's sleazy chaos, but by then we have stopped taking him seriously. Mr Williams has beckoned us into too many gaudy sideshows. Some of his inventions are extremely bright – Freda Jackson as a gipsy brothel-keeper, Ronald Barker as her beskirted bouncer, Elizabeth Seal as her daughter, who thinks, feels, and wears as little as the law will allow – but they do not really advance the author's simple thesis: that purity can survive corruption as long as it gets the hell out.

There are three attitudes that a serious writer can adopt towards the world. He can mirror its sickness without comment; he can seek to change it; or he can withdraw from it. Mr Williams, by recommending withdrawal, places himself in the third batch, along with the saints, the hermits, the junkies, and the drunks. The attitude is defensible, but it somehow sounds better in diaries and autobiographies than in a place as social and public as a theatre.

About Peter Hall's direction, however, I have no doubts,

and this despite a Kilroy (Denholm Elliott) who can manage neither the accent nor the dumbness of the part. Judged as a frenetic pageant, a circus of noise and colour, a three-ring freak show, the production generates an excitement that London has not felt in a theatre since the early extravagances of Peter Brook. The use of sound – nasal bullfight music and bleating fairground spiels – is especially striking. Mr Williams, champion of the fly-blown, the man who sold solitude to the gregarious, has never found in London a director half so bold, half so loyal.

(1957)

Requiem for a Nun

by WILLIAM FAULKNER
at the Royal Court

The curtain has just fallen on William Faulkner's *Requiem for a Nun*. It has been performed with imposing devoutness by Ruth Ford, Bertice Reading, Zachary Scott, and John Crawford. The production (by Tony Richardson) and the settings (by Motley) have been austerely hieratic. Let us now imagine that there steps from the wings the Stage Manager of Thornton Wilder's *Our Town*. Pulling on a corn-cob pipe, he speaks.

S.M.: 'Well, folks, reckon that's about it. End of another day in the city of Jefferson, Yoknapatawpha County, Mississippi. Nothin' much happened. Couple of people got raped, couple more got their teeth kicked in, but way up there those faraway old stars are still doing their old cosmic criss-cross, and there ain't a thing we can do about it. It's pretty quiet now. Folk hereabouts get to bed early, those that can still walk. Down behind the morgue a few of the young people are roastin' a nigger over an open fire, but I guess every town has its night-owls, and afore long they'll be tucked up asleep like anybody else. Nothin' stirring down at the big old plantation house – you can't even hear the hummin' of that electrified barbed-wire fence, 'cause last night some drunk ran slap into it and fused the whole works. That's where Mr Faulkner lives, and he's the fellow that thought this whole place up, kind of like God. Mr Faulkner knows everybody round these parts like the back of his hand, 'n' most everybody round these parts knows the back of Mr Faulkner's hand. But he's not home right now, he's off on a trip round the world as Uncle Sam's culture ambassador, tellin' foreigners about how we've got to love everybody, even niggers, and how integration's bound to happen in a few thousand years anyway, so we might just as well make haste slowly. Ain't a thing we can do about it.

(He takes out his watch and consults it.)

Along about now the good folk of Jefferson City usually get around to screamin' in their sleep. Just ordinary people havin' ordinary nightmares, the way most of us do most of the time.

(An agonized shrieking is briefly heard.)

Ayeah, there they go. Nothin' wrong there that an over-dose of seconal won't fix.

(He pockets his watch.)

Like I say, simple folk fussin' and botherin' over simple, eternal problems. Take this Temple Stevens, the one Mr Faulkner's been soundin' off about. 'Course, Mr Faulkner don't pretend to be a real play-writer, 'n' maybe that's why he tells the whole story backwards, 'n' why he takes up so much time gabbin' about people you never met – and what's more, ain't going to meet. By the time he's told you what happened before you got here, it's gettin' to be time to go home. But we were talkin' about Temple. Ain't nothin' special about her. Got herself mixed up in an auto accident – witnessed a killin' – got herself locked up in a sportin' house with one of those seck-sual perverts – witnessed another killin' – got herself married up 'n' bore a couple of fine kids. Then, just's she's fixing to run off with a blackmailer, her maid Nancy – that's the nigger dope-fiend she met in the cathouse – takes a notion to murder her baby boy. That's all about Temple – just a run of bad luck that could happen to anyone. And don't come askin' me why Nancy murders the kid. Accordin' to Mr Faulkner, she does it to keep him from bein' tainted by his mother's sins. Seems to me even an ignorant nigger would know a tainted child was better'n a dead one, but I guess I can't get under their skins the way Mr Faulkner can.

(He glances up at the sky.)

Movin' along towards dawn in our town. Pretty soon folks'll start up on that old diurnal round of sufferin' and expiatin' and spoutin' sentences two pages long. One way or another, an awful lot of sufferin' gets done around here. 'Specially by the black folk – 'n' that's how it should be, 'cause they don't feel it like we do, 'n' anyways, they've got that simple primitive faith to lean back on.

(He consults his watch again.)

Well, Temple's back with her husband, and in a couple of minutes they'll be hangin' Nancy. Maybe that's why darkies were born – to keep white marriages from bustin' up. Anyways, a lot of things have happened since the curtain went up tonight. Six billion gallons of water have tumbled over Niagara Falls. Three thousand boys and girls took their first puff of marijuana, 'n' a puppy-dog in a flyin' coffin was sighted over Alaska. Most of you out there've been admirin' Miss Ruth Ford's play-actin' 'n' a few of you've been wonderin' whether she left her pathos in the dressing-room or whether maybe she didn't have any to begin with. Out in Hollywood a big producer's been readin' Mr Faulkner's book and figurin' whether to buy the movie rights for Miss Joan Crawford. Right enough, all over the world, it's been quite an evening. 'N' now Nancy's due for the drop.

(A thud offstage. The Stage Manager smiles philosophically.)

Ayeah, that's it – right on time.

(He re-pockets his watch.)

That's the end of the play, friends. You can go out and push dope now, those of you that push dope. Down in our town there's a meetin' of the Deathwish Committee, 'n' a fund-raisin' rally in aid of Holocaust Relief, 'n' all over town the prettiest gals're primping themselves up for the big beauty prize – Miss Cegenation of 1957. There's always somethin' happenin'. Why – over at the schoolhouse an old-fashioned-type humanist just shot himself. *You* get a good rest, too. Good-night.'

> *(He exits. A sound of Bibles being thumped moment-arily fills the air.)* (1957)

The Iceman Cometh
by EUGENE O'NEILL
at the Arts

Cat on a Hot Tin Roof
by TENNESSEE WILLIAMS
at the Comedy

Paul Valéry once defined the true snob as a man who was afraid to admit that he was bored when he was bored; and he would be a king of snobs indeed who failed to admit to a *mauvais quart d'heure* about halfway through *The Iceman Cometh*. But perhaps, as a colleague suggests, all great art should be slightly boring. A vast structure is to be built, and in the long process there are bound to be moments of tedium: they are the price we pay for size and splendour, and we pay it gladly once the architect has convinced us that we can trust him. O'Neill convinced last Wednesday's audience in thirty minutes flat, after which no doubts remained. This was no crank, planning a folly dependent on sky-hooks: we were safe in the hands of the American theatre's nearest counterpart to Frank Lloyd Wright.

But how did he hold us in our seats through four hours and more of circular alcoholic conversation? By means of verbal magic? I think not. O'Neill writes clumsily and top-heavily. He never achieves the luminous, crystallizing phrase, nor has he the opposite virtue of earthy authenticity: his gin-mill dialogue has the stagey swagger of melodrama. If it isn't the language, then, is it the universality of the theme? Again, no. Most of the characters are special cases, confirmed alcoholics out of touch with any kind of reality that cannot be bottled. When Hickey, the reformed drunk, urges these red-eyed wet-brains to abandon their pipe-dreams and face the truth about themselves, we know that the cure will kill them; but we cannot relate this knowledge to our own lives as we can, for instance, when Gregers Werle strips Ekdal of his illusions in *The Wild Duck*. Many of us, like Ekdal, have a darkroom of the soul where we develop dreams that the light of day would obliterate. But very few of us actually live in the dark-room, so enslaved to our fantasies that we would rather have D.T.s than give them up.

No, what holds us about the play is the insight it gives us into O'Neill himself. It is a dramatized neurosis, with no holds barred, written in a vein of unsparing, implacable honesty. 'Speak, that I may see thee,' said Ben Jonson; and when O'Neill speaks, he hides nothing. Instead of listening to a story, we are shaking hands with a man, and a man whose vision of life is as profoundly dark as any since Aeschylus. It is this autobiographical intensity that grips us throughout the *longueurs* of the narrative and the gawkiness (I had almost said Gorkiness) of the style. For O'Neill, a pipe-dream is not just one alternative to despair: it is the only alternative. His bar-room derelicts comfort and sustain one another as long as each tolerates the other's illusions. Once Hickey has removed the illusions, nothing remains but guilt and mutual accusation. One may not agree with O'Neill's conclusions, but one cannot escape the look in his eye, which is as magnetic as the Ancient Mariner's. He speaks like a man who has touched bottom himself; for whom words like 'inferior' no longer have meaning. He is one of the few writers who can enter, without condescension or contempt, the world of those whom the world has rejected.

The play demands and gets superb direction. Peter Wood's production is better in many respects than the New York version I saw and admired last spring. Like all good directors, Mr Wood is loyal to the text; he is also constructively disloyal to the hysterical punctuation and overheated stage-directions of which American playwrights are so fond. His cast deserves individual attention. Nicholas Meredith plays a cashiered Blimp, making a character out of a caricature by discreet understatement; Lee Montague is funny, dour, and truthful as an Italian barkeep who cannot bring himself to admit that he is also a pimp; and Jack MacGowran, pinch-faced and baggy-trousered, plays the tetchy proprietor with a weasel brilliance I have not seen since the heyday of F. J. McCormick. In the sketchily written role of a drunken Harvard alumnus, Michael Bryant gets closer to the raw nerve of reality than any West End débutant I can remember. The pale, shaky smile, the carefully preserved sophistication, the glib, hectic delivery all converge to make a rounded, original whole, half clown, half martyr.

Of the three central characters, Patrick Magee does not quite get the rock-sombre melancholy of Larry, the disgusted nihilist who has deserted anarchism for drink: but the other two are perfect – Vivian Matalon as a guilty young stool-pigeon, pathetically ripe for suicide and Ian Bannen as Hickey, the manic salesman, driving his friends to destruction with the enthusiasm of a revivalist. I winced a bit at the Kensington cosiness of Mr Wood's three waterfront tarts. Otherwise, the production is flawless. It makes a wonderfully worrying evening.

By a useful coincidence, *Cat on a Hot Tin Roof* also explores the impact of truth on illusion, the difference being that where O'Neill thinks pipe-dreams necessary, Tennessee Williams condemns them under the generic heading of 'mendacity'. A world war separates the two plays. In jazz terms, *The Iceman Cometh* (1939) is a collective improvisation on a traditional blues theme. *Cat on a Hot Tin Roof* (1954) belongs to the modernist school, its three acts being in essence three long introspective solos (by, respectively, Maggie, Big Daddy, and Big Mama), accompanied throughout by the ground-bass of Brick's pervasive melancholy.

The first act lays bare a breaking marriage: Brick, the liquor-loving son of a Southern millionaire, can no longer sleep with Maggie, his wife. The second act tells us why, in the course of a scorching duologue between father and son which reveals that Brick is a latent homosexual, consumed with guilt because he spurned a college friend who loved him and died, shortly after the spurning, of drink. Brutally reacting to this harsh dose of truth, Brick ripostes in kind, and Big Daddy learns what the rest of the family already knows: that he is suffering from inoperable cancer. In the last act the relations gather round Big Mama to batten on the inheritance. Maggie wins it by pretending to be pregnant. To support her lie, Brick must sleep with her; and thus mendacity breeds mendacity.

A magnificent play: but modern jazz, to pursue the metaphor, calls for much greater technical virtuosity than Dixieland. Williams's quasi-tragedy needs superlative soloists, superlatively directed. After seeing Peter Hall's production I feel I owe an apology to Elia Kazan. I still prefer the author's third act (here played for the first time) to the modified version approved by Mr Kazan; but I missed, more than I would ever have thought possible, the galvanic inspiration of Mr Kazan's direction. Mr Hall's pace is lethargic: he stresses everything except what needs stressing. General sloth may account for the cutting of (among others) Big Daddy's best speech; but I cannot think what could account for the omission of the play's last vital line, in which Brick ironically queries Maggie's protestations of love, unless it was the inadequacy of the actor playing the part. Paul Massie, to whom I refer, is callow and absurdly unprepared for a searching test like Brick. All the same, he ought to have been allowed to utter, however lamely, the final clinching statement of the play.

Leo McKern, with crudely padded shoulders, uses enormous vocal exertions to become Big Daddy; but the more he tries, the more he fails, for the whole point about the character is that his cynical, animal zest should flow without effort. Which leaves us with Kim Stanley, the gifted Broadway actress who plays Maggie the Cat. Miss Stanley has all the qualities for the part, an anxious lyricism, a limpid voice, tear-puffed eyes, and indomitable gallantry; but, as pregnant women are said to be eating for two, she found herself quite early on acting for four. It was like watching a first-rate squash player hammering away at a court without walls.

(1958)

Epitaph for George Dillon

by JOHN OSBORNE and ANTHONY CREIGHTON
at the Royal Court

The second act of Epitaph for George Dillon, written four years ago by John Osborne and Anthony Creighton, contains a long duologue which in terms of human contact and mutual exploration is better than anything in Mr Osborne's later unaided works. One of the participants is Dillon himself, a farouche young actor-dramatist currently sponging on a suburban family straight out of Mr Coward's Fumed Oak. (Subject for a thesis: estimate the influence on Mr Osborne's later plays of The Vortex and Red Peppers, also bearing in mind that the dismissive use of 'little', favoured by Mr Osborne in a plethora of phrases beginning 'nasty little', 'feeble little', 'sordid little', etc., was pioneered by Mr Coward in the twenties.) Dillon has walked out on his wife, a prosperous actress whom he venomously accuses, à la Jimmy Porter, of having 'betrayed' him. In his new suburban bolt-hole he meets, as Jimmy never did, his intellectual match.

This is Aunt Ruth, the family outsider, whose life has hit the emotional doldrums. She has just ended two affairs, one of them with Communism and the other with a young writer skilled in the neurotic art of extorting love by means of pathos. The job of playing Marchbanks to her Candida is temporarily vacant. George volunteers for the part, and the scene in which they come to grips (or, rather, fail to come to grips) is an object lesson in meaty, muscular, dramatic writing.

Ruth, the born giver, slowly recognises in George a born taker. He savages her cliché-ridden family, whom he regards as part of a universal conspiracy to destroy him. 'I attract hostility,' he declares in a paranoid ecstasy, 'I'm on heat for it.' (Note the female sexual image: one would love to let a good analyst loose on George.) Whenever he goes too far, he resorts to spasms of little-boy charm and bursts of comic improvisation; but though Ruth laughs with him and is sorry for him, she has lived through such scenes before. No more of that sickness for her; no more diving to the rescue of people who scream for help while lying in puddles, achieving by the pretence of drowning a voluptuous fusion of self-pity and power over others. George's only justification for his behaviour is his talent. But where, as Ruth piercingly reminds him, is the evidence that he has any talent at all? And at length George admits to a terrible doubt. He has all the popular symptoms of genius, but perhaps not the disease itself. The admission, however, cuts no ice with Ruth, and George has to console himself by jumping into bed with her teenage niece.

Up to this point, apart from a few glaring crudities in the handling of flashbacks, the play is entirely successful – powerful, honest, and transfixing. The spirit of suburbia is lovingly captured in Stephen Doncaster's setting and the performances of Alison Leggatt, Wendy Craig, and especially Avril Elgar, whose dowdy spinster daughter, merry as a jerboa, is twin sister to Alec

Guinness's unforgotten Abel Drugger. William Gaskill's direction drives shrewdly throughout.

Yvonne Mitchell, though she lacks the years for the part, plays Ruth with a steely, sad directness that is exactly right; and one could not wish for a better George than Robert Stephens, one of the new 'red-brick actors', neither actorish in aspect nor conventionally po-voiced, to whom the English Stage Company has introduced us. Mr Stephens makes George both wolfish and wan, and there is in his voice a cawing note that may even have been modelled on Mr Osborne himself. This is the cleverest portrait I have seen of a certain kind of neurotic artist.

But what kind? Good or bad? And this is where the authors let us down. In the third act George makes one of his plays a provincial hit by spiking it with sex; simultaneously he recovers from an attack of T.B. and agrees to marry Ruth's niece, who is pregnant by him. He ends in tears. But are they the tears of a good writer frustrated by the commercial theatre and suburban morality? Or the tears of a bad writer who has at last met himself face to face? We are given no clue. If George is seriously intended to be a persecuted genius, then the whole play, not just the hero, is paranoid to the point of hysteria. If, on the other hand, he is a mediocre writer forced at length to accept his own mediocrity, it is a play of astounding courage and strength. The authors shrug and allow us to guess which answer is right, which is as if one were to write a play about the crucifixion of a miracle healer without giving the smallest hint as to whether the cures worked. Have we been rooting for a phoney or the real thing? The mere fact of doubt indicates that the play has misfired. Yet the fire is there, boiling and licking, however neurotically; and you must not miss that second act.

(1958)

The Potting Shed

by GRAHAM GREENE
at the Globe

The time is ten years hence, a decade after the London opening of Graham Greene's *The Potting Shed*. A Failed Drama
Critic lies abed in his dingy lodgings, up to here in
Scotch. Around him are the bleak and grimy symbols
of his faith – the cobwebbed bust of Brecht, the mil-
dewed model of the National Theatre, the yellowing
autograph of Stanislavsky, the drab little pot of clotted
Eulogy, the rusty Panning Pen. He looks somehow void
and empty, though of course, as we know, he is up to
here. A young Psychiatrist is interrogating him.

P.: But in that case why do you still go to the theatre?

C. (*simply, if indistinctly*): It's my job. Once a critic,
always a critic. It's my half of the promise. Sometimes I fall down during the Anthem and disappear for
acts on end, and then they have to take my pen away
for a while. But I always come back. The people need
critics, and a whisky-critic's better than none.

P.: Even if he's lost his vocation?

C.: Even then. But don't misunderstand me. I'm not
a bad critic. I go through the motions. I get out of bed
every day at seven o'clock in the evening and go to
the theatre. Sometimes there isn't a play on, but I go
anyway, in case I'm needed. It's a matter of conscience.
Have another slug of fire-water.

P.: Not just now. Can you remember exactly where
you lost your faith? When did you last have it with
you?

C.: I didn't lose it. It was taken away from me one
night ten years ago at the old Globe Theatre, before
they turned it into a car-park. John Gielgud was in the
play. Very wrought-up he was, very curt and brusque –
you know how he used to talk to other actors as if

215

he was going to tip them? Irene Worth played his ex-wife. Then there was Gwen Ffrangcon-Davies, very fierce, and a clever little pouter called Sarah Long. And Redmond Phillips – he played a frocked sot on the brink of the shakes. He was the best of a fine lot. No, you couldn't complain about the acting. But somehow that made it worse. (*He sobs controllably.*)

P. (*controllingly*): Tell me about the play. Force yourself back into the theatre. Slump now as you slumped then in D16.

C. (*in a hoarse whisper*): Graham Greene wrote it. It began with the death of a famous atheist, head of a rationalist clan. Greene made them out to be a bunch of decrepit puritans, so old-fashioned that they even enjoyed the company of dowdy dullards like Bertrand Russell. But fair enough: Greene's a Catholic, and the history of Catholicism shows that you can't make an omelette without breaking eggheads. Anti-intellectual jokes are part of the recipe. At first I thought I was in for a whodunit. The old man's son – Sir John – was kept away from the death-bed because of something nameless that had happened to him in the potting shed at the age of fourteen. There were clues all over the place. For one thing, he had recently lost his dog. . .

P. (*shrewdly*): Dog is God spelled backwards.

C.: The same crude thought occurred to me, but I rejected it (pity my complexity) as being unworthy of the author. How wrong I was! The hero's subsequent investigations into his past revealed that we were indeed dealing not with a whodunit but a God-dunit. He had hanged himself in the dread shed, and demonstrably died. And his uncle, the priest, had begged God to revive him. Make me an offer, haggled the Deity. My faith in exchange for the boy's life, said the priest: and so the repulsive bargain was struck. The boy lived, and uncle lost his faith. My first impulse on hearing these farcical revelations was to protest by the only means at my disposal: a derisive hiccup. But then I looked about me and saw row after row of rapt, attentive faces. *They were taking it seriously!* And suddenly, in a blaze of darkness, I knew that my faith in the theatre and the people who attend it had been withdrawn from me.

P.: But why?

C.: You may not now remember the theatre as it was ten years ago. It seemed on the brink of renaissance. I was one of many who were newly flushed with a great conviction. We recklessly believed that a theatre was a place where human problems could be stated in human terms, a place from which supernatural intervention as a solution to such problems had at long last been ousted. Drama for us was an affirmation of humanism, and its basic maxim was not: 'I die that you may live,' but: 'I *live* that you may live.' *The Potting Shed*, financed by two normally intelligent managements at a highly reputable theatre, shot us back overnight to the dark ages.

P.: But what about Gibbon? 'The Catholic superstition, which is always the enemy of reason, is often the parent of the arts'?

C.: Art that is not allied with reason is today the enemy of life. And now you must excuse me. You have kept me in bed long after my usual time for getting up. And I have a first-night to attend. The play, I understand, is a fearless indictment of a priest who refuses to accompany a murderer to the scaffold because of stupid, heretical, rationalist doubts about the efficacy of prayer to bring the man back to life. The bounder will no doubt be shown his error. Meanwhile (*he takes a deep draught of red-eye*), here's to good old G.G.! Who said the Pope had no divisions? (*He departs, half-clad and half-cut, to perform in a spirit of obedient humility the offices laid down for him by providence and the Society of West End Theatre Managers.*)

(1958)

A Resounding Tinkle and *The Hole*

by N. F. SIMPSON
at the Royal Court

Two years ago last Tuesday there was no English Stage Company. What a dull theatre we must have had! And what on earth did we playgoers find to argue about? After only two years I can scarcely remember the theatrical landscape as it was before George Devine set up shop in Sloane Square and called in John Osborne, the Fulham flamethrower, to scald us with his rhetoric. The climate, on the whole, was listless. We quarrelled among ourselves over Brecht and the future of poetic drama; in debates with foreign visitors we crossed our fingers, swallowed hard, and talked of Terence Rattigan; but if we were critics, we must quite often have felt that we were practising our art in a vacuum.

In two years and twenty-eight productions the Royal Court has changed all that. To an extent unknown since the Ibsen riots, it has made drama a matter of public controversy. It has button-holed us with new voices, some of them bawdy, many of them irreverent, and all of them calculated to bring gooseflesh to the evening of Aunt Edna's life. It has raised hackles, Cain, laughs, and the standards of English dramaturgy. It has given the modern repertoire a permanent London address. At times, perhaps, it has appealed too exclusively to the *côterie*-votaries (Chelsea offshoots of the North American culture-vultures). Yet in spite of this it has reached out and captured popular audiences on television and Broadway and in the West End. Once or twice, quite spectacularly, the Court has fallen on its face, but this is one of the occupational hazards you must expect if you set out to climb mountains. For the most part it has given my mind a whetstone, and my job a meaning, that the English theatre of five years ago showed few signs of providing. If (and the if is crucial) it can hold its present nucleus of talent together, it may very well change the whole course of English drama.

It has celebrated its second birthday by giving us a present: a dazzling new playwright. On the strength of his double bill, *A Resounding Tinkle* and *The Hole*, I am ready to burn my boats and pronounce N. F. Simpson the most gifted comic writer the English stage has discovered since the war. The first of his two plays, which has been drastically cut and revised since it won a third prize in *The Observer* competition, I reviewed when the Court gave it a Sunday showing last year. I indicated its affinities with M. Ionesco, M. Dhéry, and the late Robert Benchley. I tried to explain how and why it had convulsed me, this casual surrealist sketch of a suburban couple with an elephant at their front door; and, had space allowed, I would have applied to Mr Simpson what Sir Max Beerbohm said of humorists in general:

> The jester must be able to grapple his theme and hang on to it, twisting it this way and that, and making it yield magically all manner of strange and precious things, one after another, without pause. He must have invention keeping pace with utterance. He must be inexhaustible. Only so can he exhaust us.

But I wondered at the time how Mr Simpson would follow his *tour de force*. Could he bring it off again without repeating himself? *The Hole* proved triumphantly that he could; that he was no mere flash in the pen, but a true lord of language, capable of using words with the sublime, outrageous authority of Humpty Dumpty.

People who believe with John Lehmann that English writers have lost interest in verbal and stylistic experiment should see Mr Simpson's work and recant. Indeed, everyone should see it: for it is not a private highbrow joke, but pure farce, wild and liberated, on a level accessible to anyone who has ever enjoyed the radio Goons (Peter Sellers and Spike Milligan, especially) or treasured the memory of W. C. Fields. I suspect, in fact,

that Goon lovers, who are accustomed to verbal fireworks displays at which logic is burnt in effigy, may get
more sheer pleasure out of Mr Simpson than professional
intellectuals, against whose habit of worrying about the
meaning of things the play is essentially directed. At
heart it is a riotous satire at the expense of people who
deal in pigeon-holes, categories, and generalizations, seeking to pin down to a consistent pattern the unrepeatable
variety of human existence, working out comprehensive
philosophic and religious systems in which somehow one
vital thing gets forgotten: the glorious uniqueness of
everything that is.

A tramp, who describes himself as 'the nucleus of a
queue', is peering into a hole in the road. Others join
him, among them a rabid authoritarian, a drifting rub-
berneck, and a student philosopher: each has a fantastic
vision of what is going on down the hole and tries to
impose it on the others. They are interrupted, from time
to time, by two housewives, one with a husband who
desperately wants to be the same as everyone else
('There's nothing Sid wouldn't do to be *identical* with
somebody'), the other with a husband who wants, equally
desperately, to be different. . . . But here I must stop,
for I am falling into the very trap Mr Simpson has
laid for us intellectuals. I am explaining instead of experiencing. And I am in danger of letting you forget
that Mr Simpson is ceaselessly, mortally, and unpredictably funny. With Michelet, he cries: *'Mon moi! Ils
m'arrachent mon moi!'* – and if that is bourgeois individualism, long may it thrive.

(1958)

Variations on a Theme

by TERENCE RATTIGAN
at the Globe

Let us suppose that Terence Rattigan's Muse, a brisk, tweedy travelling representative of Thalia-Melpomene Co-Productions Ltd, has just returned home after four years' absence. We find her reading the reviews of Mr Rattigan's *Variations on a Theme*. After a while she flings them impatiently down. Her tone, as she addresses us, is querulous.

MUSE: This would never have happened if I'd been here. We get *Separate Tables* launched, I go off on a world cruise, and as soon as my back's turned, what happens? He tries to write a play on his own. Oh, he's threatened to do that before now, but I've always scared him out of it. 'Look what happened to Noël Coward,' I'd say. *That* usually did the trick. 'Just you wait till I'm ready,' I'd say. 'Inspiration doesn't grow on trees, you know.' But Master Terence Slyboots knows better. Thinks you can write plays just like that, haha. The minute I heard what he was up to I came beetling back, but they were already in rehearsal.

'What's the meaning of this?' I said, and I can tell you I was blazing. 'Well, darling,' he said, 'four years is a long time, and – ' 'Don't you darling me,' I said. 'I'm a busy Muse. I've got my other clients to consider. You're not the only pebble on the Non-Controversial Western Playwrights' beach, you know. Now let's get down to cases. What's this play about?' 'Well,' he said, 'the central character, who's rich and bored and lives in a villa near Cannes, gets desperately fond of a cocky young boy from the local ballet company, and – ' 'Hold your horses,' I said. 'We've never had a play banned yet, and, by George, we're not starting now. Make it a cocky young *girl*.' 'The central character,' he said, very hoity-toity, 'is a *woman*.'

Black mark to me, I must admit. But once I'd grabbed hold of the script and taken a good dekko at it, my worst fears were confirmed. About the best you could say about it was that it wouldn't be banned. This heroine (he calls her Rose Fish and then, if you please, makes jokes about whether or not she has gills) started out as a typist in Birmingham. She's married four men for money before she meets this ballet-boy. He's been keeping company with a male choreographer, but give the devil his due, Master Terence knows his Lord Chamberlain well enough to keep *that* relationship platonic.

Egged on by the choreographer, Rose gives the lad up for the good of his career. He reforms overnight, but returns to her just as she's in the last throes of succumbing to a wonky lung. And in case you haven't cottoned on to the fact that it's Marguérite Gautier all over again, Rose has a daughter whose pet author is Dumas *fils*. Master Terence makes no bones about his sources. Trouble is, he makes no flesh either. That's where I should have come in. Honestly, I could slap the scamp.

'Interesting subject, don't you think?' he said when I gave the script back to him. 'No,' I said, 'but you've made a real Camille of it, haven't you?' He ignored my barbed word-play. Ruthlessly I pressed on. 'Whatever became', I asked, 'of that subtle theatrical technique of yours we hear so much about? T.B., indeed, in this day and age! And making the boy symbolically sprain his ankle. And having Rose leave her farewell message to him on a tape-recorder. And giving her a *confidante* I'd have been ashamed to wish on Pinero. And what about that Sherman lover of hers who is talking the so comic English? If you'd written the play well, it would have been bad enough. As it is – ' 'I thought the theme would carry it,' he said, 'a young boy living off an older woman.' That made me plain ratty. 'You're not Colette,' I said, 'and don't you think it.'

Anyway, I've told Master Terence that from now on

he can whistle for his Muse. I'm not going to come crawling back to him. He thinks the play will succeed in spite of me, in spite of its lack of inspiration. He thinks it's what the public wants. But that reminds me of what Groucho Marx said when three thousand people turned up at the funeral of a rich Hollywood mogul whom everybody loathed. 'You see what I mean?' he said. 'Give the public what they want, and they'll come to see it.' I hope Master Terence heeds the warning. I can get along without him, thank you very much. But he can't get along without me.

(1958)

Hamlet

by WILLIAM SHAKESPEARE
at Stratford-on-Avon

The case of Michael Redgrave is perennially absorbing, even to those who deny that he is a great actor. On he plunges, struggling and climbing and stumbling, bursting with will and intelligence, and seeking always to widen the range of his remarkable physical and vocal equipment. Never, to my knowledge, has he run away from an acting problem: he'll wrestle with them all. A serious actor, in short.

Yet something is missing. We admire, but are not involved. 'I wish thar was winders to my Sole,' said Artemus Ward, 'so that you could see some of my feelin's.' Mr Redgrave's trouble is that his windows are opaque – one might even say frosted. Sir Laurence Olivier once said he would rather lose his voice or his arms than his eyes. Watch Mr Redgrave's: no matter how he rolls and darts them about, they remain somehow glazed and distant. We know from the evidence of our own that he has two of them, yet something about him persistently suggests the Cyclops. When he looks at other people, either actors or audience, it is as if he saw them only in two dimensions. They are simply 'things in his dream.' Try as he may (and God knows he tries), he cannot establish contact with them as human beings. Just as we think he is about to break through to us, something within him shies and bolts. He withdraws into his solitude, and when next we look, the windows are shuttered again.

Now this business of 'connecting', of getting into emotional touch with others, is at the heart of all acting. It is the very touchstone of the craft. And that is Mr Redgrave's paradox. He has in abundance all the attributes of a great actor, without the basic quality necessary to be a good one.

Even so, he is always fascinating to watch. His present *Hamlet* is a packed, compendious affair, much richer in detail than the one he gave us eight years ago at the Vic. At fifty, Mr Redgrave is the oldest Hamlet to have been seen in England since 1938, when Esmé Beringer struck a glancing blow for feminism by playing the part in her sixty-fourth summer; and it must be conceded that the actor sometimes resembles less a youth approaching murder for the first time than a seasoned Commando colonel suffering from battle fatigue. Nor is the illusion helped by a Gertrude who looks even younger than Googie Withers – a surprising achievement, considering that Miss Withers herself plays the part. Sheer intellectual agility, of which he has plenty, is what Mr Redgrave relies on. He knows the text inside out, and when he offers new readings (such as 'Nilus' for 'eisel' in the grave scene), we trust him as we would trust a walking Variorum Edition of the play. No subtlety of inflexion or punctuation escapes him; at times, indeed, he seems to be giving us three different interpretations of the same line *simultaneously*, which is a bit flustering.

In terms of character, Mr Redgrave presents a man fearful of rousing the sleeping demon within him. Cocteau described the artist as a kind of prison from which works of art escape. This Hamlet is a prison from which fury escapes, in wild frustrated spasms. His lips quake with the effort of containing it. Bottled hysteria is this actor's speciality, as the cellarage scene brilliantly proves. Mr Redgrave's Hamlet, like his Lear, is most convincing when closest to madness. It is, however, entirely unmoving, for the reason mentioned above.

Dorothy Tutin's Ophelia, a mouse on the rack, makes some illuminating minor points, chief among them her horrified reaction, in the play scene, to the mimic death of the Player King. I liked Edward Woodward's Laertes, Paul Hardwick's Rosencrantz (a nervous hearty), and the notion of playing the Second Gravedigger as a supercilious bureaucrat. Almost everything else in Glen Byam Shaw's production is dismal. The courtiers line up like mechanical waxworks, raising their hands in polite embarrassment when the royal family is exterminated before their eyes. The music is Victorian, the costumes are fussy, and the setting, an arrangement of shiny hexagonal pillars, appears to have been inspired by the foyer of the old Paramount Cinema in Birmingham. The best piece of business (Claudius's slapping the face of the Player Murderer) comes from Hugh Hunt's 1950 production. About two of the major performances my feelings are neutral : Cyril Luckham's sane, plodding Polonius and Mark Dignam's Claudius, which very nearly makes up in practical shrewdness what it lacks in dignity and sensuality.

(1958)

The Hostage

by BRENDAN BEHAN
at Stratford-atte-Bowe

At the end of N. F. Simpson's *A Resounding Tinkle* there is a passage, aberrantly omitted from the Royal Court production, in which four B.B.C. critics discuss the play.

It reads, in part:

CHAIRMAN: Denzil Pepper – what do you make of this?

PEPPER: This is a hotchpotch. I think that emerges quite clearly. The thing has been thrown together – a veritable rag-bag of last year's damp fireworks, if a mixed metaphor is in order.

MISS SALT: Yes, I suppose it *is* what we must call a hotchpotch. I do think, though – accepting Denzil Pepper's definition – I do think, and this is the point I feel we ought to make, it is, surely, isn't it, an *inspired* hotchpotch?

PEPPER: A hotchpotch de luxe. . . . A theatrical haggis.

CHAIRMAN: Isn't this what our ancestors would have delighted in calling a gallimaufry?

(Pause)

MUSTARD: Yes. I'm not sure that I don't prefer the word gallimaufry to Denzil Pepper's hodgepodge.

PEPPER: Hotchpotch. No, I stick, quite unrepentantly, to my own word. . . .

The satanic accuracy of all this is enough to make any critic's elbow fly defensively up. I quote it because it has a chilling relevance to Brendan Behan's *The Hostage*. He would, I fancy, be a pretty perjured critic who could swear that no such thoughts infested his mind while watching Mr Behan's new (careful now) – Mr Behan's new *play*. I use the word advisedly, and have since sacked my advisers – for conventional terminology is totally inept to describe the uses to which Mr Behan and his director, Joan Littlewood, are trying to put the theatre. The old pigeon-holes will no longer serve.

From a critic's point of view, the history of twentieth-century drama is the history of a collapsing vocabulary. Categories that were formerly thought sacred and separate began to melt and flow together, like images in a dream. Reaching, to steady himself, for words and concepts that had withstood the erosion of centuries, the critic found himself, more often than not, clutching a handful of dust. Already, long before 1900, tragedy and comedy had abandoned the pretence of competition and become a double act, exchanging their masks so rapidly that the effort of distinguishing one from the other was at best a pedantic exercise. Farce and satire, meanwhile, were miscegenating as busily as ever, and both were conducting affairs on the side with revue and musical comedy. Opera, with Brecht and Weill, got into everybody's act; and vaudeville, to cap everything, started to flirt with tragi-comedy in *Waiting for Godot* and *The Entertainer*.

The critic, to whom the correct assignment of compartments is as vital as it is to the employees of Wagons-Lits, reeled in poleaxed confusion. What had happened was that multi-party drama was moving towards coalition government. Polonius did not know the half of it: a modern play can, if it wishes, be tragical-comical-historical-pastoral-farcical-satirical-operatical-musical-music-hall, in any combination or all at the same time. And it is only because we have short memories that we forget that a phrase already exists to cover all these seemingly disparate breeds. It is Commedia dell'Arte. *The Hostage* is a Commedia dell'Arte production.

Its theme is Ireland, seen through the bloodshot prism of Mr Behan's talent. The action, which is noisy and incessant, takes place in a Dublin lodging-house owned by a Blimpish veteran of the Troubles whose Anglophobia is so devout that he calls himself Monsieur instead of Mr. His caretaker is Pat (Howard Goorney), a morose braggart who feels that all the gaiety departed from the cause of Irish liberty when the I.R.A. became temperate, dedicated, and holy. Already, perhaps, this sounds like a normal play; and it may well sound like a tragedy when I add that the plot concerns a kidnapped Cockney soldier who is threatened with death unless his opposite number, an I.R.A. prisoner sentenced to be hanged, is reprieved. Yet there are, in this production, more than twenty songs, many of them blasphemously or lecherously gay, and some of them sung by the hostage himself. Their authorship is attributed to Mr Behan, his uncle, and 'Trad'. Nor can one be sure how much of the dialogue is pure Behan and how much is gifted embroidery; for the whole production sounds spontaneous, a communal achievement based on Miss Littlewood's idea of theatre as a place where people talk to people, not actors to audiences. As with Brecht, actors step in and out of character so readily that phrases like 'dramatic unity' are ruled out of court; we are simply watching a group of human beings who have come together to tell a lively story in speech and song.

Some of the speech is brilliant mock-heroic; some of it is merely crude. Some of the songs are warmly ironic; others are more savagely funny. Some of the acting is sheer vaudeville; some of it (Murray Melvin as the captive, and Celia Salkeld as the country girl whom, briefly and abruptly, he loves) is tenderly realistic. The work ends in a mixed, happy jabber of styles, with a piano playing silent-screen music while the Cockney is rescued and accidentally shot by one of the lodgers, who defiantly cries, in the last line to be audibly uttered : 'I'm a secret policeman, and I don't care who knows it!'

Inchoate as it often is, this is a prophetic and joyously exciting evening. It seems to be Ireland's function, every twenty years or so, to provide a playwright who will kick English drama from the past into the present. Mr Behan may well fill the place vacated by Sean O'Casey. Perhaps more important, Miss Littlewood's production is a boisterous premonition of something we all want – a biting popular drama that does not depend on hit songs, star names, spa sophistication, or the more melodramatic aspects of homosexuality. Sean Kenny's setting, a skeleton stockade of a bedroom surrounded by a towering blind alley of slum windows, is, as often at this theatre, by far the best in London.

(1958)

Long Day's Journey into Night

by EUGENE O'NEILL
at the Globe

Eugene O'Neill died five years ago, The eclipse of reputation that commonly befalls great men as soon as they die has not yet happened to him; and now that *Long Day's Journey into Night* has followed *The Iceman Cometh* into London, I doubt if it ever will. O'Neill has conquered. We have the measure of him at last, and it is vast indeed. His work stretches like a mountain range across more than three decades, rising at the end to these two tenebrous peaks, in which the nature of his immense, hard-pressed talent most clearly reveals itself. As Johnson said of Milton, he could not carve heads upon cherry-stones; but he could cut a colossus from a rock. Sometimes the huge groups of his imagination stayed stubbornly buried within the rock; worse, they would sometimes emerge lopsided and unwieldy, so that people smiled at them – not without reason, for it is widely felt that there is nothing funnier than a deformed giant.

Many charges, during his lifetime, were levelled at O'Neill by the cherry-stone connoisseurs of criticism. That he could not think; that he was no poet; that his attempts at comedy were even more pathetic than his aspirations to tragedy. The odd thing is that all of these charges are entirely true. The defence admits them : it does not wish even to cross-examine the witnesses. Their testimony, which would be enough to annihilate most other playwrights, is in O'Neill's case irrelevant. His strength lies elsewhere. It has nothing to do with intellect, verbal beauty, or the accepted definitions of tragedy and comedy. It exists independently of them : indeed, they might even have cramped and depleted it.

What is this strength, this durable virtue? I got the

clue to it from the American critic Stark Young, into whose reviews I have lately been dipping. Mr Young is sometimes a windy writer, but the wind is usually blowing in the right direction. As early as 1926 he saw that O'Neill's theatrical power did not arise from any 'strong dramatic expertness', but that 'what moved us was *the cost to the dramatist of what he handled.*' (My italics.) Two years later, reviewing *Dynamo*, he developed this idea. He found in the play an 'individual poignancy' to which he responded no matter how tritely or unevenly it was expressed. From this it was a short step to the truth. 'Even when we are not at all touched by the feeling itself or the idea presented,' he wrote, 'we are stabbed to our depths by the importance of this feeling to him, and we are all his, not because of what he says but because saying it meant so much to him.'

Thirty years later we are stabbed in the same way, and for the same reason. The writing of *Long Day's Journey* must have cost O'Neill more than Mr Young could ever have conceived, for its subject is that rarest and most painful of all *dramatis personae*, the dramatist himself. No more honest or unsparing autobiographical play exists in dramatic literature. Yet what grips us about it is not the craft of a playwright. It is the need, the vital, driving plaint, of a human being.

We are watching a crucial day in O'Neill's late youth, covered with a thin gauze of fiction; events are telescoped, and the family's name is Tyrone. They live in a gaunt, loveless New England house. Father is a rich retired actor, now beetle-browed with drink, whose upbringing as an immigrant Irish pauper has made him a miser: he recognizes the fault, but cannot cure it. His wife suffered badly at the birth of their second son (Edmund, otherwise Eugene), and he hired a cheap quack to ease her pain, with the result that she has become a morphine addict. The elder boy is a failed actor, something of a whoremaster, and a great deal of a drunk. His brother, Edmund, who has been to sea and is ambitious to be a poet, also drinks and detests more than he wholesomely should.

We catch the quartet on the desperate day when mother, after a long abstinence, returns to drugs, and Edmund learns that he has T.B. With these urgent, terrible realities the family cannot cope. Old rows, old resentments keep boiling up; the pressures and recriminations of the past will not let the present live. Every conversation leads inexorably to the utterance of some sudden, unforgivable, scab-tearing cruelty. At every turn O'Neill points the contrast between official Irish-Catholic morality and the sordid facts of drink and dope. The family goes round and round in that worst of domestic rituals, the Blame Game. I blame my agony on you; you blame yours on her; she blames hers on me. Father blames his past; mother blames father; elder son blames both, and younger son blames all of them. If the play has a flaw, it is that O'Neill, the younger son, lets nobody blame him – though I recall, as I write this, the moment when his mother cries out that she would not be what she is had he never been born. The wheel, coming full circle, runs over all of them. Shortly after the events covered in the play, O'Neill entered a sanatorium, where, he wrote later, 'the urge to write first came to me.' It was more than an urge, it was a compulsion.

The London production is much shorter than those I saw in Berlin and New York; about a quarter of the text has been cut away. This is shrewd pruning, since a non-American English-speaking cast might not have been able to carry the full four-hour burden. Alan Bates, shock-haired and forlorn, approaches Edmund with just the right abandon. Once inside the part, however, he stumbles over a distracting North Country accent. Ian Bannen, on the other hand, gets easily to the heart of the elder brother, especially in the last-act debauch when he confesses to Edmund how much he hates and envies him : what he lacks is the exterior of the seedy Broadway masher. He falls short of his New York counterpart, Jason Robards, Jr., just as far as Anthony Quayle falls short of Fredric March. Mr March, with his corrugated face and burning eyes, looked as weighty as if he were made of iron. Mr

Quayle, though he conveys every syllable of the part's meaning, never seems to be heavier than tin.

By West End standards, let me add, all these performances are exceptionally good. That of Gwen Ffrangcon-Davies is by any standards magnificent. In this production mother is the central figure: a guileful, silver-topped doll, her hands clenched by rheumatism into claws, her voice drooping except when drugs tighten it into a tingling, bird-like, tight-rope brightness. Her sons stare at her, and she knows why they are staring, but: 'Is my hair coming down?' she pipes, warding off the truth with a defensive flirtatiousness. At the end, when the men are slumped in a stupor, she tells us in a delicate quaver how the whole mess began. 'Then I married James Tyrone, and I was happy for a time. . . .' The curtain falls on a stupendous evening. One goes expecting to hear a playwright, and one meets a man.

(1958)

Krapp's Last Tape and *End-Game*

by SAMUEL BECKETT
at the Royal Court

Slamm's Last Knock, a play inspired, if that is the word, by Samuel Beckett's double bill at the Royal Court:

The den of Slamm, the critic. Very late yesterday. Large desk with throne behind it. Two waste-paper baskets, one black, one white, filled with crumpled pieces of paper, at either side of the stage. Shambling between them – i.e., from one to the other and back again – an old man: Slamm. Bent gait. Thin, barking voice. Motionless, watching Slamm, is Seck. Bright grey face, holding pad and pencil. One crutch. Slamm goes to black basket, takes out piece of white paper, uncrumples it, reads. Short laugh.

232

SLAMM (*reading*): . . . the validity of an authentic tragic vision, at once personal and by implication cosmic . . .

Short laugh. He recrumples the paper, replaces it in basket, and crosses to other – i.e., white – basket. He takes out piece of black paper, uncrumples it, reads. Short laugh.

SLAMM (*reading*): '. . . Just another dose of nightmare gibberish from the so-called author of *Waiting for Godot*. . . .'

Short laugh. He recrumples the paper, replaces it in basket, and sits on throne. Pause. Anguished, he extends fingers of right hand and stares at them. Extends fingers of left hand. Same business. Then brings fingers of right hand towards fingers of left hand, and vice versa, so that fingertips of right hand touch fingertips of left hand. Same business. Breaks wind pensively. Seck writes feverishly on pad.

SLAMM: We're getting on. (*He sighs.*) Read that back.

SECK (*produces pince-nez with thick black lenses, places them on bridge of nose, reads*): 'A tragic dose of authentic gibberish from the so-called implication of *Waiting for Godot*.' Shall I go on?

SLAMM (*nodding head*): No. (*Pause.*) A bit of both, then.

SECK (*shaking head*): Or a little of neither.

SLAMM: There's the hell of it. (*Pause. Urgently.*) Is it time for my Roget?

SECK: There are no more Rogets. Use your loaf.

SLAMM. Then wind me up, stink-louse! Stir your stump!

Seck hobbles to Slamm, holding rusty key depending from piece of string round his (Seck's) neck, and inserts it into back of Slamm's head. Loud noise of winding.

SLAMM: Easy now. Can't you see it's hell in there?

SECK: I haven't looked. (*Pause.*) It's hell out here, too. The ceiling is zero and there's grit in my crotch. Roget and over.

He stops winding and watches. Pause.

SLAMM (*glazed stare*): Nothing is always starting to happen.

SECK: It's better than something. You're well out of that.

SLAMM: I'm badly into this. (*He tries to yawn but fails.*) It would be better if I could yawn. Or if you could yawn.

SECK: I don't feel excited enough. (*Pause.*) Anything coming?

SLAMM: Nothing, in spades. (*Pause.*) Perhaps I haven't been kissed enough. Or perhaps they put the wrong ash in my gruel. One or the other.

SECK: Nothing will come of nothing. Come again.

SLAMM (*with violence*): Purulent drudge! *You* try, if you've got so much grit in your crotch! Just one pitiless, pathetic, creatively critical phrase!

SECK: I heard you the first time.

SLAMM: You can't have been listening.

SECK: Your word's good enough for me.

SLAMM: I haven't got a word. There's just the light, going. (*Pause.*) Are you trying?

SECK: Less and less.

SLAMM: Try blowing down it.

SECK: It's coming! (*Screws up his face. Tonelessly.*) Sometimes I wonder why I spend the lonely night.

SLAMM: Too many f's. We're bitched. (*Half a pause.*)

SECK: Hold your pauses. It's coming again. (*In a raconteur's voice, dictates to himself.*) Tuesday night, seven-thirty by the paranoid barometer, curtain up at the Court, Sam Beckett unrivalled master of the unravelled revels. Item: *Krapp's Last Tape*, Krapp being a myopic not to say deaf not to say eremitical eater of one and one-half bananas listening and cackling as he listens to a tape-recording of twenty years' antiquity made on a day, the one far gone day, when he laid his hand on a girl in a boat and it worked, as it worked for Molly Bloom in Gibraltar in the long ago. Actor: Patrick Magee, bereaved and aghast-looking grunting into his Grundig, probably perfect performance, fine throughout and highly affecting at third curtain-call though not formerly. Unique, oblique, bleak experience, in other words, and would have had same effect if half the words *were* other words. Or any words. (*Pause.*)

SLAMM: Don't stop. You're boring me.

SECK (*normal voice*): Not enough. You're smiling.

SLAMM: Well, I'm still in the land of the dying.

SECK: Somehow, in spite of everything, death goes on.

SLAMM: Or because of everything. (*Pause.*) Go on.

SECK (*raconteur's voice*): Tuesday night, eight-twenty by the Fahrenheit anonymeter, *End-Game*, translated from the French with loss by excision of the vernacular word for urination and of certain doubts blasphemously cast on the legitimacy of the Deity. Themes, madam? Nay, it *is*, I know not themes. Foreground figure a blind and lordly cripple with superficial mannerisms of Churchill, W., Connolly, C., and Devine, G., director and in this case impersonator. Sawn-off parents in bins, stage right, and shuffling servant, all over the stage, played by Jack Mac-

Gowran, binster of this parish. Purpose: to analyse or rather to dissect or rather to define the nature or rather the quality or rather the intensity of the boredom inherent or rather embedded in the twentieth or rather every other century. I am bored, therefore I am. Comment, as above, except it would have the same effect if a quarter of the words were other words and another quarter omitted. Critique ended. Thesaurus and out.

SLAMM: Heavy going. I can't see.

SECK: That's because of the light going.

SLAMM: Is that all the review he's getting?

SECK: That's all the play he's written.

> *Pause.*

SLAMM: But a genius. Could you do as much?

SECK: Not as much. But as little.

> *Tableau. Pause. Curtain.*
> (1958)

The Chairs and *The Lesson*

by EUGENE IONESCO
at the Royal Court

The French theatre, about which I prophesied glumly some months ago, has now entered upon a state of emergency. An alarming article in the current issue of *Arts* reveals that during the first five months of this year the box-office receipts at Parisian theatres declined, compared with the same period last year, by nearly two-fifths. The fact to be faced is brutal and simple: French audiences are drifting away from the theatre because they feel that the theatre is drifting away from them. They are frankly bored with it; and the immediate prospect reflects their boredom. Thirty-two theatres, an unprecedented number, will close this summer. Only twelve have elected to brave the drought, most of them peddling the theatrical equivalent of scented water-ices. *Cocktail Sexy* will hold the fort at the Capucines; at the Grand-Guignol, *L'Ecole du Strip-tease*. At only one small theatre will you find, throughout the dog-days, the work of a French author of serious repute. Who is the man capable of inspiring such unique managerial confidence? Nobody but M. Ionesco, founder and headmaster of *l'école du strip-tease intellectuel, moral, et social*.

Faith in the drawing-power of this anarchic wag seems to be shared by the English Stage Company, who last week offered a double bill of *The Chairs* and *The Lesson*. Neither play is new to London. *The Chairs* is a Court revival, and the Arts Theatre taught us our lesson in 1955. The point of the programme is to demonstrate the versatility of Joan Plowright, who sheds seventy years during the interval, and to celebrate this nimble girl's return from Broadway, where she appeared in both plays under Tony Richardson's direction. Yet there was more in the applause than a mere welcome home. It had about it a blind, deafening intensity: one felt present at the consecration of a cult. Not, let me add, a Plowright cult – staggeringly though she played the crumbling hag in the first play, she simpered a little too knowingly as the crammer's prey in the second. No: this was an Ionesco cult, and in it I smell danger.

Ever since the Fry-Eliot 'poetic revival' caved in on them, the ostriches of our theatrical intelligentsia have been seeking another faith. Anything would do as long as it shook off what are known as 'the fetters of realism'. Now the broad definition of a realistic play is that its characters and events have traceable roots in life. Gorki and Chekhov, Arthur Miller and Tennessee Williams, Brecht and O'Casey, Osborne and Sartre have all written such plays. They express one man's view of the world in terms of people we can all recognize. Like all hard disciplines realism can easily be corrupted. It can sink into sentimentality (N. C. Hunter), half-truth (Terence Rattigan), or mere photographic reproduction of the trivia of human behaviour. Even so, those who have mastered it have created the lasting body of twentieth-century drama: and I have been careful not to except Brecht, who employed stylized production techniques to set off essentially realistic characters.

That, for the ostriches, was what ruled him out of court. He was too real. Similarly, they preferred Beckett's *Fin de Partie*, in which the human element was minimal, to *Waiting For Godot*, which not only contained two tramps of mephitic reality but even seemed to regard them, as human beings, with love. Veiling their disapproval, the ostriches seized on Beckett's more blatant verbal caprices and called them 'authentic images of a disintegrated society'. But it was only when M. Ionesco arrived that they hailed a messiah. Here at last was a self-proclaimed advocate of *anti-théâtre*: explicitly anti-realist, and by implication anti-reality as well. Here was a writer ready to declare that words were meaningless and that all communication between human beings was impossible. The aged (as in *The Chairs*) are wrapped in an impenetrable cocoon of hallucinatory memories; they can speak intelligibly neither to each other nor to the world. The teacher in *The Lesson* can 'get through' to his pupil only by means of sexual assault, followed by murder. Words, the magic innovation of our species, are dismissed as useless and fraudulent.

Ionesco's is a world of isolated robots conversing in cartoon-strip balloons of dialogue that are sometimes hilarious, sometimes evocative, and quite often neither, on which occasions they become profoundly tiresome. (As with shaggy-dog stories, few of M. Ionesco's plays survive a second hearing. I felt this particularly with *The Chairs*.) This world is not mine, but I recognize it to be a valid personal vision, presented with great imaginative aplomb and verbal audacity. The peril arises when it is held up for general emulation as the gateway to the theatre of the future, that bleak new world from which the humanist heresies of faith in logic and belief in man will for ever be banished.

M. Ionesco certainly offers an 'escape from realism', but an escape into what? A blind alley, perhaps, adorned with *tachiste* murals. Or a self-imposed vacuum, wherein the author ominously bids us observe the absence of air. Or, best of all, a fun-fair ride on a ghost train, all skulls and hooting waxworks, from which we emerge into the far more intimidating clamour of diurnal reality. M. Ionesco's theatre is pungent and exciting, but it remains a diversion. It is not on the main road : and we do him no good, nor the drama at large, to pretend that it is.

(1958)

Postscript on Ionesco

The position towards which M. Ionesco is moving is that which regards art as if it were something different from and independent of everything else in the world; as if it not only did not but *should* not correspond to anything outside the mind of the artist. The end of that line, of course, is Action Painting. M. Ionesco has not yet gone so far. He is stuck in an earlier groove, the groove of cubism, which has fascinated him so much that he has begun to confuse ends and means. The cubists employed distortion to make discoveries about the nature of objective reality. M. Ionesco, I fear, is on the brink of believing that his distortions are more valid and important than the external world it is their proper function to interpret. To adapt Johnson, I am not yet so lost in drama criticism as to forget that plays are the daughters of earth, and that things are the sons of heaven. But M. Ionesco is in danger of forgetting; of locking himself up in that hall of mirrors which in philosophy is known as solipsism.

Art is parasitic on life, just as criticism is parasitic on art. M. Ionesco and his followers are breaking the chain, applying the tourniquet, aspiring as writers to a condition of stasis. At their best, of course, they don't succeed; the alarming thing is that they try. As in physiology, note how quickly the brain starved of blood produces hallucinations and delusion of grandeur. 'A work of art,' says M. Ionesco, 'is the source and the raw material of ideologies to come.' *O hubris!* Art and ideology often interact on each other, but the plain fact is that both spring from a common source. Both draw on human experience to explain mankind to itself; both attempt, in very different ways, to assemble coherence from seemingly unrelated phenomena; both stand guard for us against chaos. They are brothers, not child and parent. To say, as M. Ionesco has said, that Freud was inspired by Sophocles is the direst nonsense. Freud merely found in Sophocles confirmation of a theory he had formed on the basis of empirical evidence. This does not make Sophocles a Freudian, or vice versa: it is simply a pleasing instance of fraternal corroboration.

You may wonder why M. Ionesco is so keen on this phantom notion of art as a world of its own, answerable to none but its own laws. Wonder no more: he is merely seeking to exempt himself from any kind of value-judgement. His aim is to blind us to the fact that we are all in some sense critics, who bring to the theatre not only those 'nostalgias and anxieties' by which, as he rightly says, world history has largely been governed, but also a whole series of new ideas – moral, social, psychological, political – through which we hope some day to free ourselves from the rusty hegemony of *Angst*. These fond ideas, M. Ionesco, quickly assures us, do not belong in the theatre. Our job, as critics, is just to hear the play and 'simply say whether it is true to its own nature'. Not, you notice, whether it is true to ours, or even relevant; for we, as an audience, have forfeited our right to a hearing as conscious, sentient beings. 'Clear evidence of cancer here, sir.' 'Very well, leave it alone, it's being true to its own nature.'

Whether M. Ionesco admits it or not, every play worth serious consideration is a statement. It is a statement addressed in the first person singular to the first person plural; and the latter must retain the right of dissent. I am rebuked in the current issue of *Encounter* for having disagreed with the nihilistic philosophy expressed in Strindberg's *Dream Play*. 'The important thing', says my interviewer, 'seems to me to be not the rightness of Strindberg's belief, but rather how he has expressed it. . . .' Strindberg expressed it very vividly, but there are things more important than that. If a man tells me something I believe to be an untruth, am I forbidden to do more than congratulate him on the brilliance of his lying?

Cyril Connolly once said, once and wanly, that it was closing time in the gardens of the West; but I deny the rest of that suavely cadenced sentence, which asserts that 'from now on an artist will be judged only by the resonance of his solitude or the quality of his despair.' Not by me he won't. I shall, I hope, respond to the honesty of such testimonies, but I shall be looking for something more, something harder: for evidence of the artist who is not content with the passive role of a symptom, but concerns himself, from time to time, with such things as healing. M. Ionesco correctly says that no ideology has yet abolished fear, pain, or sadness. Nor has any work of art. But both are in the business of trying. What other business is there?

(1958)

The Cherry Orchard and Three Sisters

by ANTON CHEKHOV
at Sadler's Wells

The great thing about the Moscow Art Theatre's production of The Cherry Orchard is that it blows the cobwebs off the play. And who put them there? Why, we ourselves. We have remade Chekhov's last play in our image just as drastically as the Germans have remade Hamlet in theirs. Our Cherry Orchard is a pathetic symphony, to be played in a mood of elegy. We invest it with a nostalgia for the past which, though it runs right through our culture, is alien to Chekhov's. His people are country gentry: we make them into decadent aristocrats.

Next, we romanticize them. Their silliness becomes pitiable grotesquerie; and at this point our hearts warm to them. They are not Russians at all: they belong in the great line of English eccentrics. The upstart Lopakhin, who buys up their heritage, cannot be other than a barbarous bounder. Having foisted on Chekhov a collection of patrician mental cases, we then congratulate him on having achieved honorary English citizenship. Meanwhile the calm, genial sanity of the play has flown out of the window. In M. Stanitsyn's production it is magnificently restored. Common sense is not a quality we like to attribute to our artists; we prefer them slightly deranged; but Chekhov had it in full measure, and so have his present, peerless interpreters. Did I say this was Chekhov without the cobwebs? It is more: it is a total spring-cleaning.

Part of its freshness comes from the fact that it is a brand new production, with new décor and several newly graduated players: on this tour the Art Theatre is clearly experimenting with youth. But there is more to it than that. The real novelty lies in its attitude towards Mme Ranevsky's feckless household. This is not the old regime, crazily expiring with a pathetic jest on its lips. It is a real family, capricious perhaps and irresponsible, but essentially normal and undoomed. The play becomes what Chekhov called it: a comedy. 'In places, even a farce', he added, but M. Stanitsyn does not go as far as that. He simply treats the characters as recognizable human beings in a mess, rather than as freaks trapped in a tragic *impasse*.

M. Massalsky's Gayev, for example, is no crumbling dodderer but the man of 'suavity and elegance' whom Chekhov imagined: the decay is internal and moral. Nor is there anything of the neurotic spinster in Mlle Lennikova's Varya: she is a practical, good-hearted girl who blushes too much to be easily marriageable; and her collapse, when Lopakhin lets her down, is the more moving for its lack of neurotic preparation. Lopakhin himself behaves, as Chekhov demanded, 'with the utmost courtesy and decorum': no thrusting vulgarity here, but a mature impatience which rises, in the third-act announcement that he is the master now, to an astonishing climax of dismayed exasperation. The actor, M. Lukyanov, plays like a master throughout.

One crucial test remains: what does the production invite us to make of Trofimov, the eternal student with his vision of a transformed Russia? The English habit is to present him as a hare-brained booby whom no one could possibly take seriously. Yet the Tsarist censor took him seriously enough to expunge several of his more critical speeches. M. Gubanov's performance is delicately right: a bundle of nerves, for ever fingering his spectacles, and a fumbler in matters of emotion, but intelligent and sincere withal – a true misfit, but also a true prophet. This is straight Chekhov, not propagandist distortion. It is we who, by turning the other members of Ranevsky's household into caricatures of high-born futility, have infected the text with unnecessary social significance.

There are many more actors to salute – it is in the nature of this glowing troupe that it bats all the way down the list. I think of M. Leonidov's Yasha, more cad's cad than gent's gent, embracing the maid Dunyasha and blowing cigar-smoke into her eyes as she smiles at him. Of M. Yanshin's earth-larding Pischchik, frantically feeling for his purse after the conjuring tricks have been played. Of M. Kornukov's plump Epikhodov, pocketing an apple to make up for his rejection by Dunyasha. And I have not yet mentioned Alexis Gribov, one of the great actors of the world, who plays the tiny part of Firs, the ancient butler – fixed like a statue, in jaundiced petrifaction, and held upright only by handy walking-sticks or tables. Are there no weaknesses? For me, yes: I thought Mme Tarassova inexpressive and unmoving. This is not a failure of conception; Chekhov expressly forbade the romantic agonies which most actresses bring to Mme Ranevsky. It is a failure of execution. The actress is simply monotonous.

Peter Ustinov contends that team-work and Chekhov are, in acting terms, incompatible. The characters, he maintains, are all soloists who occasionally interrupt each other's monologues but never listen to what anyone else is saying. They are deaf and blind to the world outside them – which is why they are funny and also why they are appalling. Fair comment, and in *Three Sisters*, a much more complex work than *The Cherry Orchard*, this technique is carried as far as it can go without blowing the play centrifugally apart. The very theme is estrangement: a brief brushing of lips is as close as anyone ever gets to another's soul. Of the three girls yearning for Moscow, Olga will never marry, Masha has married badly, and Irina is cheated of marriage by a tragic duel. Their brother, Andrey, is yoked to a prolific and faithless shrew. Two nihilists look on: one active – the savage Solyony, who scents his hands because, like Lear's, they smell of mortality – and the other passive: Chebutikin, the doctor, jilted by the girl's mother and now drunk past caring. And so all sit, mourning and mumbling, making out of their inconsequence a choral lament on human isolation.

The Moscow production, based on the original staging by Nemirovich-Dantchenko, gets all of this and infuses it with that strange dynamic apathy that is Chekhov's greatest demand on his actors. The sisters themselves are new to the roles and as yet unsettled in them: Mlle Yurieva's Masha comes nearest to the wry fatalism we are looking for. Her Vershinin, M. Massalsky, is unduly restrained, tarred with the pomade of the *matinée* idol; but the elder parts are filled to overflowing with beard and rasp and detail. M. Gribov's Chebutikin, in particular, is all I had heard of it; encrusted with corruption, a ponderous fish-eyed shrug of a man, he is yet capable, while remembering his dead love, of a sudden and transfixing pathos. The last act is, I suppose, the high-water mark of twentieth-century drama, yet this superb company meets its challenge as if opening the door to an old friend. The sound-effects and lighting are brilliant throughout: we weep, apart from anything else, for a lost world so lovingly revived. How these actors eat; and listen; and fail to listen; and grunt and exist, roundly and egocentrically exist! They have become, with long rehearsal, the people they are playing: they do not need, as our actors do, to depend on the lines alone for their characterization. We act with our voices, they with their lives. Where we leave off, they begin. Don't be deterred by the language barrier. This is not verbal acting, like ours, but total acting: Stanislavsky often made his players rehearse without words, to be sure that their faces and bodies were performing as well. Read the play before going, and you will be safe. Safe, and enriched.

By a shaming coincidence, our theatre last week offered what should have been its best: Edith Evans, John Gielgud, and Harry Andrews in *Henry VIII* at the Old Vic. This sprawling chronicle has four good scenes: Buckingham's downfall and Wolsey's, and Katharine's trial and death. The rest slumps without galvanic direction, which here it doesn't get. The style is ceremonial and listless, bogged down by leaden costumes and drab settings. The end of an era, I thought during the first act, when Dame Edith and Mr Andrews, ludicrously under-rehearsed, were groping for lines like children playing at blind-man's-buff. And though Sir John made good use of his poker back and door-knob face, he never for a moment suggested Wolsey the self-made 'butcher's cur': all was rigid declamation, issuing from a tense and meagre tenor.

Certes, he wept: which is to say, he moved himself. Dame Edith, by contrast, moved me. Her death scene lifted her to those serene, unassertive heights where at her best she has no rivals. The quiet, large face, with its prehensile upper lip, shifted and quaked according to the dictates of the character, an unabashed queen in great extremity. Dame Edith ignored the 'verbal music', and thereby made a truer music, having to do with the experience of dying. Alone in the company at what foreigners are wrongly encouraged to regard as our national theatre, she could have wandered on to the stage at Sadler's Wells and seemed at home.

(1958)

My Fair Lady

by FREDERICK LOEWE and ALAN JAY LERNER
at Drury Lane

'Was all the hysteria justified?' one read on Thursday morning, à propos of the uproar at Drury Lane last Wednesday night. The nerve of the question took one's breath away, coming as it did from the very journalists who had created the hysteria. Those who beat drums are in no position to complain of being deafened. Let us forget about the hysteria associated with My Fair Lady and point instead to the rare, serene pleasure it communicates, a pleasure arising from the fact that it treats both the audience and Pygmalion with civilized respect.

This winning show honours our intelligence as well as Shaw's. It does not bully us with noise: the tone throughout is intimate, light, and lyrical, and even Doolittle's lion-comique numbers are sung, not shouted. It does not go in for irrelevant displays of physical agility: the dustman's pre-nuptial rout at Covent Garden is the only choreographic set-piece. Following the film, it restores Eliza to Higgins at the end, but no other sentimental concessions are made: the score contains only two love songs. Never do we feel that numbers have been shoehorned, with a beady eye on the hit parade, into situations that do not concern them. Where most musical adaptations tend to exploit their originals, this one is content to explore.

Everything in the score grows naturally out of the text and the characters; the authors have trusted Shaw, and we, accordingly, trust them. Consider the four solo numbers they have provided for Higgins. In the first he rails against the English for neglecting their native tongue; in the second he congratulates himself on the sweetness of his disposition. In the third he damns women for their refusal to behave like men; and in the fourth, a wonderful blend of rage and regret, he furiously acknowledges his attachment to a woman who is unlike him in every respect. All four songs are right in character, and all four are written more to be acted than sung. Rex Harrison, performing them in a sort of reedy *Sprechgesang*, is not merely doing the best he can; he is doing just what the authors wanted. For all its grace and buoyancy, what holds the show together at the last is its determination to put character first.

On this resolve all its talents converge. A feeling of concord positively flows across the footlights. In a sense, the outstanding thing about the evening is that there is nothing outstanding about it, no self-assertion, no sore thumbs. The keyword is consonance. Oliver Smith's décor, lovely in itself, both enhances and is enhanced by Cecil Beaton's dashing dresses. Frederick Loewe, the composer, and Alan Jay Lerner, the lyricist, have produced a score as sensitive to Shavian nuance as litmus to acid. They have drawn song out of Shaw's people, not imposed it on them. Mr Lerner's words are wily enough for Gilbert, and Mr Loewe's contribution, enriched by the creative arrangements of Robert Russell Bennett, is far more than a series of pleasant songs: it is a tapestry of interwoven themes, criss-crossing and unexpectedly recurring, so that a late number will, by a sudden switch of tempo, echo an apt phrase from an earlier one. Apart from all this, the cast itself, directed by the hawk-eyed Moss Hart, is among the best ever assembled for *Pygmalion*.

Stanley Holloway is the fruitiest of Doolittles, Robert Coote the most subtly pompous of Pickerings. Nothing in Julie Andrews's Cockney becomes her like the leaving it; but she blossoms, once she has shed her fraudulent accent, into a first-rate Eliza, with a voice as limpid as outer space. And I don't doubt that Mr Harrison, who seemed a bit edgy on Wednesday, is by now giving the effortless, finger-tip performance I saw last year on Broadway. The moment when he, Miss Andrews, and Mr Coote erupt into that ecstatic, improvised tango, 'The Rain in Spain', is still the happiest of the night. Ten years ago, I learn,

THE AGES OF MAN

Shaw was approached for permission to turn his play into a musical. Outraged, he replied: 'If *Pygmalion* is not good enough for your friends with its own verbal music, their talent must be altogether extraordinary.' In this instance, it is.

(1958)

The Ages of Man

at the 46th Street Theatre, New York

I have always felt that Sir John Gielgud is the finest actor on earth from the neck up, and, having heard his Shakespearian recital, *Ages of Man*, I am in no mood to revise that opinion. Whenever I think of Sir John, I remember what C. E. Montague (my favourite drama critic next to Shaw) said of Coquelin; namely, that 'his power was simply the sum of the three strict elements of great acting – a plastic physical medium, a finished technical cunning, and a passion of joy in the thought of the character acted.'

Sir John has the last two qualities in abundance, and is almost entirely deficient in the first; when in motion, he is constricted, hesitant, and jerky, enmeshed in unseen cords of inhibition. His exceptional virtues of mind and voice stand out most clearly in repose, and for this reason the present display at the 46th Street Theatre seems to me one of the most satisfactory things he has ever done. Now and then, when the impulse of a speech demands it, he takes a step or two to right or left and permits his hands, which spend much of the evening protectively clasping each other, to fly up in gestures that claw the air, but for the most part he is still, and all the better for it; the voice flows freely among us, a thrilling instrument that commands the full tonal range of both viola and 'cello. Brass is absent, and this may explain why he gives us nothing of

247

Henry V or *Antony and Cleopatra* and only the briefest snatch of *Macbeth* – all of them plays that cannot readily be scored for unaccompanied strings. But what he can do he does peerlessly. Never before have I followed Richard II's slow ride down to despair with such eager, pitying attentiveness (Sir John himself wept, as Richard should), and the excerpts from *Hamlet* were delivered with a mastery of *rubato* and a controlled energy that put one in mind of Mozart. The speech before the duel ('Not a whit, we defy augury . . .') was in the nature of an epiphany, the last phrases falling on the ear in cadences of overwhelming tenderness and serenity.

I had expected successes like these from Sir John; what I had forgotten was his narrative virtuosity. To passages that tell a story – Clarence recounting his nightmare, Hotspur describing a brush with a fop on the battlefield, Cassius tempting Brutus with splenetic anecdotes about Caesar – he brings a graphic zeal that is transfixing. Like the spider's touch in Pope's poem, his voice 'feels at each thread, and lives along the line.' The impact of the performance is not, however, exclusively aural; as I've said, Sir John's physical inexpressiveness does not extend above the collar stud. Poker-backed he may be; poker-faced he certainly isn't. Wherever pride, scorn, compassion, and the more cerebral kinds of agony are called for, his features respond promptly, and memorably.

(1959)

Summing Up: 1959

As recently as five years ago, popular theatre in the West End of London was virtually dominated by a ruthless three-power coalition consisting of drawing-room comedy and its two junior henchmen, murder melodrama and barrack-room farce. Although competitive among themselves, the members of the combine were united in their determination to prevent the forces of contemporary reality from muscling in on their territory.

The average playwright had ceased trying to hold the mirror up to nature, and the fashionable playwright could not possibly hold a mirror up to anything, since genteel idiom demanded the use of the word 'looking-glass.' Nightly, in dozens of theatres, the curtain rose on the same set. French windows were its most prominent feature, backed by a sky-cloth of brilliant and perpetual blue. In the cheaper sort of production, nothing but the sky was visible through the windows, and the impression was conveyed that everyone lived on a hill. There was also a bookcase, which might even – if the producer was in a devil-may-care frame of mind – be three-dimensional and equipped with real books. If we were not at Mark Trevannion's country house in Berkshire, we were probably at Hilary Egleston's flat in Knightsbridge, and, wherever we were, we ran into the same crowd – Rodney Curzon, feeling frightful; a 'really rather nice' American named Kip, Joe, or Calvin McIlhenny III; and, of course, that audacious young Susan Mainwaring, accompanied by her Aunt Gertrude, an obligatory dragoness with strong views about modern youth, the welfare state, and her senile rip of a husband, referred to as 'your poor Uncle Edgar', who never appeared. Off-stage characters like Uncle Edgar continually cropped up in remarks such as 'This reminds me of that ghastly evening when Priscilla Mumbles took her owl to the Ritz for cocktails.' Nobody except the gardener was ever called Sidney or Bert, and names like Ethel and Myrtle were reserved for housemaids, paid companions, and pets. To pour the drinks, there was usually somebody's tweedy, middle-aged stick of a husband, who grinned tolerantly at his wife's caprices, offered brandy to her lovers, and never raised his voice above street level; a symbol of sanity in a collapsing world, he was described by the other characters as 'damn decent' or 'rather dim', and by the critics as 'that admirable actor, Cyril Raymond.' (Or any of a dozen other admirable actors.) The language of drawing-room drama was of a rigid deformity. People never just *went* anywhere; they beetled down to Godalming, hurtled up to town, nipped round to Fortnum's, and staggered off home. All bores were cracking, all asses pompous, and the dialogue was sprinkled with epithets of distaste, mostly drawn from the vocabulary of English nannies; for example, 'horrid', 'dreadful', 'nasty', 'sickening', 'disgusting', and 'nauseating.' These were often reinforced by the additional disparagement of 'little', as in 'dreadful little man', 'disgusting little creature', or 'nasty little mind'. (In other contexts, 'mind' was replaced by the classier 'mentality'; e.g., 'You have the mentality of a day-old chick.' For similar reasons, 'visualize' was generally preferred to 'imagine.') At some point in every play, the hero was required to say, 'That, Celia, is a thoroughly immoral (or 'perfectly revolting') suggestion.' Minor English place names were relied upon to tinge the baldest statements with wit. A line like 'I am spending the summer in the country' could convulse a whole audience if revised to read 'I am spending the summer at Sidcup/Herne Bay/Budleigh Salterton.'

Five years ago, anyone whose knowledge of England was restricted to its popular theatre would have come to the conclusion that its standard of living was the highest on earth. British plays about people who could not afford villas on the Côte d'Azur were very nearly as rare as British people who could afford them. The poor were seldom with us, except when making antic contributions to broad farce or venturing, tongue-tied with embarrassment and clutching cloth caps, into the gracious salons of middle-class comedy, where they were expected to preface every remark with 'Beggin' yer pardon, Mum.' To become eligible for detailed dramatic treatment, it was usually necessary either to have an annual income of more than three thousand pounds net or to be murdered in the house of someone who did. This state of affairs did not apply during the war years, when everyone pulled together and even Noël Coward wrote tributes to the patriotism of the working classes; otherwise, however, it had persisted since the mid-thirties and

Love on the Dole. And it had been noticed much earlier that that.

> If our dramatists will condescend to make our acquaintance (or rather cease from trying to persuade themselves that they don't know us), they will find that we, too, the un-mentioned by Debrett, the jaded in aspect, have brains and hearts. They will find that we, too, are capable of great joys and griefs, and that such things come our way quite often, really.

Max Beerbohm wrote that in February 1907. It might easily have been written in 1954. I do not think it could be written today.

A change, slight but unmistakable, has taken place; the English theatre has been dragged, as Adlai Stevenson once said of the Republican Party, kicking and screaming into the twentieth century. Only an Englishman, probably, would notice the difference. In the middle of summer there were twenty-one straight plays running in London. Sixteen of them were farces, light comedies, or detective stories, and one at least of the remaining five was a borderline case. I refer to Graham Greene's *The Complaisant Lover*, which bears the same relationship to Mr Greene's earlier plays that his 'entertainments' bear to his more serious novels. It deals with a suburban dentist whose wife has just started to sleep with a local bookseller. The adulterous pair arrange to spend a week-end in Amsterdam, which is interrupted – in a scene of the bitterest farce – by the sand-blind, unsuspecting cuckold. To force the issue, the lover informs the husband, by letter, of his wife's infidelity. The trick misfires. It drives the dentist to tears but not to divorce; instead, he cannily proposes a *ménage à trois* – a solution that satisfies him, assuages his wife's guilt, and utterly disconcerts the bookseller. Perhaps because John Gielgud's antiseptic direction failed to convince me that the lovers had achieved any significant carnal contact, perhaps because Ralph Richardson performed in a vein of fantasy that seemed incompatible with dentistry, I could not believe a word of it. Or, rather, I believed in many of the words – Mr Greene's lines have a startling casual candour – but not in the people who were uttering them. Mastery of dialogue, I reflected afterward, is no substitute for mastery of characterization.

Apart from *The Complaisant Lover*, plays are thriving in central London with titles like *The French Mistress*, *Caught Napping*, and *Simple Spymen*. How, then, can I support my claim that the English theatre is growing up? I do so by reference to a three-pronged suburban assault that has lately been launched on the central citadel. As in a Shakespeare history play, the western region is all afire with deep-revolving zeal, led by the English Stage Company, which set up shop in 1955 at the Royal Court Theatre, in Sloane Square, where it has since presented, in addition to well-known texts by Arthur Miller, Brecht, Giraudoux, and Ionesco, the first plays of Angus Wilson, Nigel Dennis, Doris Lessing, N. F. Simpson, and John Osborne. The Court is run by a stuffy committee and aided by a meagre subsidy from the Arts Council; even so, it managed to stage, during the 1958–9 season, two remarkable plays that would never five years ago have transferred – as these did – to the West End. One was *The Long and the Short and the Tall*, by a thirty-year-old television writer named Willis Hall. In construction this was a wartime anecdote of fairly familiar mould. A reconnaissance patrol, cut off by a Japanese advance in the middle of the Malayan jungle, debates its chances of getting back to base by breaking through the enemy lines. The argument is complicated by the fact that the men have taken a Japanese prisoner; should they let him accompany them, or shoot him out of hand? As in most British war stories, the cast is a cliché microcosm, a 'cross-section of the community' that includes a Scot, a Welshman, a North Countryman, a Cockney, a trigger-happy sadist, and a tough warmhearted sergeant. They are all, however, deeply individualized; each speaks a language so abundant in racy local metaphor that I could have kicked myself for having acquiesced in the popular myth that the British vernacular is dull wherever it is not Americanized. Mr Hall's play is not only boisterous, exuberant, and accurate; it is also beautifully written. Moreover, it is performed in what, for the London theatre, is a new style of acting. Until a few years ago the English drama schools devoted much of their energy to ironing out of their pupils' accents all trace of regional origin and to replacing it with the neutral, official dialect spoken by B.B.C. announcers. Suddenly, however, a group of plays has sprung up for which B.B.C. English is utterly useless. Out of nowhere – or perhaps out of everywhere – an ambitiously talented bunch of young provincial actors has emerged, ideally fitted to embody the new drama, which treats ordinary people not as helpless victims, Stoical jingoists, or clownish vulgarians but as rational human beings. Only two of the eight men in Mr Hall's cast had appeared in the West End, and their director, Lindsay Anderson, had no previous experience of the professional stage, although he has a high reputation as a documentary-film maker. With his actors – Kenji Takaki, Robert Shaw, Edward Judd, Ronald Fraser, David Andrews, Emrys James, Bryan Pringle, and Peter O'Toole – I could find no fault, and in the case of Mr O'Toole, as the cynical Cockney who befriends the Japanese captive, I sensed a technical authority that may, given discipline and purpose, presage greatness. To convey violence beneath banter, and a soured, embarrassed goodness beneath both, is not the simplest task for a young player, yet Mr O'Toole achieved it without sweating a drop. The play lacked stars, and it had a downbeat (that is, anti-war) ending, in which the patrol was decimated. These facts may explain why, despite enthusiastic notices, it ran in the West End for only three months. It will, anyway, be remembered as a portent.

The same can be said of *Roots*, a new piece by Arnold Wesker, who is twenty-seven years old and was born in the East End of London. The subject of his play, which opened at the Court in June and has since moved to the West End, is ignorance. The daughter of a family of agricultural labourers comes home, after a long stay in London, full of progressive ideas she has learned from her lover, who works (as Mr Wesker once worked) in the kitchen of a West End restaurant. Fruitlessly, she tries to explain art and politics to her kinfolk, who regard her with compassionate bewilderment; she plays classical music to her mother on the phonograph, and embarks on a wild dance to illustrate the release it has brought to her. Mother nods, smiling but uncomprehending; how should she care for art, fed as she is by radio pabulum, living as she does with no electricity, an outdoor toilet, and water from a garden tank, on less than £5 a week? Beatie, the daughter, has returned with a vocabulary that succeeds only in alienating her from her background. In the last scene a family gathering is reluctantly convened to welcome her urban boy-friend, who fails to turn up. A smug reaction of I-told-you-so prevents anyone from comforting the shattered Beatie. If this were an English play of the traditional kind, the jilted girl would at this point recognize the futility of her intellectual aspirations and snuggle back to the bosom of the family. Not so Beatie. She rounds on her relatives, blaming their conservatism and their suspicion of independent thought for her own inability to communicate with intelligent people. She has failed because of the *mystique* of humility that has taught her since childhood to keep her place and not waste time on books. At the end of this tirade she realizes that for once she has not been parroting the opinions of her lover but has been thinking for herself. With the wonder that is cognate with one's first sense of identity, she cries, 'I'm beginning. *I'm beginning!*' And the play is over. I stumbled out in a haze of emotion, on a sticky, baking July evening. The theatre, I noticed, was full of young men and women who had been distracted from the movies, from television, and even from love-making by the powerful lure of a show that concerned them and that could help as well as amuse. Joan Plowright played the awakened rustic, and the director was John Dexter, and in neither case can I think of an alternative half as good.

What the future has in store for the Royal Court is anyone's guess. *Roots* was followed by Vivien Leigh in *Look after Lulu!*, Noël Coward's adaptation of Feydeau's *Occupe-toi d'Amélie*, which flopped last season on Broadway. The London critics politely detested it, and I cannot imagine why it was ever staged at that address. John Osborne told me that he walked into the theatre early in July and found it full of Miss Leigh, Mr Coward, and Hugh Beaumont, the most powerful of West End producers. He wondered for a second if he had come to the wrong place. The original idea had been that the Royal Court should conquer Shaftesbury Avenue; instead, Shaftesbury Avenue seemed to have conquered the Royal Court.

Whatever doubts one may have about the Sloane Square assault on the West End, the two other spearheads look pretty formidable. It is too early yet to pass judgement on the Mermaid Theatre, at Puddle Dock, which was conceived by a dedicated actor-impresario named Bernard Miles, built by public subscription on the brink of the Thames in the financial heart of London, and opened with fanfares last spring. A great concrete hangar, with a raked auditorium, a revolving stage, and an acting area that extends from wall to wall, the Mermaid is physically a director's dream. Its inaugural production – an immediate success – was a free adaptation, augmented by music and song, of *Rape upon Rape*, an eighteenth-century comedy by Henry Fielding, a satirist whose mordancy was such that it impelled Walpole, the Prime Minister, to bring all stage performances under the censorship of the Lord Chamberlain. (Fielding subsequently took up the novel, and England, according to Shaw, was thereby deprived of its finest playwright between Shakespeare and himself.) Intended as a sour indictment of corrupt judges, the play has been adulterated by the addition of insipid tunes and acting of a prevailing coyness; perhaps only Brecht and Weill could have given

Fielding the kind of musical staging he needed. The new title, *Lock Up Your Daughters*, indicates the degree of compromise that was involved. But Mr Miles has some valiant plans for his new playhouse. Once this hit has run its course, *on verra*.

By far the most damaging dent in the West End structure has been made by Joan Littlewood, the artistic director of the company known as Theatre Workshop. Two of the smartest playhouses in London – Wyndham's and the Criterion – are occupied, as I write this, by productions that originated at the Theatre Royal, Stratford-atte-Bowe, the East End headquarters of Miss Littlewood's extraordinary troupe. At the Criterion there is *A Taste of Honey*, a first play by Shelagh Delaney, a Lancashire girl who is well over six feet tall and just over twenty years old. It deals joyfully with what might, in other hands, have been a tragic situation. The teenage heroine, who lives in a ratty tenement bed-sitter, is deserted by her nagging, peroxided mother, who is unaware that her daughter is pregnant by a Negro sailor. Played with tenderly cheeky impulsiveness by a young actress named Frances Cuka, the girl accepts the fact that her child is likely to be fatherless and makes a temporary home with a slender art student whose sexual bent is toward his own sex. Her only qualm is that her own father was mentally deficient: 'He lived in a twilight land, my dad, the land of the daft.' Eventually her mother comes home, the student is summarily evicted, and the curtain falls on preparations for the impending birth. I don't know that I like all of Miss Littlewood's production tricks; I don't see why the mother should address all her lines to the audience, like a vaudeville soloist, and I can't understand why the original ending, in which she accepted the Negro paternity of her daughter's baby, has been altered to permit her to make unattractive jokes about piccaninnies and 'bloody chocolate drops'. All the same, we have here quite a writer, and quite a director.

Brendan Behan's *The Hostage*, currently playing at

Wyndham's Theatre, is a perfect embodiment of Miss Littlewood's methods, and well deserved the prize for the best production of the 1959 Paris International Theatre Festival. It is a babble of styles, devoid of form yet full of attack – *Hellzapoppin*, you might say, with a point of view. The scene is a Dublin bawdy-house in which a British serviceman is held as hostage for an I.R.A. soldier condemned to death for shooting a policeman. As in *A Taste of Honey*, what sounds tragic turns out to be uproariously comic. The brothel becomes a sort of music-hall. The actors chat to the audience, send themselves up in the mock-heroic manner that is Ireland's least imitable contribution to world literature, and sing a number of outstandingly villainous songs, including a devastating tribute to England –

> *Old ladies with stern faces,*
> *And the captains, and the kings*

– and a life-embracing chorus called 'There's no place on earth like the world.' No dramatic unity is achieved or aimed at; the players wander in and out of character whenever they, or the events of the play, feel like it. The jokes are unpredictable and often genuinely rude. The brand name of a whisky is clarified as 'Vat 69 – the Pope's telephone number', one of the principal clowns is a male transvestite named Princess Grace, and I particularly liked the Negro prizefighter who, in a moment of exceptional tumult, strolls across the stage bearing a sign that reads 'Keep Ireland Black.' Finally, the hostage – beautifully played by Alfred Lynch – is accidentally killed in a raid, but no time is allowed for mourning. Mr Lynch jumps up again and joins all the rest of the cast in a rousing number entitled 'Oh death, where is thy sting-a-ling-a-ling, oh grave, they victor-ee!'

Miss Littlewood demands players who can improvise not only in rehearsal but before an audience. She likes the morning's headlines to be incorporated into the evening's performance – a habit that caused her last year to be haled into court and fined for contravening the censorship regulations, which insist that every word spoken on a public stage must first be submitted for approval to the Lord Chamberlain's office. Whether it is desirable for actors to usurp the writer's job and invent their own lines is something I seriously doubt. Whenever I raise the subject, Miss Littlewood starkly replies that as soon as a production is fixed, it is dead, and that she would prefer anything to the inflexible monotony of what she sees in the West End. A stocky, trenchant woman in her forties, she was born in a working-class district of South London and educated at a convent school. She went to the Royal Academy of Dramatic Art on a scholarship, and founded Theatre Workshop in 1945, warning her actors that regular salaries were out of the question; all she could promise them was that the box-office receipts would be equally divided at the end of each week. The company toured England, Germany, Norway, Sweden, and Czechoslovakia for eight years before settling down at the Theatre Royal. To Miss Littlewood's dismay, the local proletariat failed to support her enterprise, and it was not until her productions of *Arden of Faversham* and *Volpone* were thunderously acclaimed at the 1955 Paris International Theatre Festival that the senior London critics began to take her seriously. Her recent conquest of the West End pleases her, but only because it means more money with which to realize her life's obsession – a people's theatre outside the West End. Politically, she stands well to the Left. This is not, I might add, a fact of much significance; it applies to nearly every theatre company in Europe of any contemporary importance.

Stratford-on-Avon is celebrating this year its hundredth season, with a troupe of actors led by Dame Edith Evans, Sir Laurence Olivier, Paul Robeson, Charles Laughton, and Sam Wanamaker. A stylistic chaos swirled around nearly everything I saw; it was like an all-star benefit show run mad in doublet and hose and lacking, for the most part, either unity or purpose. The five guest stars seemed remote from the rest of the cast –

and not surprisingly, when you consider that Dame Edith and Mr Laughton are playing only two roles apiece in a total of five plays, while Sir Laurence and the Messrs Robeson and Wanamaker are confining themselves, respectively, to Coriolanus, Othello, and Iago. Moreover, it takes a closely knit company and dynamic direction to offer consistently good work to an audience that is mainly composed of uncritical tourists and a town that is frankly apathetic toward theatre. Peter Bull, the English character actor, has lately recorded – in a highly diverting autobiography called *I Know the Face, But . . .* – his impressions of the place:

> I am here to say, with prejudice, that I personally loathe Stratford-on-Avon. . . . The atmosphere of old Tudory and brass ornaments brings my bile to boiling-point, and I did fancy during my short stay there that no one in the town seemed frightfully keen on the actors, who are largely responsible for bringing the shop ladies and gentlemen their revenue.

Mr Bull's testimony may be slightly loaded, since he was fired during rehearsals; all the same, he has a point. *All's Well That Ends Well*, the first Stratford production I saw this year, is directed by Tyrone Guthrie with his familiar, infuriating blend of insight and madness. On the one hand we have the great conductor, the master of visual orchestration, conceivably the most striking director alive when there are more than six people on stage; on the other hand we have his zany *Doppelgänger*, darting about with his pockets full of fireworks, and giving the members of the orchestra hot-feet whenever genuine feeling threatens to impend. He has done to *All's Well* what he did a few seasons ago to *Troilus and Cressida* at the Old Vic; that is, set it in a Shavian Ruritania faintly redolent of *Arms and the Man*. This, of course, would have delighted Shaw, who always held that Helena, the lady doctor who pursues and ensnares the man of her choice, was a harbinger of his own aggressive heroines. Mr Guthrie's modernization enables him to make some telling points that Elizabethan costume often obscures. When Helena, having worked her miracle cure on the king's fistula, claims as her reward the hand of Bertram, the young man's initial reaction is to treat the whole thing as a joke; he cannot believe that the daughter of a medical practitioner could seriously contemplate marrying into the aristocracy. Meanwhile, the braggart Parolles becomes a breezy, overdressed roadhouse cad, foredoomed to failure in his social climbing by the possession of an accent that is ever so slightly 'off'. What Mr Guthrie has done is to make subtle class distinctions where Shakespeare made broad ones; one wonders whether the idea could have occurred to anyone but an Englishman. Until the evening was halfway through, I was beguiled and fascinated. Afterwards Mr Guthrie's love of horseplay obtrudes, and we get – among other things – a long scene, performed mainly in mime, wherein a deaf general reviews the French troops and exhorts them to battle through a faulty public-address system. Two hours of this can be fun; three and a quarter is too much. Lavache, the Countess of Roussillon's clown, who has some of the most haunting prose in Shakespeare, is entirely omitted; to cut a play, yet make what remains last longer than the whole, must argue, I suppose, a kind of dotty genius. The role of the Countess, curiously described by Shaw as the most beautiful old woman's part ever written (it is in fact merely the only old woman's part in Shakespeare that is neither a scold nor a murderess), is played by Dame Edith in her characteristic later manner – tranquillized benevolence cascading from a great height, like royalty opening a bazaar.

Peter Hall, the young man who will next year assume the direction of the Stratford theatre, has staged *A Midsummer Night's Dream* in a manner just as personal as the Guthrie *All's Well*. With sound historical justification, he sees the play as an occasional piece, intended for the celebration of a well-bred marriage; accordingly, he deploys the action in the great hall of an Elizabethan manor house, which gradually, through the cunning of

Lila de Nobili's décor, sprouts greenery and develops into a more or less credible forest. Foolishly, the lover's scenes are played for broad comedy; Mr Hall's sense of stage humour is not of the subtlest, and too many people stumble and fall unfunnily down. His positive contribution is in his handling of the fairies. Fatigued by sinister Oberons with sequins on their eyelids and by Junoesque Titanias attended by sinewy girls flapping romantically about to Mendelssohn, I was delighted by Mr Hall's fresh approach. His fairies are closely related to the lost boys of *Peter Pan*, with Titania as their prim, managing Wendy. Admittedly, they are clad somewhat like insects, and one of them is without doubt a diminutive old lady. But Oberon himself is pure Peter — a petulant, barefoot boy; well-meaning and genuinely magical. Puck, in this interpretation, is not so much his slave as his kid brother. Finally, we have Charles Laughton, a ginger-wigged, ginger-bearded Bottom. I confess I do not know what Mr Laughton is up to, but I am sure I would hate to share a stage with it. He certainly takes the audience into his confidence, but the process seems to exclude from his confidence everyone else in the cast. Fidgeting with a lightness that reminds one (even as one forgets what the other actors are talking about) how expertly bulky men dance, he blinks at the pit his moist, reproachful eyes, softly cajoles and suddenly roars, and behaves throughout in a manner that has nothing to do with acting, although it perfectly hits off the demeanour of a rapscallion uncle dressed up to entertain the children at a Christmas party.

Othello, as directed by Tony Richardson, is full of factitious life — jazz drumming between scenes, rampageous crowds, gestures toward symbolism, like making the Duke of Venice a cripple who has to be carried off-stage by a Negro servant, and bizarre climatic effects, as when Othello disembarks on Cyprus in a thick fog and a high wind — and totally devoid of emotional reality. Shakespeare's great indictment of circumstantial evidence comes almost suavely across, without passion or impact. None of the three leading players seems to be operating on the same wave-length as the others, or even to be speaking the same language. Two of them – Mr Robeson and Mr Wanamaker – have had very little Shakespearian experience, and the third – Mary Ure – is vocally ill-equipped for either tragedy or poetry. Miss Ure primly flutes; Mr Wanamaker clips and swallows, playing Iago in a style one would like to call conventional if only he were doing it well. Iago, above all, should be disarming. Mr Wanamaker, to coin an epithet, is profoundly arming. In more appropriate company, I am sure, Mr Robeson would rise to greater heights than he does. As things are, he seems to be murdering a butterfly on the advice of a gossip columnist. His voice, of course, is incomparable – a foundation-shaking boom. It may, however, be too resonant, too musically articulated for the very finest acting. The greatest players – Kean and Irving, for example – have seldom been singers as well. Their voices were human and imperfect, whereas the noise made by Mr Robeson is so nearly perfect as to be nearly inhuman.

We will skim over the inessentials of the Stratford *Coriolanus* as quickly as possible. Boris Aronson's setting is mountainous, which is fine, and full of mountainous steps, which is not – I recalled Alec Guinness's remark, *à propos* of Shakespearian productions in general, that he himself had very few conversations on the stairs of his own house. Harry Andrews is a stolid, muscular Menenius. As Volumnia, the hero's stifling mother, Edith Evans looks overpowering, but her fussy, warbling vibrato swamps all too often the meaning of the lines. Peter Hall's direction is straight and vigorous, with hardly any ideological slanting – a good way with a play that is best served when either everything is slanted or nothing. The lesson to be learned from *Coriolanus* is that although Shakespeare was willing to condemn anyone in the social order, no matter how low or high his position, he would never have condemned the order itself. Any rung in a ladder may be rotten, but there must be a ladder, and rungs.

We can now get down to the heart of the production, which is Olivier's performance of Coriolanus. The first thing to praise is its sheer intuitive intelligence. Olivier understands that Coriolanus is not an aristocrat; he is a professional soldier, a *Junker*, if you like, reminiscent in many ways of General de Gaulle – a rejected military saviour who returns, after a long and bodeful silence, with an army at his back. Fully aware of the gap between Coriolanus and the patricians he is serving, Olivier uses it to gain for the man an astounding degree of sympathy. With the delicacy that is his hallmark as much as power – few actors are physically as dainty, and none rolls eyes that are half as calf-like – he emphasizes Coriolanus the hater of phoneyness, the plain military man embarrassed by adulation, the awkward adult boy sickened equally by flattery and by the need to flatter. A cocky, jovial commander, he cannot bring himself to feign humility in order to become Consul, and his sulky refusal to apologize to the people takes on, in Olivier's hands, the aspect of high political comedy. We cannot applaud the man, but we like him, and thus the battle of the part is halfway won. What spurs him to betray Rome is not pride but a loathing of false servility.

Olivier also seizes on the fact that Coriolanus was brought up under his mother's thumb. 'There's no man in the world/More bound to 'a mother,' says Volumnia. Her opinion always comes first. 'I muse my mother/Does not approve me further' is our initial hint that Coriolanus is doubtful whether he is right to be so intransigent toward the plebeians. Under her persuasion, he consents to make his peace with them, and it is Volumnia who finally dissuades him from sacking Rome, the paternal city. Olivier's ashamed, hesitant collapse is among the truest moments of his performance. Sidling towards Volumnia, he grasps her hand and murmurs, 'Oh – *my mother. . . .*'

This Coriolanus is all-round Olivier. We have the wagging head, the soaring index finger, and the sly, roaming eyes of one of the world's cleverest comic actors, plus the desperate, exhausted moans of one of the world's masters of pathos. But we also confront the nonpareil of heroic tragedians, as athletically lissome as when he played Oedipus a dozen years ago. No actor uses *rubato*, stealing a beat from one line to give to the next, like Olivier. The voice is soft steel that can chill and cut, or melt and scorch. One feels the chill in the icy tirade that begins 'You common cry of curs' and ends 'There is a world elsewhere.' And one is scorched by the gargled snarl of rage with which Olivier rams home, by a wrenching upward inflexion on the last syllable, 'The fires i' th' lowest hell fold in the peo*ple*!' At the close, faithful as ever to the characterization on which he has fixed, Olivier is roused to suicidal frenzy by Aufidius's gibe – 'thou boy of tears.' '*Boy!*' shrieks the overmothered general, in an outburst of strangled fury, and leaps up a flight of precipitous steps to vent his rage. Arrived at the top, he relents and throws his sword away. After letting his voice fly high in the great, swingeing line about how he 'flutter'd your Volscians in *Cor-i-o-li*,' he allows a dozen spears to impale him. He is poised, now, on a promontory some twelve feet above the stage, from which he topples forward, to be caught by the ankles so that he dangles, inverted, like the slaughtered Mussolini. A more shocking, less sentimental death I have not seen in the theatre; it is at once proud and ignominious, as befits the titanic fool who dies it.

The image, and the echo, of this astonishing performance have taken root in my mind in the weeks that have passed since I witnessed it. The dark imprint of Olivier's stage presence is something one forgets only with an effort, but the voice is a lifelong possession of those who have heard it at its best. It sounds, distinct and barbaric, across the valley of many centuries, like a horn calling to the hunt, or the neigh of a battle-maddened charger.

(1959)

Titus Andronicus

by WILLIAM SHAKESPEARE
at the Stoll

Cymbeline

by WILLIAM SHAKESPEARE
at Stratford-on-Avon

Having closely compared Peter Brook's production of *Titus Andronicus* with Peter Hall's production of *Cymbeline*, I am persuaded that these two young directors should at once go into partnership. I have even worked out business cards for them:

Hall & Brook, Ltd, the Home of Lost Theatrical Causes. Collapsing plays shored up, unspeakable lines glossed over, unactable scenes made bearable. Wrecks salvaged, ruins refurbished: unpopular plays at popular prices. Masterpieces dealt with only if neglected. Shakespearian juvenilia and senilia our speciality: if it can walk, we'll make it run. Bad last acts no obstacle: if it peters out, call Peter in. Don't be fobbed off with Glenvilles, Woods, or Zadeks: look for the trademark – Hall & Brook.

The present examples of Hallage and Brookery come unmistakably from the same firm. In each case the director has imposed on a blood-stained, uneven play a unifying conception of his own. Messrs Brook and Hall have swathed in 'atmosphere' pieces of work which otherwise would be tedious. They have punctuated drab texts with ritual processions, barbaric music and extravagant scenic effects, thereby distracting attention from lines and situations that would be absurd without such adornment. And, by an odd coincidence, they have both been craven in the same way. Asked to produce Tamora's lost sons, Titus replies: 'Why, there they are both, baked in that pie': Mr Brook deletes the last five words. Similarly, when Caius Lucius exclaims: 'Soft ho! what trunk is here without his top?'

Mr Hall deletes the last three. This is inexcusable coward-ice. Those who devote themselves to making silk purses out of sows' ears are in duty bound to go the whole hog.

Two years ago Mr Brook's production crowned a Strat-ford season which had already seen Sir Laurence Olivier's triumphant Macbeth. After that banquet, *Titus* came as an unexpected *bonne bouche*, and also as a neat bit of directorial do-it-yourself, since Mr Brook was responsible both for the music, growling and pinging, and the décor, stately and arcane. The same production, having lately visited and apparently dumbfounded such exotic cities as Zagreb and Warsaw, is now installed at the Stoll as an established classic. This is going altogether too far. While I admire the skill with which Sir Laurence and his director have made the play palatable, I wish they had collabor-ated on something nobler than a versified atrocity report. They have done superbly something that was not worth doing at all; and I am sure that London would have pre-ferred to see its greatest actor in the highest reaches of his art, not splashing about in its shallows.

I agree that he splashes tremendously, making crested waves of mere ripples; no one can rival Sir Laurence when it comes to transports of rage, moans of grief, guttural crows of triumph and Senecan doughtiness of soul. Yet on Monday night he was well below par. His voice seemed constipated, a crafty squawk instead of a terrible bellow; he rushed and gabbled, betraying all the signs of an over-tired actor who is addressing a foreign audience and count-ing on their inability to understand what he is saying.

This symptom was noticeable in many of his col-leagues: I have never heard a Shakespeare play so unin-telligibly raced. There were two shining exceptions: Maxine Audley and Anthony Quayle as Tamora and Aaron, who ran away with the evening by the simple expedient of not running at all. Sir Laurence's London appearances are rare, and this one is not to be missed; but I hope that no one will go expecting to see him, or his author, at anything like their best.

Mr Hall tackles *Cymbeline*, a slightly better play, with

similar aplomb and comparable success; which does not mean that I think his production should forthwith be sent on an extended tour of Eastern Europe. What he has done is to weld all the play's manifold facets – its jokes and beheadings, its Roman armies and Renaissance villainies – into the same experience; and he has achieved this by throwing over the whole production a sinister veil of faery, so that it resembles a Grimm fable transmuted by the Cocteau of *La Belle et la Bête*.

He creates, in short, an ambience in which the ludicrous anomalies of the plot are believable and even lovable. Lila de Nobili helps him, with a cobwebby, tree-shaded, magic-prone Gothic setting that takes us straight into the world of momentous fantasy where alone the play can flourish. Posthumus (Richard Johnson) is a perfect white-clad knight; the Queen (Joan Miller) an Arthurian enchantress. Helmets gleam and threaten from high hillsides, and all the costumes are silvery, bulrushy or glaucous green. All but for the Romans, who wear crimson and gold: the massed advance of those embossed and glittering shields makes a stunning visual impact.

I was prepared to be entranced by Peggy Ashcroft's Imogen until I began to be obsessed by this actress's ocular mannerisms. We all know that she blinks; it was my misfortune to discover that her blinks coincide with the words she intends to emphasize. Having spotted this trick, I watched only for her blinking, and am thus in no position to assess her performance. Otherwise, my admiration for Mr Hall's production is boundless, and I was as appalled as he must have been by the off-stage engineer who prefaced every musical intervention with thirty booming seconds of gramophone hum.

(1957)

Pericles

by WILLIAM SHAKESPEARE
at Stratford-on-Avon

Johnson thought *Pericles* a 'mouldy tale', though it is hard nowadays to see why. Today the epic is back in vogue : no longer, either in the novel or the theatre, do we reject as inartistic a series of imaginary events whose only common denominator is that they all happen to the same person.

Whoever wrote the play's first two acts was plainly a sloppy poet (e.g., his constant use of 'the which' to pad out the pentameter), but I don't doubt that, were he alive today, his scripts would be all over the wide screens. There is even, as they say, a picture in *Pericles*, assuming that the censor could be soothed. The fulcrum of the action – Pericles' flight from Antioch on discovering incest at court – would need what is known as a little fixing, and the brothel in Mytilene would automatically become a sort of wild teashop, but the rest is (almost literally) plain sailing. Before long the 'working title' would be abandoned, and an item would appear in *Variety* : 'De Mille rumoured dickering with Kirk Douglas for lead in upcoming blockbuster, "Around the Med. in Eighteen Years".'

But there is more to the play than crowd-catching melodrama. From the moment in Act III when Shakespeare announces his presence with : 'Thou god of this great vast, rebuke these surges', we are in another world. The verse, hitherto skipping, begins to stride; the characters, so many antique court cards, take on a third dimension. The brothel interludes are as good as anything in *Measure for Measure*, and, outside *Lear*, Shakespeare never wrote a father-daughter scene as moving as the mutual recognition of Pericles and Marina : after this, the old voyager's rediscovery of his wife seems almost perfunctory.

Daughters, in the later plays, are the thing : sometimes

long-lost, like Marina and Perdita: sometimes, like Imogen and Cordelia, estranged from father: sometimes banished with him, as Miranda was: and once, in the case of Goneril and Regan, dedicated to his destruction. The climax of *Henry VIII* is the birth of a royal princess whose father, like Prospero, Lear and Pericles, has no male issue. Nor, at the time of his death, had Shakespeare. His only son died in 1596, and his daughters, Susanna and Judith, both survived him. To Susanna he left the bulk of his estate, while Judith got nothing. Was there no sibling rivalry here, no paternal preference? Were there no rows and reconciliations? We can only guess in the dark. My own conjecture is that Shakespeare was latterly much obsessed with his girls, which may explain why the greatest play-doctor in the history of drama chose the story of Pericles to re-vamp, and why he did it with such passion.

The Stratford production is pictorially magnificent, a restless Oriental kaleidoscope in which the crowds move horizontally and the stage lifts vertically. Tony Richardson, directing Shakespeare for the first time, deploys a visual imagination of Reinhardtian fertility: the action flows like a stream over rapids, accompanied by music that twangles and bubbles, disguising the bad bits and enlivening the good. The chorus, Gower, is Shakespeare's tribute to the earlier poet from whom he got his story: Mr Richardson brilliantly makes him a Negro fabulist, telling the strange tale to a bunch of credulous sailors.

In every respect save one Mr Richardson's Stratford début is as impressive as Peter Brook's, twelve years ago. The exception is in the matter of acting. There is nothing wrong with Richard Johnson's patient Pericles, Geraldine McEwan's sweetly candid Marina, or Patrick Wymark's oafish brothel-keeper. Nor is there anything memorably right: never do we feel that the text has been creatively pointed, jabbed into new life. And where it most matters, in the third-act storm where Shakespeare comes up like thunder, the lines are lost in mechanical uproar: I listened in vain for: 'The seaman's whistle is as a whisper in the ear of death.' 'More matter, with less art' : Gertrude had Polonius's number, and Mr Richardson's too. He will be a superb director when he gets the balance right.

(1958)

Decade in Retrospect: 1959

I offer no prognosis, since the patient's condition is still desperately enfeebled, but I do not think it deniable that at some point in the past ten years the English theatre regained its will to live, emerged from its coma, and started to show signs of interest in the world around it. Assuming that it gets the proper nourishment, it may walk again. If my optimism sounds hesitant, I ask you to remember that as recently as five years ago all the symptoms presaged disaster.

The early fifties saw the withering of the vogue for verse drama that had flowered, with so much acclamation, in the previous decade. It is absurdly easy, now that the boon of hindsight is ours, to explain why *The Cocktail Party* and the charming inventions of Mr Fry were so zealously over-touted. They gave us access to imagined worlds in which rationing and the rest of austerity's paraphernalia could be forgotten; they also reminded us that words could be put to other public uses than those of military propaganda, news bulletins and government regulations.

But as the economy revived, everyday reality became less obnoxious; and it was clear, soon after the new decade began, that audiences were ready for plays about the facts of contemporary life. This readiness amounted before long to a positive hunger. Terence Rattigan responded to it with his best plays, *The Deep Blue Sea* (1952) and *Separate Tables* (1954); Graham Greene contributed *The Living Room* in 1953; and their matinée Doppelgänger was N. C. Hunter, the author of *Waters of the Moon* and *A Day by the Sea*.

At the same time, the flood of interpretative energy that had poured since the war into productions of the classics had begun to dry up, or at least to seek diversion; in the last six years there have been few revivals worthy of mention in the same breath as Peter Brook's *Measure for Measure* and *Venice Preserv'd*, Tyrone Guthrie's *Tamburlaine*, and Douglas Seale's tripartie *Henry VI*, all of which were staged between 1950 and 1953. On both sides of the footlights one felt a movement toward something fresher, something that was connected more intimately – more journalistically, perhaps – with daily experience.

I do not wish to make extravagant claims. The movement was, and is, a minority affair, operating within an art that exerts, at best, no more than a minority appeal. The face of the West End has not been lifted overnight, detective stories and inane light comedies are as prevalent today as they were ten years ago, and our musicals (apart from *The Boy Friend*, a deliberate exercise in nostalgia) sound archaically quaint besides such post-1950 Broadway products as *Wonderful Town*, *The Pajama Game*, *My Fair Lady*, *West Side Story* and *Gypsy*. The quality of the bad shows is as low as ever. It is the quality of the good ones that has risen.

The breakthrough took place in the spring of 1956. Much as I wince at images of purulence, there is no doubt that the English Stage Company's production of *Look Back in Anger* lanced a boil that had plagued our theatre for many years. Good taste, reticence and middle-class understatement were convicted of hypocrisy and jettisoned on the spot; replacing them, John Osborne spoke out in a vein of ebullient, free-wheeling rancour that betokened the arrival of something new in the theatre – a sophisticated, articulate lower-class. Most of the critics were offended by Jimmy Porter, but not on account of his anger; a working-class hero is expected to be angry. What nettled them was something quite different: his self-confidence. This was no envious inferior whose insecurity they could pity. Jimmy Porter talked with the wit and assurance of a young man who not only knew he was right but had long since mastered the vocabulary wherewith to express his knowledge.

Osborne's success breached the dam, and there followed a cascade of plays about impoverished people. Such plays had existed before; the novelty lay in the fact that the emphasis was now on the people rather than on their poverty. For the first time it was possible for a character in English drama to be poor and intelligently amusing.

Writers like John Arden, Doris Lessing, Alun Owen and Willis Hall had their works performed at the Court, and with three plays – *Chicken Soup and Barley*, *Roots* and *The Kitchen* – Arnold Wesker came closer than any other English dramatist to demonstrating that Socialist realism was not a dogmatic formula but a uniquely powerful means of conveying sane theatrical emotion. (The last act of *Roots* is as moving as any piece of native writing I have seen on the West End stage.)

Meanwhile, after years of neglect and discouragement, Theatre Workshop was coming into its own. Joan Littlewood's craggy determination to create a people's drama bore fruit at last with Shelagh Delaney's *A Taste of Honey* and Brendan Behan's two adventures in dialogue, *The Quare Fellow* and *The Hostage*. Rowdier and less cerebral than what was going on at the Court, Theatre Workshop's productions nevertheless made a more thorough conquest of the West End. Last summer, at the Criterion and Wyndham's (the respective homes of Miss Delaney's first play and Mr Behan's second), I saw in the audience young people in flimsy dresses and open-necked shirts whose equivalents, ten years ago, would have been in a cinema, if they were indoors at all. What is more, they were cheering at the end.

How has this upsurge of – we must face the phrase – proletarian drama come about? Primarily, of course, because two theatres with liberal policies were available to give it a hearing; without the Court and Theatre Workshop it would never have happened. But what external influences can one detect? Not many, I would say, from France. Messrs Beckett and Ionesco have left their fingerprints on Harold Pinter and the mortally funny N. F. Simpson; otherwise, France is nowhere. (On the strength of his new play, *One Way Pendulum*, I suspect Mr Simpson to be the possessor of the subtlest mind ever devoted by an Englishman to the writing of farce.)

And Germany? The key name, of course, is Brecht, but the paucity of good translations, coupled with the short supply of managements who are willing and able to stage his work in the manner to which it is accustomed, has inevitably limited his impact. The brief London visit of the Berliner Ensemble recruited a multitude of admirers, but it has not, as far as one can tell, inspired any plays. We argue about Brecht's virtues and vices as an embodiment of 'committed art'; we contrast him with Shaw, whom Lenin acutely called 'a good man fallen among Fabians'; but we have borrowed little from his style beyond a few directorial tricks. Either we should perfect our German, or his translators should learn English.

In my view, the strongest and most unmistakable influence on our drama in the last ten years has been transatlantic. For the first time in its history, the English theatre has been swayed and shaped by America – by which I mean Hollywood as well as Broadway. The young people who are moulding the future of the London stage were all growing up at a time when the talking picture had established itself not merely as a viable medium of entertainment but as a primary (perhaps *the* primary) form of art. They cut their teeth on the films of Welles, Wyler, Wilder and Kazan, and on the plays (later adapted for the screen) of Arthur Miller and Tennessee Williams. Some of them prefer Williams, others Miller, but you will find very few who dislike both.

If latter-day English drama is serious in intent, contemporary in theme, and written in rasping prose, Broadway and Hollywood are part of the reason. The results, for good playwrights who are inimical to realism, have not been altogether beneficial. John Whiting appears to have abandoned the theatre; Peter Ustinov's development seems to have been arrested since *Romanoff and Juliet*; and sabre-toothed satire, which is nearly always stylized, has been represented in London only by Nigel Dennis's *Cards of Identity* and *The Making of Moo*, neither of which ran very long. ('Satire," as George Kaufman said, 'is what closes on Saturday night.') It would be sad if a healthy and belated faith in realism were to lead to a rejection of all those non-realistic forms towards which satire naturally inclines.

My hope for the sixties is the same as my hope for the fifties – that before they are out I shall see the construction of the National Theatre. Or, rather, of two National Theatres, equal in size and technical facilities. One of them would focus its attention on old plays, the other on new ones. The talent is demonstrably there. All it needs is financial succour, official status, and a permanent address.

Billy Liar

by KEITH WATERHOUSE and WILLIS HALL
at the Cambridge

The Lion in Love

by SHELAGH DELANEY
at the Belgrade, Coventry

The Happy Haven

by JOHN ARDEN
at the Royal Court

In quantity, the past week has been a bright one for supporters of the new movement in our theatre; three plays by gifted young authors cropped up on successive nights. Quality, however, is another matter; and it is here that my lips purse and the brooding begins.

We have irrevocably (and healthily) renounced the 'gentleman code' that cast its chilling blight on so much of twentieth-century English drama. No longer are we asked to judge characters by the exquisiteness of their sensibilities, or by the degree to which, in moments of crisis, their behaviour is consonant with Bloomsbury standards of tact, good form and discreetly muted sentiment. Yet to these standards, rarefied and bloodless though they were, the audience assented, and in part aspired; they formed a shared territory of belief upon which communication of a sort was possible.

Now, dive-bombed by Mr Osborne and undermined by Miss Littlewood, they have been laid low. And the question arises: With what are they to be replaced? The old code, so to speak, has been cracked: where and what are the new assumptions which, jointly held by author and audience, will enable a new kind of communication to be achieved and sustained? For without some common ground, some area of truce wherein the playwright's convictions (moral, social or political) coincide with those of his spectators, drama quickly languishes; it may, in such circumstances, provoke a scandal, or bask in a fleeting *succès d'estime*, but it is very unlikely to take root.

The present state of the English theatre is one of deadlock. Its audience is still predominantly conservative, wedded by age and habit to the old standards; its younger playwrights, meanwhile, are predominantly anti-conservative, irretrievably divorced from the ideological *status quo*. Obviously, they need a new audience; but in order to attract it they will have to define and dramatize the new values for which they severally stand. We know what they are *against* – the human consequences of class privilege, the profit motive, organized religion, and so forth – but what are they *for*?

Most of them are Socialists of one shade or another; but it is significant that Arnold Wesker, their foremost advocate of affirmation, concluded his trilogy with a play that affirmed nothing but the futility of Socialism. The only general assumption on which Mr Wesker, his colleagues and their audiences seem to be substantially agreed is that the lower strata of English society deserve a more central place on the English stage.

But this is an extremely tricky area of agreement; because English audiences (outside the Royal Court and
Theatre Workshop) instinctively associate the lower strata
of society with the lower strata of comedy. Give them half
a chance, and they'll laugh their heads off; and this creates
a great temptation to play into their hands – as, for all
its merits, *Fings Ain't Wot They Used T'be* unquestionably does. The point is that it takes a stiff injection of
social comment to persuade your average playgoer to
accept shows of this genre on any level other than that
of farce. *Roots*, which was thus inoculated, is Mr Wesker's
best work. *Billy Liar*, adapted by Keith Waterhouse and
Willis Hall from Mr Waterhouse's exuberant novel, lacks
any such injection. The broader implications of the book
are skirted or ignored; it is presented in terms of pure
farce. The first-night audience accordingly treated it as
such, and understandably found it wanting.

The eponymous hero is a provincial adolescent in a
ferment of furtive rebellion against everything that surrounds him; no explanation of his mutinous tendencies is
offered beyond the fact that he has a bellicose and hard-
cursing father. An undertaker's clerk and something of a
psychopath, Billy lives a multitude of secret lives. At the
slightest provocation he lapses into mimicry; an industrial
dynast, an Augustan fop and a legless war hero are among
his pet characterizations. His conscience is a vacuum. Three
adoring girls are vying for his hand; by some miscalcula-
tion, he is betrothed to two of them, and much of the
action concerns his efforts to relieve his official fiancée of
her engagement ring in order to transfer it to her importunate successor.

He invents elaborate lies, most of them totally unnecessary, to greet anyone who telephones or knocks at
the door; and he delights in spreading palpably false
reports about pregnancies and amputations. When his
grandmother dies – a garrulous old complainer whom in
life he detested – he suffers a single, momentary pang of
sorrow. Alone in a moonlit garden, he has been idly imit-
tating bird-calls and playing about with a bamboo stick,

which he uses first as an outsize cigarette-holder and then as a drum-major's baton; suddenly remembering the corpse upstairs, he curbs his fantasies, and begins, solemnly and in pure bugle tones, to hum the Last Post.

It is an unforgettable moment – the high point of the play, and also of Albert Finney's performance. This stocky, surly young maestro sometimes mugs as exorbitantly when playing Billy himself as he does when playing Billy imitating someone else; all the same, Mr Finney is a true fascinator, as Richard Burton was at his age. What mars the evening (apart from the adaptors' absurd decision to restrict the action to one suburban villa instead of letting it roam) is the fact that Billy Liar, as here presented, is no more than an opportunistic splicing of Jimmy Porter, minus the passion, and Lucky Jim, minus the moral awareness. The result is a ramshackle piece of purely whimsical entertainment, and Lindsay Anderson rightly directs it as such.

Shelagh Delaney's second play, The Lion in Love, has many of the negative merits of the new school. Though it deals with a Lancashire family in a state of constant emotional upheaval, it wastes no time on sentimental agonies or grand romantic outbursts. Everything is compressed, slimmed down to the hard bone of fact. Dad, a congenital bolter, leaves home for the umpteenth time, and for the umpteenth time slinks back. Banner, his son, returns rich from the prize-ring, spends all he has, and departs, almost unnoticed, for Australia. Peg, Banner's sister, is picked up by a lively young Glaswegian and whisked off to London. There are no emotional explosions; the tone throughout is cool and casual. It is also flat.

Miss Delaney prattles on like a primitive, filling her pages with traditional North Country tags, mottoes, quips and insults – the small change of Lancashire conversation, though possibly silver-sounding to Southern ears. Apart from an odd phrase here and there (e.g., the description of council houses as 'brick boxes with eyes in them'), the writing leaves no mark on one's memory. The last act is a riot of loose ends, and no hint of underlying philosophy is vouchsafed beyond the assertion that everyone is out for himself.

John Arden's *The Happy Haven* is an elephantine comedy of humours about an old people's home, run by a smug, adenoidal doctor who discovers a chemical formula for rejuvenation and wants to try it out on his patients. Already embarked on their second childhood, which seems to embody all the worst, most bitterly competitive features of their first, they shrink in horror from the idea of being young again. Eventually, they manage to pump the doctor full of his own elixir, whereupon he dwindles into a teddybear-clutching schoolboy. End of joke.

Mr Arden fails not merely because his wit is elephantine, but because his play has no anchor in normality. The characters are all unhinged, and there is no one to act as a bridge between ourselves and the grotesques across the footlights. The acting, meanwhile, is first rate; nobody could improve on the unctuous breeziness, the glottal wheedling, of Peter Bowles as the medical superintendent.

(1960)

The Caretaker

by HAROLD PINTER
at the Duchess

With *The Caretaker* Harold Pinter has begun to fulfil the promise that I signally failed to see in *The Birthday Party* two years ago.

The latter play was a clever fragment grown dropsical with symbolic content. A befuddled young lodger, lazing in a seaside boarding-house, was visited and ultimately kidnapped by a pair of sinister emissaries from the Outside World; the piece was full of those familiar paranoid overtones that seem to be inseparable from much of *avant-garde* drama. In *The Caretaker* symptoms of paranoia are still detectable – one of the characters is a near-zombie whose individuality has been forcibly effaced by a brain operation – but their intensity is considerably abated; and the symbols have mostly retired to the background.

What remains is a play about people. They are three in number, and all male. One is the mental *castrato* I have already mentioned; a sad, kindly fellow, he inhabits a suburban attic that is crammed with cherished objects of no conceivable use, among them a rusty lawn-mower and a disconnected gas-cooker (Cf. M. Ionesco's *Le Nouveau Locataire.*) He offers a bed to a mangy, homeless old tramp, who spends most of his time raging about imagined insults and planning abortive trips to Sidcup, where he has left his references and proofs of identity in charge of a quondam friend. The triangle is completed by his host's brother, a talkative, ambitious young man who owns both the attic and the crumbling house beneath it. Eager to obtain a job as caretaker, the tramp tries flattering the brothers and even attempts to play one off against the other. He succeeds only in antagonizing both, and ends up evicted.

Now it may very well be that there are symbols here. The two brothers may represent the bifurcated halves of a schizoid personality; alternatively, the landlord may stand for the Super-Ego, the tenant for the Ego, and the tramp for the Id. Either way, I am not particularly concerned. What holds one, theatrically, is Mr Pinter's bizarre use (some would call it abuse) of dramatic technique, his skill in evoking atmosphere, and his encyclopaedic command of contemporary idiom.

To take these qualities in order : where most playwrights devote their technical efforts to making us wonder what will happen *next*, Mr Pinter focuses our wonder on what is happening *now*. Who are these people? How did they meet, and why? Mr Pinter delays these disclosures until the last tenable moment; he teases us without boring us, which is quite a rare achievement. It is reinforced by his mastery of atmosphere. There is a special belt of English suburbia, spectral in its dusty shabbiness, that

exists in no other Anglo-Saxon country. America has tenement drama, penthouse drama and drama set in the exur-
banite strongholds of the middle class; but London is
unique in the *déclassé* decrepitude of its Western suburbs,
with their floating population, their indoor dustbins, their
desolate bed-sitters, their prevalent dry rot – moral as well
as structural – and their frequent, casual suicides. Mr
Pinter captures all this with the most chilling economy.

We come finally to his verbal gifts; and it is here that
cracks of doubt begin to appear in the façade of my enthusiasm. Time and again, without the least departure
from authenticity, Mr Pinter exposes the vague, repetitive
silliness of lower-class conversation. One laughs in recognition; but one's laughter is tinged with snobbism. Towards the end of the evening I found myself recalling an
experimental play I had seen some ten years before. Its
origins were Dutch, and it took place in a snowbound
hut on top of a mountain; the *dramatis personae* were The
Mother, The Daughter and Fate, who emerged from a
wardrobe in the second act and delivered a baleful tirade
about death. Rain, meanwhile, splashed into a bucket
through a hole in the roof. When the harangue was done,
the Mother lifted her eyes and said, more aptly than perhaps she knew : 'Only the drip speaks.'

Mr Pinter's play likewise has a bucket and a leaky roof;
and it occurred to me, as the curtain fell, that what I had
been watching was nothing more than an old-fashioned
avant-garde exercise, galvanized into a semblance of
novelty by the author's miraculous ear for colloquial
eccentricities. Instead of The Brother, The Other Brother
and Everyman, the characters were called Aston, Mick
and Davies; and instead of declaiming, they chatted.

Yet the quality of the chat is consistently high. Mr
Pinter is a superb manipulator of language, which he sees
not as a bridge that brings people together but as a barrier
that keeps them apart. Ideas and emotions, in the larger
sense, are not his province; he plays with words, and he
plays on our nerves, and it is thus that he grips us. Three
remarkable actors embody his vision. Donald Pleasance,

as the wild Welsh tramp, has the showiest part and gives the most spectacular performance; but I felt that he was carried, like a drunk between two policemen, by the muscular playing of his colleagues – Alan Bates, as the heartless, garrulous brother, and Peter Woodthorpe, as the stolid, pathetic one. The direction, an object lesson in the organization of nuances, is by Donald McWhinnie.

(1960)

Tamburlaine the Great

by CHRISTOPHER MARLOWE
at the Oxford University Dramatic Society

Tamburlaine the Great, cut and directed by John Duncan, is the most accomplished thing the OUDS has done for years. The lawn is alive with swirling soldiers, who stop dead in their tracks the instant anybody speaks; when the speech ends, they zoom about again, coming to rest in starkly stylized postures as soon as the next syllable has been uttered. The total effect is like a highly organized version of the game known as 'Statues', overlaid with what I take to be an intimate knowledge, on the director's part, of the Japanese cinema.

The supporting cast, studded as it is with constantly repeated names like Usumcasane, Theridamas, Mycetes, Celebinus and Callipine, got blurred in my mind, rather as if they were a horde of pills and wonder drugs bent on decimating one another:

> Young Streptomycin, take a thousand horse
> And storm the gates of Sulphacetamide!
> But who comes here? The currish Pentathol
> Doth spur his steed across the grassy plain
> With Formalin and mighty Dexamyl.
> Beard'st thou me here, thou bold Barbiturate?
> Sirrah, thy grandam's dead – old Nembutal.
> The spangled stars shall weep for Nembutal,
> As Jove himself did cry for Chlorophyll.
> She'll serve thy turn, and that of Ephedrine.

Is it not passing brave to be a king,
Aureomycin and Formaldehyde,
Is it not passing brave to be a king
And ride in triumph through Amphetamine?

(1960)

A Man For All Seasons

by ROBERT BOLT
at the Globe

In *A Man for All Seasons*, Robert Bolt has chopped the later career of Sir Thomas More into a series of short and pithy episodes, each of which is prefaced by a few words of comment and explanation, addressed directly to the audience. Changes of scene are indicated emblematically, by signs lowered from the flies; and the style throughout inclines rather to argument than to emotional appeal. There is no mistaking whose influence has been at work on Mr Bolt; the play is clearly his attempt to do for More what Brecht did for Galileo.

In both cases, the theme is persecution, and the author's purpose is to demonstrate how authority enforces its claims on the individual conscience. More was a victim of the Reformation; Galileo, a century later, fell foul of the Counter-Reformation; and both men, being contented denizens of our planet, were extremely reluctant to embrace martyrdom. Each found himself the servant of two masters. Galileo had to choose between science and the Pope, More between the Pope and the King; and each of them, after years of hair-splitting and procrastination, ended up by choosing the Pope – Galileo because he feared for his body, More because he feared for his soul. According to Brecht, Galileo was disloyal to the new science, and is therefore to be rebuked; according to Mr Bolt, More was loyal to the old religion, and is therefore to be applauded.

It is hereabouts that the two playwrights part company. I have no idea whether Mr Bolt himself is a religious man, but I am perfectly sure that if someone presented him with irrefutable evidence that every tenet of Catholicism was a palpable falsehood, his admiration for More would not be diminished in the smallest degree, nor would he feel tempted to alter a word of the text. The play's strongest scenes, all of which occur in the second half, are those in which More, employing every resource of his canny legal brain, patiently reminds his inquisitors that silence is not to be equated with treason, and that no court can compel him to reveal or defend his private convictions. His position, in short, is that he takes no position; and I have no doubt that we are meant to draw an analogy between More and those witnesses who appear before the Un-American Activities Committee and take the Fifth Amendment.

As a democrat, I detest such coercive investigations into a man's innermost ideas; as a playgoer, however, I feel entitled to know what his ideas are, and how he arrived at them. Here, where Brecht is voluble, Mr Bolt is mum. If, upon completing *Galileo*, Brecht had suddenly learned that his protagonist's hypotheses were totally untrue, he would either have torn up the manuscript or revised it from start to finish. From Mr Bolt's point of view, on the other hand, it matters little whether More's beliefs were right or wrong, all that matters is that he held them, and refused to disclose them under questioning. For Mr Bolt, in short, truth is subjective; for Brecht it is objective; and therein lies the basic difference between the two plays.

Compare them, and it soon becomes obvious that Mr Bolt's method is the more constricting. Since there can be no battle of ideologies, he must reduce everything to personal terms; the gigantic upheavals of the Reformation dwindle into a temperamental squabble between a nice lawyer who dislikes divorce and a lusty monarch who wants an heir. Our attention is focused on the legal stratagems whereby More postponed his martyrdom, and distracted from the validity of the ideas that got him into trouble to begin with. The play contains some muscular period writing, especially in the scene where More deliberately insults his old crony, the conformist Duke of Norfolk, in order to absolve him from the responsibility of breaking off their friendship; and it is history's fault, not Mr Bolt's, that his hero came to grief so much less dramatically than Brecht's. (More's fate was sealed by a perjured witness; whereas it was Galileo himself who laid low Galileo.) At bottom, however, *A Man for All Seasons* is not so much a play as an essay in hagiography. Mr Bolt looks at history exclusively through the eyes of his saintly hero. Brecht's vision is broader: he looks at Galileo through the eyes of history.

The direction, by Noel Willman, skips swiftly around a permanent setting (by Motley) of impenitently Swedish-modern design. Leo McKern plays the Chorus, a bellicose, time-serving oaf whom the programme labels, somewhat rudely, 'The Common Man'. Beery and button-holing, Mr McKern gives a reekingly good account of a highly tendentious role.

Where More himself is concerned, Mr Bolt has indulged in a lot of simplification. He has banished More the scurrilous pamphleteer, More the earthy pleasure-lover, and More the vernacular comic, whom C. S. Lewis has called 'our first great Cockney humorist'. What remains is More the gentle reasoner, and this Paul Scofield plays to the hilt, at once wily and holy, as unastonished by betrayal as he is by fidelity. He does the job beautifully; but where, in this obsequious piece of acting, is the original Scofield who burst upon us, some twelve years ago, like exquisite thunder? Perhaps time has tamed him, or security, or something unassertive in his cast of mind. It is true that he has never given a bad performance; but it was not in negatives like this that we formerly hoped to praise him. We were looking for greatness. The power is still there, though it has long been sleeping; may it soon revive and transfix us.

(1960)

The above review provoked a comment from Robert Bolt which was published in the next edition of *The Observer*. It ran:

'Mr Tynan's certainly fair and probably generous notice of my play raises incidentally a philosophic question of practical importance. I am grateful for the comparison he drew between *A Man for All Seasons* and *Galileo* – indeed I impudently challenged it by misquoting Brecht's most celebrated line at the climax of my own play. It is where the plays diverge that Mr Tynan makes the proposition which I want to query: "For Mr Bolt, in short, truth is subjective; for Brecht it is objective; and therein lies the basic difference between the two plays."

'I only roughly understand what is meant by "objective truth". It is presumably a truth which remains true regardless of who does or doesn't hold it to be true. It seems a very religious concept. But in the present context Mr Tynan's point is clear enough: "If, upon completing *Galileo*, Brecht had suddenly learned that his protagonist's hypotheses were totally untrue, he would either have torn up the manuscript or revised from start to finish." Is this Mr Tynan's guess, or did Brecht himself say he would? For what it means is that the worth of this play about Galileo is conditional upon the correctness of Galileo's hypotheses. I don't believe this, and I don't believe Mr Tynan does, really. Thus:

'The difference between the hypotheses of modern cosmology and the hypotheses of Galilean cosmology is already quite as sharp as the difference between the Galilean and the Aristotelian. If the Galilean hypotheses were "true" and showed the Aristotelian to be "untrue" then by the same token the Galilean are now shown to be untrue. If the Galilean hypotheses are untrue then, according to Mr Tynan, *Galileo* should be torn up or rewritten. In fact, Mr Tynan and I both think it a great play.

'Or, if this comparative view of the truthfulness of successive hypotheses is insufficiently "objective" for Mr Tynan, let us anticipate the dawning of that day when every feature of the Galilean cosmology has been discarded in favour of others. (I take it Mr Tynan does not deny the possibility of such a thing. If he does, he has a kindred spirit, not in Galileo but the Cardinal Inquisitor.)

If that day is tomorrow, will Brecht's absorbing, profound and illuminating play at once become boring, superficial and dull? It will continue to be as absorbing, profound and illuminating as it in fact is. But where can these virtues now reside? What is it that is left when the "objective" truth of Galileo's beliefs is removed from the play *Galileo*? Just Galileo. And that is what Brecht's play is about, as mine is about More.

'There are many differences between the two plays (apart I mean from the obvious one in sheer stature), but the *basic* difference is this. Both men were passionately and to their core convinced. Both were required by Authority to deny themselves. One complied; the other refused.

'Brecht's play shows the frightful price which may have to be paid for that compliance – the reduction of the man in his own estimation to a status where he has only the right to scratch himself and eat. My play shows the frightful price which may have to be paid for that refusal to comply – the end of life on any terms at all.

'Both plays are about uncommon individuals but both are also about organized society. As the essence of organized society, I have taken, quite overtly I think, the structure of the Law. An act of perjury in a trial for High Treason seems to me not altogether undramatic but in this case it has a wider significance, too. More, as Mr Tynan emphasizes, put his trust in the Law, that is, in organized society; this act of perjury, engineered by the Court, showed how the appointed guardians of society were ready to crack it open and let in anarchy to maintain their own advantages. As for the passive bulk of society, those with no immediate responsibility for what is done, I don't think my portrait of the Common Man is "rude" or "tendentious"; he is not actively malignant; under similar circumstances could either Mr Tynan or myself be sure of doing better?

'Here is the practical bearing of all this: Any society needs a conservative and a radical element. Without the first it flies apart, without the second it putrefies. The conservative can be taken for granted, for it only needs acceptance and a good working substitute for acceptance is sloth. But the radical rejects the *status quo*, and unless this is done in the name of a definite vision of what an individual human person is, and is not being allowed to be, rejection degenerates to a posture, no less complacent than the Establishment itself. I think this is our present position. Much ink, perhaps some blood, will flow before we arrive at a genuinely modern, genuinely credible vision of what a human person is. But I think that any artist not in some way engaged upon this task might just as well pack up and go home. The personal is not "merely" personal.'

I replied as follows:

Mr Bolt's dissenting gloss on my review of *A Man for All Seasons* is a healthy phenomenon; it is always cheering when a playwright shows that he cares more about the ideas he is expressing than about the number of paying customers he can induce to listen to them. But while I respect Mr Bolt's motives, I cannot swallow his conclusions; they seem to me to be founded on premises that expose, quite poignantly, the limitations of our Western approach to historical drama.

Mr Bolt surveys his chosen slice of the Tudor era with the right end of the telescope firmly clapped to his eye: what he sees is Sir Thomas More, in dominant close-up, with everything else out of focus. A hint, now and then, is lightly dropped that More's obduracy was not only a crafty individual challenge to Tudor law but a social and political threat to the whole process of the English Reformation. Once dropped, however, these hints are rapidly swept under the carpet and forgotten. Mr Bolt is primarily absorbed in the state of More's conscience, not in the state of More's England or More's Europe.

Brecht, on the other hand, though he gives us an intimate study of Galileo's conscience, takes pains to relate it at every turn to Galileo's world and to the universe at large. In short, he uses the wrong end of the telescope as well. He naturally worries about 'what an individual human person is'; but he also worries about the society into which that person was born, and the contributions he made (or failed to make) towards improving it. Brecht's play deals with Galileo *and* the postponed dawn of the age of reason. Mr Bolt's play deals with More, *tout court*.

As to the matter of 'objective truth': what concerns Brecht is Galileo's contention that the earth revolved around the sun, and I am not aware that anybody has yet disproved it. If they had, I have no doubt that Brecht would have written a different play, possibly based on the arrogance of scientists who fail to verify their hypotheses, or on the ways in which hubris can stunt the growth of enlightenment. 'The truth,' as he never tired of insisting, 'is concrete'; Galileo is in possession of a useful, concrete, revolutionary truth, which authority compels him to deny.

Does Mr Bolt seriously think that Brecht would have devoted the same attention to a man who held that the earth was a saucer-shaped object created in the seventh century AD? That, too, would have constituted a heresy, and the Church would unquestionably have silenced anyone who sought to spread it. Under pressure, the heretic might well have recanted, and thereby reduced himself, as Mr Bolt says of Galileo, 'in his own estimation'. But what about the estimation of history? Heartless though it may sound – and the theatre, where suffering is feigned, is the last stronghold of permissible heartlessness – I must confess that I am more interested in a persecuted scientist whose beliefs are demonstrably true than in one whose beliefs are demonstrably false.

Mr Bolt makes no such distinctions. For him, the mere fact of belief is enough, and Sir Thomas's martyrdom would have been just as tragic if the point at issue had been his refusal to admit that two plus two equalled four. We are expected to sympathize with him simply and solely because he declines to reveal his convictions. It is here that Mr Bolt and I part company. There may be evidence of temperamental bias in my preference for oppressed heroes with whose opinions I agree; but I don't think I am acting unfairly when I demand that heroes should define their opinions, regardless of whether I agree with them. Brecht tells us precisely what Galileo asserted, and why he asserted it; and the play grows out of the explanation. Mr Bolt tells us nothing about More's convictions or how he came to embrace them. In the second act Norfolk asks him whether he is willing to abandon all he possesses because of 'a theory' – namely, the idea that the Pope is St Peter's descendant.

'Why, it's a theory, yes; you can't see it, can't touch it; it's a theory,' More replies. 'But what matters to me is not whether it's true or not but whether I believe it to be true, or rather not that I *believe* it but that *I* believe it. . . . I trust I make myself obscure?'

That is as close as we get to knowing what More believes, and why. It is not, in an age as pragmatical as ours, nearly close enough. By way of a footnote: I concede that people like Mr Bolt and myself might easily behave, in comparable circumstances, as corruptly and boorishly as the character played by Leo McKern. What is 'rude' and 'tendentious' is that a character who is the essence of boorish corruption should be labelled 'The Common Man'.

Chicken Soup with Barley

by ARNOLD WESKER
at the Royal Court

Rhinoceros

by EUGENE IONESCO
at the Strand

Arnold Wesker's *Chicken Soup with Barley* is the first of his three plays about the members, friends and connections of the Kahn family; the other two – *Roots* and *I'm*

Talking About Jerusalem – will follow at intervals of a month.

The action of the trilogy takes place between the middle thirties and the late fifties, and has as its background three wars – the Spanish Civil, the Second World, and the Cold. Its purpose is to show the ways in which these huge disturbances impinge on a Jewish working-class household, altering their habits of work and thought, and thus determining the course of their lives.

The theme is a vast one, and Mr Wesker is splendidly equipped to handle it. Like many Jewish writers, he thinks internationally, yet feels domestically; and it is this combination of attributes that enables him to bring gigantic events and ordinary people into the same sharp focus. The function of drama, in Mr Wesker's view, is not just to tell a story, but to interpret history.

The subject of *Chicken Soup with Barley* is the erosion of political certainties, and their replacement by apathy. We begin in 1936; the Fascists are marching on the East End, and the Kahns are on fire with Communist zeal – all of them, that is, except Harry the *paterfamilias*, whose ardour tends to evaporate when violence impends. His sister Cissie is a union leader, and his daughter Ada a schoolgirl militant, but Harry himself skulks and evades, for which he is reviled by his wife Sarah, who is as instinctively Communist as she is instinctively maternal. The Spanish war is on, and the conflict with Fascism is imminent; for the moment, all the issues are clear.

In the subsequent acts – set in 1946–7 and 1955–6 – a fog of doubt descends; and black and white blur into grey. Fascism has been defeated, and a Labour Government has pushed through a minor social revolution; but the Kahns still find themselves living in an acquisitive, competitive jungle. One of their former comrades has become a respectable shopkeeper, and blushes to recall the pinkness of his past. Cissie, the workers' champion, slips into embittered retirement; Ada, deciding that the real enemy is not capitalism but industrialization, moves into the country to practise handicrafts *à la* William Morris;

and Harry's son Ronnie, a Socialist poet in the making, is shattered by the suppression of the Hungarian revolt. Harry himself, meanwhile, has suffered two strokes and subsided into a state of passive acceptance; convinced that he has nothing to live for, he gradually loses the will to live. Only Sarah – ignorant, intuitive, tea-brewing Sarah – survives with undiminished idealism; and it is she who brings down the curtain by pleading with Ronnie : 'If you don't care, you'll die !'

Mr Wesker's socialism is more emotional than intellectual; he is concerned less with economic analysis than with moral imperatives. His rhetoric sometimes rings hollow, and what distinguishes his style is not so much its subtlety as its sturdiness. All the same, nobody else has ever attempted to put a real, live, English Communist family on to the stage; and the important thing about Mr Wesker's attempt is that they *are* real, and they *do* live.

Some of the performances leave room for qualms. Kathleen Michael, for example, seldom conveys the intensity of feeling that keeps Sarah going, and the cast as a whole could do with a little more Jewish dynamism, not to mention a little more Jewish wit. But considering the talent on hand, I have no major quarrels with John Dexter's direction. Although the Kahns bicker incessantly, they differ in one vital respect from the theatrical characters to which we are inured. They are not arguing about a way of earning, or a way of spending, or a way of making love. They are arguing about a way of life.

Some years ago, Eugène Ionesco and I locked horns in a controversy on the subject of social drama, which I liked and he detested. In support of his antipathy, he said that he could take any 'social play' that had ever been written, and diametrically reverse its meaning simply by changing a few words here and there. That, according to M. Ionesco, was enough to demonstrate the futility of the form. I did not believe him at the time, but I believe him now, since I have recently seen *Rhinoceros*, in which he proves his point up to the hilt. This is M. Ionesco's first attempt at a 'social play', and the number of interpretations to which it is susceptible is roughly equal to the number of people in the audience.

A couple of rhinoceroses are heard thundering through the streets of an unnamed European city. They swiftly multiply, and before long it is obvious that the inhabitants themselves are turning into rhinos, some of the unicorn, others of the bicorn variety. In other words, they are turning into faceless conformists; by surrendering to the herd instinct, they are consenting to the destruction of the human ego. The hero, a tipsy little clerk, looks on in horror while all his chums desert him in favour of inhuman, thick-skinned, hard-hoofed anonymity.

But what is the rhinoceros meant to symbolize? Communism, unquestionably; but also Nazism, Socialism, Calvinism or any other ism that appears to threaten one's self-hood. You can change the meaning of *Rhinoceros* merely by switching a few words; and however you switch them, its development is monolithically unsurprising. M. Ionesco is right: there is nothing worse than a bad social play.

Ostensibly, his piece is a defence of individualism against creeping totalitarianism. In fact, it is a concealed attack on reason as a guide to political conduct, and on the very notion that logic may be used as a means of social persuasion. M. Ionesco is begging us to leave people alone to work things out for themselves, and the more alone the better – if ninety-nine per cent of the world voted for the abolition of capital punishment it would presumably be the part of the true individualist to vote for its retention rather than conform.

The play is directed, dashingly and unmistakably, by Orson Welles. I had been warned to expect a display of trickery; instead, I saw much less trickery than M. Ionesco's stage directions call for. I also saw a group of actors on whom a unified style had been emphatically – and no doubt painfully – imposed. The overlapped dialogue, the whirligig moves, the boisterously assured utterance – these are Mr Welles's trademarks, and the production as a whole is exactly what we have come to expect of him : a carefully orchestrated battle of egos, performed by actors who have learned from their director that being inhibited gets you nowhere in the theatre.

Laurence Olivier, as the last exemplar of individualism, is not so much miscast as undercast. Wearing an inexplicable Apache wig, and behaving with a determined kind of boyish, hangdog charm, Sir Laurence skitters gracefully around the stage, rolling his eyes and trying hard to seem humble and insignificant. The task is not an easy one; there is never any doubt that with one breath, one vocal blast, one surge of his enormous humanity, he could blow the part to smithereens, and with it the play. He controls himself quite splendidly; one merely laments the waste of his time.

(1960)

Roots
by ARNOLD WESKER
at the Royal Court

Improvisation, or The Shepherd's Chameleon and Victims of Duty
by EUGENE IONESCO
at the Arts

The miraculous thing about *Roots* – part two of Arnold Wesker's trilogy – is that its author has managed to build an intensely moving play out of the raw materials of old-fashioned kitchen comedy, if not of outright farce. Ignorant rustics, pap-fed on pop songs; baths taken in the kitchen; the domestic row in which Mum won't address Dad except through a third person; the family high tea, complete with trifle, mayonnaise bottle and uncomfortably brilliantined yokels; the arty daughter with ideas above her station; the wife who tells her ailing husband that he has indigestion between the shoulderblades – mention any of these inventions to your average playgoer, and he will instantly assume that there's fun in the offing; the kind of fun, as it happens, that ruined the Abbey Theatre.

And indeed, Mr Wesker does want us to smile; but he makes sure that condescension, in our smiling, is replaced by compassion, and that we are always aware of the sad, hard facts underlying the behaviour we find so hilarious. Taken separately, the details he accumulates are frequently comic; his achievement is to have set them in a context of such tangible reality that sympathy banishes belly-laughs. It is Chekhov's method, applied not to the country gentry but to the peasants at the gate.

Like N. F. Simpson, Mr Wesker can amuse us with the vacuous redundancies of everyday chit-chat; unlike Mr Simpson, he draws our attention to the causes of mental apathy – among them television, the Light Programme and the popular Press – as well as to its effects. Mum squabbles with Dad over the use of an electric cooker; but we know what Dad earns, and realize that for him electricity is a luxury. And the comedy of a chronic stomach-ache wanes when we learn that it can cost a man his job.

Above all, Mr Wesker shows his mastery in the way he handles Beatie, the heroine. Long absent in London, Beatie has fallen in love with Ronnie Kahn (the East End poet of *Chicken Soup with Barley*); she comes home bursting with his ideas about the necessity of convincing ordinary people that art is intended for them, and not merely for the intellectually privileged. She postures and proselytizes, like a hot-gospeller among Eskimos, while her relations look on, impassively bewildered. The rules of conventional dramaturgy demand that she should get her come-uppance; in the final scene, she is jilted by Ronnie, and all seems set for her to abandon her pretensions and return to the simple life. We expect capitulation. Instead, Mr Wesker gives us triumph. By losing Ronnie, Beatie finds herself, and proclaims, now with unassailable certainty, that she has been right all along. Her astonished cry of self-discovery brings down the curtain on the most affecting last act in contemporary English drama. It would be wrong to describe *Roots* as a Socialist play, but if anyone were to tell me that a Tory had written it, I should be mightily amazed.

Among living playwrights Mr Wesker has few peers when it comes to evoking an atmosphere of family cohesiveness; his characters belong together, even when they are not on speaking terms with each other. Under John Dexter's direction, the Royal Court team performs in a spirit of what might be called unromantic realism, though it is in fact – to revive an unfashionable word – nothing more or less than naturalism.

Joan Plowright's Beatie seemed to me a touch too pawky, suggestive less of rural Norfolk than of urban Lancs. One suspected at times that Miss Plowright thought Beatie rather a silly girl; and by imitating Ronnie as if he talked like a well-bred phoney, she made it hard to believe that the two had ever met. All the same, she grips one's attention throughout, and rises glowing to the challenge of the final scene.

In *Improvisation, or The Shepherd's Chameleon*, the first half of the double bill at the Arts, M. Ionesco rails against those who question the validity of his dramatic method. 'The critic', he asserts, 'should describe, and not prescribe.' In *Victims of Duty*, the second half of the bill, he shows us the kind of play that the critics are presumably trying to keep him from writing. It deals with a persecuted little man (Chaplinesque) who is forced by a mysterious 'detective (Kafkaesque) to uncover the secrets of his past. After about fifteen minutes, caprice takes over – the concept of art as the product of accident, the theory that communication can be achieved only by sacrificing integrity.

'It is in my dreams, my anguish, my dark desires, my inner contradictions,' says M. Ionesco in the curtain-raiser, 'that I reserve the right to find the stuff of my plays.' I do not doubt that *Victims of Duty* is stuffed with dreams, anguish and the rest; but I reserve the right to deny that the result is more than a cloudy and befuddled *mélange*. When you've seen all of Ionesco's plays, I felt at the end, you've seen one of them.

For a professed enemy of didacticism, he is strangely didactic himself. In *The Shepherd's Chameleon* he appears as a harassed author whose creative flow is interrupted by three pedants who seek to baffle him with talk of Brecht and science; and the play embodies his protest against their attempts to label him and define the nature of his art. Yet in these matters M. Ionesco himself is the supreme dogmatist. In his view of drama there is no room for rational qualms or for the ambiguities he so much despises in Brecht; either a playwright is a total individualist, utterly unconcerned with ideology, or he is not a playwright at all.

Or so M. Ionesco insists. It is probably unfair to take his absolutism quite seriously; more charitably, perhaps, one should regard him as a brilliant improviser, raging against the world of ideas into which fame has dragged him, and determined to place his work beyond the reach of criticism – and also of thought. One can't help feeling that he ought to follow Ring Lardner's example and stay out of critical debates. I mention Lardner because he wrote, in the twenties, a number of short nonsense plays that easily outdo M. Ionesco in the extravagance of their non-sequiturs, and contrive to be shatteringly and disturbingly funny without claiming to have been born out of private agony. (1960)

I'm Talking About Jerusalem

by ARNOLD WESKER
at the Royal Court

As a rule, Harold Pinter's characters live immured in a room, vaguely intimidated by the world outside, fearful of direct communication with each other, and therefore talking about everything except what most deeply concerns them. As representatives of our way of life, they precisely complement Arnold Wesker's characters, who rush out to grapple with the world, bent on communicating with each other and anyone else who will listen, and seldom talking about anything but their deepest concerns. Yet what do they accomplish? *I'm Talking About Jerusalem*, the last instalment of Mr Wesker's trilogy, suggests that his answer is: almost nothing. The members of the Kahn family end up with their hopes baffled and their ideals defeated. The world outside has let them down; they feel alienated and rejected. No doubt they will 'carry on', but their passion for causes has abated, and they are no longer quite sure where they are going. One more disastrous adventure, you feel, and the path might well lead straight to Mr Pinter's room. Mr. Wesker's conclusion, in short, is not very far from Mr Pinter's starting-point: that there is something in our society that is irrevocably hostile to the idea of human brotherhood.

At the beginning of *Chicken Soup with Barley* the Kahns, like Lincoln Steffens, 'have seen the future, and it works'. By the end of *I'm Talking About Jerusalem*, twenty-three years later, they have decided that it doesn't. Their early allegiance to Communism has long since disintegrated; and although Beatie Bryant emerges from *Roots* with a new sense of purpose and identity, we are not told exactly what she is going to do with it.

This last play deals with a frustrated attempt to translate Socialist theory into practice. Ada Kahn and her husband Dave, haters of mass production and readers of William Morris, move out of the East End into a lonely Norfolk cottage, where Dave proposes to manufacture furniture of his own design, thereby – as he hopes – reviving the tradition of pride in craftsmanship that industrialization has stifled.

The first two acts, in which he and his wife are struggling to establish themselves, pleasantly remind us that Mr Wesker is one of the few Western dramatists who can write about political idealists without mockery or condescension. The moving-in process, accompanied by the forebodings of Ada's mother and the soaring enthusiasm of Ronnie Kahn; Dave's momentary qualms when a wartime chum turns out to have developed into a cynical 'realist'; the family game wherein Ada and her young son pretend to be lumps of clay into which Dave, mimicking the Deity, solemnly breathes life – all this is lovingly observed, and lambently acted, especially by Frank Finlay as the cynic. Mr Finlay's assault on Dave's ideals – and, by extension, on his own past – is an unforgettable set piece, full of implied self-hatred; even his laughter sounds like a kind of weeping.

In the third act the dream fades. Dave's prices are too high to compete with factory products, the bank refuses him a loan, and he is forced to go back to the city, while Ronnie looks on, tearfully wondering what went wrong. Two full-blooded minor characters, Aunt Cissie and Aunt Esther, barge amusingly in; but the play as a whole tails off into something between a whimper and a shrug. An experiment in medievalism has collapsed, and everyone behaves as if it were the end of the world. Nobody points out to Dave or Ronnie that the failure of a privately owned furniture business can hardly be equated with the failure of Socialism; all that happens is that Ronnie, after a bout of weeping, brings down the curtain by bellowing to the fields: 'We're bloody mad to cry!' One can only agree. This final outburst of affirmation comes across as an empty gesture, utterly devoid of intellectual substance; and its effect, I am afraid, is to strengthen John Whiting's recent animadversions on the new movement in our theatre. Mr Whiting conceded that it had a heart: 'All the throbbing emotionalism proves it. . . . It is that little tiny head that worries me.'

It worries me, too. All the same, I part company with Mr Whiting when he derides Beatie Bryant (and through her, Mr Wesker) because she 'seems to see art as an educative influence, something which uplifts, does you good. Nonsense! Some of the best art teaches nothing and can do irreparable harm, if not actually deprave.' I will not embarrass Mr Whiting by asking him to give examples, but I do beg him to ponder the following remarks of John Berger's:

... why should an artist's way of looking at the world have any meaning for us? Why does it give us pleasure? Because, I believe, it increases our awareness of our own potentiality. ... The important point is that a valid work of art promises in some way or another the possibility of an increase, of an improvement. Nor need the work be optimistic to achieve this; indeed, its subject may be tragic. For it is not the subject that makes the promise, it is the artist's way of viewing his subject.

Mr Wesker's view of his subject is blurred, at the end, by sentimentality and intellectual flabbiness, for which I have chided him. But he cannot legitimately be condemned for having tried to 'do us good'. I have been emotionally enlarged, and morally roused, by the experience of hearing Mr Wesker talk about Jerusalem. This is not, perhaps what Mr Whiting means by art; but it is what most of us mean by theatre.

(1960)

The Duchess of Malfi
by JOHN WEBSTER
at the Aldwych

With a rattle of skeletons and a fanfare of maniacal screams, the Stratford-on-Avon company has opened its first London season. *The Duchess of Malfi* is a play for which exaggerated claims have sometimes been made; as a traumatic experience, branding the mind with panic, it is not to be compared with Alfred Hitchcock's grisly masterpiece, *Psycho*, and G. H. Lewes was right, though turbid in utterance, when he condemned 'the irredeemable mediocrity of its dramatic evolution of human passion'.

Webster is not concerned with humanity. He is the poet of bile and brainstorm, the sweet singer of apoplexy; ideally, one feels, he would have had all his characters drowned in a sea of cold sweat. His muse drew nourishment from Bedlam, and might, a few centuries later, have done the same from Belsen. I picture him plagued with hypochondria, probably homosexual, and consumed by feelings of persecution – an intensely neurotic mind, in short, at large in the richest, most teeming vocabulary that any age ever offered to a writer.

One imagines his contemporaries dismissing him as 'that charnelhouse poet', much as we nowadays dub Beckett the dramatist of the dustbin. And although we cannot call him the inventor of the sick joke (a field in which Kyd, Marlowe and Shakespeare were all ahead of him), he certainly rolled back the frontiers of the new genre – as witness the scene in which Duke Ferdinand extends a hand for his sister to shake, omitting to warn her that it has lately been severed from a corpse. In the whole of Webster's work, scarcely an act is committed that is not motivated by greed, revenge or sexual rapacity.

Yet his characters die superbly, asserting their self-hood to the last breath – even the least of them, such as the Duchess's maid, who expires with a sudden, plaintive cry of : 'I am quick with child!' Webster's people are most themselves when the knife, noose or potion is nearest; you might say that his plays come alive the closer they get to death. *The Duchess of Malfi* is an intricate tale of the vengeance sought and obtained by two brothers – one ducal and incestuous, the other ecclesiastical and more normally lecherous – on their widowed sister, who has offended by remarrying beneath her.

The present production, by Donald McWhinnie, is a forthright, noisy affair, played all out for melodrama; effective enough in its way, but far from the subtle, imaginative interpretation of which I for one went in hopes. Peggy Ashcroft's Duchess is more ripely moving than her Haymarket performance of fifteen years ago; but I wished, as I listened to Eric Porter's strangled ranting, that Gieldgud were still playing Ferdinand, still imparting the same thrill of finality to the line : 'I will never see thee more.' There are no blatant weaknesses in the cast, and nothing is lacking in the production, save finesse and originality.   (1960)

A Gap Defined: 1960

Permit me, in a thin week, to pursue a general topic. To begin with a postulate : theatre sustains itself by a process of cross-fertilization to which all of its species contribute. From this it follows that a weakness in any particular species, however humble, will sooner or later be transmitted to the rest. Not at all frivolously, I am going to suggest that our theatre as a whole has been infected, and injured, by our weakness in the tiny, ancillary department of satirical cabaret.

Where else but in a small room, late at night, before an audience more notable for its mind than its money, can the true satirist – whether writer or performer or both – practise his art and polish his weapons? In such an atmosphere he need not restrict himself to the hints and nudges that masquerade as satire in West End revues. He can be outrageous and uninhibited; he can pierce to the quick of the ulcer without bothering to administer sedation; he can speak freely on any subject from the Cuban revolution to the Immaculate Conception.

Cabaret of this sort is not only satirical in itself, but the cause that satire is in other theatrical forms. The London stage has always excelled in turning out samples of complacent, self-congratulating and fundamentally inoffensive wit; and it has lately been exploring the comic potentialities of surrealism. But whenever it attempts satire, in the full, corrosive sense of the word, it looks blundering and amateurish. It is out of practice. It has no training-ground, no source.

Compare, for instance, the German theatre in the twenties, nourished by the stinging, acidulous wit of the Berlin *Nachtlokalen*, on which Brecht and Weill founded their method and based their style. In Paris, meanwhile, one has the *chansonniers*, which have always been outposts of opposition to whatever regime chanced to be in power, and which have reserved their right to dissent, even under de Gaulle. The French theatre has many failings, but it has never wanted for satirists.

Since the war, however, the prime incubator of non-conformist night-club wit has been American. Adolph Green and Betty Comden, who wrote the lyrics of *On The Town* and *Wonderful Town*, made their reputations in the *boîtes* of Greenwich Village; and Abe Burrows, the co-author of *Guys and Dolls*, started his career as a cabaret parodist. More recently, a new group, higher of brow and redder in tooth and claw than its predecessors, has taken control. It is led, of course, by Mort Sahl, an avid sceptic who might be defined as a liberal nihilist; he is quoted, I see, as having said that, whereas the last presidential election produced a bumper crop of male children christened Dwight or Adlai, the present one should yield an even larger number named Undecided.

There is also Lenny Bruce, to whom nothing either human or inhuman is alien. This cool iconoclast includes among his pet targets the bomb, sexual hypocrisy, racial intolerance, the profit motive and organized religion; as an ice-breaker, he sometimes uses a routine in which a Madison Avenue publicist telephones the Pope, addressing him as Johnny, urging him to 'wear the big ring' when he visits America and assuring him that: 'Nobody knows you're a Jew.' By way of finale, he often employs a Negro associate, to whom he explains that in the great big yonder racial barriers will collapse and we shall all be united – Negroes, Italians, Jews, Puerto Ricans, Germans, everyone. 'And then,' he adds, his eyes shining, 'we'll all go out and beat up the Polacks.'

Messrs Sahl and Bruce rose to fame from a cellar-club in San Francisco called 'the hungry i'; at the same time, a similar haunt in Chicago was fostering the talents of Mike Nichols and Elaine May, in whose work delicate verbal surgery replaces the machine-gun of Sahl and the cobra-fangs of Bruce. Mr Nichols is blond and reflective, Miss May dark and intense. Their act is an unnerving display of mutual empathy, since much of their material is improvised; Odets, Wilder, Joyce, Pirandello and

Dostoevsky are some of the authors whose styles I have heard them simulate, impromptu and by audience request.

Among their contemporaries and competitors are such unsettling wags as Shelley Berman, Jonathan Winters and Bob Newhart, all cabaret-bred; and a new generation of satirists is in active training. For proof, consider a sketch I saw last spring in a Chicago dive known as 'The Second City'. It showed Richard Nixon coming down to breakfast wearing his new, liberal mask, to which his daughter reacted with a scream of : 'Momma, *who's* that *man*?'

We, meanwhile, have strip-joints with acres of goose-flesh, and clip-joints with sequinned, androgynous floor-shows.

As a nation we are not devoid of satiric gifts. Our suburbs and provinces abound in fledgling Jimmy Porters and Billy Liars, fast-talking, quick-thinking young intellectuals who specialize in informed derision; but there is nowhere for them to develop their skill. We lack a place in which intelligent, likeminded people can spend a cheap evening listening to forthright cabaret that is socially, sexually and politically pungent. Lacking it, we have a theatre in which lumbering charades are gravely acclaimed for their unsparing mordancy. Thus is the great name of satire neglected, degraded and traduced.

Romeo and Juliet

by WILLIAM SHAKESPEARE
at the Old Vic

'This is as't should be' – *Romeo and Juliet*, IV, 2.

In the past half-century nothing has plagued the English classical theatre more than the problem of coping with its permanent responsibility, its matrix and its millstone – the works of William Shakespeare.

Fashions in Shakespearian production have succeeded

each other as swiftly as Picassovian phases. Modern-dress enthusiasts have vied with platform-stage purists; the plays have been staged as Jacobean masques, neo-Victorian extravaganzas, exercises in Tudor rhetoric, expositions of Freudian dogma, and Ruritanian charades. Contemporary scholarship, with its heavy emphasis on the conventional element in Elizabethan drama, has not gone unnoticed; and it is nowadays an axiom, even among non-experimental directors, that the production style (sometimes known as the chosen convention or the overall concept) takes precedence over everything else. Individual characterization – that square old Bradleyan obsession – has sharply declined in status; nobody has any ideas on the subject beyond a vague and unquestioned assumption that all Shakespearian characters are 'larger than life'.

Last Tuesday at the Old Vic a foreign director approached Shakespeare with fresh eyes, quick wits and no stylistic preconceptions; and what he worked was a miracle. The characters were neither larger nor smaller than life; they were precisely life-size, and we watched them living, spontaneously and unpredictably. The director had taken the simple and startling course of treating them as if they were real people in a real situation; and of asking himself just how those people, in that situation, would behave.

It sounds obvious enough; yet the result, in Franco Zeffirelli's production of *Romeo and Juliet*, is a revelation, even perhaps a revolution. Nobody on stage seems to be aware that he is appearing in an immortal tragedy, or indeed in a tragedy of any kind; instead, the actors behave like ordinary human beings, trapped in a quandary whose outcome they cannot foretell. Handled thus realistically, it is sometimes said, Shakespeare's essential quality gets lost. I passionately demur. What gets lost is not Shakespeare but the formal, dehumanized stereotype that we have so often made of him.

It is likewise urged that Signor Zeffirelli robs Shakespeare of his poetry; but this argument is valid only if one agrees with those blinkered zealots who insist that poetry is an arrangement of sounds, instead of an arrangement of words. Last Tuesday I heard every syllable; meaning and character were wedded, and out of their interaction poetry arose. The production evoked a whole town, a whole riotous manner of living; so abundant and compelling was the life on stage that I could not wait to find out what happened next. The Vic has done nothing better for a decade. A young English director of my acquaintance made a true comment in one of the intervals. 'Every director in the audience,' he said, 'is biting his nails and wondering why he never thought of this before.'

It is hard to know where to begin the catalogue of particular praise. The sets (also by Signor Zeffirelli) are spaciously atmospheric, composed of peeling, flaking walls that serve equally well for interiors or exteriors. Children scuffle in the alleys and vendors bawl their wares. We are unmistakably in Verona, or anyway in Italy; the director has even taught his English cast how to shrug. The rival factions are gangs of dawdlers with time on their hands; captives of the streets, like the boys in Fellini's film, I Vitelloni. Mercutio (electrically played by Alec McCowen) is their unquestioned idol, an intense, fierce, sourly witty young man, always conscious of his intellectual supremacy. His death comes as a chilling shock, since Signor Zeffirelli has caused it to occur by accident. His bout with Tybalt, a basically playful affair, is already over when the mortal thrust is delivered; it is a chance and unintended stroke, yet it kills him, whereafter the feud between the families takes on a new dimension of seriousness. They have squabbled immemorially, but this is their first murder, and it tilts the action towards tragedy.

Romeo, meanwhile, is an idler lured out of sulks into love. His meeting with Juliet at the Capulets' ball is staged with marvellous tact. A crowd has gathered to hear someone sing; around the fringe of it the lovers tentatively edge, ending up together, quietly pressing palm to palm. The balcony scene is heartrendingly good. Here, as everywhere else in the production, grace is subordinated to circumstance, the ideal to the real. Instead of leaping ballet-ically up a conveniently placed creeper, John Stride (as Romeo) has to concentrate prosaically on climbing a highly unco-operative little tree. Judi Dench, a calm, wise little Juliet, awaits him aloft; their encounter is grave, awkward and extremely beautiful.

Romeo's departure for exile is staged with even greater earthiness. The bedroom setting is dominated by a lofty four-poster, in which the couple lie; and no doubt is left in one's mind that it is sheer, newly-wedded exhaustion, more than anything else, that delays Romeo's leave-taking.

The latter part of the evening suffers from some damaging excisions. One of them is superbly economic – the almost filmic cut from Juliet's feigned death to Romeo in Mantua, declaiming: 'Then I defy you, stars.' Many of the others, however, are confusing, especially in the last act, which looked slightly under-rehearsed. But the major fault hereabouts lies with the play. It lets the director down. In the world of tangible, credible reality that he has created, magic potions have no place.

(1960)

Crystal Balls: 1960

Today – there being no new West End shows to discuss – we improvise. The theme is prophecy. Basing our predictions on current and recent form, let us look ahead at next season, and at some of the plays that our more prominent contemporaries may have in store for us (any resemblance to the plays they actually write, living or dead, is purely uncanny).

As my imagination sees it, the season begins with a new comedy by T. S. Eliot, two years in the polishing and completed just too late for Edinburgh. Entitled 'The Tradesmen's Entrance', it represents Mr Eliot's first attempt to deal with the aspirations of the proletariat. Hard on its heels comes Graham Greene's 'The Purifying

Agent', a thriller with mystical overtones, set in Hull, about a Middle-European spy who finds himself hounded by Heaven as well as by M.I.5. Both are respectfully received, but neither rivals in popular acclaim the latest work of Lionel Bart, who follows up the success of *Oliver!* by turning *Bleak House* into a new Cockney musical called *Bleak!*

From across the Channel we have 'Cirque d'Automme', a sour yet fragrant tragicomedy in which M. Anouilh recaptures the creative mood, redolent of anguish and provincial railway stations, that moved him to write *La Sauvage* and *Eurydice*. 'Cirque d'Automne' has to do with a travelling circus that is stranded in Perpignan on New Year's Eve; its central characters are a philosophic ringmaster, a pretty trapeze *artiste* of all too pliable morality, and the latter's drunken catcher, who wants – as he puts it – 'to drop everything'. Translated as 'Autumn Circus', the play instantly runs into copyright trouble with the legal advisers of Miss Dodie Smith. Litigation of a similar kind also awaits the season's first transatlantic hit – a satirical farce adapted from episodes in the career of the inspired clown who founded *The New Yorker*. Terence Rattigan's lawyers immediately move into action against its title, 'Ross'.

Meanwhile, Tennessee Williams enters the lists with a romantic dithyramb in one act, unearthed from some forgotten bottom drawer. Its hero is a sensitive cadet who runs away from West Point to become a hungover beachcomber in Ischia; and it is called 'A Year of Dry Mornings'. From Arthur Miller, no play emerges; although there is strenuous controversy in the pages of *Encore* about a lecture he delivers to the Yale Drama School on the theatrical implications of Bertrand Russell's latest book, 'The Ethics of Catastrophe', and Aldous Huxley's new collection of apocalyptic essays, 'The Ending Revel'. In other quarters, pious attention is paid to Sir Michael Redgrave's autobiography, 'Aloof in the Theatre'.

But even when we have saluted 'The Undertaker' (John Osborne's blistering attack on Martin Luther) and 'Falling

Over Backwards' (Arnold Wesker's biographical play about Ezra Pound), no doubt remains that the most vociferously debated theatrical offering of the season is Harold Pinter's smash hit, 'The Area'. In accordance with the pattern set by Mr Pinter's previous plays, it begins as follows:

Scene: A room. A camp-bed, unmade, centre. ALF, reading a telegram, wanders up and down. TAFF, wearing a cap and a Manchester United rosette, sits on the bed, dismantling a tin-opener. No doors, left, right or centre.

ALF: What you want to do, see, you want to watch out for that lot, or they'll have you round the twist. Right round the twist, they will, and then where are you? Up the wall, that's where you are, that's where they'll have you, if you don't watch out for them. See, I know that lot. I've had my eye on the lot of them. What I mean, I've seen them bellocking up and down Ladbroke Grove the minute the shops are shut. I know that sort inside out. They'll play Old Harry with you, that lot will. Not a spark of respect from top to bottom.

TAFF: You mean Old Nick.

ALF: What do you mean, I mean Old Nick?

TAFF: They'll play Old Nick with you. That's what you call proper usage.

ALF: What's that got to do with it, then?

Silence.

You're a bit of what they call a live wire, aren't you? You don't want to come the idiomatic over me, if that's what you think you're doing. I've bought and sold better men than you with one hand held behind my back, any day of the week, right, left and centre, until it's coming out of my ears. You want to be bloody careful, mate, I'm warning you.

TAFF: That tin of Heinz vegetable salad wants seeing to. Got a bit of rust on it.

ALF: You can whistle for your Heinz vegetable salad when that lot comes round after you. They'll give you Heinz vegetable salad all right, that lot will. What you want to do, see, you want to watch out for that lot. . . .

Beyond the Fringe

at the Fortune

The curtain rises on what might be a crypt, or perhaps an efficiently looted wine-cellar. It is anyway the kind of place into which the late Tod Slaughter used to lure his leading ladies, preparatory to hurling them down a disused sump. On the righthand side of the stage a flight of stone steps leads up to some sort of battlement. To the left of centre, and partly hidden beneath the platform, is a grand piano. Somewhere to the rear a flying buttress is distinctly visible.

Strewn (it is the only word) about the stage are three young men. One of them is gawky and angular, with large feet and carrot-coloured hair; he has wild eyes, and might just possibly be a Jew. (Later in the evening he is to deny this. 'I'm not a Jew,' he explains, 'I'm Jew-*ish*. I don't go the whole hog.') His real name is Jonathan Miller; I do not know what his other name is. Of his two companions, one looks like a well-kept minor poet, all lanky elegance and clearly as sly as they come. Like his friends, he is wearing casuals, ideal for lounging around crypts. To avoid confusion, we will call him Peter Cook.

The remaining member of the trio, better known (though only slightly better) as Alan Bennett, has spectacles, flaxen hair and the beginnings of a lantern jaw. With his kindly, puzzled face, he resembles a plain-clothes friar, badly in need of a tonsure. What he and his companions are doing in the cellar is immediately obvious: they are doing nothing. A right crew, one murmurs to oneself, of layabouts. Half a minute passes in silence, which worries them not at all. They shift easily, not uneasily, in their semi-sleep.

All of a sudden, there enters a smaller young man with twinkling dark eyes and twinkling dark hair, later identified as Dudley Moore. Seating himself at the piano, he plays the national anthem, and briskly departs. The others, who have leapt to attention, lapse once more into in-attention. Idly, and a little querulously, they discuss the mystery pianist, and his habit of coming in every few minutes to play the national anthem. It emerges that he belongs to the Moscow State Circus. They resolve to win him over to the Western way of life by teaching him to blow a raspberry whenever Mr Khrushchev's name is mentioned. Soon afterwards the musician reappears; and before long all four of them are busily engaged in blow-ing rhythmic raspberries at Mr Macmillan. Plainly, some-one has bungled, though in what way I cannot now remember.

The entire scene lasts only a few minutes; I have des-cribed it at such length and in such detail because it is the exordium of *Beyond the Fringe*, which I take to be the funniest revue that London has seen since the Allies dropped the bomb on Hiroshima. Future historians may well thank me for providing them with a full account of the moment when English comedy took its first decisive step into the second half of the twentieth century.

The show began as a late-night experiment at last year's Edinburgh Festival, since when it has been shrewdly revised and much expanded. Only four men are involved, and they are the authors of all they perform. The set is unchanged throughout. Among other marvels, Mr Miller gives us a hearty, broadminded vicar, exhorting his lads to 'get the violence off the streets and into the churches where it belongs'; a squirming teacher of linguistic philos-ophy, frenetically distinguishing between 'why-questions' and 'how-questions'; and an implacable African politician, whom Mr Miller mocks with the probing intensity that an equal deserves. More seriously (the show is nothing if not morally committed), he appears as a condemned man, persistently asking the question we would all ask in that extremity: 'Will it hurt?'

Mr Moore satirizes folk-singers, fashionable composers, and the collaboration of Peter Pears and Benjamin Britten;

during the interval, he crops up in the orchestra pit, tinkling away like a local incarnation of Erroll Garner. Mr Cook, meanwhile, qualifies at least thrice for the revue anthologies: once as a Beaverbrook journalist, nervously protesting that he has not ditched his liberal principles, and proudly declaring that he still dares, when drunk, to snigger at his employer; again as the Prime Minister, casually tearing up a letter from an old-age pensioner; and again as a Pinteresque outcast who would have liked to be a judge, if he had only had enough Latin. 'The trappings of extreme poverty', says Mr Cook in this characterization, 'are *rotten*.'

Mr Bennett, in manner the mildest of the quartet, is perhaps the most pungent in effect. His man-to-man chat about Dr Verwoerd ('a bit of a rough diamond') and his opponents ('crypto-Socialists') in the Foreign Office is wickedly accurate; and one will not readily forget the oleaginous blandness with which Mr Bennett delivers a sermon on the text: 'My brother Esau is an hairy man, but I am a smooth man.'

I have omitted the collective numbers, among them a devastating attack on civil defence, and the only successful parody of Shakespeare that I have ever heard. Certainly, *Beyond the Fringe* lacks a great deal. It has no slick coffee-bar scenery, no glib one-line blackouts, no twirling dancers in tight trousers, no sad ballets for fisherwomen clad in fishnet stockings, no saleable Kitsch. For these virtues of omission we must all be grateful; but it can be justly urged against the show that it is too parochial, too much obsessed with B.B.C. voices and B.B.C. attitudes, too exclusively concerned with taunting the accents and values of John Betjeman's suburbia. *Beyond the Fringe* is anti-reactionary without being wholeheartedly progressive. It goes less far than one could have hoped, but immeasurably farther than one had any right to expect.

(1961)

The Dumb Waiter

by HAROLD PINTER
at the Theatre Royal, Stratford-atte-Bowe

The Pinter vogue continues to spread. Not since Christopher Fry in the late forties has an English playwright so powerfully influenced the style of his contemporaries. Mr Pinter has a whole school of dramatists speaking in his very accents; his is the new small talk, and very small, on lips stiffer than his, it can sound.

Its distinguishing features can be easily listed. First, the aimlessly iterated phrases: what I tell you three times is art. Next, the sudden use of an outlandish word in a sentence otherwise drab and demotic. (No wonder Coward is a Pinter admirer; he played similar tricks with upper-class idiom in the twenties.) And thirdly, a calculated gulf between the dramatic situation – usually one of undefined threat – and the language, numb and inexpressive, in which the characters respond to it.

The trouble with Mr Pinter's people is not that they cannot communicate with each other but that they leave the vital things unspoken, deliberately missing the points they are too scared to face or even to imagine; and what is left unsaid often erupts, at the end, into violence. Mr Pinter's ear ranks with Jenkins's and Van Gogh's among the great ears of history: his characters are robots whose conversation is so intimately real that it reconciles us to the frequent unreality of their behaviour. Menaced by nameless terrors, they chat idly about bus routes; but when he is writing at his best – as in *The Caretaker* – with a strict formal shape and a strong emotional impetus, they cease to be merely odd and become at once funny and frightening.

Last week brought a ham-fisted production of Mr Pinter's *The Dumb Waiter*, listening to which with half an ear I suddenly realized that I knew the source of the

Pinter style. Consider this colloquy between the two killers :

BEN : When he sees you behind him –
GUS : Me behind him –
BEN : And me in front of him –
GUS : And you in front of him –
BEN : He'll feel uncertain –
GUS : Uneasy.
BEN : He won't know what to do.
GUS : So what will he do?
BEN : He'll look at me and he'll look at you.
GUS : We won't say a word.
BEN : We'll look at him.
GUS : We won't say a word.
BEN : He'll look at us.
GUS : And we'll look at him.
BEN : Nobody says a word.

And compare it with this :

SWEENEY : Nobody came.
And nobody went
But he took in the milk and he paid the rent.
SWARTS : What did he do?
All that time, what did he do?
SWEENEY : What did he do! What did he do?
That don't apply.
Talk to live men about what they do . . .
I gotta use words when I talk to you
But if you understand or if you don't
That's nothing to me and nothing to you . . .

In *Sweeney Agonistes*, too, we note the same lurking violence ('I knew a man once did a girl in . . .'). Who would have thought that Mr Pinter shared a literary progenitor with Mr Prufrock !

(1961)

Luther

by JOHN OSBORNE
at the Théâtre des Nations

Why, it was asked on all sides at the opening night of
Luther in Paris, should John Osborne have wanted to write
a play about the founder of Protestantism? I can think of
a number of reasons that might have drawn the two men
together across the centuries.

Luther in Christendom, like Mr Osborne in the microcosm of the theatre, was a stubborn iconoclast of lowly
birth, resentful of authority and blind to compromise.
Rather than retract a syllable of his writings he would
defy the Pope; one is reminded of Mr Osborne's brushes
with the Lord Chamberlain. To his surprise and alarm,
Luther caused an international tumult with his attacks
on indulgences, and was hailed as a popular hero by
people of whose causes he thoroughly disapproved: is
there not something here that might speak to the author
of *Look Back in Anger*, embarrassed to find himself
dubbed an apostle of social revolution when in fact, like
Luther, he preached nothing but revolutionary individualism?

'In many ways, life began for Luther all over again
when the world . . . forced him into the role of rebel
reformer and spiritual dictator': thus Erik H. Erikson,
the author of *Young Man Luther*, a psychiatric study that
could have served as the germinal text for Mr Osborne's
play. Dr Erikson, like Mr Osborne, seizes on the fact that
Luther was plagued throughout his life by constipation,
and habitually expressed himself in anal imagery. Oppressed and frequently beaten by his father, he became
'inhibited and reined in by a tight retentiveness'; the
celebrated 'revelation in the tower', wherein he first felt
himself flooded and illuminated by the Holy Spirit, took
place while he was in the privy – 'a revelation', Dr Erikson

adds, 'is always associated with a repudiation, a cleansing . . .'

Once he had solved the riddle of the sphincter, his way was free to solve the problem of man's relationship with divinity. To some extent (for he was a great beer drinker) Luther made a god of his stomach, but to a much larger extent he made a stomach of his God. To break wind in the face of Satan and the Pope became an obsession with this superb vernacular poet; in Dr Erikson's words, 'a transference had taken place from a parent figure to universal personages, and . . . a central theme in this transference was anal defiance'.

This aspect of Luther, the neurotic haunter of lavatories, is brilliantly conveyed by Mr Osborne, and as brilliantly linked with the Luther we all know – the fractious, self-lacerating monk who refused to concede that the Church could wash away his guilt, and thus bequeathed to us the chronic Angst of Protestantism. Nothing is more typical of Luther than the fact, omitted by Mr Osborne, that he commissioned a series of woodcuts in which Rome was portrayed as a prostitute giving rectal birth to a swarm of misshapen demons; in this he is closer to Bosch than to Calvin. It was beguiling to observe, at last Thursday's première, that the lines by which a presumably sophisticated audience was most shocked were nearly all direct translations from the hero's own works.

In form, the play is sedulously Brechtian, an epic succession of *tableaux* conceived in the manner of *Galileo*; and the graph of its development is likewise Galilean – a rebel against papist dogma publishes heresies, and is asked by velvet-gloved officialdom to recant. The difference is that Luther rejects the demand; all the same, Mr Osborne's final scene is an obvious echo of Brecht's. The protagonist, having settled for domesticity, is seen smacking his lips over a good meal, conscious the while that he has betrayed the peasants who revolted in his name, just as Galileo betrayed the cause of scientific enlightenment. We are left with a powerful impression of a man who invented the idea of the individual conscience, responsible to no earthly authority, and was racked by his own invention; a man, as Cardinal Cajetan puts it, who hates himself and can only love others.

The language is urgent and sinewy, packed with images that derive from bone, blood and marrow; the prose, especially in Luther's sermons, throbs with a rhetorical zeal that has not often been heard in English historical drama since the seventeenth century, mingling gutter candour with cadences that might have come from the pulpit oratory of Donne. And it can readily swerve into comedy, as in the long harangue of the indulgence sales-man, offering snake-bite remedies against the mortal nip of the serpent in Eden.

Always the play informs; one's reservation must be that it too seldom excites; the thrusting vigour of its style goes into exposition rather than action. Yet I count it (to burn a boat or two) the most eloquent piece of dramatic writing to have dignified our theatre since *Look Back in Anger*. The direction, by Tony Richardson, is simple and hiera-tic, and no finer Luther could be imagined than the clod, the lump, the infinitely vulnerable Everyman presented by Albert Finney, who looks, in his moments of pallor and lip-gnawing doubt, like a reincarnation of the young Irving, fattened up for some cannibal feast.

Julian Glover, Peter Bull and George Devine are the best of the lesser folk, and Jocelyn Herbert's décor is worthy, in its glowing restraint, of the Berliner Ensemble.

(1961)

Stop the World—I Want to Get Off!

by ANTHONY NEWLEY *and* LESLIE BRICUSSE
at the Queen's

One of the things that distinguish comedy today from comedy in the past is that today the comedians them-selves tend to write it. Gone, increasingly, are the gag-smiths on whose lips the star would hang; instead of being spokesmen for committees, like Bob Hope or Jack Benny, the new clowns speak for themselves; and their craft, in consequence, has become more perilous and nerve-racked. In America, Mort Sahl, Lenny Bruce, Elaine May and Mike Nichols are of this breed; in England, Spike Milligan, and the four 'agile and mellifluous quodlibetarians' (to pluralize Max Beerbohm's phrase for Professor C. E. M. Joad) of *Beyond the Fringe*.

For this crack regiment Anthony Newley has now volunteered. In collaboration with Leslie Bricusse, he is responsible for the book, music and lyrics of *Stop the World — I Want to Get Off*, of which he is also, quite emphatically, the star. Nor, had the gallery booed, could he have exculpated himself by blaming the direction, since it was he who staged the show. He did not, of course, design it; after all, Sean Kenny was free, and it is universally agreed that the principal function of English stage design is to enable Mr Kenny to continue his momentous experiments in the use of surplus timber. Otherwise, the evening is Mr Newley's : his the laurels, his the thorns.

The verdict, I fear, must be thorns. From his past record (if not from his recent records) we know Mr Newley to be one of our brightest young performers, dapper and sly and capable of provoking a worried, modern kind of laughter. What perturbs me, in *Stop the World*, is the influence of those other Mr Newleys, the writer, the composer and the director : one man in his time plays many parts, but not all on the same night. The show concerns an average man named Mr Littlechap who marries the boss's daughter, gets rich, has affairs, enters politics, bags a peerage and decides, as he dies, that he has led a selfish life. It all takes place in a circus tent, symbolizing the human condition. To convey some idea of its quality, let me give you a list of the things without which, in the theatre, I can most easily do. They include :

(*a*) All plays in which circus tents symbolize the human condition (e.g.: *J.B.*).

(*b*) All protagonists with names like Mr Zero, Mr Adam,

He, The Little Man and Mr Littlechap. To be theatrically interesting, Everyman must be Someone, not just Anyone.

(c) All mimes except Marcel Marceau. It was clear as soon as he shuffled in, pigeon-toed and baggy-trousered (a gait and garb that never varied), with a hopeless, prognathous grin on his white-painted face, that Mr Newley had been subjected to a massive overdose of Bip. When he spoke, one was startled; it was like being present at a miracle cure. In addition to walking without moving forwards, Mr Newley had the gall to end the show in the same foetal posture that M. Marceau adopts in the final moment of his most celebrated number – man's progress from birth to death.

(d) All plays in which the hero is represented as falling in love with the same eternal woman, who reappears throughout his life in various disguises (vide Terence Rattigan's Who is Sylvia?). In Stop the World, the Eve-figure has four identities; a Russian, a German, an American, and an Englishwoman called Evie. They are played by Anna Quayle, a Junoesque redhead who might, in happier circumstances, be extremely droll.

(e) All jokes about Russia that involve the mention of tractors.

(f) All puns except the very best. There is no excuse for horrors like 'a sour little Kraut' or 'the ig-Nobel Prize-winner'; and I hope I have now heard the last of the Steppes-steps homophone.

(g) All plays that carry political impartiality to the length of implying that there is no difference between Right and Left.

(h) All plays of which the director is also the protagonist.

(i) All plays of which the protagonist is also the author.

In sum, a sad, pretentious evening, visually monotonous and redeemed only by glimmers of potentiality from Mr Newley (that tinny, plaintive voice) and Miss Quayle. After this escapade, I hope Mr Bricusse will manage to persuade his talented partner to modify the demands of his ego. There were periods, especially in the second half, when one sensed an ominous coldness settling on the house; the audience, one felt, was sitting on its hands, while Mr Newley was sitting on the right hand of God.

(1961)

A Breakthrough Breaks Down: 1961

In a week void of London *premières*, I scan the list of available productions and am shocked. So little, in ten years, seems to have changed. The Royal Court has arrived and survived, a beach-head for our splashing new wave; but one beach-head, it becomes chillingly clear, doesn't make a breakthrough.

A decade ago, roughly two out of three London theatres were inhabited by detective stories, Pineroesque melodramas, quarter-witted farces, debutante comedies, overweight musicals and unreviewable revues; the same is true today. The accepted new playwrights then were Fry, Eliot and Anouilh; of this threesome Anouilh is still represented on the playbills of London, and the other two have been replaced by Arnold Wesker (*The Kitchen*) and John Osborne (*Luther*).

As for Theatre Workshop, it is almost as if it had never been. Unknown in London ten years ago, and recently decapitated by the loss of Joan Littlewood, it has no West End memorial except what must by now be a fairly apathetic production of *Fings Ain't Wot They Used T'Be*. Theatrically, though not otherwise, Brendan Behan has been silent since *The Hostage*: Shelagh Delaney has not yet fulfilled the glowing promise of *A Taste of Honey*; and Alun Owen, all-conquering on television, failed to conquer Shaftesbury Avenue with *Progress to the Park*.

Harold Pinter's newest piece, *A Night Out*, was originally commissioned by, and performed on, television; and the flock of Pinter mimics – or *Pinteretti*, as I sometimes think of them – have made no impact at all on the theatre. Nor, if we are talking about public acclaim, has Mr Wesker, whom the West End persistently shuns. Our new school of regional actors has two leaders, of whom one, Albert Finney, can be seen in *Luther*, but only for a limited season, while the other, Peter O'Toole, is busy filming in Arabia.

Dispassionately eyed, the great proletarian upsurge of which we bragged so freely (and of which so many foreign critics wrote so enviously) looks very much like a frost. Its symbols are Willis Hall and Keith Waterhouse, the authors of *Billy Liar* – two working-class playwrights who owe their London success to a middle-class parlour farce.

Perhaps we expected too much; perhaps that is why the breakthrough broke down. In our rage against conventional theatre, we should have remembered the *caveat* of that incomparable critic, Trotsky :

> It is fundamentally wrong to oppose proletarian to bourgeois culture and art. Proletarian culture and art will never exist. The proletarian regime is temporary and transitory. Our revolution derives its historic significance and moral greatness from the fact that it lays the foundations for a classless society and for the first truly universal culture.

In other words, the worker's task is purely militant – to build a new society from which a new kind of art will emerge. Until then, we should not repine, we should even rejoice if working-class art shows signs of being influenced by the best of bourgeois culture. It was by publicly expressing sentiments like these that Trotsky hastened his expulsion from the Soviet Union. Too many of our younger playwrights have forgotten, in their passion for novelty of content, the ancient disciplines of style. Rightly determined to look beyond the drawing-room for their subject matter, they have poured the baby out with the bath-water. In the battle for content, form has been sacrificed.

What I look for in working-class drama is the sort of play that is not ashamed to assimilate and acknowledge the bourgeois tradition, which includes a multiplicity of styles, not all of them wholly despicable. Otherwise, the drift of writers towards television and the cinema will swell to flood proportions; dialogue composed in eaves-dropped snippets will always be easier to write than dialogue orchestrated into acts. Moreover, I would remind aspiring prole satirists that the tone, background and terms of reference of *Beyond the Fringe*, the sharpest London revue I have ever seen, are entirely middle-class. To sum up, nothing is more crucially stupid than to deride the artistic achievements of a social class because one deplores its historical record.

Those achievements belong to the past. Between them and the work of people now living a link must be forged and maintained: between Strindberg and Osborne, Chekhov and Shelagh Delaney, Stanislavski and Joan Littlewood, Galsworthy and Wesker, Büchner and John Arden, and other such pairings. But these connections can rarely be made, since the opportunities for comparison so seldom arise. Lacking a National Theatre, London has no playhouse in which the best of world drama is constantly on tap, available for immediate ingestion by spectators of eclectic tastes. One function of such a theatre would be to bridge the gap between those elements of bourgeois theatre that lean towards the future and those elements of the new drama that extend a hand towards the past.

That is the ideal, and at present it is impracticable. One resorts to statistics. Last night the London theatre was to all intents and purposes cut off from history. Of thirty-four playhouses, only three were staging plays that were written more than ten years ago – *Dr Faustus*, at the Old Vic, *'Tis Pity She's a Whore*, at the Mermaid, and *The Rehearsal*, by Anouilh, at the Globe. This trio apart, the oldest play in London last night was Agatha Christie's *The Mousetrap*. I am all for modernity; but this is ridiculous.

Let Coward Flinch

At a time when the talk is all of youth in the theatre, I
should like to pose a question: Where are the *old* playwrights? Never, perhaps, in its history has our theatre
been so thinly equipped with active, established dramatists
past their thirties. We have Messrs Greene and Rattigan,
of course, but most of their coevals and seniors are either
inactive or unperformed, forced into silence by the swift,
radical change in the theatrical climate. Shaw went on
writing into his nineties, and Ibsen into his seventies; nowadays, 'too old at forty' is increasingly the rule. Where,
for instance, is Mr Fry? And how is Mr Eliot? And who
is N. C. Hunter?

I see that I have omitted Mr Coward. We know where
he is, all right; he is rebuking history in the pages of *The
Sunday Times*, wagging his finger at the theatre's 'new
wave' and daring it to drown him. Last week, in the first
of three articles, he accused the younger playwrights of
having failed in the cardinal task of attracting large
audiences – an ambitious charge, coming at a time when
A Taste of Honey and *The Hostage* are prospering on
Broadway, when *The Caretaker* and *Billy Liar* are coining
it in London, and when it has just been announced that
Mr Coward's latest play will shortly be withdrawn after
a run of less than six months.

The bridge of a sinking ship, one feels, is scarcely the
ideal place from which to deliver a lecture on the technique of keeping afloat. While flaying the new dramatists
for boring their audiences with dirt, dustbins and Socialist
dogma, Mr Coward observed that 'political or social propaganda in the theatre, as a general rule, is a cracking
bore'. The exceptions, presumably, include such of his
own works as *Peace in Our Time*, wherein a 'progressive'
English intellectual eagerly collaborates with the Nazis,
and *Relative Values*, which ends with a climactic toast to
'The final inglorious disintegration of the most unlikely

dream that ever troubled the foolish heart of man – Social Equality'.

Mr Coward's second article, we were promised, would deal with 'the Scratch-and-Mumble School' of acting. Sentences at once began to form in my mind:

Heretical though it may be to say so, I maintain that if a tax-ridden English playgoer coughs up a guinea for the privilege of occupying an orchestra stall, he is entitled to expect something slightly more glamorous than the spectacle of an extremely cross young gentleman, execrably attired, reeking of fried onions, and behaving like one of the less inhibited inmates of the London Zoo. . . . Since I myself would never dream of embarrassing my under-privileged brethren by inviting them to discuss their squalid and monotonous problems under my roof, I see no reason why I should pay good money to hear the same problems discussed in the theatre. There are, I believe, Citizens' Advice Bureaux which exist for that very purpose.

. . . Nowadays, apparently, it is considered unpardonably right-wing for an actor to wear anything more seductive than a bedraggled T-shirt and a pair of inconveniently tight blue-jeans, while to speak the Queen's English clearly enough to be understood by the honest souls in the gallery is proof positive that one has 'sold out' to the forces of reaction. . . .

I am senile enough to remember the time when West End actors were not ashamed to be better dressed than their audiences. . . .

It is doubtless too much to suggest that the ironing-boards which clutter up so many London stages might be used with advantage to give the actors' costumes a brisk pressing. . . .

I feel now as I have always felt, that acting should be larger, and if possible prettier, than life. . . . It is both bigoted and snobbish to insist that the company of a vulgar, illiterate skivvy is preferable to that of a woman who, deprived of the benefits of a proletarian upbringing, has had to make do with elegance, breeding and wit. . . . Whatever may be the taste of the regimented hordes of playgoers outside London, Paris and New York, it is immensely gratifying to reflect that in these three cities at least there remains a hard core of loyal, middle-aged theatre-lovers who have had quite enough of the 'new drama', thank you very much, and frantically yearn for the day when the theatre will pull itself together and rise above it. . . .

And here I give in, because nothing of my invention could rival the following authentic excerpt from Mr Coward's opening blast:

'The first allegiance of a young playwright should be not to his political convictions, nor to his moral or social conscience, but to his talent.' This wins my medal for the false antithesis of the month; for what if the author's 'talent' is inseparable from his conscience and convictions, as in the best writers it is?

(1961)

Queen after Death

by HENRY DE MONTHERLANT
at the Oxford Playhouse

Talking about our younger playwrights in the new issue of *The Twentieth Century*, George Devine remarks: 'There's a movement away from modern dress naturalism. To begin with, they had to write what was close to them, from their own experience. Now they're starting to explore a much wider territory . . .' He cites John Osborne's *Luther*, and adds that Shelagh Delaney has plans for a play about Derby in the fifteenth century; he might also have mentioned John Whiting's *The Devils*, Peter Shaffer's long-gestated chronicle play about the Incas, and – upping the age-limit a little – Christopher Fry's *Curtmantle*.

If Mr Devine is right, and a resurgence of historical drama is imminent, we should all be grateful to the Oxford Playhouse for having chosen such a moment to present Henry de Montherlant's *Queen After Death*, one of the most numbing examples of the genre in modern dramatic literature, and an object lesson in how not to do it.

For Montherlant, history is dignified, and dignity is sententious; every speech comes tripping across the footlights with a ball and chain of pseudo-profundity attached to its ankle. The characters, so many robed machines for the production of densely scrambled platitude, exchange lectures on the state of their souls, the danger of love, the nature of power, the claims of justice, the necessity of duty, and other topics calculated to exploit the full capacity of the French language for exquisite, lapidary emptiness.

Quite often the people on stage seem to be engaged in earnest discussion of a play that is not in fact taking place. They express formal opinions; they swap sentiments, anecdotes and metaphors; but outside the printed text they have no existence at all. They are walking figures of speech, syntactical fictions. Stung by a crafty stroke of litotes, they may riposte with a shrewd oxymoron to the bread-basket; but it is all shadow-boxing, a sort of Tussaud tournament.

In English drama (I generalize), character reveals itself and is presented for judgement mostly in terms of class; in Continental drama (I generalize again), mostly in terms of temperament and ideas. But on bookshelves everywhere, accumulating dust and scholarly revaluations, one comes across a third kind of play, in which character consists merely in verbal gesture. It is to this category that *Queen After Death* belongs.

It was Montherlant's first dramatic attempt, written for the Comédie Française in the early years of the Occupation, and it is precisely the sort of play one would not expect from an eminent novelist; the theatre, he seems to have felt, was no place for the realistic disciplines of prose fiction. Alternatively, he may have been under the misapprehension that it was the Opéra, and not the Comédie Française, who had commissioned the piece; which would explain the fact that it reads less like a play in need of actors than a libretto in need of a composer. I have no doubt that a surge of Germanic orchestration would lift the words up to heights befitting, and falsely ennobling, their glacial pretentiousness.

The plot is basic, heroic enough to have entranced Corneille or Schiller, and brief enough to be summarized in the manner of a hastily Englished opera-synopsis. Ferrante, the tyrannic king of Portugal, wishes that his Crown Prince son, Don Pedro, would marry the important Infanta of Navarra, who is maltreated by that son's refusal. (Aria: ''Tis not the woman in me who is insulted, it is the Infanta.') It is transpired that Don Pedro has already himself a wife in secret, and pregnant for him, who is entitled Dona Inez. This news is rending the king choleric, whereabouts he ordains his son to break his contract and lose that wife. But Don Pedro would not lose her, and she him, and then the king causes her to be slain for reason of state. In that moment, with an irony of fate, nature cracked his heart (Aria: 'A king is like a huge tree'), so that he is dead afterwards.

Into this straightforward piece of *Realpolitik* Montherlant imports all sorts of tragic motives; it is a latterday French custom to unearth complex philosophical justifications for simple acts of cruelty or cowardice, with the result that villains, in the contemporary French theatre, often end up as unrecognized martyrs. The king, for instance, has Inez killed not because policy demands it but because he is a dying man, resentful of her youth and fertility.

But one's main objection to *Queen After Death* as a historical play is that it totally neglects historical circumstance. Its wordiness is modern wordiness, disguised in Renaissance trappings, and the result is that spurious brand of 'universality' which assumes that all human beings are always the same, whether ancient or modern, pagan or Christian, Negro or Caucasian, landlord or serf.

A play set in the past needs much fuller documentation than one set in the present; we cannot understand it unless we know the broad social context in which the action is laid. In the normal, conventional theatre, said Brecht, 'Thought determines Being'. In the epic theatre, on the other hand, 'Social Being determines thought'. Montherlant's play is a normal, conventional, and hence utterly frivolous treatment of a thoroughly epic theme.

(1961)

Ross

by TERENCE RATTIGAN
at the Haymarket

I was out of the country when Mr Rattigan's *Ross* opened nine months ago, and though I saw it soon afterwards, no pretext for writing about it arose until last week, when Michael Bryant replaced Sir Alec Guinness as the scourge of the Turks. Ever since I heard Peter Sellers's impersonation of Sir Eric Goodness, a famous actor whose latest role is that of a Persian mystic named Smith, I have been unable to picture anyone else in the part; but Mr Bryant copes doughtily, and has the grace to seem decently embarrassed by Lawrence's last line – 'God will give you peace' – and the bugle-call that accompanies it.

Reduced to essentials, Mr Rattigan's play is a Jack Harkaway adventure with a Freudian core. The villain is a bestial Turk who sprawls on a couch instead of sitting up like a gentleman; alone in the cast, and on top of his other vices, he sweats. Our side includes well-read General Allenby, perceptive Sir Ronald Storrs, and venal but lovable Auda Abu Tayi, a bloodthirsty sheikh with his heart in the right place. With one sickening exception (a public schoolboy gone rotten), T. E.'s mates in the RAF are likewise a first-rate crew – rough diamonds, perhaps, but one would thank one's stars for them in a tight corner.

In the middle of the picture is Lawrence, with his madcap dream, at which fools scoff, of a free, united Arab State. He's a queer one, is T. E., but you must admit the fellow's got guts; he's a man apart from other men, singled out by destiny, born to be fortune's fool. It turns out, early in the second half, that he knew all along about the Anglo-French agreement to carve up Arabia between them after the war. This would seem to invalidate everything he has so far professed, and to make him a cheat and a liar as well as a fool; but you must not imagine that he loses faith in his mission on grounds as rational as these.

Although it tells us nothing about Lawrence's childhood or upbringing, this is a psychological play. For the second time in his career (*Adventure Story* was the first), Mr Rattigan shows us a conquering hero who is stopped dead in his tracks by a revelation of sexual abnormality somewhere east of Suez. In the earlier work, Alexander the Great is stunned to discover that he has a mother-complex; in *Ross*, Lawrence the puritan learns, through being forcibly subjected to sodomy, that he is a non-practising homosexual. Guilt is the spur that has raised his clear spirit. He has done the right things for the wrong reasons. What shall it profit a man if he shall gain the world and lose his virginity? Convinced that his idealism is no more than a by-product of his perversion, Lawrence backs out of the limelight and espouses anonymity.

One would like to think that Mr Rattigan had read what Christopher Caudwell had to say about Lawrence's loathing of the Western way of life: 'He had desired to be just and friendly and brave and to hate pomp and ceremony and wealth, and to love the essence of a man simply as it realised itself in action . . .' and about how he betrayed his ideal by bringing to Arabia 'the very evil he had fled';

> Soon his desert Arabs would have money, businesses, investments, loud-speakers, and regular employment. But he could not realise this consciously, for he had never been fully conscious that it was bourgeois social relations he was fleeing. . . . He was in fact like a man who, fleeing blindly from a deadly disease to a healthy land, himself afflicts it with the plague.

But my main objection to *Ross* is not that its view of history is petty and blinkered; so, it might be urged, is Shakespeare's in *Henry V*. What clinches my distaste is its verbal aridity, its flatness of phrase, and – above all –

its pat reliance on the same antithetical device in moments of crisis. For examples, see below :

1. 'I've an idea you don't care for authority, Ross.'
   'I care for discipline, sir.'
2. 'There's nothing in the world worse than self-pity.'
   'Oh yes there is. Self-knowledge.'
3. 'And so he will win his battles by not fighting them?'
   'Yes. And his war too – by not waging it.'
4. 'And is this only the beginning?'
   'It may be the ending, too.'
5. 'I think I must remind you that I have not yet offered you this appointment.'
   'No. Nor you have. And I haven't accepted it, either.'
6. 'Your man must believe in them and their destiny.'
   'What about your own country and *its* destiny?'
7. 'You're going to make it hard for me, are you?'
   'I see no reason to make it easy.'
8. 'You sicken me.'
   'I sicken myself.'

I will refrain from pressing the case, though it might be worth quoting, by way of conclusion, one spectator's comment on this most fashionable of chronicle plays. 'It was too episodic,' he said, 'to be really picaresque.' Non commitment could hardly go further.

(1961)

The Lady from the Sea

by HENRIK IBSEN
at the Queen's

Listening to *The Lady from the Sea* one thinks of Melville's exalted hymn, in the first chapter of *Moby Dick*, to the lure of great waters :

> Why did the old Persians hold the sea holy? Why did the Greeks give it a separate deity, and own brother of Jove?

Surely all this is not without meaning. And still deeper the meaning of that story of Narcissus, who because he could not grasp the tormenting, mild image he saw in the fountain, plunged into it and was drowned. But that same image, we ourselves see in all rivers and oceans. It is the image of the ungraspable phantom of life. . . .

Ibsen's Ellida, the lighthouse-keeper's daughter, might echo all of this. Hydrophilia, fortified by more than a touch of narcissism, has long since claimed her for its own. Not a day of summer passes but she must take her ritual dip in the fjord, an undine restless for her native element. In imagination a sea-creature, she is in fact the second wife of a provincial doctor – one of those well-meaning fumblers whom Ibsen, most sadistic of theatrical match-makers, delights to saddle with women they can neither comprehend nor satisfy.

In Dr Wangel's home Ellida feels superfluous, unwanted by her step-daughters and unable to compete with her dead predecessor; she has come to despise her marriage as a squalid business arrangement, of no significance beside the pagan compact into which she entered, years before, with a mysterious, long-vanished sailor. His image has grown in her mind to obsessive proportions; and it is his return, almost as if she had telepathically summoned him, that precipitates the play's crisis. Speaking in terms of oracular starkness, he declares that he has come to claim his bride : Ellida must choose between her soul-mate and her legal husband.

But there is more to it than that. The choice is also between fantasy and reality. True, the sailor exists objectively; but so do the *revenants* in *The Turn of the Screw*; and I found my thoughts straying to that interpretation of James's novel which holds that the malevolent phantoms are projections of the heroine's repressed sexual desires. In Ibsen's play, it is not enough to regard the sailor merely as a symbol of Ellida's yearning for the sea; the basic symbol is the sea itself, which stands for all the elemental forces that bourgeois society frustrates and inhibits. Not least among them is sex; we know that Ellida no longer sleeps with her husband. Emotionally stifled, and lacking other outlets for her energies, she almost literally *creates* the sailor, as an objective manifestation of her discontent.

If we miss the point, it may be because Ibsen compromised; in other words, he hesitated to introduce a wholly unreal character into an otherwise realistic setting. (A contemporary playwright would have no such qualms; e.g. the Match-Seller in Mr Pinter's *A Slight Ache*.) Hence the trouble he takes to deck the sailor's behaviour with the trappings of authenticity – a murder charge to account for his long absence, a newspaper report of Ellida's marriage to explain his sudden return. For me, the play's frailty lies here and not, as many critics have urged, in the *dénouement*. Ellida finally elects to stay with her husband, her reason being that he has allowed her, for the first time, to make a choice 'in freedom and on her own responsibility'. Being free to choose, she is able to reject. That, anyway, is her story, and one must admit that it constitutes a pretty feeble excuse for persisting in a marriage that has been unequivocally exposed as a sham. But what if she is rationalizing? What if she is incapable of facing freedom and responsibility, and prefers the opportunities for neurotic self-indulgence that are offered by a life of irresponsible confinement? On that supposition, which nothing in the text contradicts, the play becomes an exercise in irony, with Ellida unmasked as a Nora who will never quit her doll's house. Or in this case, perhaps, her bird-bath.

Although it follows the conventional, affirmative reading of the last scene, the present production is a fine one, with settings by Motley that would not disgrace the Moscow Art Theatre. This is the only Ibsen play that Chekhov might have written, and Glen Byam Shaw has directed it with a Chekhovian feeling for its sunsets and nostalgias; the high mountain air we associate with Ibsen is here thickened by a river mist, intermittently pierced by the mournful hooting of steamers.

For Vanessa Redgrave, who plays Wangel's elder

daughter, a Chekhov season must forthwith be mounted, with special emphasis on *The Seagull* and *The Three Sisters*. To witness the scene in which Miss Redgrave embraces her tutor's offer of financial help, rejects it upon learning that it involves marriage, and eventually, tentatively, reaccepts it, as her need to escape stagnation overrides her distaste for an unpropitious match, is to relive the painful, illusion-shedding transition that marks the end of youth. If there is better acting than this in London, I should like to hear of it.

As the mermaid manquée, Margaret Leighton is exquisitely distraught; a bit too actressy, now and then, a bit too conscious that this was one of Duse's greatest parts; but brilliant in many passages that call for controlled hysteria and/or abject melancholia.

(1961)

Becket

by JEAN ANOUILH
at the Aldwych

The Royal Shakespeare Theatre pursues its royalist course; after *The Hollow Crown*, written by the monarchs of England, we have M. Anouilh's *Becket*, which is about one of them. Not that one would recognize Henry II from this Parisian portrait, any more than one would recognize Joan of Arc in Shakespeare's termagant Pucelle; M. Anouilh gives us the Plantagenet bully-boy who was half of Henry, but omits the great judicial reformer who was the other.

More, perhaps, than any other sovereign of his century, Henry deserved the title of intellectual. M. Anouilh ignores this altogether; indeed, in a foreword to the play, he explains that he never bothered to find out what Henry and Becket were really like. What he sought to tell was the story of a friendship sundered by the rival claims of Caesar and God; and the obvious way to simplify the contest was to make the king a man of passion and the archbishop a man of principle. It is the artist's privilege thus to tamper with fact; all the same, one may regret that M. Anouilh shied away from the harder task of showing a conflict between intellectual equals who differed only in their definitions of loyalty.

So much for the play M. Anouilh didn't write. The one he did write is a clever, *insouciant* chronicle, glossed with neat jokes and flawed as an entertainment only when it attempts high seriousness. This author's forte is the sentimental-satirical, not the tragic; a master of pinpricks, he has no gift for swordplay. His Becket is a Saxon who torments himself for having collaborated with the Norman invader. Such intense self-disgust, almost a century after the Conquest, strikes one as a trifle excessive; something here smacks less of pre-Renaissance England than of post-war France.

The early scenes sketch in the enigmatic relationship between Henry and his favourite Saxon; exorbitant in all things, the king makes emotional demands on Becket that the latter, a worldly but passionless creature, cannot possibly meet. Henry needs love, and Becket gives him companionship. M. Anouilh's study of a master increasingly dependent on his servant, unable to comprehend that there are limits to what royalty can command, and flying into tantrums whenever his whims are frustrated, provides the piece with its best and showiest moments, which Christopher Plummer takes in his swaggering stride. This is an actor of real stage-seizing power, unafraid of the big gesture, and endowed with a stabbing voice of kaleido-phonic virtuosity.

One enjoys M. Anouilh when he is being sour (as in Henry's rancorous encounters with his wife and children) or wistful (as in the last wintry meeting between the king and his erstwhile pal). It is when he goes in for profundity that one wishes M. Anouilh would turn it up. He is a quick but shallow thinker; the access of sanctity that over-comes Becket on his appointment as archbishop, compel-ling him to take God's side against the king, is something M. Anouilh's temperament cannot grasp nor his talent express, except on the tritest level. In these mysteries he is not so much a child (which would be tolerable) as a quiz kid. The higher the play aims, the more abjectedly it fails.

Becket, in short, is just what one would expect of an author who can write, as M. Anouilh does in his preface: 'I suppose I am not very serious; after all, I work in the theatre. . . .' By such wry disclaimers as this does the second-rater declare himself.

Peter Hall's production is stronger and more unified in style than the Broadway version I saw some months ago. Eric Porter, whom few actors excel in the difficult art of conveying to an audience the specific gravity of moral scruples, is a superbly worried Becket; Olivier, who created the part in New York, was a much less convincing candidate for martyrdom. Later, however, Sir Laurence took over the role of the king, on which he worked the kind of magic that is the great actor's prerogative: he imposed on a minor play a major act of reinterpretation.

His Henry was devoured by a passion that confused him even as it consumed him: the actor implied what the character never suspected, namely, that his attachment to Becket was homosexual. Hence the sulks into which he is thrown by Becket's coolness; hence, too, the oafish malice with which he steals his friend's mistress; he wants to deprive Becket of a female bedfellow, and at the same time to be close to someone whom Becket has loved. When the girl kills herself, Henry is convulsed by a frenzy of guilt and begs permission to spend the night in Becket's bed: in this scene Sir Laurence was so nakedly, pathetically vulnerable that one felt ashamed to be watching. And he made it quite clear, by some interlinear stealth, that Henry raised Becket to the see of Canterbury in order to unsex him.

The keystone of this amazing performance fell into place just before the final curtain. The penitent king, having undergone a ritual scourging, quits the cathedral to acknowledge the cheers of his people. Sir Laurence paused halfway to the door and, turning towards the martyr's tomb, elaborately winked and blew in its direction a heartfelt farewell kiss. These intimacies concluded, he swept out into history.

(1961)

Happy Days

by SAMUEL BECKETT
at the Royal Court

Samuel Beckett's new work, the latest bulletin from the Arctic latitudes of his particular hell, the starkest portrait he has yet drawn of the slow burial that begins with birth, is called *Happy Days*.

It is much too long, too full of infertile pauses, and should really have been staged in one act, as a feminine counterpart to *Krapp's Last Tape*. It is a dramatic metaphor extended beyond its capacities. That said, I urge you to see it. But go early, and study the author's photograph that stares out of the programme.

Note the wrinkles between his eyebrows, converging in a crossroads of anxiety; and the look on his face, at once accusing and aghast, as of a man about to be struck by lightning, or a child who has been spat on without warning. This head, one feels, has been cropped for execution, and in its eyes the guillotine looms. This is our author, a prophet who cannot help seeing beyond creature comforts to the engulfing grave.

He shows us Winnie, a middle-aged woman buried up to her waist in a mound of sun-baked earth. Already death has half-claimed her; she refers to the earth that is sucking her under, inch by inch, as 'the old extinguisher'. Yet she is jolly: despite her nostalgic chatter about the passing of 'the old style', she chuckles a lot, is grateful for the mercy of survival, and hails each new day as another free gift of happiness.

Her husband Willie lives in a burrow behind the mound

from which he sometimes emerges to scan a news-sheet or a pornographic picture, and into which he must always crawl backwards. With his bald head and pointed skull, Willie represents the ageing phallus, just as Winnie stands for the ageing breast. Now and then they share a laugh. Winnie sees an ant bearing eggs, and Willie ventures a pun about 'formication'. 'I suppose some people might think us a trifle irreverent,' his wife observes, 'but I doubt it. How can one better magnify the Almighty than by sniggering with him at his little jokes, particularly the poorer ones?'

But, of course, both she and Willie, and all mankind, are among the Almighty's poorer jokes; the earth will inter our dreams as ineluctably as it rises around Winnie's neck. She mentions death's 'pale flag' and unexpectedly quotes 'Fear no more the heat o' the sun'; time and again the text refers back to Shakespeare and his contemporaries, the supreme poets of transience.

Brenda Bruce, peaked and wan but resilient to the last, sustains the evening with dogged valour, and ends up almost *looking* like Beckett; she is self-effacingly partnered by Peter Duguid, whose role is confined to a few shouts and murmurs, and a silent expedition on all fours.

Anyone disposed to scoff at the thought of an actress waist-deep in earth should know that Beckett has anticipated such mockery. Winnie describes a man and woman who once came to gape at her:

> 'What's she doing? he says – What's the idea? he says – stuck up to her diddies in the bleeding ground . . . What does it mean? he says – What's it meant to mean? – and so on – lot more stuff like that – usual drivel – Do you hear me? he says – I do, she says, God help me – What do you mean? he says, God help you?'

Here Winnie gazes straight at the audience. 'And you, she says, what's the idea of you, she says, what are you meant to mean?'

Only those who are sure of the answer can afford to miss the play.

(1962)

The Broken Heart

by JOHN FORD
at the Chichester Festival Theatre

Dear Sir Laurence:

I have now seen all but one of the three inaugural productions you have directed at the Chichester Festival Theatre, and I have to report a general feeling that all is not well with your dashing hexagonal playhouse. When you opened your season with *The Chances*, a flimsy Jacobethan prank by Beaumont and Fletcher, one shrugged and wrote it off as a caprice; but when *The Broken Heart*, a far more challenging piece, likewise fails to kindle one's reflexes, it is time to stop shrugging and start worrying. Something has clearly gone wrong: but how? Who put the hex on the hexagon? Does the fault lie in the play, in the theatre, or in you, its artistic director?

First things first. The play is Ford's best tragedy, and history rightly says that Ford is not bunk. It also says (and here you may not agree) that on this occasion he composed a series of agonized tableaux rather than a continuously developing action. Nearly all the principal characters are mismated or sexually deprived: we see them as if lit by magnesium flares, pleading, brooding, repining and expiring.

Young Orgilus yearns for Penthea, but cannot have her: during a feud between their two families she married someone else. Her brother Ithocles, who fixed the match and thereby drove Orgilus to despair, yearns just as vainly for Calantha, heiress to the throne of Sparta. At the end (forgive me this recapping) all four of them have died, the men by straightforward blood-letting and the girls by such recherché means as delayed-action heart failure and voluntary starvation.

Did you feel, as I did, a strange undertow of incest running beneath the text? Orgilus, for example, behaves like a cuckold when his little sister falls in love; and halfway through a scene between Ithocles and Penthea, who are twins, the latter's husband bursts in and accuses them of unnatural leanings. Whenever he writes about death or sin, Ford is marmoreal and unforgettable: his work is a scattering of noble fragments awaiting some genius of theatrical archaeology to reassemble it as a monument.

Given a script so awkwardly split between nobility and banality, did you find a production style that might weld it together? I think not. You went all out for anonymous rhetoric, 'fuyant le naturel' – as a French critic once put it – 'sans trouver la grandeur'. A lot of vocal brandishing took place in a vacuum. 'Vehemence without real emotion,' said G. H. Lewes, 'is rant; vehemence with real emotion, but without art, is turbulence.' One noted both kinds of vehemence in your *Broken Heart*.

When in doubt about the precise emotion behind a speech, have it delivered in tones of ungovernable rage: was this, as I suspected, your watchword? I liked your handling of Rosemary Harris, a calm, unpainted Penthea, looking at once ravaged and ravishing; and some of the crowd scenes had a solemn, collective splendour. But how do you account for Joan Greenwood's Calantha, a stoical heroine reduced to the stature of a baritone Joyce Grenfell? And Roger Furse's décor, three layers of gaudy wedding-cake propped up against the back wall? And your own performance as Miss Harris's enforced husband? Surely Bassanes is a stupid, self-deluding dotard at whose ridiculous jealousy we are supposed to laugh until, in the course of time, it becomes pathetic. You played him from the first as a sombre old victim bound for the slaughter, too noble and too tragic ever to be funny. Ford's tragedy was thus robbed of its essential comedy.

Most remarkable of all, you were indistinct: one lost more than half of what you said. And here begins my sad indictment of the peninsular Chichester stage. Shakespeare's actors performed on an out-thrust platform because they needed illumination from the sun's rays; the least desirable seats in the Globe Theatre – those occupied by the groundlings – were the ones nearest the stage. Proximity was a disadvantage. Nothing so quickly dispels one's sense of reality as a daubed and bedizened actor standing four feet from one's face and declaiming right over one's head. The picture-frame stage was invented in the seventeenth century to give all the spectators the same sightlines and the same viewpoint; but it encouraged expensive décor, and in the last fifty years we have been urged to revive the projecting stage, ostensibly for artistic reasons but actually because it cuts scenic costs to a minimum.

Chichester is a product of our gullibility : instead of letting the whole audience see the actors' faces (however distantly), we now prefer to bring them closer to the actors' backs. The Chichester stage is so vast that even the proximity argument falls down : an actor on the opposite side of the apron is farther away from one's front-row seat than he would be from the twelfth row of a proscenium theatre – where in any case he would not deliver a crucial speech with his rear turned towards one's face.

The more-or-less straight-edged stage (preferably stripped of its proscenium framing) remains the most cunning and intimate method yet devised for transmitting plays to playgoers : and it was on stages like this that you spent a quarter of a century polishing your technique. Alas, at Chichester your silky throwaway lines, flicked at the audience like leg-glances by Ranjitsinhji, are literally thrown away : they go for nothing and die unheard.

In a small theatre, where sound and sight present no problems, the promontory stage is perfectly viable. In a large theatre like Chichester's, it simply does not work, above all if the plays one is performing depend for their effect on verbal nuance. You might point out to the National Theatre Committee that, by recommending a stuck-out stage for the main playhouse and a proscenium for its junior partner, they have got things exactly the wrong way round.

(1962)

Plays for England

by JOHN OSBORNE
at the Royal Court

The pastime of sado-masochism – whereby one gains pleasure from dominating or being dominated – is deeply ingrained in English sexual life; so much so that the French call it *le vice anglais*. Whether it springs from faulty toilet-training or public-school brutality is not here our concern: the point is that it exists, that it inspires much of our pornography, and that it makes its first overt appearance on the English stage in *Under Plain Cover*, the second half of John Osborne's new double bill, *Plays for England*.

Mr Osborne's courage is doubly flabbergasting: not only does he state the facts about a sado-masochistic *ménage*, he also refrains from condemning it. The Turners, Tim and Jenny, are a provincial couple who never go out; they are much too absorbed in fetishist fantasies. They dress up in a variety of interchangeable roles – doctor and patient, strict master and meek housemaid, leather-clad motor-cyclist and docile Girl Guide. They are both obsessed with underwear, summed up in the wife's elaborate tribute to what she and her husband delight to call 'knickers'.

They persistently joke and improvise: when the wife, in her housemaid garb, threatens to hand in her notice rather than be chastised, the husband ripostes by declaring that the time is the thirties, and no other jobs are available. 'What a good idea!' she cries, bending to his inventive whim. Commodes, corsets and rubber in all its forms are among their other preoccupations, which they discuss as gaily as other couples discuss the garden, the curtains and the new car.

In the midst of a characteristically off-beat experiment, Tim asks Jenny whether she would like to have another baby. She says at once that she would. We suddenly realize that this is not only a thriving affair but a genuine, working marriage: an anal-sadistic relationship need not preclude love. This is perhaps the most audacious statement ever made on the English stage.

The *dénouement* is hasty and strained: Tim and Jenny are revealed to be brother and sister, the Press prises them apart and Jenny marries another, whom she swiftly deserts to rejoin Tim. Anton Rodgers and Ann Beach (particularly the latter) are superb as the mutually hypnotized couple. The script should immediately be sent to every *avant-garde* writer, with special reference to Genet: what they leave opaque or translate into evasive poetic symbols is reduced by Mr Osborne to basic, unambiguous sexual fact. The result is not, perhaps, a work of art; but as a document it is unique and unmissable. It is also genuinely shocking.

(1962)

Blitz!

by LIONEL BART
at the Adelphi

Mawkish where it tries to be poignant, flat where it means to be funny, and secondhand where it aims at period authenticity, Lionel Bart's *Blitz!* is a misfire on the grand scale, despite the devoted salvage work of Amelia Bayntun and a supporting cast of between twenty-eight and ninety-seven players. (Amid so much smoke, it is hard to be sure.)

All the obvious gestures of verisimilitude are made. We hear Sir Winston exhorting and Vera Lynn consoling; while in the background, accompanied by sumptuous detonations, London is unquestionably burning. Yet all this seems utterly detached from what is going on in the foreground – a trite squabble between two East End families (one Jewish, one Gentile) that could have taken place at any time in the last fifty years. True, the Jewish girl is blinded in an air raid, but her face is miraculously unscarred and, after a brief lapse into drunkenness, her Gentile boy-friend comes to his senses and marries her; meanwhile, to preserve moral parity between the households, Mr Bart makes the girl's brother a deserter, who ultimately repents. An Irish trio, some homeless Indians and a couple of Chinese crop up in the crowd scenes to symbolize multiracial amity : and Mr Bart permits himself one 'daring' touch – a Negro spiv.

The songs are straightforward music-hall stuff, spiced now and then with hints that the composer-lyricist is aware, if only telepathically, of the achievements of composers whose work is less well known in England than his own; by a sort of osmosis, phrases and cadences from minor American musicals seep into his melodies; and there is one tune – a lively children's number called 'Mums and Dads' – that sounds exactly like a reject from *Oliver!*

In all, I cannot feel that Mr Bart's theme has inspired him; nor can I honestly say I am sorry. Twenty-two years have passed since the blitz began, and I see no fruitful point in being nostalgic about it : after all, nobody was writing musicals about trench warfare in 1940. A bookmaker repeatedly quoted by James Agate once said that Marie Lloyd had a heart as big as Waterloo Station. *Blitz!* is as big as Waterloo Station, but it has no heart.

It does, however, have Sean Kenny's scenery, and herein may lie its true significance. Belasco and Novello went pretty far in the direction of spectacular realism; but in *Blitz!* there are distinct signs that the sets are taking over. They swoop down on the actors and snatch them aloft; four motor-driven towers prowl the stage, converging menacingly on any performer who threatens to hog the limelight; and whenever the human element looks like gaining control, they collapse on it in a mass of flaming timber.

In short, they let the cast know who's boss. They are magnificent, and they are war : who (they tacitly inquire) needs Lionel Bart? I have a fearful premonition of the next show Mr Kenny designs. As soon as the curtain rises, the sets will advance in a phalanx on the audience and summarily expel it from the theatre. After that, the next step is clear : Mr Kenny will invent sets that applaud.

(1962)

King Lear

by WILLIAM SHAKESPEARE
at Stratford-on-Avon and later in London

Lay him to rest, the royal Lear with whom generations of star actors have made us reverently familiar; the majestic ancient, wronged and maddened by his vicious daughters; the felled giant, beside whose bulk the other characters crouch like pygmies. Lay also to rest the archaic notion that Lear is automatically entitled to our sympathy because he is a king who suffers.

A great director (Peter Brook) has scanned the text with fresh eyes and discovered a new protagonist – not the booming, righteously indignant Titan of old, but an edgy, capricious old man, intensely difficult to live with. In short, he has dared to direct *King Lear* from a standpoint of moral neutrality.

The results are revolutionary. Instead of assuming that Lear is right, and therefore pitiable, we are forced to make judgements – to decide between his claims and those of his kin. And the balance, in this uniquely magnanimous production, is almost even. Though he disposes of his kingdom, Lear insists on retaining authority; he wants to exercise power without responsibility, without fulfilling his part of the feudal contract. He is wilfully arrogant, and deserves much of what he gets.

Conversely, his daughters are not fiends. Goneril is genuinely upset by her father's irrational behaviour, and nobody could fault her for carping at the conduct of

Lear's knights, who are here presented as a rabble of bellicose tipplers. After all, what use has a self-deposed monarch for a hundred armed men? Wouldn't twenty-five be enough? We begin to understand Regan's weary inquiry: 'What need one?'

Such is Mr Brook's impartiality, so cool the moral scrutiny he applies to the text, that we can laugh at Lear's crazy obtuseness without endangering the play's basic purpose, which is tragic; but generally tragic, not individually so. Mr Brook has done for *Lear* what he did for Alec Clunes's Claudius in *Hamlet* some years ago: he has taught the 'unsympathetic' characters to project themselves from their own point of view, not from that of the inevitably jaundiced hero.

Writing about this incomparable production, I cannot pretend to the tranquillity in which emotion should properly be recollected. To convey my impressions, I prefer to quote a slightly revised version of the programme notes I scrawled in the Stratford dark.

Flat white setting, combining Brecht and Oriental theatre, against which ponderous abstract objects dangle. Everyone clad in luminous leather. Paul Scofield enters with grey crew-cut and peering gait; one notes at once the old man's trick of dwelling on unexpected vowels and lurching through phrases as if his voice were barely under rational control. . . . Brook means us to condemn his stupidity, and to respect the Fool (Alec McCowen) who repeatedly tries to din his message into the deaf royal ears. . . . The knights are tight, and Goneril (Irene Worth) is right to be annoyed; but won't this wreck the scene in which Kent takes his revenge on Goneril's uppish steward? . . .

Later: Kent certainly loses his laughs, but the scene reveals him as an unreflecting bully who is unable to give a coherent answer to Cornwall's patiently iterated question: 'Why art thou angry?' This is the alienation effect in full operation: a beloved character seen from a strange and unlovely angle. . . . Gloucester (Alan Webb), so often Lear's understudy and rival moaner, has taken on a separate identity: a shifty old rake and something of a trimmer, capable of switching his allegiance from Lear to Cornwall and back again. . . .

Spurned by his daughters, Lear loses his wits purely in order to punish them: 'I shall go mad!' is a threat, not a pathetic prediction. 'Blow, winds' is an aria of fury, the ecstasy of vengeful madness; as Scofield howls it, three copper thunder-sheets descend behind him, rumbling and quivering. . . .

Top marks for his drained, unsentimental reading of the lines about 'unaccommodated man'. (Lear by now is a rustic vagabond: cf. the classless derelicts of Samuel Beckett, and especially the crippled hero of *Endgame*.) High marks, too, for Brook's decision to stage Gloucester's trial in the same hovel where Lear has recently arraigned his daughters.

The blinding of Gloucester could hardly be more shocking. 'Upon these eyes of thine,' says Cornwall, 'I'll set my foot': and Brook, responding to the ghastly hint, gives Cornwall a pair of golden spurs with which to carry the threat into literal effect. . . .

Am baffled as always by Edgar's inexplicable failure to reveal himself to his blinded father; Shakespeare is here milking a situation for more than it is worth. . . .

And suddenly, greatness. Scofield's halting, apologetic delivery of 'I fear I am not in my perfect mind'; sightless Gloucester, sitting cross-legged on the empty stage while the noise of battle resounds in the wings; and the closing epiphany, wherein Lear achieves a wisdom denied him in his sanity – a Stoic determination, long in the moulding, to endure his going hence. . . .

But even Brook is defeated by Edmund's tangled liaisons with Regan and Goneril: mainly because James Booth handles verse with the finesse of a gloved pugilist picking up pins, but also because the minutiae of sexual jealousy seem puny beside Lear's enormous pain. . . . Lighting deliberately bright throughout, even during the nocturnal scenes, as in the Chinese theatre; and no music except towards the end, when the text demands it. . . .

This production brings me closer to Lear than I have ever been; from now on, I not only know him but can place him in his harsh and unforgiving world.

Last month, reviewing Peter Brook's bleak and beautiful production of *King Lear* before it moved from Stratford to London, I stressed its moral neutrality: the way in which, by presenting Lear as a cranky old despot who deserved a come-uppance from Goneril and Regan, Mr Brook had balanced the scales, so that the characters were neither 'bad' nor 'good' but equally entitled to our attentive concern.

They were not doomed by vice or predestinately driven; they were merely people, varying manifestations of 'the thing itself'. Not much nobility was permitted them; often they took the stage kneeling, grovelling, stumbling, squirming, wriggling about like worms, forced into graceless postures, slumped in the stocks, or shoved on their backs to be tortured.

I see now a clue to the nature of Mr Brook's cruel, unsparing egalitarianism; his production is amoral because it is set in an amoral universe. For him the play is a mighty philosophic farce in which the leading figures enact their roles on a gradually denuded stage that resembles, at the end, a desert graveyard or unpeopled planet. It is an ungoverned world; for the first time in tragedy, a world without gods, with no possibility of hopeful resolution. No Malcolm or Fortinbras is on hand to rebuild this ruined kingdom: Albany, the heir-apparent, resigns his inheritance to be shared between Kent, who promptly rejects it, and Edgar, who responds with a brief and highly ambiguous speech about obeying 'the weight of this sad time'.

Mr Brook never tries to compel our tears, though we may weep if we wish; as when Paul Scofield's growling king shares a bench with Alec McCowen's sniping fool, the latter anxiously gauging how close his master is to madness; or when Lear and Gloucester, respectively mindless and eyeless, meet at Dover and huddle together for comfort. But in general the tone is as starkly detached as

Albany's, on hearing that Regan and Goneril are dead :

> This judgement of the heavens, that makes us tremble.
> Touches us not with pity.

The key to Mr Brook's approach may be found in an essay by Jan Kott, the Polish critic, comparing *Lear* to Beckett's *Endgame*; I have cited it before in these columns, and it is now available in *Shakespeare Notre Contemporain*, a collection of M. Kott's essays.

In brief, his argument is that Beckett and Shakespeare have more in common with each other than either has with the romantic, naturalistic theatre that historically separates them. For one thing, they have a sense of the grotesque, of the absurd discrepancy between the idea of absolute values and the fact of human fragility. Tragedy in the cathartic sense occurs only when there are fixed gods, fates, moral principles or laws of nature to which a man's acts can be opposed and by which they can be judged. Where no such absolutes obtain, the effect is not tragic but grotesque. It brings with it no consolation. 'Tragedy is the theatre of priests,' says Kott, 'the grotesque is the theatre of clowns.'

In *Lear*, he insists, the stage must be empty and sterile, a bare space of hostile earth Gloucester's mock suicide is a tragic situation transmuted into farce; unless the gods exist, it is a comic irrelevance, a sacrifice made to a Godot who shows no signs of arriving. 'In both versions of *Endgame*, Shakespeare's and Beckett's, the Book of Job is played by clowns.' Shakespeare employs a quartet of near-buffoons – a madman, a fool, a blind man and a feigned demon. As for Beckett: 'The two couples – Pozzo blinded and Lucky struck dumb, Hamm who cannot rise and Clov who cannot sit – are drawn from the "endgame" of *King Lear*.'

Mr Brook, reversing the process, bases his *Lear* on Beckett. At times the measurements fail to tally; there is nothing remotely Beckettian, for example, in the Edmund-Regan-Goneril triangle or the battle scenes. But where the concept fits, as it mostly does, the production burns itself into your mind; you forget poor over-parted Edmund (James Booth), and remember only that you will seldom see such another Gloucester, and never such another Lear. Nor are you likely to emerge from a theatre with a sharper or more worrying sense of mortality.

(1962)

Giselle

at Covent Garden

Ballet is not my business, nor poaching my practice; but the sudden offer, in a week scarcely bulging with theatrical goodies, of two seats for Giselle was too tempting to decline: so much has been written about the purely dramatic impact of the Fonteyn-Nureyev partnership that I felt justified in trespassing.

Unlike many of my friends, I do not subscribe to the view that ballet, as a separate art form, is a passing fad. That it is young I admit (one can hardly do otherwise, since nothing in its surviving repertoire is much more than 130 years old); but this does not necessarily mean that the gods love it.

I do not underrate the arguments against it – that it is essentially a court entertainment which the nineteenth-century bourgeoisie adopted in order to raise themselves to the level of kings; that it got above itself when it claimed artistic independence and sought to be more than the handmaiden of drama and opera; and that it is out of all proportion for a single ballet company to consume (at a rough but conservative estimate) more than twice as much public money every year as the whole of the London theatre.

I also concede that Giselle itself is something of a hoax: where else but in the ballet world would you find a grown-up audience ready to believe that the betrayal of a village maid by a nobleman in mufti, played out to sweetly whimpering music in a pantomime setting of canvas cottages packed with scampering peasants, was an emotional experience comparable in intensity to *Hamlet*?

All the same, if faced with a question like: 'Must we scrap ballet?' I would certainly answer no. As practised in Britain, it blithely insults my intelligence and leaves my deeper sensibilities untouched; but it does appeal to my sense of occasion, which was profoundly stirred last Tuesday night. In her own way, that dark-haired woman, signalling madness while spinning so prettily, was every bit as poignant as Mary Pickford at her peak; as Stark Young said of another American actress, she was 'all music and security of outline, like a swan on water'; but what moved me more than anything else in her performance was the fact that I knew she was Margot Fonteyn.

As for Nureyev, I mistimed my emotional response, owing to the pressure of thrilled expectation in the house, and began to be moved just *before* he made his entrance. When he paced into sight, like a *dégagé* faun, I instantly recognized the physical ideal of romantic ballet and its audience: a frail, wild young animal, 'poetic' in the archaic sense of 'possibly prone to TB.'

In the second act, down on one knee with his head cradled in his arms, he presented a perfect, fleeting image of contrition; and his face, which is that of a wide-eyed, mutinous orphan with a shock of ungoverned hair, reminded me throughout of the youthful Johnnie Ray, who had the same kind of delinquent pathos. Talent like this is born to flower in close-up; sooner or later Nureyev must surely migrate from the ballet to the cinema.

Meanwhile, I defy anyone not to be affected by the curtain-calls of *Giselle*; here, more than anywhere else, romantic ballet justifies its existence. Embracing bouquets, Dame Margot curtsies; Nureyev bows deeply from the neck, while the other men bow from the waist; Dame Margot proffers a bloom or two; Nureyev accepts them and kisses her hand; solo calls alternate with dual calls; and applause, the incessant obbligato, rhythmically swells and subsides. The more one claps, the more one's eyes mist with tears – tears of gratitude, perhaps, that art can be as undemanding, and at the same time as status-spawning, as this.

(1963)

Who's Afraid of Virginia Woolf?

by EDWARD ALBEE
at the Billy Rose Theatre, New York

The pride of the New York season, acclaimed alike by critics and civilians, is Edward Albee's *Who's Afraid of Virginia Woolf?* Every year there is at least one Broadway play to carp at which is tantamount to blasphemy; and this year Mr Albee's is it. Smiles freeze on hitherto friendly faces when I say that I found it too funny. 'You mean you think people destroying themselves are funny?' said one frozen face, to which I replied that I didn't and that that was exactly the point.

Mr Albee's piece is a marathon dissection of that familiar corpse, the married life of middle-class intellectuals; it is a microcosm of a microcosm, a cloistered game of ill-mixed doubles played out by a cast of four in three acrimonious acts. They are tipsy when it starts – just after a faculty party on a New England campus – and barely controllable when it ends; the action covers the small hours of their ripening intoxication.

The host is George, a middle-aged historian despised by his wife Martha, whose father founded the University; an adroit wielder of the castrating snippers, she enjoys reminding him that his academic life is a failure. No slouch where verbal sadism is concerned, he habitually retorts, with an eager, bonhomous smile creasing his face, that Martha is six years his senior, upset by the menopause, and therefore to be pitied. They sharpen their claws on two visitors – a square young biologist, ruthlessly bent on success, and his idiot bride, whom he married only because she developed a hysterical pregnancy.

Having humiliated each other to their mutual satisfaction, George and his wife turn their attention to a new game, which George calls 'getting the guests'. Before dawn breaks, the biologist has tried and physically failed to go to bed with Martha, and his bride, between vomiting fits, has learned from George that the reason for her hasty marriage is common knowledge. Another piece of bourgeois debris now comes crashing down : to compensate for their sterility, George and Martha have long since connived at a private pretence that they have a grown-up son. To revenge himself for Martha's attempted infidelity, George exposes this fantasy as an outright lie.

The false son, on whom the last act rests, is a strained and implausible gimmick; and the implied debate between humanism (the neurotic historian) and science (the heartless biologist) is too heavily loaded in the former's favour to be of much dialectical interest. What perturbed me most of all, however, was the author's respect for his audience; on the threshold of making them wince, he retreats and lets them off with a laugh. And the cast assists him, scoring quick comic points wherever the chance is offered, fearful (as Broadway actors too often are) of losing, even for a moment, the customers' rapt, approving attention. By signs like these we recognize a panicky theatre.

Mr Albee's text advances the great American art of insult; it is full of brilliant poetic invective and soaring cadenzas of spite, and it could not be better acted than by Uta Hagen, lecherously booming, and Arthur Hill as her blithely destructive mate; but it leaves one's heart unbruised and unmoved. It is too funny by half.

It also dwells on impotence, a long-established Broadway theme that has lately hardened (or softened) into an obsession. No serious play is complete without it. Mr Albee's scientist cannot make love to Miss Hagen; nor could Brick to his wife in *Cat on a Hot Tin Roof*; nor could Edward G. Robinson to his mistress in Paddy

Chayeksy's *Middle of the Night*; nor could Jason Robards to his child-bride in Lillian Hellman's *Toys in the Attic*; nor could Paul Newman to Geraldine Page in *Sweet Bird of Youth*. In fact, since Stanley Kowalsky hit the sack with Blanche Dubois some sixteen years ago, the number of Broadway heroes who have proved their sexual prowess in the course of the action could probably be counted on the fingers of one hand.

(1963)

The National Theatre: A Speech to the Royal Society of Arts

On the north bank of the Thames, alongside Hungerford Bridge, there is a building originally intended for theatrical performance. Over the door you can still read its name: the Playhouse. It closed down as a commercial theatre many years ago and became a B.B.C. studio. Directly opposite, on the south bank of the river, also alongside Hungerford Bridge, there is an empty site. On it, in the course of the next few years, the National Theatre will be built – a permanent, non-commercial home for the British theatre, whose doors (except during holidays, fires, floods, plagues and nuclear wars) will never thereafter be closed.

In this riverside confrontation there are the makings of a hopeful symbol. On the rich northern bank, we have the money-making theatre that the public failed to support; on the poorer southern bank, the non-money-making theatre that the public is paying to build. If this is a valid symbol, if the people of this country have really switched their allegiance from the commercial to the non-commercial theatre, then I find myself in the unwonted posture of arguing with the tide of accepted opinion instead of against it.

But of course it isn't as clearcut as that. Official opinion, in the course of the past hundred years or so, has slowly been coaxed, cajoled and pressured into taking the view that we ought to have a National Theatre. But even today, I am convinced that the great majority of people have only the vaguest idea of why we needed it. I doubt if they will actively attempt to sabotage the construction of the new theatre that Denys Lasdun, our architect, is designing – but then, they did nothing to sabotage the appalling Shell building that broods over the site like a bullet-riddled cenotaph. Apathy in these matters is no evidence of good judgement. Moreover, a few weeks ago I ran into outright hostility to the very idea of state-subsidized culture in a quarter where I had taken some kind of qualified sympathy for granted. I was talking to a well-known English novelist, who shall be Amis, about the National Theatre. He astonished me by saying that he objected on principle to all artistic ventures that were financed by the government. Art, he said, should rely on the laws of supply and demand: what the public wanted it would pay for out of its private pocket, and anything that could not pay its way was probably not good art. He challenged me to name a single great artist who did not prosper in his own lifetime. I whispered Mozart, whom he brushed aside as an exception; and I might have mentioned Brecht, who only achieved recognition when the East German government gave him a subsidized theatre to run.

Finally, my novelist chum told me that he would rather rely on the judgement of publishers who were profit-minded individualists than submit his manuscripts to a panel of faceless do-gooders employed by a Ministry of Culture. I tried to point out that public patronage was not intended to exclude private patronage – when suddenly I realized that we were arguing from different premises. He was talking as a novelist, who needs only time, talent and a typewriter to produce a work of art. I, on the other hand, was concerned with the theatre, where, apart from this trio of prerequisites, a writer needs actors, directors, designers, carpenters, costumiers, wig-makers, stagehands, electricians and possibly singers, dancers and musicians as well, before his work can take on life and present itself for critical assessment. It costs infinitely less to publish a bad novel than to put on a bad play in the commercial theatre. And as soon as you begin to apply commercial criteria to the drama, you find that a play with two characters and one set, which runs for six months, must be considered 'better' – in inverted commas – than a play with fifty characters and twelve sets, which runs for a year : since the former will undoubtedly show a larger profit.

Ever since I had this unsettling chat, I have refrained from taking anything on trust when talking about the National Theatre. Hence the first question I'd like to deal with is : why do we need it?

Britain came late to the whole idea of state-aided theatre. One of the reasons for this is that our rulers have never officially concerned themselves with drama – and by rulers I mean royalty. Queen Elizabeth I enjoyed Shakespeare's plays, but she never paid for their upkeep. Louis XIV, by contrast, took Molière's actors under his fiscal wing and gave France the Comédie Française. Similarly, it was the rulers of the German city-states who founded the great German tradition of subsidized theatre; the provincial centres of German culture still compete with each other for theatrical supremacy.

Another reason for British backwardness is the lasting damage inflicted on the theatre by the Puritans in the seventeenth century. After their moral lacerations, acting came to be regarded as a form of clothed prostitution; and though Charles II subsidized actresses, he did not subsidize plays. Until Irving got his knighthood in 1895, acting remained a dubious profession, barely a stone's cast away from the brothel. And this mighty backlog of Puritan disapproval had to be dislodged before a British government could be persuaded to spend a penny of public money on an art so trivial. Nobody realized that the theatre had become trivial precisely because no public money had been spent to make it otherwise.

Twenty years ago a prominent American playwright summed up what he felt about the Broadway theatre :

'That the most exalted of the arts should have fallen into the receivership of businessmen and gamblers is a situation parallel in absurdity to the conduct of worship becoming the responsibility of a herd of water-buffaloes. It is one of those things that a man of reason had rather not think about until the means of redemption is more apparent.'

That was Tennessee Williams, talking about the American theatre in 1944. People in Britain have been arguing in the same way for more than a century, and elsewhere in Europe for more than three hundred years. The means of redemption became apparent a long time ago. The very idea that good theatre should be required to show a profit would seem indecent in Sweden, Denmark, Poland, Czechoslovakia, Hungary, Yugoslavia, Norway, Russia, Italy, both the Germanies and France. You might as well insist that public libraries should profiteer or that the educational system should pay its way. Theatre in these countries is an amenity for which the state or the municipality – which are simply the individual writ large – must hold itself responsible. It is something the public needs and deserves, like art galleries, zoos and parks for recreation.

Henry James wrote in 1872 : 'It is impossible to spend many weeks in Paris without observing that the theatre plays a very important part in French civilization; and it is impossible to go much to the theatre without finding it a copious source of instruction as to French ideas, manners and philosophy.'

The same could not have been said of the British or the American theatre in the late nineteenth century. In London and New York drama had been forced into the market-place, there to compete with every other huckster. It had inevitably become a short-term art, dependent on quick financial returns, concerned only to produce what the public wants now – not what it might want over a period of five, ten or twenty years. It was compelled to concentrate on easily digestible, uncontroversial, ego-massaging, audience-ingratiating trifles – relieved on occasion by classical revivals tailored to fit star personalities. Box-office tyranny was absolute; and has remained so – apart from latterday trickles of patronage from bodies like the Arts Council – ever since.

Subsidy offers what commercialism negates: the idea of continuity, the guarantee of permanence. If a new production fails on first showing, it need not be lost for ever; it can be shelved for a while and then, if public opinion changes, be revived on the crest of a new wave. Subsidy also enables the theatre to build a durable bridge, with free passage for traffic in both directions, between the past and the present. If Broadway were subsidized, for instance, we should still be able to see Elia Kazan's productions of *A Streetcar Named Desire* and *Death of a Salesman* – they would still be on view, alternating with a dozen other plays, old and new, performed by permanent acting troupes. The plays of Chekhov and Gorky have been in the repertoire of the Moscow Art Theatre for sixty years, with occasional changes of cast. In this way each new generation of playgoers is kept in touch with history. The storehouse of past achievement is always open to the public, instead of being irrevocably burned down at the end of every season.

People sometimes fear that state subsidy may bring with it state control and censorship, and in totalitarian countries this has often been the case. The truth is that governments have two equally effective means of controlling their artists. One is by direct censorship. The other is more oblique but not less potent – it is censorship imposed by *withholding* subsidies, thereby enslaving the artist to the box-office and forcing him, unless he is a genius, to turn out lovable, undisturbing after-dinner entertainments.

What can happen to a theatre without subsidy was vividly animated for me at the Edinburgh Drama Conference. Ninety people attended it, speaking twenty-odd languages, and among them was a young American director who wanted to stage, on the last day of the conference, a 'Happening'. He explained it to me thus: 'You see, Ken, Broadway is like a jungle. If you want to experiment you have to go out into the streets.' He wanted to use the Conference audience in the following experimental way: 'First of all, there'll be no chairs in the hall. Not one. Just a couple of thousand used automobile tyres lying around on the floor. In the middle of the auditorium there'll be four monumental towers of gasoline cans. At the exits there will be four men in black sitting on motorcycles with the motors idling ominously. I shall then invite the audience to build a mountain of tyres in the centre of the floor. Next, and simultaneously, the lowest and the highest notes on the organ will be sounded, thereby creating a sense of unease. The cyclists, at this point, start to circle around the people building the mountain. The guys on the towers of gasoline cans will begin to strike them with hammers on the off-beat. The audience will then dismantle the mountain.' I asked him where they would sit. 'On the tyres, where else?' But (I pointed out) they had paid money and booked seats with numbers. . . .

At length I persuaded him to stage the Happening outside the hall in the courtyard, after the Conference was over. I stood on a balcony and watched it with a group of Eastern European directors – people who worked in theatres that subsidized experiment, and were not faced with the stark choice between commercialism and cut-price improvisation masquerading as art. Looking down, we felt like Louis XVI and his court with the revolutionary mob howling beneath. Except that this was not a genuine revolution; it was a gesture born of economic necessity. I learned afterwards what the young American was trying to do. He explained that he wanted to restore a sense of ritual and participation to the act of playgoing. But it was ritual without content, a party game instead of a communal festivity. It was do-it-yourself art – the only alternative, in an entirely profit-based society, to commodity art, art considered as a saleable product.

Subsidy is the missing link, the third force which can occupy and colonize the great intermediate area between minority theatre based on private whim and and majority theatre based on private profits. This is precisely the area that the National Theatre exists to inhabit and develop; and our hope is that it will be the first, not of the few, but of the many – the beginning of a chain reaction that will set up a national grid of subsidized theatres in London and in every provincial centre.

In the British theatre as a whole, chaos still prevails. The notion that an ideal playhouse is a place where you can see a permanent company of first-rate actors appearing in a large and varied repertoire of first-rate plays is generally accepted; but the notion that such a playhouse must inevitably incur an enormous financial loss, even if it plays to capacity, is less widely embraced. The formation of the National Theatre company was a step towards sanity – towards placing the theatre on the same footing as art galleries and public libraries. The pioneers of the National Theatre movement – people like Shaw, William Archer and Harley Granville Barker – confidently expected that their battle would be won in time for the tercentenary of Shakespeare's death. That was in 1916. Victory was delayed until October 1963, when the National Theatre presented its inaugural production just in time for the quatercentenary of Shakespeare's birth.

There are many other serious legitimate theatres in Britain which are supported to a certain extent by public funds. The National Theatre gets more money than any of the others; but I should like to emphasize that none of them gets enough. To support our first year's operations, we received a Treasury grant of £130,000 – only £50,000 more than the sum allotted the year before to the Old Vic. And the Old Vic employed a much smaller company at much lower salaries, and presented a much shorter list of plays. To keep our standards as high as our output, we shall need more money soon. The same applies to our friendly rivals, the Royal Shakespeare Company. I should like them to be able to compete with us on equal terms; because artistic competition usually makes for better art, whereas commercial competition seldom makes anything but money. The National Theatre and the Royal Shakespeare Company should be able to live side by side in the same kind of relationship as that which exists between the Comédie Française and Jean-Louis Barrault's Théâtre de France.

The tap of public patronage is not exactly gushing, but at least it has been connected. To borrow a dictum beloved of American Negro leaders: 'We ain't where we ought to be, and we ain't where we're going to be, but we sure ain't where we were.' The National Theatre, as a company, exists; the great *de facto* hurdle has been surmounted. It has acquired a brilliant architect in Denys Lasdun, and before long its permanent home will begin to creep up on the South Bank, mercifully obscuring at least part of the Shell penitentiary. What form the theatre will take is something on which I cannot pronounce. Anything I say here reflects personal bias, not official consensus. It is accepted that there should be two auditoriums; it is also accepted that if you try to cram more than a thousand people into a single auditorium, you are entering an area where audibility or visibility or both are sure to be imperfect. Neither on nor outside the Building Committee of the National Theatre is there absolute agreement as to how deeply the stage should project into the auditorium – how far, you might say, it should put its tongue out at the audience – but it is generally felt that actors and spectators should seem to be in one room, without the separating guillotine of the proscenium frame. Beyond this common ground, all is doubt and guesswork.

Speaking for myself and not for the National Theatre, I have two cherished hopes. One concerns the relative sizes of the two projected playhouses. Tradition, based on continental models and Harley Granville Barker's proposals, dictates that one should be large, reserved for the major classics, and the other small, devoted to experimental work. I believe this dichotomy to be artificial and archaic. It derives from the days when all reputable theatres had to be large in order to be commercial; and when plays of doubtful commercial value were forced into converted cellars, attics or church halls that could be cheaply rented. According to this viewpoint, there are two separate kinds of theatre: majority theatre, performed for money, and minority theatre, performed for kicks. This division, originally imposed by economic necessity, tends to survive in the minds and attitudes of those who are planning a theatre from which economic necessity has been removed. Instead of a big house holding a thousand and a little one holding three hundred or so, I would therefore propose two theatres much closer in relative capacity – eight hundred, let us say, and six hundred. Otherwise we may tend to perpetuate the class-conscious notion that there is one kind of drama for the many and another kind, implicitly superior, for the few. Any theatrical experience that cannot be communicated to six hundred people at a sitting is not, on the face of it, the sort of experience that a National Theatre exists to provide. I would hope, of course, for a third auditorium – a workshop or studio devoted to far-out experiment, such as the Schiller Theatre has in West Berlin – but the priority, in my mind, rests with the other two.

Next, there is the anguished question of how far the stage should jut out into the audience; and this is bound up with what we have just considered. The aim is to get as many people as possible as close as possible to the stage. Geometrically, this means that the larger the prospective audience, the more you have to push the acting area out into their midst. Reduce the audience, and at once you reduce the necessity of shoving out a peninsular stage – which even at its best imposes on the customers a number of dire deprivations, such as staring at an actor's rear view when most you need to look at his face and hear the words he is saying. I have heard it speciously argued that a projecting stage adds 'a third dimension' to acting. What a grotesque abuse of language! *All* live acting is in three dimensions, as opposed to screen and television acting, which has two; and I cannot understand how the ability to see one's fellow-spectators behind the actors materially adds to the sculptural roundness of the experience. If we erected a few rows of seats behind the actors on the stage of the Old Vic, would it really make the productions more three-dimensional? The truth, I suspect, is that *proximity* creates the illusion of an extra dimension. And in a theatre of reasonable size, you don't need a tongue-shaped stage to achieve proximity. It exists, after an improvised fashion, in that brilliant conversion job, the Mermaid Theatre in Puddle Dock, where the edge of the stage is straight.

All of us at the National Theatre worry about architectural problems, whether or not it is our business to do so. We also fret over our immediate task, which is to assemble the best available actors and put them into a snow-balling repertoire of the best available plays, ancient and modern, comic and tragic, native and foreign. But we have also stumbled across an additional problem. It has to do with re-education; slowly and patiently, we have had to set about re-educating actors, directors, playwrights and audiences alike. You would be surprised how hard it is, in a society where 'theatre' means 'theatre for private profit', to explain to people that *this* theatre actually belongs to them, and is not in any way stirred by the need or desire to show a profit. I have had to point out to playwrights that in our *modus operandi* they must take the long-term, not the short-term view; although we cannot offer them the quick financial gains of a West End run, we can offer them instead a repertory run that might last for decades. The base on which our enterprises rests can be simply stated: we are not selling a product, we are providing a service. Success at the box office is no longer the only criterion. We would rather have a first-rate work playing to less than capacity than a third-rate one filling the house. Instead of fearing criticism, we can learn from it without rancour, since we do not depend—as the commercial theatre must—on rave reviews for survival.

So far we have opened six productions in the space of five months. On the whole, the critics have applauded and the public has flocked. I don't doubt that this is partly due to the patriotic euphoria that clusters around the launching of any great national venture, and we are sure to run into an iceberg or two before long. But we have not fulfilled the cynical prophecy that the National Theatre would be a plush-lined museum; the names of Laurence Olivier, John Dexter and William Gaskill are not exactly renowned for reverent conventionality, and I am no conservative myself.

Equally, we have not established a 'style' of our own. This is because we never intended to. Good repertory theatres fall into two main categories. One is the kind that is founded by a great director or playwright with a novel and often revolutionary approach to dramatic art. He creates a style for his own special purpose. Examples of this process would include Stanislavsky's Moscow Art Theatre, Bertolt Brecht's Berliner Ensemble and Joan Littlewood's Theatre Workshop. The other category consists of theatres with a broader, less personal *raison d'être* : whose function – more basic though not more valuable – is simply to present to the public the widest possible selection of good plays from all periods and places. In this group you can place the Schiller Theatre in West Berlin; the Royal Dramatic Theatre in Stockholm; and the National Theatre in the Waterloo Road. Their aim is to present each play in the style appropriate to it – and that is an ambition by no means as modest as it sounds.

A year or so ago, I noticed that out of more than two dozen plays running in the West End, only three had been written before 1950. This is the kind of fantastic imbalance that the National Theatre exists to correct. By the end of our first year we shall have staged twelve plays – eight British, four foreign; nine by dead authors, three by living. Of these, roughly half will remain in next autumn's repertoire – some of them, hopefully, for periods of many years. In 1964–5 a dozen more productions have been chosen to join the list. Shakespeare is a necessity, though not in bulk; we are content to leave the lion's share of the bard to the Royal Shakespeare Company. To test the stamina of plays that were praised in the fairly recent past is part of National Theatre policy – hence our decision to revive Noël Coward's *Hay Fever*, directed by the author. Other productions in active preparation include Congreve's *Love for Love*, Strindberg's *Dance of Death*, *The Dutch Courtesan* by John Marston, Brecht's *Mother Courage* (which, apart from the Berliner Ensemble's short but cataclysmic visit in 1956, has never been professionally performed in London), Chekhov's *Three Sisters*, a play by John Osborne based on Lope's *La Fianza Satisfecha* (a strange and startling moral fable), and *The Royal Hunt of the Sun*, by Peter Shaffer. The list is long and various, and only high subsidy makes it even conceivable.

You may ask whether the public wants the theatrical goods we have chosen for them and for which their taxes have paid. The answer is that it looks that way; up to last week the average attendance at the Old Vic was not far short of ninety per cent. And who are these playgoers? Where do they come from and what do they want? We have some information on this subject, derived from a questionnaire that we appended to the programme of Max Frisch's *Andorra*. Ten per cent of the audience, to date, have filled it in and returned it; and you may like to hear some of the results – bearing always in mind that the audience for a play like *Andorra* is likely to be younger and more experimentally inclined than the audience for an established classic.

The *Andorra* figures show that thirty-five per cent of the audience is either teaching or being taught. A further twenty-four per cent consists of clerical or other white-collar workers. Point three per cent (0.3%) are manual workers. The last figure is the most distressing, demonstrating as it does that live theatre is socially beyond the desires and financially beyond the means of working-class audiences. Something must be done to remedy this, the obvious course being to reduce the prices of admission, which would involve either an increase of subsidy or a lowering of artistic standards. The former would clearly be preferable. Encouragingly, fifty-five per cent of the audience is thirty-five years old or younger, which implies that we are not tailoring our programme to meet the demands of gerontophile nostalgia. Many of our spectators are addicts, obsessed with theatre to the point (in some cases) of mania. Thirty-seven per cent of them go to the theatre more than thirty times a year; and fifteen per cent more than fifty times. One realizes that the theatre is kept alive by a hard core of absolute fanatics. Nine per cent of the audience, paying more than seventy-five visits a year, buy far more tickets than the thirty per cent who come fifteen times or less.

Geographically, the figures reveal an overwhelming majority of National Theatre-goers in London and the Home Counties – eighty-nine per cent, as against a tiny minority from the rest of Britain and the world. Obviously, we must tour as much and as widely as we can if we are to deserve the epithet 'National'. Replying to a question about the plays they would most like to see added to the repertoire of the National Theatre, the audience voted for Ibsen, Shaw, Brecht, Marlowe, Wilde, O'Neill and Jonson, in that descending order. Sixty per cent of them liked *Andorra* with only twenty-two per cent of hostility – not bad, considering that it was the first new play (and an awkward, foreign one at that) which the National Theatre had ever presented.

I have tried, in this headlong survey, to give some idea of the direction in which the National Theatre is moving. My conclusions, of course, are those of a navigator and not of a pilot. I once defined a critic as a man who knew the way but couldn't drive the car. As a back-seat driver at the National Theatre, I am putting that maxim to the test.   (1964)

The Royal Smut-Hound

For 'wind from a duck's behind', substitute 'wind from Mount Zion'.
Omit 'crap', substitute 'jazz'.
Omit 'balls of the Medici' : 'testicles of the Medici' would be acceptable.

Delete 'postcoital', substitute 'late evening'.

For 'the Vicar's got the clappers', substitute 'the Vicar's dropped a clanger'.

Omit 'piss off, piss off, piss off', substitute 'Shut your steaming gob'.

These staccato commands are authentic and typical extracts from letters dispatched in recent years from the office of the Lord Chamberlain of Great Britain, second ranking dignitary of Her Majesty's Court. He is the official in charge of the royal household, responsible for receiving visiting potentates and for arranging all state ceremonies from christenings to coronations. He also appoints the Keeper of the Royal Swans. On no account must he be confused with the Lord *Great* Chamberlain – a lowly sixth in the dignitary ratings – who supervises royal openings of Parliament and helps the monarch (if the latter is male) to dress on coronation mornings.

Among the other duties of the Lord Small Chamberlain, as we may call him in passing, is that of censoring all plays presented for public performance in the United Kingdom; and it is this which explains the obscene correspondence that issues from his headquarters in St James's Palace. On royally embossed note-paper, producers all over the country are gravely informed that 'fart', 'tits', 'sod', 'sperm', 'arse', 'Jesus!', etc., are illicit expressions, and that 'the Lord Chamberlain cannot accept the word "screwed" in place of the word "shagged"'. It is something of a wonder that no one has lodged a complaint against His Lordship for corrupting and depraving the innocent secretaries to whom this spicy stuff is dictated; at the very least, the Post Office might intervene to prevent what looks to me like a flagrant misuse of the mails.

At the moment there is nothing we can do about it. The Lord Chamberlain's role as legal censor dates back to 1737, when Sir Robert Walpole's administration – probably the most venal in British history – rushed an Act through Parliament to protect itself from criticism in the theatre. Ever since Tudor times, the Chamberlain (or his subordinate, the Master of the Revels) had been empowered by royal proclamation to regulate dramatic entertainments, but he had mainly confined his cuts to matters of heresy or sedition that might offend the monarch. It was Walpole's panicky vengefulness that gave statutory recognition and legislative force to the Chamberlain's powers, and established a Court official as the sole dictator of the British theatre. Henceforth, no new plays or additions to old ones could be staged without his approval.

This authority was toughened and extended by the Theatres Act of 1843, a repellent piece of legislation that is still in force. Under its provisions, anything previously unperformed must be submitted to 'the Malvolio of St James's Palace' (Bernard Shaw's phrase) at least a week before opening night; a reading fee of two guineas is charged, so that you pay for the privilege of being banned; licences already granted may be revoked if the Chamberlain changes his mind (or if there is a change of Chamberlain); and any theatre presenting an unlicensed work to a paying audience will be summarily closed down. His Lordship can impose a ban 'whenever he shall be of opinion that it is fitting for the Preservation of Good Manners, Decorum, or of the Public Peace'. He need give no reason for his decisions, from which there is no appeal. Since he is appointed directly by the sovereign, he is not responsible to the House of Commons. He inhabits a limbo aloof from democracy, answerable only to his own hunches. The rules by which he judges plays are nowhere defined in law; to quote Shaw again and not for the last time, 'they simply codify the present and most of the past prejudices of the class he represents'.

Since he is always recruited from the peerage, he naturally tends to forbid attacks on institutions like the Church and the Crown. He never permits plays about eminent British subjects, living or recently dead, no matter how harmless the content and despite the fact that Britain's libel laws are about the strictest on earth.

Above all, he feels a paternal need to protect his flock from exposure to words or gestures relating to bodily functions below the navel and above the upper thigh. This – the bedding-*cum*-liquid-and-solid-eliminating area – is what preoccupies him most, and involves the writers and producers who have to deal with him in the largest amount of wasted time.

The normal procedure is as follows: enclosing the two-guinea fee, you submit your script, which is then read by one of three 'Examiners' – anonymous part-time workers, occasionally with some theatrical background. The Examiner passes it on with his comments to the Chamberlain's two Comptrollers – army officers in early middle-age – who add their own observations before referring it to the boss himself. Then begins the salty correspondence, which may go on for months. The Comptroller lists the required cuts and changes; the producer replies, agreeing, protesting or proposing alternatives. (A fine recent protest was penned by the director of John Osborne's *Inadmissible Evidence*: 'We find that the cutting of the words "menstrual periods" is blocking the flow of the scene.')

If postal deadlock is reached, the next stage is a chat with the Comptroller, who usually comes on as a breezy man of the world who knows as much about four letter words as the next man but somehow feels that the next man should be prevented from hearing them. Insane bargaining takes place: the Comptroller may permit you a 'pee' in Act One so long as you delete a 'Christ!' in Act Three. Discussing a one-line gag about the hero's mother-in-law in Osborne's *Look Back in Anger* ('She's as rough as a night in a Bombay brothel'), the Comptroller roared with laughter and said: 'That's a splendid phrase and I shall use it in the Guards' Club, but it won't do for the theatre, where people don't know one another.' If the author still declines to be slashed and rewritten by strangers, he can apply for an interview with the Chamberlain himself; but unless he has a pretty powerful management behind him, he is unlikely to get one; and it has seldom been known to do any good.

Chamberlains are rarely garrulous. Shaw said of the one who held office in his youth that he made only two recorded pronouncements: 'I am not an agricultural labourer', and 'Who is Tolstoy?' The present incumbent is more of a loose-mouth. In the spring of 1965 he gave an interview to the London *Sunday Times*, in the course of which he said: 'You'd be surprised to see the number of four-letter words and I think I can say obscenities, that are sometimes included in scripts by the most reputable people.' (He meant, of course, 'piss', 'arse' and 'shit' as well as the obvious venereal monosyllables.) 'We normally cut certain expletives, for example, "Christ" and "Jesus" ', he went on, 'which are admittedly used in common parlance . . . but still do give offence to a great number of people.' When asked by the interviewer which subject – sex, religion or politics – raised the most problems, he replied that in terms of quantity, sex was the most troublesome, although: 'I have personally found the religious ones most difficult of all.' He admitted that, if faced with a play that satirized Christianity, 'I would start with a bias against it'. In the six months immediately preceding this colloquy, his office had received 441 scripts, of which sixty-three had been returned for cutting and changing. In eighteen cases the proposed alterations were radical. One of the latter group was John Osborne's *A Patriot for Me*, a play factually based on the career of a homosexual colonel in the Austro-Hungarian army who was blackmailed into spying for the Russians and finally committed suicide. The Chamberlain demanded the excision of five whole scenes. The author refused; and the producers had to turn their theatre into a private club in order to present a major new work by one of Britain's leading dramatists.

Who is the Lord Chamberlain? As I write, he is Cameron Fromanteel, first Baron Cobbold, educated at Eton and Cambridge, and a former Governor of the Bank of England: a cheerful, toothy, soothing chap in his early sixties. His predecessor, who retired in 1963, was the 11th Earl of Scarbrough, educated at Eton and Oxford, and a former Governor of Bombay. Unlike Lord Cobbold, he could boast first-hand experience of artistic endeavour, having written, in 1936, *The History of the Eleventh Hussars*.

These are the men who have exercised absolute power over British drama for the past fourteen years. As a highly respected director once put it: 'Why should a colonial administrator be allowed to put fig leaves on statues? Or a banker to paint out the bits of pictures that he doesn't like?' He is not alone in his bewilderment, which history amply supports. Around the turn of the century, the poet Swinburne declared that the Lord Chamberlain had exposed the English stage 'to the contempt and compassion of civilized Europe'. To cite a few other spokesmen from the same period:

> All I can say is that something or other – which probably is consciousness of the Censor – appears to deter men of letters who have other channels for communicating with the public, from writing for the stage. (Thomas Hardy)

> The censorship, with its quite wanton power of suppression, has always been one of the reasons why I haven't ventured into playwriting. (H. G. Wells)

> I am certain that a dramatic author may be shamefully hindered, and that such a situation is intolerable; a disgrace to the tone, to the character, of this country's civilization. (Joseph Conrad)

> There is not perhaps another field so fine in the England of today for a man or woman of letters, but all the other literary fields are free. This one alone has a blind bull in it. (From a protest signed by many writers, including Henry James, J. M. Barrie, Galsworthy, Conan Doyle and Shaw)

All of which suggests that Shaw was right when he argued that the dearth of good English plays between the early eighteenth century and his own début in the late nineteenth was entirely due to the existence of the Lord Chamberlain, a baleful deterrent lurking on the threshold of creativity. After all, why should a first-rate writer venture into a theatre where Sophocles' *Oedipus Rex* was

banned? Just before World War One, Sir Herbert Beerbohm Tree wanted to stage this great tragedy of incest;
the censor brusquely turned him down, a decision which
moved the popular playwright Henry Arthur Jones to
publish a suave letter of complaint. It read in part:

> Now, of course, if any considerable body of Englishmen
> are arranging to marry their mothers, whether by accident
> or design, it must be stopped at once. But it is not a fre-
> quent occurrence in any class of English society. Through-
> out the course of my life I have not met more than six
> men who were anxious to do it.

We know very little about the qualities the sovereign
looks for when he or she appoints a Chamberlain. According to the current holder of the office, whose opinion may
not be wholly disinterested, they include 'wide experience,
a knowledge of what is going on in the contemporary
world, and the habit of sifting advice, reaching decisions
and taking responsibility'. Of the methods employed by
the Chamberlain to select an Examiner of plays, we know
nothing at all. Shaw wrote in 1899:

> It will be inferred that no pains are spared to secure the
> services of a very highly qualified and distinguished person
> to wield this astonishing power – say the holder of a
> University chair of Literature and Dramaturgy. The in-
> ference is erroneous. You are not allowed to sell stamps
> in an English post office without previously passing an
> examination; but you may become Examiner of plays
> without necessarily knowing how to read or write.

This is not to say that a fully qualified Examiner would
be an improvement. Rather the contrary: a censor with
a first-rate mind, capable of penetrating the elaborate disguises under which contraband ideas are smuggled to the
public, and shrewd enough to detect potential non-con-
formity in the foetal stage, could castrate the drama far
more effectively than the present posse of numbskulls. All
censors are bad, but clever ones are the worst.

In Elizabethan times and throughout the seventeenth
century, when censorship was mostly carried out by the

Master of the Revels, the chief qualification for the job was greed. The fee for reading a script rose during this period from five shillings to one pound, and in the 1660s a particularly corrupt Master attempted to raise his income by claiming authority over such public pleasures as cockfights, billiards and ninepins. But although the censor was grasping, he was relatively harmless; he did not see himself as the nation's moral guardian, and as long as authors refrained from advocating the overthrow of the monarchy and the established church, their freedom – especially in sexual matters – was virtually complete.

The rot that still plagues the British theatre set in with Walpole, who began to get worried in 1728, when John Gay pilloried the ruling classes with tremendous popular success in *The Beggar's Opera*. Detailed and specific attacks on Walpole's premiership followed in the plays of Henry Fielding; and the result was the crippling, muzzling Censorship Act of 1737. Thereafter Fielding gave up the theatre in favour of the novel: English literature gained the author of *Tom Jones*, but English drama lost the services of a man who might well have developed into the greatest playwright since Shakespeare.

Britain did not at first take kindly to Walpole's encroachment on freedom of speech. Lord Chesterfield argued vainly against it in a majestic and permanently valid speech to the House of Lords:

> If Poets and Players are to be restrained, let them be restrained as other Subjects are, by the known Laws of their Country; if they offend, let them be tried as every Englishman ought to be, by God and their Country. Do not let us subject them to the arbitrary Will and Pleasure of any one Man. A Power lodged in the hands of one single Man, to judge and determine, without any Limitation, without any Control or Appeal, is a sort of Power unknown to our Laws, inconsistent with our Constitution. It is a higher, a more absolute Power than we trust even to the King himself; and therefore I must think we ought not to vest any such Power in his Majesty's Lord Chamberlain.

And Samuel Johnson wrote an essay ironically defending the censorship against a playwright who objected that the Chamberlain had banned one of his works without giving a reason:

> Is it for a Poet to demand a Licenser's reason for his proceedings? Is he not rather to acquiesce in the decision of Authority and conclude that there are reasons he cannot comprehend? Unhappy would it be for men in power were they always obliged to publish the motives of their conduct. What is power but the liberty of acting without being accountable?

Johnson went on to propose that the censor's power should be extended to the press, and that it should be made a felony for a citizen to *read* without the Chamberlain's licence.

But idiocy triumphed and swiftly entrenched itself. The nineteenth century was the censor's paradise and playground. In 1832 the Examiner of plays was quizzed by a royal commission. He said it was indecent for a dramatic hero to call his mistress an 'angel', because angels were characters in Scripture, and Scripture was 'much too sacred for the stage'. When asked why he forbade oaths like 'Damme', he replied: 'I think it is immoral and improper, to say nothing of the vulgarity of it in assemblies where high characters and females congregate.'

The same Examiner had lately banned a meek little play about Charles I, whom the British people had decapitated two centuries earlier. He realized (he said) that its intentions were harmless, 'but mischief may be unconsciously done, as a house may be set on fire by a little innocent in the nursery'. This tone of lofty condescension resounded through the rest of the century. *La Dame aux Camélias* was condemned because it might inflame the public to acts of sexual riot. A stage version of Disraeli's novel *Coningsby* was banned on the eve of its opening. 'You see,' the Chamberlain explained to the baffled adapter, 'you are writing a kind of quasi-political piece, and here you are exhibiting a sort of contrast between the manufacturing people and the lower classes. Don't you think, now, that that would be a pity?' When Henry Irving sought to appear in a poetic play about the life of Mohammed, he was tetchily informed that Queen Victoria's subjects included millions of Mohammedans who would be outraged if the Prophet were represented on stage. The Chamberlain's nervousness about holy metaphysics is notorious; as late as 1912, an extremely godly play was rejected because it contained such blasphemous lines as 'Christ comfort you' and 'The real Good Friday would be that which brought the cure for cancer'.

The arch-fiends, however, were Ibsen and Shaw – social critics who brutally exposed the hypocrisies of official morality and their destructive effect on personal relationships. Both suffered from the censor's gag. 'I have studied Ibsen's plays pretty carefully,' said the Chamberlain's Examiner in 1891, 'and all the characters appear to me morally deranged.' Two years later he ambushed Shaw by banning *Mrs Warren's Profession*; and when he died in 1895, Shaw wrote a cruel and classic obituary:

> The late Mr Piggot is declared on all hands to have been the best reader of plays we have ever had; and yet he was a walking compendium of vulgar insular prejudice. . . . He had French immorality on the brain; he had American indecency on the brain; he had the womanly woman on the brain; he had the divorce court on the brain; he had 'not before a mixed audience' on the brain; his official career in relation to the higher drama was one long folly and panic. . . . It is a frightening thing to see the great thinkers, poets and authors of modern Europe – men like Ibsen, Wagner, Tolstoy and the leaders of our own literature – delivered into the vulgar hands of such a noodle as this amiable old gentlemen – this despised, incapable old official – most notoriously was.

Seventy years have passed since then, but appallingly little has changed. Less than a decade ago, the Chamberlain stamped on Arthur Miller's *A View from the Bridge* and Tennessee Williams's *Cat on a Hot Tin Roof* because he thought them tainted with homosexuality. These ludicrous bans have now been lifted, but the censor still forbids all theatrical representations of queer characters who follow their sexual leanings without being tragically punished or revealing any sense of guilt. Everything remotely anal, no matter how far removed from sensual enjoyment, is automatically prohibited. In 1964 the Royal Shakespeare Company (Patron: the Queen) put on a French surrealist play of the 1920s in which a stately Edwardian beauty, symbolizing death, was required to break wind at regular intervals. The stage directions indicated that the effect could be made by a bass trombone in the wings, but this was not precise enough for the Chamberlain. He passed the script only when the director agreed to let the trombonist play the Destiny Theme from Beethoven's Fifth Symphony. This apparently made farting respectable.

John Osborne, probably the most important British dramatist since Shaw, has naturally been singled out for the censor's special attention. His first play, an assault on McCarthyism, was presented by a provincial repertory company in 1951; it contained a scene in which one of the characters was falsely smeared as a homosexual. The Chamberlain cut the imputation of queerness and thus crippled the play. 'It's the sheer humiliation that's bad for the artist,' Osborne said to me not long ago. 'I know playwrights who almost seem to be *living* with the Lord Chamberlain – it's like an affair. There's a virgin period when you aren't aware of him, but eventually you can't avoid thinking of him while you're writing. He sits on your shoulder, like a terrible nanny.'

In 1959 Osborne wrote and directed a musical called *The World of Paul Slickey*. Before it opened on tour, the usual exchange of letters with the censor had taken place, including the following concession from Osborne's lawyer:

> My client is prepared to substitute for:
>> 'Leaping from the bridal bed,
>> He preferred his youthful squire instead,'
>
> the line:
>
>> 'He preferred the *companionship* of his
>> youthful squire instead.'

But while the show was on its way to London the Chamberlain received one or two complaints that prompted him to demand new cuts and revisions. Among several offending lines, there was a lyric that ran :

> And before I make a pass,
> I'll tell her that the sun shines out of her – face.

On this the censor's comment was curt and final. 'If the pause before "face" is retained, this couplet will be unacceptable.' Osborne sat down in fury to register a general protest :

> Your office seems intent on treating me as if I were the producer of a third-rate nude revue. What I find most bewildering is the lack of moral consistency and objectivity which seems to characterize your recent decisions – decisions which seem to be reversed and changed because of the whim of any twisted neurotic who cares to write to you and exploit his own particular sexual frustration or moral oddity. In paying attention to what is without question an infinitesimal and lunatic minority, you are doing a grave injustice not only to myself but to the general public and your own office.

I sympathize with Osborne's rage, while regretting that he let it trap him into implying that special privileges should be granted to serious drama and withheld from 'third-rate nude revues'. Erotic stimulation is a perfectly legitimate function of bad art as well as good, and a censor who bans a stripper is behaving just as illiberally and indefensibly as one who eviscerates a masterpiece.

Osborne returned to the attack in 1960, when the Chamberlain blue-pencilled eighteen passages – many of them entire speeches – from his chronicle play, *Luther*, in which Albert Finney was to conquer the West End and Broadway. Osborne stated his terms in a white-hot letter to the London producer :

> I cannot agree to any of the cuts demanded, *under any circumstances*. Nor will I agree to any possible substitutions. I don't write plays to have them rewritten by someone else. I intend to make a clear unequivocal stand

on this because (a) I think it is high time that someone did so, and (b) . . . the suggested cuts or alternatives would result in such damage to the psychological structure, meaning and depth of the play that the result would be a travesty. . . . I will not even contemplate any compromise . . . I am quite prepared to withdraw the play from production altogether and wait for the day when Lord Scarbrough [at that time the Lord Chamberlain] is no more. . . . I have made up my mind and, in fact, did so long ago.

This blast had its effect. For once, the censor crumpled; and *Luther* went on with only five small verbal changes, three of them involving the substitution of 'urine' or 'kidney juice' for 'piss'. Osborne wrote to the producer congratulating him on an 'astonishing victory'. His present belief, shared by most of his contemporaries in the British theatre, is that censorship is not only offensive but superfluous: the existing laws relating to libel and obscenity are already ferocious enough to warm any bigot's heart, and constitute, in themselves, quite a sizeable deterrent to freedom of speech. Would Osborne allow a Black Muslim play to be performed in a community of white supremacists? 'Yes – anything that creates energy and vitality is good for the theatre.' When I posed the ultimate question – would he permit sexual intercourse on stage? – Osborne replied: 'It might make me ill, and I'd like to know beforehand what I was in for. But I'm prepared to be exposed to it – although I might want a seat on the aisle.'

Improvisation – the utterance of words unfiltered by the authorized sin-sieve – is one of the Chamberlain's abiding hates. A few years ago, when the off-Broadway revue called *The Premise* came to London, he forbade the cast to improvise, despite the fact that at least half of the show (according to its publicity) was made up on the moment's spur. On this occasion, mindful perhaps of Anglo-American relations, he took no legal action; but in 1958 there were convictions and fines when the producers of a play entitled *You Won't Always Be on Top* enhanced the text with an unlicensed impersonation of Sir Winston Churchill opening a public lavatory.

With these anomalies in mind, consider an antic sequence of events which unfolded in April 1965. The management of an Australian revue called *Guarding the Change* was instructed by the Chamberlain, three hours before the curtain was due to rise at the New Lyric Theatre in London, that two sketches would have to be omitted. One concerned Scott of the Antarctic, who died half a century ago, and the other was a parody of a characteristically radiant royal address which ended with the words:

> Our thoughts/good wishes/carpet salesmen/aircraft car-
> riers are on their way toward you. And so, on this beau-
> tiful morning/afternoon/evening, what is there for us
> to say but hello/how-do-you-do/goodbye/well done/arise,
> Sir Robert Menzies.

This, like the bit about Scott, was expunged on the grounds of good taste. The management at once tele-phoned to ask whether they could fill the gap left in their programme by reading to the audience the letter in which the Chamberlain imposed his ban. The request was re-fused. 'Without fear or favour,' as a wag later remarked, 'the Lord Chamberlain also banned his own letter.'

That same evening, however, the royal family them-selves were rocking with laughter at an inspired Irish clown named Spike Milligan, most of whose gags are famously impromptu. To quote at length the wag cited above (Michael Frayn of *The Observer*):

> They were at the Comedy Theatre, watching *Son of Oblomov*, with Spike Milligan departing from the script to make jokes in which he mentioned their names, like 'Why does Prince Philip wear red, white and blue braces?' (Answer: 'To keep his trousers up.') . . . But the point is, what is the Lord Chamberlain going to do about Mr Milligan? Mentioning Prince Philip or his braces on the West End stage is not allowed. . . . And what will he do about the royal family? If the reporters saw correctly through their night glasses in the darkness, the whole party seem to have aided and abetted Mr Milligan by providing sensible evidence of appreciation. In other words, they are

all accessories after the fact. Will the Lord Chamberlain revoke *their* licences? . . .

Mr Milligan has in his files what may well be the strangest single document in the history of theatre censorship. In 1962 he collaborated with John Antrobus on a clearly deranged but maniacally funny comedy called *The Bed-Sitting Room*. In January 1963, the joint authors received a communication from the Lord Chamberlain, from which I quote:

This Licence is issued on the understanding that the following alterations are made to the script:

ACT I

Page 1: Omit the name of the Prime Minister: no representation of his voice is allowed.

Page 16: Omit '. . . clockwork Virgin Mary made in Hong Kong, whistles the Twist.' Omit references to the Royal Family, the Queen's Christmas Message, and the Duke's shooting. . . .

Page 21: The detergent song. Omit 'You get all the dirt off the tail of your shirt.' Substitute 'You get all the dirt off the front of your shirt.'

ACT II

Page 8: The mock priest must not wear a crucifix on his snorkel. It must be immediately made clear that the book the priest handles is not the Bible.

Page 10: Omit from 'We've just consummated our marriage' to and inclusive of 'a steaming hot summer's night.'

Page 13: Omit from 'In return they are willing . . .' to and inclusive of 'the Duke of Edinburgh is a wow with Greek dishes.' Substitute 'Hark ye! Hark ye! The Day of Judgment is at hand.'

ACT III

Pages 12–13: Omit the song 'Plastic Mac Man' and substitute 'Oh you dirty young devil, how dare you presume to wet the bed when

the po's in the room. I'll wallop your bum
with a dirty great broom when I get up
in the morning.'

Page 14: Omit 'the perversions of the rubber'. Substitute 'the kreurpels and blinges of the
rubber'. Omit the chamber pot under bed.

No argument I have yet heard in favour of dramatic
censorship is strong enough to withstand the armour-
plated case against it, which I can sum up in three
quotations:

To purchase freedom of thought with human blood and
then delegate its exercise to a censor at £400 a year is a
proceeding which must make the gods laugh. (Frank
Fowell and Frank Palmer, authors of *Censorship in England*, 1912)

What, then, is to be done with the Censorship? Nothing
can be simpler. Abolish it, root and branch, throwing the
whole legal responsibility for plays on the author and
manager, precisely as the legal responsibility for a book is
thrown on the author, the printer and the publisher. The
managers will not like this; their present slavery is safer
and easier; but it will be good for them, and good for the
Drama. (Bernard Shaw, 1909)

The Stage, my Lords, and the Press are two of our Out-
sentries; if we remove them – if we hoodwink them – if
we throw them in Fetters – the Enemy may surprise us.
Therefore I must look upon the Bill now before us as a Step,
and a most necessary Step too, for introducing arbitrary
Power into this Kingdom. It is a Step so necessary, that if
ever any future ambitious King, or guilty Minister, should
form to himself so wicked a Design, he will have reason
to thank us for having done so much of the work to his
Hand; but such Thanks I am convinced every one of your
Lordships would blush to receive – and scorn to deserve.
(Lord Chesterfield to the House of Lords, 1737)

Chesterfield was right when he carried the case against
the Lord Chamberlain beyond the boundaries of dramatic
art into the broader domain of civil liberties and demo-
cratic rights. The fundamental objection to censorship is

not that it is exercised against artists, but that it is exercised at all.

Sixty-odd years ago, Shaw was alarmed to hear a rumour that the United States was proposing to censor the theatre. 'O my friends across the sea,' he wrote with a passion I echo today, 'remember how the censorship works in England, and DON'T.'

(1965)

Index

*References to works only

385